ISBN 978-0-428-13231-6
PIBN 11215959

This book is a reproduction of an important historical work. Forgotten Books uses state-of-the-art technology to digitally reconstruct the work, preserving the original format whilst repairing imperfections present in the aged copy. In rare cases, an imperfection in the original, such as a blemish or missing page, may be replicated in our edition. We do, however, repair the vast majority of imperfections successfully; any imperfections that remain are intentionally left to preserve the state of such historical works.

1 MONTH OF
FREE
READING

at
www.ForgottenBooks.com

By purchasing this book you are eligible for one month membership to ForgottenBooks.com, giving you unlimited access to our entire collection of over 1,000,000 titles via our web site and mobile apps.

To claim your free month visit:

www.forgottenbooks.com/free1215959

GEORGE BUCHANAN.

Engraved by W. H. Lizars from an Original Picture in the Library of the University of Edinburgh.

MEMOIRS

OF THE

Life and Writings

OF

GEORGE BUCHANAN.

BY

DAVID IRVING, LL. D.

THE SECOND EDITION.

EDINBURGH;

PRINTED FOR WILLIAM BLACKWOOD, PRINCE'S STREET: AND
T. CADELL AND W. DAVIES, STRAND, LONDON.

1817.

144#3, 26
6

PREFACE

The taste and genius of Buchanan reflect the highest reputation on his native country; nor can Scotland boast of another name equally illustrious in the general history of literature. The most learned and ·fastidious of his contemporaries regarded him as the best Latin poet of the age; and, by a rare felicity of talent, he ·attained to the same preëminence as a writer of prose. His history of Scotland, composed in the full maturity of his vigorous mind, is distinguished from other productions of the same class, not merely by its elegance of style, but by a conspicuous air of originality, and by the sagacity and penetration which it almost uniformly displays. His profound and masterly work *De Jure Regni*, excited the universal odium of those who imagined it unwarrantable to resist even the wildest encroachments of arbitrary power; but it has taught modern philosophers to discuss the principles of political science with new freedom and energy.

The history of Buchanan may therefore be considered as the history of an individual who, in his own department, stands unrivalled in modern times. The materials for such a work are neither very scanty nor superabundant. Buchanan, at the request of some of his friends, composed a brief account of his long and variegated life. This biographical tract, which I have reprinted in the appendix, is written with modesty and reserve: it descends no later than the period of his final return to Scotland, and the whole of it only occupies a very few pages. Nor is the author sufficiently careful to mark the chronology of the events which he there records. This rapid sketch, so far as it extends, is however our safest guide. An edition of it was long afterwards published by Sir Robert Sibbald; who added several biographical notices, and augmented the number of the testimonies collected by Sir Thomas Pope Blount.

The name of Buchanan, it may be almost superfluous to remark, occurs in every collection of general biography. The article inserted in the very curious work of Bayle, is extremely defective: this acute and singular man seems to have been but little acquainted with the productions of Buchanan, and still less with the genuine character of their author. But to the learned and indefatigable Le Clerc our obligations are not inconsiderable. This writer, who, in the year 1706, inserted in one of his periodical publications a dissertation *De George Buchanan et de ses Ouvrages*,[a] had evidently perused his works with attention, and had formed no injudicious estimate of his personal and literary merits.

Still however no other separate memoir had been undertaken, or at least had made its appearance. During the earlier part of last century, George Crawfurd addressed to the gentlemen of the name of Buchanan, proposals for writing and publishing the life of this illustrious scholar; but his project does not seem to have met with

---

[a] Bibliotheque Choisie, tom. viii, p. 106.

adequate encouragement. He proceeded however to the completion of his work: and in the year 1751, after the author's decease, proposals for printing it were issued at Glasgow, but with no better success. With the subsequent fate of Crawfurd's work I am not acquainted. A biographical account of Buchanan, was also composed by the Rev. Robert Wodrow; and the original manuscript is now in the library of the university of Glasgow. It consists of one hundred and thirty-two quarto pages, very closely written, and displays the author's usual industry and love of truth. The only information which I have derived from it, consists of some notices which Wodrow has transcribed from the records of the church, and from Calderwood's unpublished history of Scotland. At a more recent period, the task of writing the life of Buchanan was successively recommended, by the earl of Buchan, to Dr Stuart and to Dr Dunbar; and either of those able men could have invested the subject with attractions, which the reader will in vain expect to discover in the subsequent pages. If, however we consider the complexion of Dr Stuart's history of

Scotland, his declining this undertaking can
certainly excite very little regret : but the
liberality and eloquence of. Dr. Dunbar
would have enabled him to display the variegated excellence of Buchanan with powerful effect.

Although no regular account of his life
was composed by Mr. Ruddiman, yet from
the labours of that learned and worthy man
I have derived very important aid. His edition of the works of Buchanan[b] is entitled
to high commendation. The plan of such a
collection was originally formed by George
Mosman ; and the impression was actually proceeding in the year 1702.[c] After
a few sheets had been completed, the property was transferred to Robert Freebairn,
printer to the king, and Ruddiman was by
him engaged in the undertaking ;[d] but the
edition did not make its appearance till
the year 1715. It reflects equal credit on
the printer and on the editor. Ruddiman's
masterly acquaintance with philology, and
with the history of his native country, had
eminently qualified him for his laborious

[b] Edinb. 1715, 2 tom. fol.
[c] Sibbaldi Comment. in Vitam Buchanani, præf.
[d] Ruddiman's Antîcrisis, p. 22.

task. The accuracy of the text, and the utility of his illustrations, are equally conspicuous. He has prefixed a copious and satisfactory preface; and, among other appendages, has added a curious and critical dissertation *De Metris Buchandnœis*. His annotations on Buchanan's history are particularly elaborate and valuable; but it is to be lamented that his narrow politics should so frequently have diverted him from the more useful tracts of enquiry. Where political prejudices intervene, he is too eager to contradict his author; and he often attempts, by very slender and incompetent proofs, to extenuate the authenticity of his narration. In illustrating the moral and literary character of Buchanan, he spent many years of his life. With great zeal and success, he afterwards vindicated his paraphrase of the psalms against the objections of Mr Benson; but his political prejudices seem to have increased with the number of his years. His controversies with Mr Love and Mr Man were conducted with sufficient pertinacity; though it must be acknowledged that the advantage of learning, and even of candour, generally inclines to Ruddiman's side. The perusal

of his controversial works in the order of
their composition, is a task of considerable
interest and edification. When he concluded his annotations on the life of Buchanan, he was disposed to regard him, with
Nathan Chytræus, as " a most excellent
and most innocent man, and entitled to
perpetual remembrance on account of his
exquisite learning and dignity;" but when
galled by his antagonists, and mortified by
the fading hopes of the house of Stewart,
he gradually adopted new opinions which
were not founded on any new evidence.
It must frequently have occurred to his reflections, that Buchanan had essentially
contributed to the dissemination of those
doctrines which led to the revolution; and
after the hopes of the Jacobites were completely blasted, he expressed himself with
a degree of asperity which is chiefly to be
regretted on his own account. One example will probably be deemed sufficient.
" But, alas! what will his great admirers
gain by that concession? Only this, that
they make him die an hardened and impe-
nitent sinner; and rather than his reputation, or more truly that of their own cause,
should suffer in this world, they choose

(horresco referens!) to let him drop into hell in the next."[e] On various topics connected with the personal character of Buchanan, his reasoning is very loose and inconclusive; nor is this to be imputed to his want of acuteness, but to his eagerness in defending opinions which had been fiercely attacked, and which in reality were indefencible.

The political tendency of his preface and notes was so far from being agreeable to the admirers of Buchanan, that an association, consisting of Mr Anderson, the Rev. George Logan, and many other adherents of the Whig party, was speedily formed at Edinburgh for the express purpose of vindicating their favourite author in a new edition of his works.[f] Their efforts however proved abortive, and the task of editorship devolved into more able hands. Ten years after the appearance of Ruddiman's edition, another was published by the learned Dr Peter Burman of Leyden;[g] a most indefatigable and useful labourer in the province of philology. Arrested by the fre-

---

[e] Ruddiman's Animadversions, p. 13.
[f] Chalmers, p. 74.
[g] Lugd. Bat. 1725, 2 tom. 4to.

quent and wide variance between the author and his *jure divino* editor, Burman had nearly been induced to relinquish his undertaking, and to advise his printer Langerak to procure assistance from Scotland, where the authenticity of the facts could best be ascertained. Of the new edition meditated at Edinburgh he was likewise apprized; though it does not appear, as some authors aver, that the associated critics made him a voluntary offer of private assistance. The printer however urging him to proceed without waiting for this vindicatory edition, he at length republished the works of Buchanan, together with Ruddiman's preface, notes, dissertation, and other appendages. The annotations which he himself subjoined are almost entirely of the philological kind. His other engagements did not permit him to undertake the office of superintending the press; and accordingly his edition is somewhat less correct than that of Ruddiman. The general value of his predecessor's labours he acknowledges in terms of due respect;[h] but he occasionally rejects

[h] " Sine controversia ab omnibus eruditis insignem iniit gratiam, vir et rerum patriarum scientia, et elegantioris doctrinæ copiis instructissimus, Thomas Ruddimannus; cum hanc

his particular opinions in a manner which that learned man was disposed to regard as contemptuous; and some of his expressions relative to British literature, and to the country of Buchanan, were such as could not easily be forgotten. Two years afterwards, when Ruddiman edited the poems of Dr Pitcairne, he eagerly embraced an opportunity of asserting the honour of his native land; and the same topics were yet fresh in his recollection when he resumed his long labours at the venerable age of eighty-one. "It came very ill from a Dutch professor," he remarks, "to undervalue a people or country, to whose valour his republick is so much indebted for its flourishing condition, and from whose troops it has received so much benefit and advantage. And I will add too that it was both ingrate and impertinent in him to speak to the disadvantage of a country, from whence so many young noblemen and gentlemen yearly repaired to him for improvement in their studies; and by whom, no doubt, he was liberally rewarded for his instructions. But as Mr Burman was glad, as I am told, to

in se provinciam, plenam tædii et molestiarum, suscipere non recusaret." (Burmanni *Præf. in Buchananum.*)

own himself in the wrong, to several Scots
gentlemen, who had been his disciples, and
has been pretty roundly chastised for it by
others. I shall say no more of it in this
place."[i] To these circumstances I merely
allude as characteristic of the excellent old
man, and without any very strong inclination to adopt the full measure of his resentment. The inhabitants of every country
have been undervalued in their turn; and
few nations of ancient or modern Europe
have experienced greater injustice than
that to which Buchanan himself belonged.

These Memoirs have undergone such
essential alterations, that this new edition
may almost be considered as a new work.
I am willing to believe that it is improved
by what is added, as well as by what is suppressed. The appendix, with the exception of the last number, is entirely new. It
includes a collection of Buchanan's Scotish
tracts; one of which is extremely rare, and
another is now printed for the first time.
His *Admonitioun*, originally published under
the inspection of the author, exhibits a

---

[i] Ruddiman's Further Vindication, p. 54.

more genuine specimen of the language of that period, than either the *Chamæleon* or the plan for new-modelling the university of St Andrews. The latter tract, which I have printed from a MS. in the Advocates' Library, seems to have been materially injured by some unskilful transcriber; and the orthography must evidently have undergone many alterations. Among other papers, the appendix likewise contains some curious notices of Buchanan, which were very politely communicated by the Rev. Dr Lee, rector of the university of St Andrews; and this, I trust, will not be his only contribution to the literary and ecclesiastical history of his country. If I had been so fortunate as to receive this communication a little earlier, it would have enabled me to avoid some errors, into which I have been betrayed by relying on the authority of former writers.

The embellishments are likewise peculiar to this edition. The portrait of Buchanan is engraved from an old painting on wood, preserved in the library of the university of Edinburgh. This picture has every appearance of an original, and no doubt can reasonably be entertained of its genuineness. It has also been thought expedient to exhibit, in two different aspects, an outline of the skull which has long been supposed to be Buchanan's, and which is now deposited in the museum of the university. To these engravings the facsimiles form an interesting addition. The inscription by Ascham, and the verses by Buchanan, were traced from a copy, in Williams's Library, of the work of Fulvius Ursinus entitled " Virgilius Collatione Scriptorum Græcorum Illustratus." Buchanan's signature is copied from the original report of the commissioners, appointed, in the year 1579, for reforming the university of St Andrews. This document, engrossed on parchment, is preserved in the archives of New College.

Edinburgh, 25 *March* 1817.

Rogerus Aschamus Georgio Buchana-
nano, Anglus Scoto, Amicus amico, hunc Poetam omnis veteris memoriæ optimum, Poetæ huius nostræ
ætatis optimo, amoris ergo, dono dat:

cum hoc monasticho /

φιλει Φιλου μνημοσυνον ὁμιλιας δείξυ.

R̸A̸

apud Hampton Court
M° D° LX·V·III°

20. Nouemb.

mplector legere tuum vehementer amorem.
Et tuum doctum pignus amoris amo.
ec minus est animus gemitor mihi gratus amo
Lucecῳ animum virtus ornat, amatῳ tuum.
c minus est gratus magni omnes error amo
Quo pectus nimio coetus amore mei.
cum multa probem virtute, minimus, am
Et nimio foetum pectus amore mei.
q errore meo uellem fors esset amare
Errorem de me candide amice tuam

G Buchanan ⸭

MEMOIRS

OF THE

LIFE AND WRITINGS

OF

GEORGE BUCHANAN.

GEORGE BUCHANAN was born in an age of little refinement, and enjoyed none of the early advantages which result from hereditary wealth; but his intrinsic greatness of mind enabled him to emerge from original obscurity, and to acquire a reputation that can only decay with literature itself. He was born about the beginning of February in the year 1506. His father was Thomas, the second son of Thomas Buchanan of Drummikill; his mother Agnes Heriot of the family of Trabroun. The house from which he descended, he has himself characterized as more remarkable for its antiquity than for its opulence. Thomas Buchanan the younger is said to

A

have óbtained from his father a grant of the farm
of Mid-Leowen, or, as it is more commonly called, the Moss,[a] situated in the parish of Killearn,
and county of Stirling.   During the lifetime of
the late proprietor, William Finlay, who died in
1808, in the ninety-fourth year of his age, the
farm-house in which Buchanan was born was
twice rebuilt : but on each occasion, its original
dimensions and characteristics were studiously
preserved; and an oak beam, together with an
inner wall, has even retained its ancient position.
The present building, which may be considered
as a correct model of Buchanan's paternal residence, is a lowly cottage thatched with straw;
but this cottage is still visited with a kind of religious veneration.   A fragment of the oak is
regarded as a precious relique; and an Irish
student, who thirsted for a portion of Buchanan's
inspiration, is known to have travelled from
Glasgow, for the purpose of visiting the house,
and passing a night directly under the original
beam.[b]

Buchanan's father died of the stone at a premature age; and, about the same period, his
grandfather found himself in a state of insolven-
cy.[c]   The family, which had never been opulent,

---

[a] W. Buchanan's Historical and Genealogical Essay upon the Family
and Sirname of Buchanan. Glasgow, 1723, 4to.

[b] Nimmo's Hist. of Stirlingshire, p. 368. Edinb. 1777, 8vo.

[c] It may however be inferred that he did not alienate his estate. In
1582, Thomas Buchanan was served heir to his father Walter Buchanan
of Drummikill. (*Inquisitionum Abbreviatio*, vol. ii, Dumb. 29.)

was thus reduced to extreme poverty : but his mother struggled hard with the misery of her condition; and all her children, five sons and three daughters, arrived at the age of maturity. She seems to have been long engaged in the pursuits of agriculture; for in the year 1531, a lease of two farms near Cardross was granted by Robert Erskine, commendator of Dryburgh and Inchmahome, to Agnes Heriot and three of her sons, Patrick, Alexander, and George.[d] One of her daughters appears to have married a person of the name of Morison. Alexander Morison, the son of Buchanan's sister, published an edition of his uncle's paraphrase of the psalms.[e] Her third son, whose extraordinary attainments have rendered the family illustrious, is reported by oral tradition, which must not however be too rashly credited, to have been indebted for the rudiments of learning to the public school of Killearn; which long continued to maintain a very considerable degree of celebrity. Mid-Leowen, which stands on the banks of the Blane, is situated at the distance of about two miles from the village; and it may be conjectured that the future poet and statesman daily walked to school, and carried along with him his homely repast. A considerable number of trees, which he

[d] Anderson's Life of Smollett, p. 12, 5th edit. Edinb. 1806, 8vo.
[e] Jos. Scaligeri Opuscula, p. 287. Paris. 1610, 4to.

is said to have planted in his school-boy days, are
still to be seen in the immediate vicinity of his
native cottage: a mountain ash, conspicuous for
its age and magnitude, was lately torn from its
roots by the violence of a storm; but two fresh
scions which arose from its ruins, have been nou-
rished and protected with anxious care. Nor is
the name of his mother without its rural memorial; a place which had been adapted to the purpose of shielding her flock, is still denominated
Heriot's Shiels.[f]

Buchanan, if we may credit a writer whose
authority is extremely slender, was afterwards
removed to the school of Dunbarton.[g] His un-
folding genius recommended him to the favour
and protection of his maternal uncle James Heriot; who, apparently in the year 1520, sent him
to prosecute his studies in the university of Paris.
It was here that he began to cultivate his poetical talents; partly impelled, as he informs us, by
the natural temperament of his mind, partly by
the necessity of performing the usual exercises
prescribed to younger students. Some of the
French writers, most capable of estimating his
attainments, have not neglected to record his obligations to their country: Vavasseur has remarked that, although a Scotchman by birth, he
might well pass for a French poet; since all that
he knew of polite literature, and particularly of

Sinclair's Statistical Account of Scotland, vol. xvi, p. 105.
[g] Mackenzie's Lives of Scots Writers, vol. iii, p. 156.

poetry, he had acquired in France.[h]   Buchanan
did not profess to be one of those bright geniuses
who can master a new language every six weeks :
he incidentally suggests that his knowledge of
Latin was the result of much juvenile labour.[i]
The Greek tongue, in which he likewise attained to proficiency, he acquired without the aid of
a preceptor.[k]   The current speech of his native
district at that period may be supposed to have
been Gaelic.   Of this language it is at least certain that he possessed some knowledge ; and an
anecdote has been related which at once confirms
the supposition, and illustrates his peculiar vein
of humour.   Having met, when in France, with
a woman who was said to be possessed with the
devil, and who professed to speak all languages,
he accosted her in Gaelie.   As neither she nor
her familiar returned any answer, he entered a
protest that the devil was ignorant of that language.[l]

Within the space of two years after his arrival

[h] Vavassoris Opera, p. 689.   Amst. 1709, fol.

[i] Buchanani Rerum Scotic. Hist. p. 4.

[k] Buchanani Epistolæ, p. 25.—Fruterius seems to extol his eloquence in
the Greek as well as in the Latin language ; but if he composed Greek
verses, he certainly did not publish them.

> Ille, Buchanani felix cognomine, vates,
>   Se eriperet nostris perpetuum ex oculis ?
> Ille, cui geminæ dives facundia linguæ
>   Ponit honoratis æmula serta comis ;
> Quemque adeo Musæ (sic sint mea gloria Musæ)
>   Et docuere sacros et didicere modos.
>
> FRUTERII Reliquiæ, p. 141.

[l] Man's Censure of Ruddiman, p. 329.

in Paris, his uncle died, and left him exposed to want in a foreign country. His misery was increased by a violent distemper, which had perhaps been occasioned by poverty and mortification. And in this state of hopeless languor, he returned to Scotland at the critical age of sixteen. Having devoted the best part of a year to the care of his health, he next assumed the character of a soldier, and served along with the auxiliaries whom the duke of Albany had conducted from France. The Scotish forces, commanded by the regent in person, marched towards the borders of England; and, about the end of October 1523, laid siege to the castle of Werk. The auxiliaries carried the exterior wall by assault, but could not long occupy the station which they had gained. The large area between the two ramparts, intended as a receptacle, during the time of war, for the cattle and stores of the neighbouring peasantry, was at this crisis replenished with materials of a combustible nature. When the garrison found themselves repulsed by the French soldiers, they set fire to the straw, and speedily expelled their enemies by the flames and smoke. During the two following days, the assailants persisted in battering the inner wall: when they had effected a sufficient breach, the French auxiliaries again rushed to the attack, and surmounted the ruins; but were so fiercely assaulted by missile weapons from the inner tower, which was yet entire, that after having sustained some loss, they were compelled to retreat, and repassed the Tweed. The duke, finding his native troops disaffected, and the army on the English frontiers too formidable from its numbers, removed his camp on the eleventh of November; and as he marched towards Lauder after midnight, his army was terribly annoyed by a sudden storm of snow.[m]

Buchanan, who belonged to a fierce and warlike nation, seems to have caught some portion of the military ardour. It was his youthful curiosity respecting the profession of arms which had prompted him thus to mingle in danger; and he was persuaded that between the studies of literature and of war a very close affinity obtains.[n] In his history of Scotland, written at an advanced age, he often describes feats of chivalry with great animation. But his experience in the course of this inglorious campaign, did not render him more enamoured of a military life: the hardships which he had undergone, reduced him to his former state of languor; and during the rest of the winter he was confined to bed.

In the beginning of the ensuing spring, when he had completed the eighteenth year of his age,

---

[m] Buchanani Rerum Scotic. Hist. p. 265.

[n] " Cum in patria valetudini curandæ prope annum dedisset, cum auxiliis Gallorum qui tum in Scotiam appulerant, *studio rei militaris cognoscendæ* in castra est profectus." (*Buchanani Vita, ab ipso scripta*, p. 2.) In his dedication of *Jephthes*, he expresses himself thus: " Neque enim inter rei militaris et literarum studium ea est, quam plerique falso putant, discordia; sed summa potius concordia, et occulta quædam naturæ conspiratio."

he was sent to the university of St Andrews.
Patrick Buchanan, his eldest brother, was matriculated at the same time.[o] On the third of October 1525, George Buchanan took the degree
of bachelor of arts; and it appears from the faculty register, that he was then a *pauper*, or ex-
hibitioner.[p] About this period, John Mair, a famous doctor of the Sorbonne, taught logic in St.
Salvator's College. Buchanan informs us that it
was to hear his prelections that he had been sent
to St. Andrews, and that he afterwards followed
Mair to France.[q] It has been very confidently
stated, that he was now a dependant on the
bounty of this venerable commentator on Peter
of Lombardy.[r] If the fact could be established

[o] Sibbaldi Comment. in Vitam Buchanani, p. 65.—The verses which Buchanan has devoted to his brother's memory are equally honourable to both.
(*Epigram.* lib. ii, 23.)

[p] Chalmers's Life of Ruddiman, p. 312.

[q] " Hunc in Galliam aestate proxima sequutus, in flammam Lutheranæ
sectæ, jam late se spargentem, incidit : ac biennium fere cum iniquitate fortunæ colluctatus, tandem in Collegium Barbaranum accitus, prope triennium classi grammaticam discentium præfuit." (*Buchanani Vita*, p. 2.) The
context might lead us to suppose, that Buchanan followed Mair to France
in the summer of 1524 : but the meaning of the passage must be, that he
returned to France the summer after Mair. From a subsequent note, it
will appear that his appointment to a regency in the College of St Barbe
took place in 1529. His return to that country must therefore be referred
to the year 1527.

[r] Dr Mackenzie's account of the connection between Mair and Buchanan is extremely curious. " Being informed that he was a youth of excellent parts, and reduced to great necessities, he sent for him in the beginning
of the year 1524, and took him into his service, he being then in the 18th
year of his age. The next summer his master going over to Paris, he took
Buchanan alongst with him, and kept him in his service there for two years,
but not thinking his service a suitable encouragement for so great a genius,

by any competent evidence, the character of Buchanan must be subjected to severe reprehension; for he mentions his supposed benefactor in terms which convey no suggestion of gratitude. Of this generous patronage however there is not even the faintest shadow of evidence; and such a tale manifestly originated from the misinterpretation of a very unequivocal passage in Buchanan's account of his own life.

Upon his return to France, he became a student in the Scotish College of Paris. On the tenth of October 1527, he was incorporated a bachelor of arts, and he took the higher degree

he procured for him a regency in the College of St Barbe, in the year 1526. For all which good offices done to him by his learned and worthy master, he returned his thanks in the following scandalous epigram, [lib. i, 51.] And this was the first time he showed his ingratitude to his benefactors, which, as we shall show, was the great and unpardonable blemish of his whole life." (*Lives of Scots Writers*, vol. iii, p. 157.) This account is to be regarded as little better than pure fiction; but the praise of invention is not solely due to Mackenzie. "He who had eat his bread," says Dr Christopher Irving, "and liv'd under his discipline, both in St. Andrews, and in the Sorbon, the space of five years, might have afforded him an handsomer character than, *solo cognomine Major*." (*Historiæ Scoticæ Nomenclatura*, p. 163. Edinb. 1682, 8vo.) Irving and Mackenzie have deduced all these preposterous inferences from the subsequent passage in Buchanan's account of his own life. "Primo vere ad Fanum Andreæ missus est, ad Joannem Majorem audiendum, qui tum ibi dialecticen, aut verius sophisticen, in extrema senectute docebat. Hunc in Galliam æstate proxima sequutus," &c.

Hector Boyce regarded the writings of Mair in a more favourable light than Buchanan: "Joannes Major theologus eruditissimus, cujus scripta haud aliter quam illuminatissimæ faces magnum Christianæ religioni attulere fulgorem." (*Aberdonensium Episcoporum Vitæ*, f. xxvii, b. Paris. 1522, 4to.) See likewise Du Pin, *Bibliotheque des Auteurs Ecclesiastiques*, tom. xiii, p. 160, and Launoi, *Regii Navarræ Gymnasii Parisiensis Historia*, tom. ii, p. 652. Paris. 1677, 2 tom. 4to.

next March.[*] During the following year, 1529, he was a candidate for the office of procurator of the German nation; but his blind compatriot Robert Wauchope, who was afterwards titular archbishop of Armagh, and who sat in the council of Trent,[t] was then elected for the ninth time. Buchanan was thus repulsed on the fifth of May, but on the third of June he was more successful.[u] The university of Paris being frequented by students from various countries, they were distributed into four classes or nations. What

---

* Chalmers's Life of Ruddiman, p. 313.

t Paolo, Istoria del Concilio Tridentino, lib. ii. Londra, 1619, fol.— Dr Cosin, bishop of Durham, describes him as " blind Sir Robert the Scot; of whom it was then commonly said, that as poreblind as he was, yet had he the commendation to ride post the best in the world." (Scholastical Hist. of the Canon of the Holy Scripture, p. 213, 2d edit. Lond. 1672, 4to.) See Miræus De Scriptoribus Ecclesiasticis, p. 266, edit. Fabricii, and George Con, or Conæus, De Duplici Statu Religionis apud Scotos, p. 112. Romæ, 1628, 4to.

u " Georgius Buchananus Scotus," says Bulæus, " nationis Germanicæ procurator electus anno 1533." (Hist. Universitatis Parisiensis, tom. v, p. 935.) This date is most probably erroneous; for Buchanan was then tutor to the earl of Cassillis. Mr Chalmers quotes the authority of the register of the Scotish College, which the late Principal Gordon had inspected at his request. A man who had only to ascertain the chronology of a single academic, was less obnoxious to negligence or inadvertency, than he who had to ascertain that of five hundred. Bulæus has exhibited many dates which are manifestly inaccurate; but his work consists of six volumes in folio. Mr Innes, who was a member of the university of Paris, varies from both these writers. Buchanan, he remarks, " came back to Paris A. D. 1527, and upon proof of his being made batchelor of arts in the university of St Andrews, he was, according to the privilege our Scotish universities enjoyed in those times in Paris, admitted to the same degree in that university, and commenced master of arts in April 1528, and in June 1530, he was elected one of the four procurators." (Critical Essay on the Ancient Inhabitants of Scotland, vol. i, p. 314. Lond. 1729, 2 vols. 8vo.)

was termed the German nation, comprehended the Scotish students.

Before this period, the tenets of Luther had begun to be widely disseminated, and to second the prepossessions of young and ingenuous minds. Buchanan, on his return to Paris, was caught by the spreading flame. His Lutheranism seems to have exposed him to new mortifications; for after he had discovered his attachment, he continued for the space of nearly two years to struggle with the iniquity of fortune. At the expiration of that term, he was appointed a regent or professor in the College of St. Barbe, where he taught grammar for about three years. His eminent qualifications for such an employment will not be questioned; but his services seem to have procured him a very inadequate remuneration. In an elegy apparently composed during this period of his life, he exhibits a dismal picture of the miseries to which the Parisian professors of humanity were then exposed. It opens with the subsequent lines.

> Ite leves nugæ, sterilesque valete Camœnæ,
>   Grataque Phœbæo Castalis unda choro:
> Ite, sat est: primos vobiscum absumpsimus annos,
>   Optima pars vitæ deperiitque meæ.
> Quærite quem capiat jejuna cantus in umbra:
>   Quærite qui pota carmina cantet aqua.
> Dulcibus illecebris tenerum vos fallitis ævum,
>   Dum sequitur blandæ carmen inerme lyræ.
> Debita militiæ molli languescit in umbra,
>   Et fluit ignavis fracta juventa sonis.

Ante diem curvos senium grave contrahit artus,
  Imminet ante suum mors properata diem :
Ora notat pallor, macies in corpore toto est,
  Et tetrico in vultu mortis imago sedet.
Otia dum captas, præceps in mille labores
  Irruis, et curis angeris usque novis.
Nocte leves somnos resolutus compede fossor
  Carpit, et in mediis nauta quiescit aquis :
Nocte leves somnos carpit defessus arator,
  Nocte quies ventis, Ionioque mari :
Nocte tibi nigræ fuligo bibenda lucernæ,
  Si modo Calliopea castra sequenda putes :
Et tanquam Libyco serves curvata metallo
  Robora, et Herculea poma ferenda manú,
Pervigil in lucem lecta atque relecta revolves,
  Et putri excuties scripta sepulta situ.
Sæpe caput scalpes, et vivos roseris ungues,
  Irata feries pulpita sæpe manu.
Hinc subitæ mortes, et spes prærepta senectæ,
  Nec tibi fert Clio, nec tibi Phœbus opem. [x]

The poverty which then attended the professors
of polite literature,[y] he has delineated more forcibly towards the close.

[x] This verse strongly resembles one of Lotichius, *Carminum* lib. i, 23,
edit. Burman.

  Nec tulit hic Clio, nec mihi Phœbus opem.

The coincidence seems however to have been accidental. Lotichius died
in 1560 ; and the poem in which this line occurs was first printed in 1754.
Buchanan's elegies were not published till 1567. Of these two poets, there
are several other coincidences ; not one of which is pointed out in the younger Burman's elaborate and splendid edition of Lotichius. In the composition of elegiac verse, Lotichius is a great proficient ; and is indeed the
best of all the German poets who have written in Latin. He died at the
premature age of thirty-two.

  [y] " Quis porro non indignetur," says Budæus, " eam disciplinam et pro-
fessionem quæ omneis alias complectitur, atque intra suum orbem coercet,

Denique quicquid agis, comes assidet improba egestas,
  Sive poema canis, sive poema doces.
Bella gerunt urbes septem de patria Homeri:
  Nulla domus vivo, patria nulla fuit.
Æger, inops patrios deplorat Tityrus agros,
  Statius instantem vix fugat arte famem.
Exul Hyperboreum Naso projectus ad axem,
  Exilium Musis imputat ille suum.
Ipse Deus vatum vaccas pavisse Pheræas
  Creditur, Æmonios et numerasse greges.
Calliope longum cœlebs cur vixit in ævum?
  Nempe nihil doti quod numeraret erat.
Interea celeri cursu delabitur ætas,
  Et queritur duram tarda senecta famem:
Et dolet ignavis studiis lusisse juventam,
  Jactaque in infidam semina mœret humum;
Nullaque maturis congesta viatica canis,
  Nec faciles portus jam reperire ratem.
Ite igitur Musæ steriles, aliumque ministrum
  Quærite: nos alio sors animusque vocat.[1]

This elegy, which is the first in the order of
arrangement, was perhaps the first in the order
of composition. It was apparently in the year

---

quæ suis finibus singulas quasi architectonico jure circumscribit, a schola.
Parisiensi (quæ ut metropolis sit ipsa omnium scholarum, et censeatur: omnium (ut opinor) ipsarum bona venia et assensione licet) inscitia temporum,
et pauperie in re literaria facta, e numero disciplinarum exauctoratam esse?
e præsidiisque ejectam Palladis atque ejus ære dirutam?" *(De Philologia,*
f. xxii. Excudebat Jodocus Badius Ascensius, 1532, 4to.) Budæus and
Cardinal du Bellay induced Francis the first to allot an annual stipend to
public professors of the learned languages; and Castellanus afterwards exerted his influence with the same munificent prince to confirm so useful an es-
tablishment. (Regii *Vita Guilicimi Budæi,* p. 44. Paris. 1540, 4to.
Gallandii *Vita Petri Castellani,* p. 49. Paris. 1674, 8vo.)

  [1] Buchanani Elegia i. *Quam misera sit conditio docentium literas humaniores Lutetiæ.*

1529 that he began to teach in the College of St Barbe : he must therefore have commenced his professorial functions about the age of twenty-three. Muretus began to teach in the archiepiscopal College of Auch at the earlier age of eighteen ;[a] and at the same age Philelphus read lectures on eloquence to a numerous auditory in the university of Padua.[b]

If the elegy was actually composed about this period, the new employment to which the author alludes was evidently that of superintending the studies of a young Scotish nobleman. Gilbert Kennedy, earl of Cassillis, who was residing near the College of St. Barbe, having become acquainted with Buchanan, admired his literary talents, and was delighted with his conversation. He was therefore solicitous to retain so accomplished a preceptor ; and their closer connection probably commenced in the year 1532. The first work that Buchanan committed to the press, was a translation of the famous Thomas Linacre's rudiments of Latin grammar ; which he inscribed to Lord Cassillis, " a youth of the most promising talents, and of an excellent disposition." This Latin version was printed by R. Stephanus in 1533.

After he had resided with his pupil for the term of five years, they both returned to Scot-

---

[a] Jos. Scaligeri Confutatio Fabulæ Burdonum, p. 451.
[b] Shepherd's Life of Poggio Bracciolini, p. 264. Liverpool, 1802, 4to.

land.[c] At this period the earl had reached the age of majority ; and Buchanan might only embrace a favourable opportunity of revisiting his relations and friends. Their connection however did not immediately dissolve. While he was residing at the earl's seat in Ayrshire, he composed a little poem which rendered him extremely obnoxious to the ecclesiastics, an order of men whom it is generally hazardous to provoke. In this poem, which bears the title of *Somnium*, and is a happy imitation of Dunbar,[d]

[c] The chronology is still unsettled. Mr Ruddiman supposes him to have begun teaching in the College of St Barbe in the year 1526; but for the office of a professor he was not qualified till 1528, when he took the degree of master of arts ; and even under the date of June the third 1529, his name, according to Mr Chalmers, occurs in the register of the Scotish College. Buchanan relates that in the former seminary he taught about three years, and at the expiration of that term, was engaged by Lord Cassillis. In the dedication of his version of Linacre, published in 1533, he remarks that he had been employed in superintending that nobleman's studies during the preceding year. From a comparison of these dates, it is obvious that he was admitted as a regent or professor in 1529, and resigned his office in 1532. The biographical narrative proceeds thus : " Interea cum Gilbertus Cassilisaeae comes, adolescens nobilis, in eâ vicinia diversaretur, atque ingenio et consuetudine ejus oblectaretur, eum quinquennium secum retinuit, atque in Scotiam una reduxit. Inde cum in Galliam ad pristina studia redire cogitaret, a rege est retentus." Lord Cassillis retained him as his domestic tutor from 1532 till 1537, and having then completed the course of his studies, carried him to Scotland. Buchanan does not aver that their former relation still subsisted. Towards the close of the year 1536, King James found the earl of Cassillis residing in France. (Leslaeus *De Rebus Gestis Scotorum*, p. 442.) He returned to Scotland in the ensuing May, and was most probably accompanied by that young nobleman and his preceptor. This supposition will readily account for Buchanan's subsequent connection with the court.

[d] Compare Buchanan's *Somnium* (*Frat. Frater.* xxxiv.) with the poem entitled, " How Dunbar was desyred to be ane Frier;" which occurs in Lord Hailes's *Ancient Scottish Poems*, p. 25. Edinb. 1770, 12mo.

he expresses his own abhorrence of a monastic
life, and stigmatizes the impudence and hypocrisy of the Franciscan friars. The holy fathers,
when they became acquainted with this specimen of his sarcastic wit, resolved to convince
him of his presumption in disparaging the sacred institutions of the church. It has repeatedly been alleged that Buchanan had himself
belonged to a religious order which he has so
frequently exposed with the most admirable
powers of ridicule ;[e] but this seems to have been
a tale fabricated by the malice of his theological
enemies.   That he had actually assumed the
cowl, has never been affirmed by any early writer sufficiently acquainted with his history.   It
is not however improbable that during the convenient season of his youthful misfortunes, the
friars were anxious to allure so promising a no-
vice; and this suggestion is even countenanced
by a passage in one of his poems.[f]

[e] " *Georgius Buchananus Minorita excucullatus, Bacchicus histrio, et atheus
poeta*, inquit Gilbertus Genebrardus Chronologia ad annum M.D.LXXII.
De religione enim Catholica pessime est meritus, et ideo cohtumeliosas voces
facile viro religioso dono, cui majoris fuit momenti pietas quam eruditio."
(Dempsteri *Hist. Ecclesiast. Gentis Scotorum*, p. 108.   Bononiæ, 1627,
4to.)   *Vir religiosus* must be translated, a man who wore a certain habit ;
for such impudent defamation exhibits a curious proof of his religion.   The
same passage is quoted with seeming-approbation by Spondanus, *Annalium
Baronii Continuatio*, tom. ii, p. 456.

[f] Ergo cave ne te falso sub nomine mendax
        Simplicitas fors transversum seducat, et illuc
        Unde referre pedem nequeas, trahat : et puerum olim
        Me quoque pene suis gens hæc in retia mendax

The earl of Cassillis seems to have reflected no discredit on his preceptor. . When he afterwards mingled in the political transactions of those turbulent times, he distinguished himself by his sagacity, his firmness, and his integrity : but his country did not long reap the benefit of his services ; and Buchanan lived to record his virtues and his premature death.[g] The father had been assassinated in Scotland,[h] and the son was supposed to have been poisoned in France. , In the year 1558 he was associated in a splendid embassy to the French court ; but after they had concluded their mission, the earl of Cassillis and three of his colleagues, together with several of their retinue, were suddenly arrested by one common destiny.

Buchanan had determined to resume his former occupations in France ; but King James, the fifth of that name, retained him in the capacity of preceptor to one of his natural sons. This son was not, as has generally been supposed, the celebrated James Stewart who afterwards obtained the regency, but another who bore the same baptis-

Traxerat illecebris, nisi opem mihi forte tulisset
Cœlitus oblata Eubuli sapientia cani.

BUCHANANI Franciscanus, p. 2.

g Buchanani Hist. p. 268, 283, 306, 310.—In the *Chamæleon*, he mentions the earls of Murray and Cassillis as " men excellent in the tyme, in all virtuus perteining to ane nobill man, and speciall in lufe of the common welth of thair cuntre."

h Buchanani Hist. p. 268. Epigram. lib. ii, 9.

B

mal name.[i] His mother was Elisabeth Shaw, of
the family of Sauchie ; and he died in the year
1548. It was perhaps in the year 1537 that
Buchanan entered upon his new charge ; for in
the course of that year, the king made an arrangement with respect to his four sons.[k] The ab-
bacies of Melrose and Kelso were secured in the
name of Buchanan's pupil, who was the eldest.

What lettered society he now enjoyed in his
native country, can only be gleaned from his
poems. Notwithstanding the complexion of his
religious sentiments, he was admitted to the hos-
pitable table of Gavin Dunbar, archbishop of
Glasgow ; who probably was not aware that his
inviting Buchanan to a banquet would contribute more to the perpetuation of his fame, than
all the ecclesiastical and civil honours to which
he attained. The poet has recorded his gratification in glowing terms.[l] In his history, Buchanan commemorates this prelate as a learned
and worthy man. He had been preceptor to
James the fifth ; obtained the archbishopric in
1522 ;[m] and in 1527 was nominated chancellor.[n]

Sir Adam Otterburn, a poet and a statesman,
also occurs in the list of his friends. Buchanan
has addressed him in one of his epigrams, and

[i] Man's Censure of Ruddiman, p. 349.
[k] Leslæus de Rebus Gestis Scotorum, p. 447. Romæ, 1578, 4to.
[l] Buchanani Epigram. lib. i, 43.
[m] Leslæus de Rebus Gestis Scotorum, p. 399.
[n] Buchanani Rerum Scotic. Hist. p. 270.

another of them is professedly transformed from Otterburn's hexameters.[o] Of his poetical works however, not a single fragment is known to exist; and his name has only glided into the history of Scotish literature, because he was the friend of Buchanan; who was equally capable of bestowing reputation, and of affixing perpetual ridicule.

But he soon experienced the danger of extending his ridicule to the orthodox. The preferment of a profane scoffer at priests must have augmented their spleen; and the Franciscan friars, still smarting from his *Somnium*, found means of representing him to the king as a man of depraved morals, and of dubious faith.[p] But on this occasion their zeal recoiled upon themselves. James had formerly begun to discover their genuine character; and the part which he supposed them to have acted in a late conspiracy against his own life, had not contribu-

---

[o] Buchanani Epigram. lib. ii, 15, 16.—Sir Adam Otterburn must be carefully distinguished from the king's advocate. A commission, dated 16th Feb. 1583-4, describes the former as Sir Adam Otterburn of Reidhall; but the latter is styled Adam Otterburn of Auldhame so late as the year 1542-3. (Rymer, *Foedera*, tom. xiv, p. 483. *Acts of the Parliaments of Scotland*, vol. ii, p. 594.) The names of both are frequently to be found in the commissions and acts of that period. Some original letters of A. Otterburn and of Archbishop Dunbar are preserved among the Cotton MSS. A copy of a letter from Dr. Thomas Magnus to the former, occurs in Calig. B. vii, 121.

[p] " *Et cum non satis justas irae suae immodicae causas invenirent, ad communae religionis crimen, quod omnibus quibus male propitii erant intentabant, decurrunt.*" (Buchanani Vita, p. 3.) See also the dedication of his *Franciscanus*.

ted to diminish his antipathy. Instead of con-
signing the poet to disgrace or punishment, the
king, who was aware that private resentment
would improve the edge of his satire,^{q} enjoined
him in the presence of many courtiers to renew
his well-directed attack on the same pious fathers. Buchanan's late experience had however
taught him the importance of caution : he determined at once to gratify the king's resentment
against the friars, and to avoid increasing the
resentment of the friars against himself. In
pursuance of this project, he composed a kind
of recantation, which he supposed might delude
the Franciscans by its ambiguity of phrase.^{r}
But he found himself doubly deceived : the indignation of the king, who was himself a satirical poet,^{s} could not so easily be gratified ; and

---

^{q} " Rex Buchananum, forte tum in aula agentem, ad se advocat, et ignarus offensionis quæ ei cum Franciscanis esset, jubet adversus eos carmen
scribere." (*Buchanani Vita*, p. 3.) Instead of *ignarus*, read *gnarus* or
non ignarus. It was King James's knowledge, not his ignorance, of the
poet's warfare with the Franciscans, that must have suggested him as already prepared to second his own resentment. Buchanan's biographical sketch
was a posthumous publication ; but in the dedication of his *Franciscanus*,
which he himself committed to the press, the story is related with that con-
sistency which a very slight correction will impart to the preceding passage.
" Is mihi continuo multis audientibus imperavit, ut in Franciscanos aliquid,
idque etiam acriter, scriberem : non quod mihi in eo genere facultatem ex-
istimaret esse præcipuam, sed quod me, opinor, stimulis privati doloris inci-
tatum, acriorem injuriæ publicæ fore vindicem speraret."

^{r} The poem to which he alludes, is apparently the *Palinodia* at the end of
his *Fratres Fraterrimi*, consisting of two parts. It is not however surprising that the friars declined such a compliment.

^{s} Sir David Lindsay's " Answer to the Kingis Flyting" verifies this assertion ; but no genuine productions of the royal author are known to be ex-

the friars were now impelled to a higher pitch of resentment. James requested him to compose another satire, which should exhibit their vices in a more glaring light. The subject was copi-. ous, and well adapted to the poet's talents and views. He accordingly applied himself to the composition of the poem afterwards published under the title of *Franciscanus;* and to satisfy the king's impatience, soon presented him with a specimen. This production, as it now appears in its finished state, may without hazard be pronounced one of the most skilful and pungent satires which any nation or language can exhibit. He has not servilely adhered to the model of any ancient poet, but is himself original, and almost unequalled. To a masterly command of classical phraseology, he unites uncommon felicity of versification ; and his diction often rises with his increasing indignation to majesty and splendour. The combinations of his wit are variegated and original ; and he evinces himself a most sagacious observer of human life. No class of men was ever more completely exposed to ridicule and infamy ; nor is it astonishing that the Popish clergy afterwards regarded the author with implacable hatred. The impurities and the absurdities which he rendered so notorious, were not the

tant. " Christis Kirk of the Grene," appears with sufficient evidence to have been composed by James the first ; and "The Gaberlunzieman," as well as " The Jollie Beggar," is imputed to his descendant without any competent authority. These two ballads, which possess uncommon merit, may be found in Mr Pinkerton's *Select Scotish Ballads,* vol. ii, p. 28, 33,

spontaneous production of a prolific brain; their ignorance and irreligion presented an ample and inviting harvest. Of the validity of his poetical accusations, many historical documents still remain. Buchanan has himself related in plain prose, that about this period some of the Scotish ecclesiastics were so deplorably ignorant, as to suppose Mártin Luther to be the author of a dangerous book, called the *New* Testament.[t]

But the church being infallible, he speedily recognized the danger of accosting its retainers by their proper names. At the beginning of the year 1539, many individuals suspected of Lutheranism were involved in the horrors of persecution. Towards the close of February, five were committed to the flames, nine made a formal recantation of their supposed errors, and many were driven into exile. Buchanan had been comprehended in the general arrest; and to the perpetual infamy of the nation, his invaluable life might have been sacrificed to the rancour of an unholy priesthood.[u] After he was committed to

[t] Buchanani Rerum Scotic. Hist. p. 291. Perizonli Hist. Sæculi Sextidecimi, p. 233. Lugd. Bat. 1710, 8vo.

[u] James Laing, a most zealous doctor of the Sorbonne, has recorded a story of Buchanan's being convicted of eating the paschal lamb like a Jew. "A Jacobo quinto...est vocatus, et de quæstione proposita examinatus, atque interrogatus, quomodo ausus fuisset quicquam tale contra consuetudinem ecclesiæ Catholicæ tentare. Homo sacrarum literarum imperitissimus, simulque impudentissimus ita regi respondit; Tu domine similiter debes agnum paschæ comedere, si vis salutem consequi: quo audito responso rex statim obstupuit, et admiratus est audaciam sive potius hominis insaniam." (*De Vita et Moribus atque Rebus Gestis Hæreticorum nostri Temporis*, f. 39.

custody, Cardinal Beaton endeavoured to accelerate his doom, by tendering to the king a sum of
money as the price of his innocent blood. Of
this circumstance Buchanan was apprized by
some of his friends at court; and his knowledge
of the king's unfortunate propensity to avarice
must have augmented all the terrors of his situation. Stimulated by the thoughts of increasing
danger, he made a successful effort to regain
his liberty; while his keepers were asleep, he
escaped through the window of the apartment
in which he was confined.[x] Directing his wan-
dering steps towards the southern part of the
island, he had soon to encounter new disasters.
When he reached the frontier of the two king-
doms, he was molested by the freebooters who

Paris. 1581, 8vo.) This tale has been repeated by various other writers;
and among the rest by David Chalmers. (Camerarius *De Scotorum Fortitudine,.Doctrina, et Pietate*, p. 269. Paris. 1631, 4to.) It is too ridiculous to demand a serious refutation.

Bale, who supposes Buchanan to have been a fervent preacher of the gospel, had caught some vague rumour with respect to his suffering martyrdom:
" A Sodomæ tyrannis, mitratis, rasis, et unctis, ob divinæ veritatis asser-
tionem, igne tandem sublatum ferunt." (*Scriptores Britanniæ*, cent. xiv, p.
226. Basil. 1557-9, fol.)

2 " The poet," says Mr Chalmers, " was imprisoned in the castle of St.
Andrews, from which he was delivered by the interposition of Beaton, a
nephew of the archbishop of Glasgow." (*Life of Ruddiman*, p. 315.) In
support of these assertions, he refers to the collection of Dr Jebb, vol. ii,
p. 466; but the passage in question relates the captivity, not of Buchanan,
but of Queen Mary. " Ils ne consererent jamais qu' *elle* ne fut mise en prison dans un fort chasteau; on dit que c'est Saint André en Escosse; et ay-
ant demeuré miserablement captive pres d'un an, fut delivrée par le moyen
d'un fort honneste et brave gentil-homme du pays, et de bonne maison,
nommé Monsieur de Beton, &c. Voilà donc *cette reyne* en liberté." See
Brantome, *Vies des Dames Illustres de France*, p. 135.

at that time were its sole inhabitants; and his life was again exposed to jeopardy from the contagion of a pestilential disease, which then raged in the north of England. On his arrival in London, he experienced the friendship of Sir John Rainsford, an English knight; who is recorded to have been the only person that protected him against the fury of the Papists.[y] Of this generous support, Buchanan was not afterwards unmindful; he has immortalized his benefactor by consecrating a poem to his memory.[z] It was apparently at this unpropitious crisis, that he addressed himself to Thomas Cromwell, afterwards earl of Essex, and to King Henry;[a] from whom he however seems to have obtained no relief. Several of his little poems remain as memorials of his necessities; for his untoward fate frequently compelled him to resort to this humiliating exercise of his exalted genius. No man was however less disposed to the servility of adulation; and when the iniquity of fortune subjected him to the direful expedient of thus soliciting patronage, it must have cost his proud spirit many a bitter pang. During the age of Buchanan, and indeed at a much later period, men of letters were not extremely jealous of their independence:[b] from the peculiar state of society, they

<hr/>

[y] Epistolæ, p. 20.   [z] Epigram. lib. ii, 24.   [a] Miscell. xiii, xv.
[b] Nec tamen interea sua pauper carmina vates
  Vendere, nec blandus circum strepere ostia cessat
  Nobilium, et prohibere suis a faucibus atram

were very frequently thrown upon the immedi.
ate protection of some great personage; and the
prevalent notions relative to prerogative and subordination were such as mankind are now ashamed to recognize. The royal ears of Elizabeth
and her successor were regaled with language of
the most absurd denomination :—how meanly did
Bacon stoop from the sublimity of his genius, to
nurse the vanity of a monarch, whose elevation
had only rendered him contemptible!

· The aspect of political affairs in England was
not calculated to secure Buchanan's attachment
to that nation; he was anxious to escape from a
country which he saw exposed to the wanton
cruelties of a brutal tyrant. The civilization of
France, as well as the particular intimacies which
he had formed in that country, led him to adopt
the resolution of returning to Paris. But he
found on his arrival that Cardinal Beaton was
residing there in the character of an ambassador.[c]

Obscœnamque famem: quid enim, quid speret ab illis.
Amplius? O meritis impar sed gratia tantis!

HOSPITALII Carmina, p. 123.

[c] Mr Pinkerton has proposed some chronological objections to which it
will here be necessary to advert. "The date 1539 on the margin is erroneous; and, not to mention that it occurs again afterwards, it disagrees with
the 'brevi post' in the text, after transactions of 1537: nor does Buchanan
mention Mary of Guise, who arrived in June 1538, after he had left Scotland: nor was Cardinal Beaton in France in 1539, though Buchanan
found him there in 1538, the real year of his escape. Yet, in his unchro-
nological history, he dates the event 1539: if not an error of the press in
the vitiated first edition." (Hist. of Scotland, vol. ii, p. 352.) In this part
at least of his history, Buchanan's chronology seems unexceptionable; and
would indeed have been singular if he had forgotten a year which to him

Andrew Govea, a native of Portugal, invited him
to Bordeaux; nor did he hesitate to embrace an
opportunity of removing himself beyond the influence of the cardinal's deadly hatred. Of the
College of Guienne, lately founded in that city,
Govea had been nominated principal; and Buchanan, evidently through his interest, was now
appointed one of the professors. Here he must
have fixed his residence before the close of the
year; for to Charles the fifth, who made his solemn entry into Bordeaux on the first of December 1539,[d] he presented a poem in the name
of the college.[e]

---

was so eventful. Nor is there the smallest room for suspecting an error of
the press: having mentioned the transactions of 1537, he proceeds to relate
an event " proximo qui hunc secutus est anno ;" and afterwards introduces
the persecution which ensued " initio anni proximi." " Initio anni proximi, qui fuit M.D.XXXIX. Lutheranismi suspecti complures capti sunt:
sub finem Februarii, quisque cremati : novem recantarunt : complures ex-
ilio damnati. In his fuit Georgius Buchananus, qui, sopitis custodibus,
per cubiculi fenestram evaserat." (Buchanani *Rerum Scotic. Hist.* p. 277.)
That this persecution occurred in 1539, is almost as certain as any event in
Scotish history; and Buchanan may safely be supposed to have known
what relation it bore to his own troubles. The purport of Mr Pinkerton's
suggestion, " nor does Buchanan mention Mary of Guise," is not sufficiently obvious: Mary of Guise had no particular title to be mentioned in
the life of George Buchanan. It is indeed certain that Cardinal Beaton
was in France in 1538, but it is not therefore certain that he was not in
France in 1539. It is not the province of an historian to record every little
embassy of every denomination. The cardinal would gladly embrace any
proper opportunity of visiting that country; where he had been dexterous
enough to obtain the bishopric of Mirepoix. (Lesleus *De Rebus Gestis Scotorum,* p. 447.)

　[d] De Lurbe, Chronique Bourdeloise, f. 42, b.

　[e] Buchanani Silvæ, i. *Ad Carolum V. Imperatorem, Burdegalæ hospi-
tio publico susceptum, nomine Scholæ Burdegalensis, anno* M.D.XXXIX.

The task assigned him at Bordeaux was that
of teaching the Latin language. For an occupation of this kind, he seems to have entertained
no particular affection; but although sufficiently
laborious, it never impaired the native elevation
of his mind.   He now prosecuted his poetical
studies with a degree of ardour which may excite admiration; during the three years of his
residence at Bordeaux, he completed four tragedies, together with various other poems on
miscellaneous subjects.   It was then, and indeed
at a much later period, the common practice of
academical students to exercise themselves in
the representation of Latin dramas.   In dramatic
poetry, the taste of the French nation was still
rude and grotesque; for they had not begun to
extricate themselves from the absurdities of the
early mysteries and allegories.   With the view
of familiarizing the students to the more correct
and elegant models of the ancient theatre, Buchanan made a sudden incursion into this province of literature.   The earliest of his dramatic
compositions bears the title of *Baptistes*.   He
had applied himself to the study of the Greek
language without the aid of a preceptor, and
as an useful exercise had executed a translation
of the *Medea* of Euripides.   This version he
now delivered to the academical stage, and afterwards, at the earnest request of his friends,
suffered it to be printed.   Those two tragedies
were performed with a degree of applause which

almost exceeded his hopes. He afterwards composed his *Jephthes,* and translated the *Alcestis,*
another drama of his favourite author. These
last productions, as he originally intended them
for publication, were elaborated with superior di-
ligence.ᶠ

The tragedy of *Jephthes* is conformable to the
models of the Grecian theatre, and is not destitute of interest. The subject is highly dramatic;
it is a subject which Buchanan's great exemplar
Euripides might have been inclined to select.
The situation of a father who had unwarily subjected himself to the dreadful necessity of sacri-
ficing a beloved and only child,ᵍ the repugnant

ᶠ The *Medea* was originally printed with the two versions of Erasmus.
" Hecuba et Iphigenia in Aulide, Euripidis Tragœdiæ, in Latinum tra-
latæ, Erasmo Roterodamo interprete. Medea ejusdem, Georgio Buchanano Scoto interprete." *Parisiis ex officina Michaelis Vascosani,* 1544, 8vo.
At the end of Buchanan's version is the following notice : " Acta fuit Burdegalæ an. 1543." The earliest edition of *Jephthes* which has been traced
is that of Paris, 1554, 4to, *Apud Guil. Morellum.* His version of the
Alcestis was printed there in the same form in 1557, *Apud Mich. Vascosanum.* The two translated dramas occur in a collection entitled " Tragœdiæ
Selectæ Æschyli, Sophoclis, Euripidis." *Excudebat H. Stephanus,* 1567,
8vo. The *Baptistes* was published by H. Charters in 1578, 8vo; and in
the course of the same year was reprinted at Frankfort in the same form by
Andrew Wechel. There is a collective edition of Buchanan's " Tragœdiæ
Sacræ et Exteræ," *Apud Petrum Sanctandreanum,* 1597, 8vo. Mr Ruddiman edited the versions from Euripides with the original text. Edinb.
1722, 8vo. Buchanan's translation is subjoined to Professor Monk's edition of the *Alcestis.* Cantab. 1816, 8vo. Of his tragedies there are many
other editions, which it would be superfluous to enumerate.

ᵍ " Jephtha's daughter," says Dr Jortin, " was devoted to God, and to
the service of the high priest, and of the tabernacle. It is strange that any
commentator should have imagined that she was sacrificed." (Jortin's
Tracts, vol. i, p. 380.) The commentators who adopt that opinion are justified by the respectable authority of Josephus. Selden could discover no

and excruciating sensations of the mother, the daughter's mingled sentiments of heroism and timidity, are delineated with considerable felicity of dramatic conception. The tender or pathetic was not however the peculiar province of Buchanan; whose talents were bold, masculine, and commanding. It has been urged by Heinsius and by Vossius, that in this tragedy the ancient rule respecting unity of time is grossly violated; because the daughter of Jephtha is known to have bewailed her virginity for the space of two months.[h] But in Buchanan's drama there is no allusion to that circumstance; and if he has exposed himself to critical reprehension, it is only because he has neglected such scrupulous advertency to the national rites of his personages.

The *Baptistes,* although inferior to the other tragedy in dramatic interest, is more strongly impregnated with the author's characteristic sentiments. Its great theme is civil and religious liberty. The poet frequently expresses himself with astonishing boldness: his language relative to tyranny and priestcraft is so strong and un-

vestige of any paternal power of thus devoting children who did not belong to the tribe of Levi. It is not pretended that Jephtha sacrificed his daughter " ex jure aliquo," but merely to fulfil a vow which it would have been piety to violate. On the subject of this vow, a chapter occurs in Selden *De Jure Naturali et Gentium juxta Disciplinam Ebræorum,* p. 530. Lond. 1640, fol.

[h] Heinsius de Tragœdiæ Constitutione, p. 204. Vossii Institutiones Poeticæ, p. 13.

disguised, that it could not then have been toler-
ated in many colleges; and the acquiescence of
Buchanan's learned auditory suggests no unfavourable opinion of the flourishing seminary to·
which he belonged. Some of his expressions
bear a very easy application to the late conduct
of Cardinal Beaton.

In the tragedies of the ancient Greek poets,
what is termed the prologue is always an essential
part of the drama; but the prologue of the *Baptistes* resembles those of Terence. Buchanan
seems to have adopted this method, because it
afforded him an opportunity of preparing his auditors for the bold sentiments which they were
about to hear.

· The same subject was afterwards selected by
several other poets. A drama with the title of
Baptistes occurs among the works of Schonæus;
and another, written by Nicholas Grimoald, and
entitled *Archipropheta, sive Johannes Baptista,*
was published at London in the year 1591. [i]
Milton had directed his attention to no fewer
than one hundred different subjects for tragedy,
and among others to that of John the Baptist.
Of this projected drama he has sketched a faint
outline; [k] which it may be no uninteresting task
to compare with the plan of Buchanan.

Grotius has remarked that Buchanan, so ad-

---

[i] Warton's Hist. of English Poetry, vol. iii, p. 60.
[k] Milton's Poetical Works, by Todd, vol. iv, p. 504.

mirable in other respects, has not sufficiently
maintained the gravity of the ancient buskin ;[1]
and it is indeed obvious that his tragedies are not
the most perfect of his compositions. The disapprobation of Heinsius, who like Grotius was
also a dramatic poet, is however expressed too
forcibly : the tragedies of Buchanan he mentions
not merely without applause, but even with some
degree of contempt.[m] Some of his objections are
manifestly frivolous ; and he might almost be
suspected of an oblique intention to establish
his own superiority. Buchanan, who was distinguished for the elevation of his genius, was certainly capable of imparting to his tragic heroes
sufficient pomp of diction ; but he was too competent a judge of propriety to invest every scene
with the same heroic swell. The diction of Euripides, whom he apparently selected as his model, is very remote from the standard which
some modern critics have attempted to introduce.
The original tragedies of the Scotish poet are not

[1] Grotius to Thuanus : " Tibi hæc mittuntur, Præses Illustrissime, qui
post Scotiæ illud numen redivivam nobis reduxisti tragœdiam : nisi quod et
Buchananus ipse, in aliis vir maximus, a cothurni gravitate degenerare videtur." (Epistolæ, p. 1. Amst. 1687, fol.)

[m] " Duos certe excellentes hac ætate viros M. Antonium Muretum, Latinæ puritatis nostro ævo principem, Georgium item Buchananum, poetam
eximium, quorum ingeniis nihil impervium fuisse dicas, nemo hodie non
novit : qui cum se huic scenæ crediderunt, alterum in cothurno, alterum in
socco pedem habuisse dicas ; adeo nec legem se tenere putant, neque mentem ad antiquitatis regulam deflectunt. Illius Cæsare equidem, hujus autem Jephte humilius vix quicquam dici potest ; cum vix unquam assur-
gant." (Heinsius De Tragœdiæ Constitutione, p. 200, edit. Lugd. Bat.
1643, 12mo.)

however free from considerable blemishes. Although his subjects are scriptural, he frequently alludes to classical mythology, and to physical objects with which the Hebrews were totally unacquainted. To some of the characters in *Jephthes* he assigns Greek names; and the chorus in very familiar terms mention the wealth of Crœsus, who was not born till about six hundred years after Jephtha. These will be considered as glaring examples of impropriety; but it may at least be pleaded that similar errors have been committed by the ancient poets. The Persians of Æschylus speak of Jupiter and Hermes: in the *Electra* of Sophocles, the characters are very familiar with the Pythian games; and in the *Phœnissæ* of Euripides, the war between Eumolpus and the Athenians is placed in the same period with the contention between the sons of Œdipus, that is, about four generations too late.[a] In the *Amphitruo* of Plautus, the characters swear by Hercules before he is supposed to be born. Nor is it unworthy of remark that Heinsius, who claimed the honour of being the first critic that comprehended the system of Aristotle,[o] and

---

[a] Grotii prolegomena in Euripidis Phœniss. Paris. 1630, 8vo. Valckenaer ad Phœniss. v. 861. Franeq. 1755, 4to.—" 'Αναχρονισμοὶ et μεταχρονισμοὶ," says Valckenaer, " nimis sunt frequentes apud quosvis, ne Homero quidem excepto, poëtas, tragicos præsertim, sed et apud philosophos, Platonem et Xenophontem."

[o] Heinsii Responsio ad Balsacium, p. 4, 25.—" L'art de la poësie," says De Croi, " qu' Aristote et qu' Homere nous avoyent laissé, avoit esté ignoré jusqu' à luy." (*Response au Discours de Balsac*, p. 10.)

who censured his predecessors with such freedom, has himself exhibited many gross violations
of propriety; has in the same tragedy blended
angels with the Furies, Michaël with Alecto,
Tesiphone with Gabriël, and Megæra with Ra-
phaël.[p]

Of his dramatic performances Buchanan entertained a very modest opinion; but if we recollect the circumstances under which they originated, they cannot fail of exciting a considerable
degree of admiration. Their composition was
partly a task which his academical station imposed: he completed the four tragedies in the compass of three years, while engaged in the laborious
occupation of teaching grammar to young students, and while he even regarded his life as inse-
cure from the deadly malice of Cardinal Beaton
and the grey friars. Whatever may be the defects

[p] Salmasii Epistola ad Menagium, p. 77, 4to.—This tragedy of Daniel
Heinsius is entitled *Herodes Infanticida.* Lugd. Bat. 1632, 8vo. Balzac published a " Discours sur une Tragedie, intitulée *Herodes Infanticida,*" (Paris, 1636, 8vo.) in which the merits of that composition were very
fairly discussed. The poet was however of a different opinion; as he soon
afterwards testified by his " Epistola, qua Dissertationi Balsacii ad Heroden
Infanticidam, respondetur." Lugd. Bat. 1636, 8vo. Jean de Croi, who
afterwards assailed him in another quarter, was eager on this occasion to vindicate his fame: his work bears the title of " Response à la Lettre, et au
Discours de Balzac, sur une Tragedie de Heins, intitulée *Herodes Infanticida.*" Geneve? 1642, 8vo. The controversy was terminated by the formidable interference of Salmasius ; who had recently been engaged in another contest with Heinsius, respecting what is termed the Hellenistic language. His tract is entitled " Ad Ægidium Menagium Epistola, super
Herode Infanticida viri celeberrimi Tragœdia, et Censura Balsacii." Paris.
1644, 8vo. It is reprinted in the collection of his *Epistolæ.* Lugd. Bat.
1656, 4to. Balzac's dissertation occurs in his *Oeuvres Diverses,* p. 110.

C

of those productions, they are at least superior to any of the Latin dramas which had been composed by modern poets. This province had been sufficiently cultivated by the scholars of Italy[q] and Germany; but with a degree of success which leaves them very far behind the author of *Jephthes*. Most of their performances, when compared with those of Buchanan, will appear extremely unclassical and grotesque. At the period when he was thus reforming the classical theatre, the productions of Betuleius and Macropedius were received with much applause.[r]

His translations from Euripides must have contributed, as well as his original compositions, to revive the genius of the ancient drama. These versions are executed with no inconsiderable felicity. The diction of *Alcestis* surpasses that of *Medea*; yet to his learned contemporaries the last appeared so highly classical, that strong suspicions were entertained of his having published in his own name a genuine relique of antiquity.[s]

---

[q] See Mr Walker's Historical and Critical Essay on the Revival of the Drama in Italy. Edinb. 1805, 8vo.

[r] " Some in Englande, moe in France, Germanie, and Italie also, have written tragedies in our tyme: of which, not one, I am sure, is able to abyde the trew touch of Aristotle's preceptes, and Euripides' example, save onely two, that ever I saw, M. Watson's *Absalon*, and Georgius Buchananus' *Jephthes*." (Ascham's *Works*, p. 320.)

[s] " Eodem certe modo," says H. Stephanus, " furti insimulatum fuisse Georgium Buchananum audivi, quum ejus Medea (id est Euripidis Medea ab eo Latine versa) in lucem prodiit. In aliqua enim bibliotheca latentem hanc Latinam Medeam surripuisse, ac suam tandem fecisse. Sed quum talis sit haec versio ut vel dignissima antiquitate (ad multos praesertim locos

The same tragedy had been translated by Ennius, whose version is not preserved.[t] At a later period two tragedies of Euripides were translated by Erasmus ;[u] and his attempt is mentioned with becoming respect by his accomplished successor. It was probably the example of Buchanan that prompted other excellent scholars to similar enterprizes : translations from the Greek dramatists were afterwards executed by Jos. Scaliger, Chrestien, and Grotius.[x]

Buchanan's original tragedies have been translated into several languages.[y] One of Milton's

quod attinet) dici queat, habent quo suam accusationem excusent." (*De bene Instituendis Græcæ Linguæ Studiis*, p. 116. 1587, 4to.)

[t] Ennii Fragmenta, p. 307, edit. Columnæ. Neapoli, 1590, 4to.

[u] Erasmi Opera, tom. i, col. 1131, edit. Clerici.

[x] Dr. Bentley remarks that Buchanan, Scaliger, Grotius, and other modern poets, have not sufficiently adverted to the prosody of the Greek dramatists. " All the moderns before had supposed, that the last syllable of every verse was common, as well in anapæsts, as they are known to be in hexameters and others : so that in poems of their own composing, the last foot of their anapæsts was very frequently a tribrachys, or a trochee, or a cretic ; or the foot ended in a vowel or an *m*, while the next verse began with a vowel or an *h*. In every one of which cases an error was committed : because there was no licence allowed by the ancients to the last syllable of anapæsts ; but the anapæst feet run on to the parœmiac, that is, to the end of the sett, as if the whole had been a single verse. This, I said, was a general rule among the Greek poets ; and even Seneca, the Latin tragedian (to shew he was conscious of this rule, that I have now discover'd) never ends an anapæstic verse with a cretic, as Buchanan, Scaliger, Grotius, &c. usually do ; though sometimes indeed he does it with a trochee, but even that very seldom, and generally at the close of a sentence." (*Dissertation upon Phalaris*, p. 132. Lond. 1699, 8vo.)—See likewise Bentley's Epistola ad Millium, p. 23, Ruddiman de Metris Buchananæis, p. 8, and Gaisford ad Hephæstionem, p. 261. Oxon. 1810, 8vo.

[y] For the subsequent notices relative to the Italian and French translations, I am almost entirely indebted to the distinguished politeness of the

biographers has ascribed to that immortal poet an English version of the *Baptistes:* but his opinion is not authorized by the slightest vestige of evidence, either historical or internal; and his persevering observations on the subject exhibit a very curious and entertaining specimen of antiquarian reasoning.[z]

late Joseph Cooper Walker, Esq. who was very minutely acquainted with the history of the drama, and was always disposed to communicate literary information.

" L'Iefte, Tragedia di Giorgio Bucanano, recata di Latino in Volgare da Scipione Bargagli." In Venezia per Matteo Valentini, 1600, 18vo.

" Jephté, ou le Vœu, Tragedie traduite du Latin de Buchanan par Florent Chrestien." Printed with " Le Premier Chapitre des Lamentations de Jerémie en vers." Orleans, Loys Rabier, 1567, 4to. Paris, Robert Estienne, 1573, 8vo. Mamert Patisson, 1587, 12mo. With the " Fragmens de Loüis de Masures." M. Patisson, 1595, 12mo. A specimen of this version may be found in the late excellent edition of Du Verdier's *Bibliotheque Françoise,* tom. i, p. 585. The same tragedy was translated into French by François Perrin, and by Nicholas le Digne, Sieur de Condes ; but neither of their versions is known to have been printed.—In one of his curious publications, Mr Walker informs us that on the same subject with this drama of Buchanan, a French opera and an Italian tragedy were composed during the last century. (*Historical Memoir on Italian Tragedy,* p. 264, 338. Lond. 1799, 4to.)

" Baptiste, ou la Calomnie, Tragedie traduite du Latin de Buchanan, par M. Brinon." Jean Osmont, 1613, 12mo. " I believe," says Mr Walker, " Brinon translated also *Jephthes.*"

[a] Peck's New Memoirs of the Life and Poetical Works of Mr. John Milton. Lond. 1740, 4to.—The translation originally appeared with this title : " Tyrannical Government Anatomised : or, a discourse concerning evil counsellors ; being the Life and Death of John the Baptist." 1642. Mr Peck not being at first aware that this is only a version of the *Baptistes,* had employed a very curious series of arguments to prove that as it could not possibly be composed by any body else, it must consequently have been composed by *Mr* Milton ; and he had moreover compiled many historical annotations to illustrate *Mr* Milton's evident allusions to contemporary transactions. Though he at length discovered his error in supposing it to be an original work, he was sorry to lose his arguments and his annota-

. In the learned dramas represented in the College of Guienne, the well-known Michel de Montagne was a frequent performer. About the period when Buchanan was appointed a professor, he there commenced his academical studies at the early age of six years. Before his return home, which took place in his thirteenth year, he personated the principal characters in the Latin tragedies of Buchanan, Muretus, and Garentæus. Those learned men, together with Gru-

. . . .

tions: he therefore published this version as Milton's, and retained all that he had formerly written, interspersed indeed with some qualifying phrases which only serve to heighten the ridicule. The preface to his new edition opens in the following manner. " His Baptistes is the sixth of Mr John Milton's nine *most celebrated* English poems; and one of the *hitherto unknown* pieces of his whereof I am now to give an account." The following specimen of the translation is one of the most favourable that are to be found; but it certainly comprehends nothing unattainable by talents very inferior to those of Milton.

> Te quicquid aer continet laxo sinu ;
> Quæcunque tellus, &c.

> Whatere the ayre in its loose bosome bears ;
> Whatere the earth can procreate, or sea
> Within it waters nourish ; thee their God
> All do acknowledge, and by thee alone
> Finde their creation. In a constant way,
> Thy lawe once given, freely they obey.
> At thy command the spring with flowers paints
> The fertile fields, and fruits the summer yields ;
> Autumne pure wine abundantly affords,
> And winter with white frost the hills attires ;
> The crooked rivers rolle into the sea
> Huge heaps of waters ; the sea ebbs and flows ;
> The silver moon illuminates the night,
> The golden sun the day ; and views this orb
> With never-resting brightnesse.

chius, he has commemorated as his domestic preceptors.[a]

Montagne relates that when he afterwards saw Buchanan in the train of Marshal de Brissac, that illustrious poet alluded to his having formed a project of composing a work on education, in which he intended to exhibit the discipline of his old pupil as a proper exemplar. This project he seems never to have executed. It was perhaps his intention to write a philosophical poem on the subject; but he might relinquish the design in consequence of having commenced another didactic work soon after the period to which Montagne refers.

Buchanan's attention to the interests of elegant and useful learning was unremitting. In a Sapphic ode addressed to the youth of Bordeaux, he reminds them of the dignity and importance of the liberal arts, and particularly of that art which he had himself cultivated with such eminent success.[b] The exertions of such a precep-

---

[a] Essais de Montagne, liv. i, chap. xxv.—Sir Robert Sibbald supposes Buchanan to have resided in the country as Montagne's tutor. (*Comment. in Vitam Buchanani*, p. 13.) Montagne has also mentioned Muretus, Gruchius, and Garentæus, as his domestic preceptors. Like Buchanan, they were professors in the College of Guienne, where he was domesticated for several years; but that any of the four was entertained in his father's house, is a conjecture manifestly devoid of foundation. Mr Ruddiman, who likewise adopts this conjecture, places Buchanan's supposed rustication with Montagne between 1542 and 1544. But it is evident from the essay to which I have referred, that Montagne did not leave the College of Guienne before the year 1546.

[b] Buchanani Miscell. ix.

tor could not fail of improving the taste of his pupils; but the splendour of his poetry seems to have conferred upon the college a substantial benefit of another kind. This seminary was more remarkable for the learning of its members, than for the opulence of its endowments. The scantiness of their provision was so sensibly felt that Buchanan, probably at the suggestion of his colleagues, addressed a poetical representation to Francis Olivier, chancellor of the kingdom.[c] On this occasion the powerful influence of the ancient lyre was revived: Buchanan afterwards inscribed to the chancellor an elegant ode, in which he commemorates his liberality and promptitude in ameliorating their condition.[d] Olivier seems to have been warmly attached to the interests of polite literature, and of its professors. He is highly celebrated in the poems of De l'Hôpital, the most distinguished of his successors in the, chancellorship. Turnebus addressed to him a similar petition in behalf of the royal professors at Paris.[e]

The social intercourse which Buchanan enjoyed at Bordeaux may be supposed to have been neither inelegant nor uninteresting. That city had long evinced its respect for learning. In ancient times it could boast of a flourishing acade-

[c] Buchanani Elegia v.
[d] Buchanani Miscell. iv.
[e] Delitiæ Poetarum Gallorum, tom. iii, p. 1045.

my,[f] and of the poetical talents of its citizen Ausonius, by whom the merits of several contemporary professors have been commemorated. The
foundation of the college to which Buchanan belonged was completed in the year 1584, when his
friend Govea was invited from Paris to officiate
as principal.[g] In 1573, the College of the Jesu-
its was instituted by the liberality of M. de Ban-
lon, a counsellor in the provincial parliament;[h]
and it was not perhaps till about that period that
the schools of Bordeaux received the privileges of
a university.[i] In the year 1555 however the College of Guienne maintained fifteen professors or
public teachers.[k] The accomplishments of Buchanan and of the able scholars with whom he
was associated had established its reputation;
and it was once regarded as the best seminary in
France for the elementary instruction of youth.[l]
Several of his associates were men of eminent talents and erudition: among them he had formed

---

[f] Bulæi Hist. Universitatis Parisiensis, tom. i, p. 46.

[g] Gabriel de Lurbe, Chronique Bourdeloise, f. 42. Bourdeaux, 1594,
4to.—This work, originally written in Latin, was translated by the author;
who was an advocate of Bordeaux. The French edition is more copious.
—A work entitled L'Antiquité de Bourdeaus, et de Bourg, was published
by Vinetus. A second edition, corrected and enlarged, was printed at Bordeaux in quarto in the year 1574.

[h] De Lurbe, Chronique Bourdeloise, f. 48.

[i] Miræus mentions Bordeaux as the seat of a university. (Notitia Epis-
copatuum Orbis Christiani, p. 275, edit. Antverp. 1613, 8vo.)

[k] Schotti Bibliotheca Hispanica, p. 618.

[l] Du Chesne, Antiquitez et Recherches des Villes, Chasteaux, et Places
plus remarquables de toute la France, p. 751.

intimacies which he recollected with pleasure during the last years of his life; and in his poetical
works he commemorates his regard for some of
the distinguished lawyers who then resided at
Bordeaux. He has written in very favourable
terms the epitaphs of François de Belcier, first
president of the parliament, Briand de Vallée,
one of the king's counsellors in the same court,
and of Innocentius Fontanus, a lawyer and a
poet.[m] To De Vallée, whom he has extolled as
one of the most worthy as well as most learned
men whom the sun had beheld,[n] he addressed an
elegy written with too much freedom.

Buchanan's social intercourse was not confined
to the college and to the city; it was at this period that he occasionally enjoyed the society of a
very extraordinary personage who resided at a
considerable distance. At Agen the elder Scaliger was now exercising the profession of a physician. That city, when he there fixed his residence, could not furnish him with a single individual capable of supporting literary conversation; and he was therefore led to cultivate an
intimacy with some of the more enlightened in-

---

[m] Buchanani Epigram. lib. ii, 17, 5, 19. *Innocentio Fontano Burdega-*
lensi Poetæ et Caussidico.

[n] Briand de Vallée is thus mentioned in an epistle by one Pierre de Vallée, appended to Franciscus Bonadus's Latin version of the psalms, Paris,
1531, 8vo: " Imprimis scripturienti mihi occurrit Briandus ille Valla,
Burdegalensis senatus consul ut vigilantissimus, ita utriusque literaturæ ornatissimus." This friend of Buchanan endowed a lecture of theology in
the College of Guienne. (De Lurbe, f. 42.)

habitants of Bordeaux. Buchanan, Tevius, and other accomplished scholars who then belonged to the College of Guienne, were accustomed to pay him an annual visit during the autumnal vacation. They were hospitably entertained in his house; and he declared that he forgot the torture of his gout whenever he had an opportunity of discussing topics of learning with such guests.[o] He has composed two poems in celebration of his illustrious friend.[p] They are not distinguished by any peculiar felicity of expression; but they possess some value, as testimonials of the favourable opinion entertained of Buchanan by a critic who despised most of his learned contemporaries. For the society of this singular man, who possessed some bad and many good qualities, Buchanan has expressed a mutual relish.[q]

Julius Cæsar Scaliger, according to the narrative of his son Joseph, was born on Friday the twenty-third of April 1484, in the castle of Ripa, situated at the head of the Lago di Garda.

[o] "In Gymnasio autem Aquitanico Burdegalensi tunc erat Buchananus, Muretus, Tevius, alii: at qui viri? Ii quotannis feriis vindemialibus Aginnum Julii Cæsaris visendi commeabant, quos et tecto et mensa excipiebat. Negabat enim sibi rem cum podagra esse, quoties tales convivas haberet, quibuscum de literis loqui posset." (Jos. Scaliger *De Vetustate et Splendore Gentis Scaligeræ*, p. 51.) In a later publication Scaliger denies that Muretus ever came to Agen after his settlement at Bordeaux: "Quum Burdegalam, relicta schola Villanova, profectus, sibi in una classium Gymnasii Aquitanici doceret, circiter annum Christi MDXLVII. neque ex eo unquam aut Aginnum repetivit, aut Julium postea vidit." (*Confutatio Fabulæ Burdonum*, p. 453.) These two passages are evidently irreconcilable.

[p] Jul. Scaligeri Poemata, tom. i, p. 166, 321.

[q] Buchanani Epigram. lib. i, 49.

He was the second son of Benedetto della Scala, descended of the royal house of Verona; which was despoiled of its principality by the republic of Venice. As Benedetto had commanded the armies of Matthias king of Hungary, and likewise enjoyed the favour of the emperor Frederick, the Venetians regarded him as a dangerous remnant of his illustrious family. Two days after his wife had been delivered of this child, they made an attempt to seize the mother and her two sons; but notwithstanding her critical situation, she escaped from the castle, and fled to her father the count of Lodronio.—Such is the genealogy which Joseph Scaliger has claimed in his unfortunate epistle to Janus Dousa;[r] and his father very frequently alludes to the same splendour of ancestry. But the validity of their pretensions is extremely dubious. The Italian scholars, as one of them has remarked,[s] were generally disposed to consider their royalty as purely fictitious. Scioppius, who attacked the dead father and the living son in a most atrocious manner, advanced many arguments in proof of their mean extraction.[t] The character of this author

[r] Jos. Scaliger de Vetustate et Splendore Gentis Scaligeræ. Lugd. Bat. 1594, 4to.—This epistle occupies the first fifty-seven pages of the collection of the author's *Epistolæ.* Lugd. Bat. 1627, 8vo.

[s] Imperialis Museum Historicum, p. 64. Venet. 1640, 4to.—See likewise Maffei, Verona Illustrata, par. ii, p. 300, and Tiraboschi, Storia della Letteratura Italiana, tom. vii, p. 1483.

[t] Scioppii Scaliger Hypobolimæus. Moguntiæ, 1607, 4to.—In the course of the following year Scioppius was exposed, in a volume entitled *" Satiræ duæ, Hercules tuam Fidem sive Munsterus Hypobolimæus, et*

renders every thing connected with his private veracity sufficiently equivocal : but on the other hand, many circumstances contribute to undermine the credit of the younger Scaliger's hyperbolical and romantic narrations ; nor can the answer which he returned to Scioppius be deemed satisfactory with respect to any of the material points of debate.   It is not true that his father was born in the castle of Ripa ; he was born in the city of Verona.[u]   If he was actually knighted

Virgula Divina." The author of the two satires, as Scaliger has often remarked in his epistles, was Daniel Heinsius, who was then in the twenty-seventh year of his age. He was born at Ghent in 1581. Placcius has improperly ascribed the " Confutatio Fabulæ Burdonum" to Janus Rutgersius. *(Theatrum Anonymorum et Pseudonymorum,* tom. i, p. 37. Hamb. 1708, 2 tom. fol.) The title indeed bears " J. R. Batavus, Juris Studiosus ;" but Scaliger has repeatedly mentioned it as his own production. On the eleventh of June 1606 he thus wrote to Janus Gruterus : " Occupatissimus hos dies fui in scripto quod adversus Burdonistas adorno. Nomen non apponam, neque meum qui scripsi, neque ejus quem anonymum hujus auctorem facio." (*Scaligeri Epistolæ,* p. 793.) He was willing that it should be considered as the composition of Rutgersius, a young scholar of the highest promise. To some editions is likewise appended a tract entitled " Vita et Parentes Gasp. Schoppii, a Germano quodam contubernali ejus conscripta." This German was perhaps Eilhardus Lubinus ; who appears to have written some tract in disparagement of Scioppius. (*Ibid.* p. 725.) Scioppius afterwards published a work, which he pretended had long been suppressed by the artifices of the Calvinists. It bears the title of " Oporini Grubini Amphotides Scioppianæ ; hoc est Responsio ad Satyram Menippæam Josephi Burdonis Pseudo-Scaligeri pro Vita et Moribus Gasp. Scioppii." *Paris.* 1611, 8vo.—Dr Foster mentions Scioppius as a " very judicious and discerning scholar." (*Essay on Accent and Quantity,* p. 213. Eton, 1762, 8vo.)

[u] Bayle, in his short account of Verona, has published the letters of naturalization which Scaliger obtained from Francis the first ; and he is there denominated " natif de *la Ville de Veronne* en Itallie." In those letters, his name and addition were unquestionably recited from his own memorial or petition.

by the emperor, it is certainly an extraordinary circumstance that he should never have assumed so honourable a distinction. It is apparently false that his original appellation was either Julius Cæsar Scaliger of Burden, or count of Burden.[x] To accuse these very learned men of downright falsehood, may perhaps appear extremely harsh and indecent; but it is not easy to admit many of their assertions relative to this subject, which seems to have interested them above all others. With all their splendid endowments, they were subject to errors which might serve to reconcile the more obscure part of mankind to their obscurity.

The father's original profession was that of arms; and he is represented as having performed prodigious feats of strength and valour. After having fought under the banners of the emperor, he retired to Ferrara, where he experienced the

---

[x] Gyraldus, the contemporary and friend of Scaliger, denominates him " Jul. Scaliger, qui prius *Burdonis* cognomine fuit, Veronensis, apprime eruditus." (*De Poetis suorum Temporum*, dial. ii, p. 415.) In the letters of naturalization he is termed " Julius Cæsar de l'Escalla de Bordoms, Docteur en Medecine." M. de la Monnoye conjectures with great probability, that instead of *Bordoms* we ought to read *Bordonis*, and that the omission of a point over the letter i in the manuscript occasioned the mistake. (*Menagiana*, tom. iii, p. 452.) Those letters contain no hint of his being descended of royal ancestors, born in the castle of Ripa, and adorned with the honour of knighthood. If Scaliger's high pretensions had been well-founded, he would not have failed to state them in his memorial; and if they had been thus stated, the titles of so honourable a subject must certainly have been recited in the instrument which constituted him a citizen of France. The date of this curious document is 1528. Bayle published it from a copy communicated by Baluzius.

liberality of the reigning duke. It was here perhaps that he became a pupil of the famous Ludovicus Cælius Rhodiginus, whom he has repeatedly mentioned as his preceptor,[y] and who was professor of eloquence in that university before his removal to Padua.[z] The poverty of his present condition led Scaliger to form a determination of assuming the habit of St. Francis: he accordingly went to the university of Bologna, and commenced his acquaintance with the writings of the subtile doctor; but his affection for a monastic life soon began to cool. The Franciscans he afterwards hated with as much cordiality as his friend Buchanan; and never willingly interchanged a single word with any member of that fraternity. Having passed into Piedmont for the purpose of visiting some of his fellow-students to whom he was much attached, he obtained the command of a troop of light horse from the French general who presided in that province; and, according to the report of his son, he performed such gallant service that he recommended himself to the personal notice of Francis the first. In the midst of his warlike broils he did not forget the pursuits of literature. His acquaintance with a physician of Turin produced an accidental bias towards the study of medicine; which he began to prosecute with all the ardour incident to so vigorous a mind. His military

---

[y] Jul. Scaligeri Poetice, lib. iii, cap. cxxvi, Poemata, tom. i, p. 306.
[z] Tomasini Elogia Virorum Illustrium, tom. ii, p. 63.

duty and nocturnal lucubrations, added to the inclemency of the sky, subjected him to a violent attack of the gout; but he had no sooner recovered his strength than he recurred with his wonted eagerness to the occupations of war and letters. Hitherto he was unacquainted with the Greek tongue; and although he had already exceeded the thirty-fifth year of his age, he applied himself to its acquisition with the utmost pertinacity and success. This intenseness of study having excited a fit of the gout more excruciating than the former, he determined to abandon the profession of a soldier. The bishop of Agen, who was related to some of his particular friends in Piedmont, having persuaded Scaliger to accompany him to his diocese as a military protector, it was the learned warrior's destiny to be there arrested by the charms of Andiette de Roques Lobeiac, a hopeful damsel of thirteen. Scaliger was more than triple that age, but he was a scholar and a soldier, and possessed the still superior recommendation of a tall and noble person. It is not however astonishing that the relations of Andiette, who was descended of a good family, should hesitate as to the expediency of her accepting the hand of a wrong-headed adventurer. They contrived to defer the match for the space of three years; but having persisted in his scheme with that pertinacity which characterised all his actions, he was at length successful. With this amiable woman, who became

4

the mother of fifteen children, his union was fortunate in every respect; she not only inherited landed property, but possessed other recommendations of a more valuable nature. Scaliger now established himself as a physician at Agen, where he spent the remainder of his days. His name was yet unknown in the republic of letters; but notwithstanding the irregular tenor of his life, he had provided a large fund of erudition, and panted to signalize himself as a literary gladiator. Erasmus had attained to the highest reputation, and Scaliger selected him as an antagonist not altogether unworthy of himself. In the year 1528 Erasmus had published his *Ciceronianus*, a very ingenious dialogue in which he exposes the laborious trifling of the professed Ciceronians; and in 1531 Scaliger published what he terms an oration in defence of Cicero against Erasmus. The very title of his work affords a proof of his having mistaken the question; for it was not the scope of the other production to extenuate the merits of Cicero himself, but to explode the preposterous notions of those servile admirers who hesitated to employ a single word or phrase, unless it had been sanctioned by the authority of their favourite author. But if Erasmus had called Cicero a blockhead and a rascal, and had himself been entitled to those appellations, Scaliger could hardly have attacked him in a more ferocious manner. His interference was the more impertinent, as he defended Cicero in a style by no means Ciceronian. Erasmus had hitherto been unacquainted even with the name of the writer who now assailed him with such rudeness; and from internal evidence he was firmly persuaded that at least the principal part of the oration had been composed by Hieronymus Aleander.[a] As he did not condescend to reply, his conduct was the most mortifying that he could have adopted. Scaliger finding himself thus treated with silent contempt, prepared a second oration still more injurious than the first; but it was not printed till after the death of the illustrious man whom he had loaded with insults equally unmerited and unprovoked.[b] In his subsequent productions, he alternately mentions Erasmus with admiration and contempt. He

[a] Jortin's Life of Erasmus, vol. i, p. 517.

[b] Scaliger's invectives were afterwards republished by the learned Maussac. "Jul. Cæs. Scaligeri adversus Desid. Erasmum Orationes duæ, Eloquentiæ Romanæ vindices: una cum ejusdem Epistolis, et Opusculis aliquot nondum vulgatis." Tolosæ, 1621, 4to. Sixteen of his letters relative to this contest occur in the *Amœnitates Literariæ*, tom. vi, p. 508, tom. viii, p. 554. Of Scaliger's principal works, exclusive of his Latin poems, I shall subjoin a catalogue.

1. De Causis Linguæ Latinæ libri tredecim. Lugduni, 1540, 4to.

2. Exotericarum Exercitationum liber quintus decimus, de Subtilitate, ad Hieronymum Cardanum. Lutetiæ, 1557, 4to.

3. Poetices libri septem, ad Sylvium filium. Apud Antonium Vincentium, 1561, fol.

4. Commentarii in sex libros de Causis Plantarum Theophrasti, et in libros Aristotelis de Plantis. Lugduni, 1566, fol.

5. Animadversiones in Historias Theophrasti. Lugduni, 1584, 8vo.

6. Aristotelis Historia de Animalibus, J. C. Scaligero interprete, cum ejusdem Commentariis. Tolosæ, 1619, fol.—This posthumous work was edited by Maussac.

D

afterwards commenced an attack on Cardan, in
a work entitled *De Subtilitate;* and a more dog-
matical or captious book never made its appearance. The productions which have chiefly per-
petuated his fame are the two treatises on poetry, and the principles of the Latin language:
in these he displays wonderful sagacity and erudition, but is frequently misled by an inherent
love of paradox and contradiction. Huet represents him as a man of a vast and elevated genius, but of a very bad taste in poetry;[c] and it
must be acknowledged that the judgments which
he pronounces on some of the principal poets of
antiquity, have deservedly superseded his claims
of infallibility. His own efforts as a poet have
but little tendency to recommend him as a critic:
his verses, which amount to a very formidable
number, are for the most part elaborately composed, and frequently are pregnant with ingenious and subtile thought; but they are inelegant,
harsh, and obscure. The style of his prose is
however greatly superior: though not altogether
free from barbarisms, it possesses much force and
elevation. Having exceeded the seventy-fourth
year of his age, this singular man was numbered
with the dead on the twenty-first day of October 1558. Josephus Justus Scaliger, who was
his tenth child, had then completed his eighteenth year. During the last four years of his

* Huetiana, p. 90.

life, Julius was half a Lutheran; and Joseph renounced the Popish doctrines at an early crisis.
Morhoff awards to the father the praise of superior genius;[d] but Jortin characterizes the son
as " the best critic and the greatest scholar that
ever was born."[e] His knowledge of languages
was prodigious; and yet Latin was almost the
only one which he did not acquire without the
aid of a preceptor. For the short space of two
months he attended the Greek lectures of Turnebus at Paris; and afterwards by his undirect-
ed exertions surmounted the difficulties of that
tongue with incredible rapidity.[f] His Greek

---

[d] Morhofius de Pura Dictione Latina, p. 366.

[e] Jortin's Tracts, vol. ii, p. 147.—Rutgersius describes him as " vir omnium ætatum maximus." (Variæ Lectiones, p. 123. Lugd. Bat. 1617,
4to.) Of the life of Joseph Scaliger, no very satisfactory account has yet
appeared. The best materials occur in his own correspondence, and in that
of his learned contemporaries. Heinsius published two orations on his death,
Lugd. Bat. 1609, 4to. Another on the same subject was pronounced by
Baudius, who writes very elegantly in prose and in verse. (Baudii Epistolæ et Orationes, p. 632.) The opinions of many authors relative to Scaliger have been industriously collected by Colomiés. (Gallia Orientalis, p.
118.) A sketch of his life may be found in Niceron, tom. xxiii, p. 279,
and in Chauffepié, Nouveau Dictionnaire Historique et Critique, tom. iv, p.
194. Of his powerful influence on the literature of his adopted country,
Ruhnkenius speaks in the following terms: " Mox enim tanquam cœlo
missus Josephus Scaliger, cui Batavi prope omnem rectum ingenii cultum,
quem ex eo tempore ceperint, si grati esse velint, acceptum referre debent,
Scaliger igitur cum ceteras ingenuas artes, tum Græcas literas, earumque
cum Latinis conjunctionem, in his regionibus fundavit." (Elogium Tibe-
rii Hemsterhusii: Opuscula, p. 23. Lugd. Bat. 1807, 8vo.)

[f] " Igitur vix delibatis conjugationibus Græcia," says Jos. Scaliger,
" Homerum cum interpretatione, arreptum uno et viginti diebus totum didici: poeticæ vero dialecti vestigiis insistens grammaticam mihi ipse forma-
vi: neque ullam aliam didici, quam quæ mihi ex analogia verborum Ho-
mericorum observata fuit. Reliquos vero poetas Græcos omnes intra qua-

have been preferred to his Latin verses. The reflection that Scaliger, Cujacius, Muretus, and Ramus, were self-taught scholars, ought to operate as a most powerful incentive on the mind of the ingenuous youth debarred from the usual avenues of intellectual improvement.

About the period when Buchanan was accustomed to visit Agen, Joseph Scaliger was yet in his infancy; but he inherited his father's high admiration of the Scotish poet. To Buchanan he awarded a decided superiority over all the Latin poets of those times.[e]

During the term of his residence in the College of Guienne, the satirist of the Scotish clergy did not find himself totally secure from danger. Cardinal Beaton, in a letter addressed to the archbishop of Bordeaux, requested him to secure the person of the heretical poet; but as this letter had been entrusted to the care of some individual much interested in the welfare of Buchanan, he was suffered to remain without mo-

---

tuor menses devoravi." (*Epistolæ*, p. 51.) This is certainly astonishing enough; but Huet's mode of refutation is not less singular. " *Experimento* tandem *meo* comperi inania hæc esse Scaligeranæ ostentationis specimina; qualia multa sparsim adspersit operibus suis vir ille, excellentis cæteroquin doctrinæ et ingenii, sed nimium admirator et prædicator sui." (Huetii *Commentarius de Rebus ad eum pertinentibus*, p. 38. Hag. Com. 1718, 12mo.) Here the vanity of Scaliger is exposed with equal vanity; for unless Huet supposed his capacity equal to Scaliger's, he could not thus have appealed to his own experience.

[e] " Buchananus unus est in tota Europa omnes post se relinquens in Latina poesi." (*Prima Scaligerana*, p. 37.) In the history of Scotland, p. 42, Buchanan mentions the son of his deceased friend.

lestation. Still however he found himself annoyed by the threats of the cardinal and the grey friars : but the death of King James, and the appearance of a dreadful plague in Guienne, alleviated his former apprehensions.

Having resided three years at Bordeaux, he afterwards returned to Paris. In 1544 he was officiating as a regent in the College of Cardinal le Moine ;[h] and he apparently retained the same station till 1547. About the former of these periods he was miserably tormented with the gout. The ardour of his fancy was however undiminished : in an interesting elegy, composed in 1544, and addressed to his late colleagues Tastæus and Tevius, he exhibits a dismal picture of his own situation ; and gratefully commemorates the assiduous attentions of his present associates Turnebus and Gelida.

> O animæ, Ptolemæe, meæ pars altera, tuque
> Altera pars animæ, Tevi Jacobe, meæ,
> Scire juvat quid agam? vivo modo, si modo vivit
> Pondus iners, animæ corpus inane suæ.

[h] In the very brief sketch of his own life, Buchanan makes no allusion to his having taught in that college: the fact may however be established by several circumstances. In his fourth elegy, he mentions Gelida as his associate ; and that learned Spaniard is known to have belonged to the College of Cardinal le Moine. Moreri asserts that Buchanan, Turnebus, and Muretus, taught in that college at the same time ; and though the general accuracy of this writer is not conspicuous, yet his testimony may be added to the other indications. Nicholas Bourbon, royal professor of Greek at Paris, who died at a very advanced age in 1644, assured Menage of the same circumstance. (*Anti-Baillet*, tom. i, p. 328.)

Sed tamen ingratas ceu vivi ducimus auras,
    Et trahit exanimem languida vita moram.
Ignea vis febris rapido sic perfurit æstu,
    Ut minus Ætnæi sæviat ira rogi.
Torrida concretis lapidescunt viscera grumis,
    Et latebras renum calculus urit atrox:[l]
Ut Cereris possint, ut Bacchi munera credi
    Tacta Medusæis obriguisse comis.
Sed tamen hæc nostri levis est accessio morbi,
    Et pars immensi vix numeranda mali :
Humor enim cunctos late diffusus in artus,
    Qua jungunt flexus ossibus ossa suos,
Obsedit cæcas pigro marcore lacunas,
    Cunctaque torpenti frigore membra ligat.
Ex humeris pendent sine robore brachia laxa,
    Nec fluidum cervix sustinet ægra caput:
Genua labant, et crura tremunt, lassique recusant,
    Tam celeres nuper, me modo ferre pedes.
Sic ego defunctus jam vivo, mihique superstes,
    Et vitæ amisso munere fata moror :
Quodque mihi superest fugitivæ lucis, id omne
    Dividit in pœnas Parca severa meas.[k]

Having finished the description of his *case*, he

---

[l] Dr. Stuart specifies the stone as Buchanan's mortal disease : " Afflicted with the stone, and pressed down by the infirmities of old age, he felt
the approach of his dissolution, and prepared for it like a philosopher."
(*Hist. of Scotland*, vol. ii, p. 242.) This seems to be one of the bold assertions for which his work is so remarkable. His character of Buchanan
is admirably delineated, but it is considerably indebted to the aid of a good
invention.

[k] Buchanani Eleg. iv. *Ad Ptolemæum Luxium Tastæum, et Jacobum Tevium, cum articulari morbo laboraret.* M.D.XLIV.—The second of Buchanan's *Silvæ* is a pastoral entitled " Desiderium P. L. Tastæi." From these
two productions it may be collected that Tastæus was a native of Gas-
cony, and that he had been associated with Buchanan in the College of
Guienne.

introduces the names of several individuals to whom he seems to have been attached.

Denique vos animis talem me fingite, quales
    Ad tumulos manes credit adesse timor;
Qualia pinguntur miseris simulacra figuris
    Terrificæ Mortis, mortiferæque Famis.
At neque Tastæus, nec Tevius assidet, ore
    Suaviloquo longum qui vetet esse diem :
Nec mihi delicias blandi facit oris Alanus,
    Nec lepida alludit garrulitate Petrus :
Nec recreant animum doctis sermonibus ægrum
    Cætera Vasconicæ turba diserta scholæ.
Sed nec amicitiæ mihi pectora cognita certæ
    In mediis hic me deseruere malis.
Sæpe mihi medicas Groscollius explicat herbas,
    Et spe languentem consilioque juvat :
Sæpe mihi *Stephani* solertia provida *Carli*
    Ad mala præsentem tristia portat opem.
TURNEBUS Aonii rarissima gloria cœtus
    Officiis vacuum non sinit ire diem :
Cæteraque ut cessent, GELIDÆ pia cura sodalis
    Et patris et patriæ sustinet usque vicem.

Carolus Stephanus, whose medical aid Buchanan has thus acknowledged, was a doctor of physic of the faculty of Paris; and, like many of his
relations, was equally distinguished as a scholar
and as a printer.[1] After having produced various

---

[1] Henricus Stephanus, or *Estienne*, established a press at Paris about the year 1500. His son Robertus was born in 1503, and died in 1559. He had continued the same business at Paris; but in 1552 he betook himself to Geneva, where he died in the communion of the reformed church. He was eminently skilled in the Hebrew, Greek, and Latin languages. He chiefly distinguished himself by his editions of the original scriptures, and by his *Thesaurus Linguæ Latinæ*. His brothers Franciscus and Carolus

works in the Latin and French languages, he died at Paris in the year 1564.

In the College of Cardinal le Moine, Buchanan was associated with colleagues worthy of himself; with Turnebus and Muretus, two of the most eminent scholars of modern times; and with Joannes Gelida, who, though of inferior

were printers at Paris. The former was also a bookseller; and in the printing business was associated with his step-father Simon Colinæus. Carolus, among other works of his own composition, published the *Thesaurus M. Tullii Ciceronis.* 1556, fol. This book is now sold " insano pretio." The second Henricus Stephanus, who was the son of Robertus, was born at Paris in 1528, and died at Lyons in 1598. Most of his impressions were executed at Paris, but he had also a press at Geneva. Notwithstanding his eminence as a printer and as a scholar, he failed to amass riches; and he is even reported to have closed his long and useful life in an hospital. " Cum patriam oblivisci non posset," says Cornelius Tollius, " Lugdunum se contulit; ubi opibus, atque ipso etiam ingenio destitutus, vitæ, et tot exantlatis pro republica literaria laboribus, in nosocomio finem fecit." (*Appendix ad Pierium de Literatorum Infelicitate,* p. 88.) For this assertion Tollius quotes no authority; and it is to be hoped that he had been misinformed. Robertus the brother of H. Stephanus was disinherited on account of his attachment to Popery; but he succeeded his father at Paris as printer to the king. He wrote various fugitive poems in Greek and Latin. He is supposed by Maittaire to have died in 1588. His son Franciscus having embraced the reformed religion, established a press at Geneva. Paulus the son of the second H. Stephanus was also a Protestant: having settled at Geneva, he printed various works in a correct manner, and contributed to support the reputation of the family. He is the author of several Latin poems. The third Robertus, son of the second, began to be distinguished at Paris as a printer about the year 1588. He was a writer of Greek and Latin verses; and translated into French the first two books of Aristotle's rhetoric. The version was completed by a nephew who bore the same name. Antonius the son of Paulus was printer to the French king during the earlier part of the seventeenth century. Of the name of Stephanus there were other printers, whose history cannot be traced with sufficient accuracy. Consult Almeloveen *De Vitis Stephanorum,* Amst. 1683, 8vo; and more particularly Maittaire's *Historia Stephanorum.* Lond. 1709, 8vo.

fame, has also been characterized as a man of great acuteness and erudition. It is remarked by a French historian that three of the most learned men in the world then taught humanity in the same college.[m] The first class was taught by Turnebus, the second by Buchanan, and the third by Muretus.[n]

Adrianus Turnebus, if any reliance may be placed on the dubious authority of Dempster, was the descendant of Scotish ancestors;[o] and it is at least certain that his original name furnishes us with a plausible argument of his compatriotism. His French name, it seems to be admitted, was originally Tournebeuf;[p] which is a correct translation of the Scotish Turnbull. He was born however at Andely near Rouen in Normandy in the year 1512. Having been sent to Paris in the eleventh year of his age, he soon rose to great distinction as an elegant and profound scholar. The history of his academical promotions has not been very accurately detailed;- but he is known to have taught humanity at Toulouse, and af﹒ terwards, through the influence of 'Petrus Gal﹒

---

[m] Marolles, Abregé de l' Hist. de France, p. 324, quoted by Teissier.

[n] Moreri, Dictionaire Historique, art. *Muret.*

[o] " Scotum fuisse," says Dempster, " acta familiæ leguntur, ut mihi sæpe referebat v. cl. filius ipsius, summus Lutetiæ senator, quem virtutum non nominis modo hæredem immaturum ex sacro ordine ante triennium mors rapuit." (*Hist. Ecclesiast. Gent. Scotorum,* p. 624.) If Dempster had quoted the authority of a living voucher, it would have been less suspicious.

[p] Mollerus de Scriptoribus Homonymis, p. 790. Hamb. 1697, 8vo.

[q] Turnebi Adversaria, lib. ii, cap. i, Oratio habita post J. Tusani Mortem, cum in ejus locum suffactus est, p. 18. Lutetiæ, 1595, 8vo.—Jacobus Tusanus died in the year 1547.

landius, to have obtained a Greek professorship
at Paris. To this was added, in 1552, the appointment of Greek printer to the king; but on
being nominated, in 1555, royal professor of philosophy and of the Greek language, he resigned
his typographical charge.[r] To the infinite regret
of learning and virtue, he died on the twelfth of
June 1565. It was his earnest request that his
body should be interred without the usual cere-
monies of the Popish church; and at nine o'clock
in the evening of the same day, it was accordingly deposited in the earth by a small number of
his friends. He had lived without any open
avowal of his affection for the reformation;[s]
but on being interrogated a few days previous to
his death, he professed his abhorrence of Popery.[t]
The earnestness with which both parties claimed
him as their associate, affords a strong proof of
the importance attached to his name. He has
been described as a man adorned by every virtue; and no scholar seems to have been more
generally revered by his contemporaries. In several of the German universities, it was custom-

---

[r] Maittaire, Historia Typographorum aliquot Parisiensium, p. 50, 56.
Lond. 1717, 8vo.

[s] Leodegarii a Quercu Oratio Funebris de Vita et Morte Adriani Turnebi, p. 102.—This oration occurs among the miscellaneous works of Turnebus. Argentorati, 1600, fol. His Adversaria form a separate volume
of the same size. Ibid. 1599. His poems are reprinted in the Deliciæ Poetarum Gallorum, tom. iii. Le Laboureur has republished a poem entitled
"Poltrotus Meræus Adriani Turnebi." (Additions aux Memoires de
Michel de Castelnau, tom. ii, p. 226.)

[t] Epistola quæ vere exponit Obitum Adriani Turnebi. Paris. 1565, 4to.

ary for the professors, when in their public lectures they quoted the authority of Turnebus and Cujacius, to move the right hand to their cap, in token of the profound veneration with which they regarded their memory.[u] His unabating ardour of study rendered him conspicuous at a period when study was a general passion ; and, like Budæus, he even devoted several hours of his wedding day to the pursuits of literature. His learning was variegated, elegant, and profound. He was equally a master of Greek and Roman philology. It was the great object of his labours to illustrate the reliques of ancient genius ; and for this department he was eminently qualified by his sagacity and erudition. It was indeed objected by a contemporary scholar of high reputation, that in reviewing the writings of the ancients, he was too fond of proposing conjectural emendations.[x] This fault is incident to many critics of prompt and keen discernment: they are more apt to render suspected passages what they might have been, than what they originally were. His Latin versions are executed with great fidelity and skill.[y]

One of his accomplished friends has remarked, that in his writings he was as violent against those

---

[u] Pasquier, Recherches de la France, p. 834, edit. Paris, 1621, fol.— Lipsius has described Turnebus as " optimus unus omnium quos sol vidit." (Epistolicæ Quæstiones, lib. v, epist. xvii.)

[x] Victorii Variæ Lectiones, p. 435, edit. Florent. 1582, fol.

[y] Hustius de Interpretatione, p. 158. Paris. 1661, 4to.

who merited his indignation, as he was gentle in
his manners towards men of worth and learning.[a]
On several occasions he has indeed manifested
considerable warmth. Respecting some of. the
works of Cicero which he had illustrated by his
observations, he was led into a controversy with
Ramus and his admirer Audomarus Talæus.
Though in an earlier work he had mentioned him
with high respect,[a] it must be acknowledged that
he now treated Ramus with much contempt.
Turnebus was also embroiled with Bodin, another writer of superior. endowments. Bodin
published an edition of the Cynegetics ascribed
to Oppian, accompanied with emendations which
Turnebus immediately claimed as his.[b] He hew-

---

[a] Lettres d'Etienne Pasquier, tom. i, p. 586.

[a] Turnebus de Methodo, f. 2. Paris. 1600, 8vo.

[b] Bodin's edition includes a poetical version, and a commentary. "Op-
piani de Venatione libri IIII. Joan. Bodino Andegavensi interprete. Ad
D. Gabrielem Boverium Andium Episcopum. His accessit Commentarius
varius et multiplex, ejusdem interpretis." *Lutetiæ, apud Michaelem Vascosanum*, 1555, 4to. The edition of Turnebus soon followed. 'Οππιανῦ
'Αναζαρβίως 'Αλιευτικῶν βιϐλία ί. Κυνηγετικῶν βιϐλία ϒ. *Parisiis, apud Adr.
Turnebum typographum regium*, 1555, 4to. After the various readings
and emendations, Turnebus has subjoined an address which evidently alludes
to the conduct of Bodin. " Septem abhinc annis leviter emendaveram Oppianum de Venatione, partim animi conjectura, partim libri veteris ope. Eas
emendationes quidam usurpavit, et sibi donavit, quas tamen non putabam
tanti, ut in furtivis rebus esse deberent : eas a nobis vindicatas et recuperatas
esse nemo conqueri debebit. Nam rerum furtivarum lege æterna est auctoritas. Non me latet," &c. The following manuscript notice occurs in the
margin of the copy which belonged to Isaac Casaubon, and which is now deposited in the British Museum. " Is est Jo. Bodinus, qui tamen hoc ne-
gat, et de Turnebo conqueritur. Ego Turnebum verum scio loqui." The
complaint to which Casaubon refers is a passage in Bodin's *Methodus ad
Facilem Historiarum Cognitionem*, p. 94. Paris. 1566, 4to. " Quos ego

ever claimed them without that violence of invective which philologers have so frequently displayed on similar occasions; and according to Bongars, this plagiarism of Bodin was notorious among their countrymen.[c]

Marcus Antonius Muretus was considerably younger than Buchanan and Turnebus. He was born at the village of Muret near Limoges, on the twelfth of April 1526. Like several other scholars of the greatest name, he was his own preceptor.[d] He was successively a public teacher of humanity, philosophy, or jurisprudence, at Auch, Villeneuve d'Agen, Paris, Bordeaux, Poitiers, and Toulouse. At Toulouse he fell under suspicion of an abominable crime, and even incurred some hazard of being committed to the flames; but a counsellor of the parliament having communicated to him a dark intimation of his danger by a single line of Virgil,[e] he fled towards Italy with the utmost terror and precipitation. His consternation, among other effects, produced a mobility in his ears.[f] Having thus

libros eam Latino versu et commentariis illustrassem, quidam grammaticus eosdem libros oratione soluta, quantum libuit de meo labore detrahens, iterum pervulgavit."

[c] " Jam edidisse illum lectiones Turnebi in Oppianum pro suis, nemo nostrorum ignorat." See a letter from Bongars to Ritterahusius, published by Colomiés, *Gallia Orientalis*, p. 83. Hagæ Comitis, 1665, 4to.

[d] Sammarthani Elogia Gallorum Doctrina Illustrium, p. 85.

[e] Heu fuge crudeles terras, fuge littus avarum.

[f] Casauboni Animadversiones in Athenæum, lib. x, cap. i. Colomesii Opuscula, p. 39. P. Petiti Commentarii in tres priores Aretæi libros, p. 17. Lond. 1726, 4to.—Procopius, who represents Justinian as a mere ass,

abandoned his native country in the year 1554,
he fixed his residence at Venice, where he opened a public lecture in the Franciscan monastery.ᵍ
He afterwards removed to Padua, and received
pupils into his house ;ʰ and here he was again
suspected of the same foul crime.ⁱ Six years after his settlement in Italy, he was invited to
Rome by Cardinal Ippolito d'Este; and in the
house of that illustrious churchman, and of his
brother Lodovico, who had arrived at the same
high preferment, he continued till the time of his
death. By his various writings, and by his prelections in the Roman university, he now acquired a reputation almost unrivalled. He successively filled with the same applause, the departments of philosophy, civil law, and humanity.ᵏ
At the sedate age of fifty, he entered into holy
orders. The younger Scaliger, if his sentiments
be faithfully represented, was disposed to regard
him as a mere atheist; nor is it difficult to con-

---

has averred that the resemblance also obtained in the article of moving ears.
Ἠλίθιός τε γὰρ ὑπερφυῶς ἦν, καὶ ταῦθα ἦσῃ ἐμφερὴς μάλιστα. καὶ οἷος τῷ τὸν
χαλινὸν Ἴλασοντι ἐπισθαι. συχνά οἱ σωμάτων τῶν ὄντων. (Historia Arcana, p. 36,
edit. Alemanni. Lugd. 1623, fol.) Justinian however did not literally
wear a bridle; and perhaps these last expressions are also to be received in a
figurative sense.

ᵍ Ghilini, Teatro d'Huomini Letterati, vol. i, p. 165.

ʰ Joan. Mich. Bruti Epistolæ Clarorum Virorum, p. 401, 403. Lugd.
1561, 8vo.—The correspondence of Muretus and Lambinus, reprinted from
the very rare collection of Brutus, may be found in Ruhnkenius's edition of
Muretus, tom. i, p. 379.

ⁱ Mureti Opera, tom. i, p. 390.

ᵏ Bencii Orationes, p. 241. Erythræi Pinacotheca, tom. i, p. 11.

ceive that the rank soil of Rome produced atheis-
tical priests in great abundance. Erythræus, who
extols his piety with much grimace, has recorded
it as a memorable circumstance that when his
health permitted, he daily celebrated mass with
many tears. He died at Rome on the fourth of
June 1585, and left a moral character which it is
not too harsh to consider as extremely dubious.[1]
Of the abominable crime repeatedly laid to his
charge he was perhaps innocent: he must either
have been very guilty, or very unfortunate.[m] A
rumor likewise prevailed of his having polluted
his hands with blood. He was besides accused
of an intemperate use of wine;[n] and when a be-
nefice suddenly converted him into a saint, he

[1] Gallia quod peperit, pepulit quod Gallia monstrum,
    Quem Veneti profugum non potuere pati,
    Muretum esse sibi civem jussere Quirites,
    Et tumulo extinctum componere suo.
    Vivere nam potius qua debuit urbe cinædus ?
    Impius et quanam dignius urbe mori ?
                                BEZÆ Poemata Varia, p. 144.

[m] There is one charge of which Muretus may very readily be acquitted ;
namely that of having composed an impious book, *De Tribus Impostoribus*,
on the three impostors, Moses, Jesus, and Mahomet. This book has with
the utmost confidence been imputed to many authors, of different ages, and
of the most opposite denominations ; but it is extremely evident that such a
book did not at that time exist. See M. de la Monnoye's " Lettre à M.
Bouhier sur le prétendu livre des trois Imposteurs" (*Menagiana*, tom. iv,
p. 374.), and a note in Dr Maclaine's translation of Mosheim's *Ecclesiastical
History*, vol. iii, p. 147.

[n] " Sed crimen istud," says Erythræus, " illudque, quod in Gallia hominem occiderit, et interdum vino se ad ebrietatem onerarit, si vera forent,
posset aliquis *juventutis excusatione* defendere." (*Pinacotheca*, tom. i, p. 13.)
Sodomy and murder being mere peccadilloes, ought by all means to be excu-
sed in a lad of spirit. " Nec ludos puero abnuimus."

himself acknowledged that the former part of his
life had been sensual and gross.[o] The evidence
of his speculative atheism is certainly incompetent; but the injurious imputations attached to
his personal character, derive the strongest confirmation from the profligate strain of his writings.[p] The obsequiousness with which he adapted himself to the pestiferous meridian of Rome,
cannot but be regarded as an indication of practical atheism: in two of his elegant orations, he
has exerted all his skill to embalm the loathsome
putrescence of Charles the ninth; and his elaborate encomium on the massacre of St. Bartholomew must be remembered to his eternal infamy.[q]
The guilt of those execrable politicians who produced this unparalleled scene of butchery, is
hardly to be compared to that of the enlightened scholar who could calmly extol so damnable a
deed.[r]

[o] Mureti Opera, tom. i, p. 766.

[p] The conduct of Muretus was Jesuitical enough; but the excellent Dr
Jortin is mistaken in supposing that he was literally a Jesuit. (Life of
Erasmus, vol. ii, p. 13.) This mistake, which had also been committed by
Thomasius, seems to have arisen from the circumstance of his funeral
oration having been pronounced by the Jesuit Bencius.

[q] " O noctem illam memorabilem et in fastis eximiæ alicujus notæ adjec-
tione signandam, quæ paucorum seditiosorum interitu regem a præsenti cædis
periculo, regnum a perpetua civilium bellorum formidine liberavit! Qua
quidem nocte stellas equidem ipsas luxisse solito nitidius arbitror; et flumen
Sequanam majores undas volvisse, quo citius illa impurorum hominum ca-
davera evolveret et exoneraret in mare. O fœlicissimam mulierem Cathari-
nam regis matrem," &c. (Mureti Opera, tom. i, p. 177.)

[r] Menage professes to regard his memory with " toute sorte de veneration: aiant appris du Jésuite Bencius, que les neuf dernieres années de sa vie

These disgraceful characteristics of the man render the most elegant of his works less palatable. He was however a scholar of the first magnitude. He has written in prose and in verse with the same purity and elegance: but his chief distinction is that of an excellent philologer; for although his diction is seldom or never unclassical, yet he rarely evinces the native elevation of a poet or orator. Before he had been accused at Toulouse, and consequently before he had assumed the consummate hypocrisy of a Roman courtier, Buchanan addressed to him a little poem in commendation of his tragedy of *Julius Cæsar.* [a]

It may be mentioned as a striking proof of his classical attainments, that he imposed upon Joseph Scaliger some verses of his own as the compositions of two ancient Latin poets. This great critic was so firmly persuaded of their genuineness, that he published them in one edition of his notes on Varro; [b] and when Muretus soon afterwards acknowledged the imposition, he felt a degree of resentment which only a critic could feel.

il étoit d'une dévotion si fervente qu'il pleuroit en disant la messe." (*Anti-Baillet*, tom. i, p. 319.) A funeral oration, composed by a Jesuit, and delivered in Rome, is certainly the most slender authority that could easily be produced in favour of clerical piety. All that can be concluded from the elegant flourishes of Bencius is, that Muretus never dreamed of piety till he became a priest. (*Orationes*, p. 246.)

[a] This tragedy of Muretus was printed among his *Juvenilia*. Paris. 1553, 8vo.—The edition of his works which I use is that published by the very learned David Ruhnkenius. Lugd. Bat. 1789, 4 tom. 8vo.

[b] Jos. Scaliger ad Varronem, p. 212, edit. H. Stephani, 1573, 8vo.

E

It was one act of his revenge to write an epigram in allusion to the scandalous affair of Toulouse.[u] Both fragments are founded on a passage of Philemon, preserved by Plutarch and Stobæus:[x] the first was ascribed to Attius, the other to Trabea.

> Nam si lamentis allevaretur dolor,
> Longoque fletu minueretur miseria,
> Tum turpe lacrumis indulgere non foret,
> Fractaque voce divum obtestare fidem,
> Tabifica donec pectore excessit lues.
> Nunc hæc neque hilum de dolore detrahunt,
> Potiusque cumulum miseris adjiciunt mali,
> Et indecoram mentis mollitiam arguunt.

> Here, si querelis, ejulatu, fletibus
> Medicina fieret miseriis mortalium,
> Auro parandæ lacrumæ contra forent :
> Nunc hæc ad minuenda mala non magis valent,
> Quam nænia preficæ ad excitandos mortuos.
> Res turbidæ consilium, non fletum expetunt.[y]

Buchanan, Turnebus, and Muretus, although they spent the best part of their lives in scholastic occupations, contracted none of the peculiari-

---

[b] Jos. Scaligeri Poemata, p. 24. Lugd. Bat. 1615, 16to.

[x] Menandri et Philemonis Reliquiæ, a J. Clerico, p. 328. Amst. 1709, 8vo. Bentleii Emendationes in Menandri et Philemonis Reliquias, p. 137, edit. Cantab. 1713, 8vo.—The genuine fragments of Attius, or Accius, and Trabea may be found in Stephanus's *Fragmenta Poetarum Veterum Latinorum*, p. 5,424. Excudebat H. Stephanus, 1564, 8vo. Those of Attius occur in Scriverius's *Collectanea Veterum Tragicorum*, p. 89. Lugd. Bat. 1620, 8vo.

[y] Mureti Hymnorum Sacrorum liber : ejusdem alia quædam Poematia, p. 56. Venetiis, apud Aldum, 1575, 8vo.

ties incident to their profession. It was a customary remark of the famous poet Ronsard that those admirable scholars, together with Anthony Govea, all of whom were his intimate friends, presented nothing of the pedagogue except the gown and cap.[*] Ronsard had been accustomed to live with men of courtly manners, and may be considered as a competent judge of politeness.

Joannes Gelida, another member of the same college, and an associate to whose pious care Buchanan acknowledges himself to have been so much indebted, was a native of Valentia. He emigrated from Spain at an early period of life, and prosecuted his academical studies at Paris. In that university, his talents procured him the appointment of a public teacher of what was then called philosophy. His stature was somewhat diminutive; but as his natural acuteness was accompanied with powerful lungs and a clear voice, he appeared to great advantage in the disputations. But the unprofitable and barbarous science in which he had been initiated, was now beginning to be exploded: the exertions of Jacobus Faber Stapulensis, and other champions, had at length introduced into that flourishing seminary a more genuine species of philosophy. Gelida, at the mature age of forty, began to discover that he had hitherto been exercised in laborious trifles ; but his mind still retained its youthful

* Thuani Hist. sui Temporis, tom. iv, p. 99.

elasticity, and he determined to retrace the course of his studies. He now applied himself, for the first time, to the attentive perusal of Cicero and other Roman authors of classical fame; and afterwards, with great avidity, to the acquisition of the Greek tongue, which he had entirely neglected in his earlier years. His strenuous perseverence soon conducted him to uncommon proficiency as a polite scholar; and it is this useful part of his history that entitles him to a more conspicuous station among the accomplished friends of Buchanan. Gelida is said to have presided over the college to which Buchanan now belonged; but as it is certain that he afterwards removed to Bordeaux to act as Govea's surrogate, this statement may be suspected of inaccuracy. Leaving a widow and a little daughter, he died at Bordeaux on the nineteenth of February 1556, after having exceeded the age of sixty.[a]

In the college where he found such able coadjutors, Buchanan seems to have remained several years. The king of Portugal had lately founded the university of Coimbra; and as his own dominions could not readily supply competent professors, he invited Andrew Govea to accept the principality, and to conduct from France a considerable number of proficients in philosophy and

[a] Schotti Bibliotheca Hispanica, p. 616. Thuani Hist. sui Temporis, tom. i, p. 610. Niceron, Memoires pour servir à l'Histoire des Hommes Illustres dans la Republique des Lettres, tom. xxii, p. 104.

ancient literature. Govea accordingly returned to his native country in the year 1547, accompanied by Buchanan and other associates. The affairs of Europe presented an alarming aspect; and Portugal seemed to be almost the only corner free from tumults. To the proposals of Govea he had not only lent a prompt ear, but was so much satisfied with the character of his associates, that he also persuaded his brother Patrick to join this famous colony. To several of its members he had formerly been attached by the strictest ties of friendship; these were Gruchius, Garentæus, Tevius, and Vinetus, who have all distinguished themselves by the publication of learned works.[b] The other scholars of whom it consisted, were Arnoldus Fabricius,[c] John Cos-

---

[*] " Erant enim plerique per multos annos summa benevolentia conjuncti, ut qui ex suis monumentis orbi claruerunt, Nicolaus Gruchius, Gulielmus Garentæus, Jacobus Tevius, et Elias Vinetus. Itaque non solum se comitem libenter dedit, sed et Patricio fratri persuasit, ut se tam præclaro cœtui conjungeret." (*Buchanani Vita*, p. 6.) Of Tevius and Vinetus some account will afterwards be given. Garentæus, or Guerente, is commemorated by Montagne as a commentator on Aristotle, and as a writer of Latin tragedy. (*Essais*, liv. i, chap. xxv.) Gruchius, who was a native of Rouen, distinguished himself by the publication of several very learned works on Roman antiquities; and even Sigonius found him a formidable antagonist. Their rival productions occur in the collection of Grævius. (*Thesaurus Antiquitatum Romanarum*, tom. i.) Onuphrius Panvinius mentions Gruchius in terms of high commendation. (*Imperium Romanum*, p. 304.) He was not less familiarly conversant with the Greek philosophy than with Roman antiquities: he taught Aristotle in the schools with high reputation; and he corrected some of the errors committed by Perionius in translating a portion of his works. He died at Rochelle in the year 1572. (Thuani *Hist. sui Temporis*, tom. iii, p. 209. Sammarthani *Elogia*, p. 52.)

[*] " Arnoldi Fabricii Vasatensis Epistolæ aliquot" are printed with the

ta, and Anthony Mendez, who are not known as
authors : the first was a native of Bazats, the
other two were Portuguese. All these professors,
except P. Buchanan and Fabricius, had taught
in the College of Guienne.[d]   To this authentic
catalogue Dempster has added, probably without
sufficient authority, other two Scotish names;
those of John Rutherford and William Ramsay.[e]

Govea had relinquished his office at Bordeaux
in the intention of resuming it after an interval
of two years; and in the mean time had delegat-
ed his authority to Gelida.   But death arrested
him in his native country.   Gelida was then appointed principal of the College of Guienne,
which he continued to govern till the time of his

epistles of Gelida. His name is therefore inserted in the catalogue of J. A.
Fabricius, who has however collected no particulars of his life. (*Centuria
Fabriciorum Scriptis Clarorum*, p. 12. Hamb. 1709, 8vo.) Of this little
work a continuation was published by the author in 1727, entitled " Fabriciorum Centuria secunda, cum` prioris Supplemento."—" Joannis Costæ
ad Lusitaniam Carmen" is prefixed to the historical production of his countryman Tevius.

   [d] Schotti Bibliotheca Hispanica, p. 617.

   [e] Dempster, p. 564-6. Mackenzie, vol. iii. p. 137.—John Rutherford
was provost of St. Salvator's College at St. Andrews about the year 1572.
(Bannatyne's *Journal*, p, 375.) He published a commentary on Aristotle's poetics, and a work entitled " Commentariorum de Arte Disserendi
libri quatuor. Joanne Retorforti Jedburgæo Scoto authore. Et nunc de-
mum ab eodem diligenter recogniti et emendati." Edinburgi, apud Henricum Charteris, 1577, 4to. Pp. 78. From this title he appears to have been
a native of Jedburgh. See Appendix, No. vi.—Dempster asserts that
William Ramsay was afterwards a professor in the university of Leyden.
Jacobus Ramseius, J. C. is enumerated by Meursius among the Leyden
professors of philosophy and eloquence. (*Athenæ Batavæ*, p. 351.) Gif-
nius mentions one Ramsay, a very learned friend of Buchanan's, who had
formerly been a professor at Wittemberg. (*Buchanani Epistolæ*, p. 7.)

decease. Govea died in the year 1548; and Buchanan, in a short epitaph, gratefully commemorated the services which he had rendered to literature. [f] During the lifetime of this worthy man, Buchanan and his associates had found their situation at Coimbra sufficiently agreeable; but after they were deprived of his protection, the Portugueze began to persecute them with unrelenting bigotry. They were first assailed by the secret weapons of calumny, and were at length accused of imaginary crimes. Three of their number were thrown into the dungeons of the inquisition, and after having been subjected to a tedious imprisonment, were at length arraigned at this inhuman tribunal. According to the usual practice, they were not confronted with their accusers; of whose very names they were ignorant. As they could not be convicted of any crime, they were overwhelmed with reproaches, and again committed to custody.

Buchanan had attracted an unusual degree of indignation. He was accused of having written an impious poem against the Franciscans; yet with the nature of that poem the inquisitors were totally unacquainted. The only copy which he had suffered to escape, was presented to his native sovereign; and before he ventured beyond the borders of France, he had even adopted the pre-

[f] Buchanani Epigram. lib. ii, 18.

caution of having the circumstances of its composition properly represented to the Portugueze
monarch. He was also charged with the heinous
crime of eating flesh in Lent; and yet with respect to that very article, not a single individual
in Portugal deemed it necessary to practise ab-
stinence. Some of his strictures relative to monks
were registered against him; but they were such
as monks only could regard as criminal. He was
moreover accused of having alleged, in a conversation with some young Portugueze, that with
respect to the eucharist, St. Augustin appeared
to him to be strongly inclined towards the opinion condemned by the church of Rome.s Two
witnesses, whom he afterwards discovered to be
Ferrerius and Talpin, made a formal deposition
of their having been assured by several respectable informants, that Buchanan was disaffected
to the Romish faith.[h]

After the inquisitors had harassed Buchanan

g See Dr M'Crie's Life of Knox, vol. ii, p. 295.

h " Alii duo testes Joannes *Tolpinus* Normannus, et Joannes Ferrerius
e Subalpina Liguria," &c. (*Buchanani Vita*, p. 6.) Read *Talpinus*.
" Jean Talpin, Docteur et Chanoine Theologal à Perigueux l'an 1570,"
was a native of Normandy. He is the author of various works in the French
language, enumerated by La Croix du Maine, tom. i, p. 591, and by Du
Verdier, tom. ii, p. 520. Ferrerius had formerly visited Scotland, where he
resided in the monastery of Kinloss. In a very juvenile work, I have mentioned several of his literary productions. (*Dissertation on the Literary
History of Scotland*, p. 80.) The catalogue may however be augmented
from Conrad Gesner's *Pandectæ sive Partitiones Universales*, f. 29, 65, 72.
Tiguri, 1548, fol. Gesner mentions him with respect in his correspondence. (*Epistolæ Medicinales*, f. 124, b. Tiguri, 1577, 4to.) See also
Menage, *Remarques sur la Vie de Pierre Ayrault*, p. 148.

and themselves for the space of nearly a year
and a half, they confined him to a monastery, for
the purpose of receiving edifying lessons from the
monks; whom, with due discrimination, he represents as men by no means destitute of humanity, but totally unacquainted with religion. In
their custody he continued several months ; and
it was about this period that he began his version of the psalms, afterwards brought to so happy a conclusion. That this translation was a
penance imposed upon him by his illiterate guardians, is only to be considered as an idle tale.[i] It
is much more probable that a large proportion
of the good monks were incapable of reading the
psalms in their native language. The rational
and elevated mind of Buchanan had received
deep impressions of religion; and the gloom of
a monastery, superadded to the persecution which
he had so long sustained, would naturally tend

[i] " Cum quæstores," says Buchanan, " prope sesquiannum et se et illum fatigassent, tandem, ne frustra hominem non ignotum vexasse crederentur, eum in monasterium ad aliquot menses recludunt, ut exactius erudiretur a monachis, hominibus quidem alioqui nec inhumanis nec malis, sed
omnis religionis ignaris. Hoc maxime tempore psalmorum Davidicorum
complures vario carminum genere in numeros redegit." (Buchanani Vita,
p. 6.) Dr Mackenzie's commentary on this passage is not unworthy of attention. " But here he gives us another specimen of his gratitude to his
benefactors, for he says, that they were altogether ignorant and void of religion. Now how improbable this is, will appear from these monks having
imposed upon him as a penance, that he should turn the psalms of David
into Latin verse." (Lives of Scots Writers, vol. iii, p. 162.) But how
will it appear that the monks imposed this penance ? No such conclusion
can be drawn from Buchanan's words ; and Dr Mackenzie had no other
authority to produce.

to foster a spirit of devotion. His frequent re-
currence to the hopes of another world, and his
recollection of the solace which his favourite art
had so often afforded him in this, may not unreasonably be supposed to have led him to the
formation of a plan, which he has executed with
piety equal to his genius. For the reputation
which he acquired by this admirable production,
he might therefore be indebted to " his good
friends and benefactors the Portugueze;" to
whom Dr Mackenzie has accused him of flagrant
ingratitude. This unintentional favour seems to
have been the only benefaction which he received.

In that country, the direful tribunal of the inquisition was formally established in the year
1536. The second inquisitor general was the
Infant Henry, afterwards king of Portugal; who
retained the office from 1539 to 1579.[k] It is asserted by a furious apostate from the Protestant
faith, that this royal inquisitor was personally
concerned in the examination of the Scotish heretic, and that in his presence Buchanan conducted himself with abject submission.[l] But the
manner in which this story is related, gives it
the air of a complete fiction; and most of the
kindred tales of the same author are so mani-

[k] Ludovicus a Paramo de Origine et Progressu Officii Sanctæ Inquisi-
tionis, ejusque Dignitate et Utilitate, p. 233. Matriti, 1598, fol.
[l] Hamiltonii Demonstratio Calvinianæ Confusionis, f. 252, b. Paris.
1581, 8vo.

festly devoid of truth, and even of probability, that they are not entitled to a serious refutation. When Buchanan was at length restored to liberty, he solicited the king's permission to return to France. He was however requested to protract his residence in Portugal; and was presented with a small supply of money, till he should be promoted to some station worthy of his talents. But his ambition of Portugueze preferment was not perhaps very violent; for he still remembered with regret the learned and interesting society of Paris. In a beautiful poem entitled *Desiderium Lutetiæ*,[m] and apparently composed before his retreat from Portugal, he pathetically bewails his absence from that metropolis, which he represents under the allegory of a pastoral mistress.

Portugal certainly could not vie with France in letters and refinement; but it was not entirely destitute of individuals conspicuous for their original and acquired talents.[n] The history of classical learning in Portugal is but little known to my countrymen; and as it is to a certain extent blended with the history of Buchanan, it ·

[m] Buchanani Silvæ, iii.—This poem has been imitated by the amiable and ingenious Dr Blacklock. (*Poems*, p. 85, Mackenzie's edit.)

[n] " Possum enim ostendere Lusitanos et philologos esse, et intra quinquaginta proximos hos annos non pauciores triginta floruisse, etiam scriptis editis, qui veteribus quum dictionis elegantia tum rerum gravitate, possint jure conferri. Possum mulieres quoque ostendere quæ cum omni vetustate certent eruditione." (Resendii *Opera*, tom. ii, p. 281.)

evidently claims a share of our present attention.

Osorius informs us that the Latin tongue was much cultivated in that country, from the reign of Alphonzo the first[*] till that of Denys; and commemorates Alphonzo himself as the author of a Latin book, written with tolerable propriety.[p] Barbarism, he adds, afterwards ensued, and the purity of that language was miserably contaminated. King Denys died in the year 1325. De Macedo and other Portugueze writers have affirmed that it was he who founded the university of Coimbra;[q] but this is an assertion which cannot fail to excite considerable suspicion. That a respectable school was established there by King Denys, is sufficiently credible: but the original founder of the university was undoubtedly John the third; and it probably assumed its regular form about the year 1540.[r] The other Portugueze university, that of Evora, was also founded during the reign of King John; whom

[*] Don Alphonzo, count of Portugal, having in the year 1139 obtained a decisive victory over the Moors, was saluted king in the field of battle. (Mariana *De Rebus Hispaniæ*, tom. i, p. 441.)

[p] Osorius de Regis Institutione et Disciplina, f. 199, b. Olysippone, 1571, 4to.

[q] Antonii de Macedo Lusitania Infulata et Purpurata, p. 37. Paris. 1663, 4to.

[r] "Veni Conimbricam," says Nicolaus Clenardus; "nova hæc est inter Lusitanos academia, quam magno et plane regis animo rex noster molitus." (Clenardi *Epistolarum libri duo*, p. 25. Antverp. 1566, 8vo.) This extract is from an epistle written in the year 1539.

his countrymen have, with one voice, extolled as a liberal patron of literature.

The great restorers of polite learning in Portugal and Spain were Arius Barbosa and Ælius Antonius Nebrissensis. Barbosa, a native of Aveiro in Portugal, after having studied in the university of Salamanca, betook himself to Florence for the purpose of attending the prelections of Politian. He became a proficient in classical literature, and was the first who introduced the Greek language into modern Spain.* In the year 1495 he returned to Salamanca, where he taught for the space of twenty years. He was afterwards attracted to his native country to undertake the tuition of Don Alphonzo, the brother of King John. He has left several works in verse and in prose; and has often been commemorated as a man of talents. His learned friend Nebrissensis, who was born at Lebrixa in Spain in the year 1444, likewise prosecuted his studies at Salamanca and in Italy. He was successively a professor at Salamanca and Alcala; and was engaged by Cardinal Ximenez in the famous Alcala edition of the bible. His various erudition has been commemorated by Erasmus, and by other scholars of that century;† but in the know-

* Gyraldus de Poetis suorum Temporum, p. 403.

† Erasmi Ciceronianus, p. 185. Christophorus Mylæus de Scribenda Universitatis Rerum Historia, p. 304. Basil. 1551, fol.—" Jacebant itaque bonæ litteræ," says Sanctius in the dedication of his acute and learned treatise on the principles of the Latin language, " quum abhinc annis centum Antonius Nebrissensis hos rebelles conatus est castigare. Sed adeo

ledge of the Greek language he was inferior to
Barbosa.[u] He died in the year 1522.[x]

Lucius Andreas Resendius, who seems to have
taught in the university of Colmbra, and at the
same period with Buchanan,[y] was the earliest
Portugueze author who investigated the antiquities of his native country with erudition and
judgment.[z] He composed various works in verse
as well as in prose ; and, in the opinion of a learn-

malum hoc radices egerat altas, ut innumeris monstris debellatis multo plu-
ra debellanda remanserint. Quod si ille iterum aut sæpius rediret, non dubito (quæ erat illius solertia) quin omnia facillime composuisset." (Minerva, seu de Causis Linguæ Latinæ. Salmanticæ, 1587, 8vo.) His eulogy
occurs among those of Paulus Jovius. (Elogia Virorum Literis Illustrium,
p. 121, edit. Basil. 1577, fol.) See also Vossius De Historicis Latinis, p.
657, and Colomesii Italia et Hispania Orientalis, p. 223.

[u] Schotti Bibliotheca Hispanica, p. 471. Francof. 1608, 4to.

[x] Antonii Bibliotheca Hispana, tom. i, p. 105. Romæ, 1672, 2 tom.
fol.—This must not be confounded with a similar work of the same author,
entitled Bibliotheca Hispana Vetus. Romæ, 1696, 2 tom. fol. These two
volumes comprehend the period from the reign of Augustus to the year
1500. Nicolaus Antonius, a very laborious and useful writer, was born at
Seville in 1617, and died at Madrid in 1684.

[y] Resendii Opera, tom. ii, p. 264. Col. Agrip. 1600, 2 tom. 8vo.

[z] Libri quatuor de Antiquitatibus Lusitaniæ a Lucio Andrea Resendio
olim inchoati, et a Jacobo Menœtio Vasconcello recogniti, atque absoluti.
Eboræ, 1593, fol.—This work was reprinted at Rome in 1597 ; and, with
other productions of the author, at Cologne in 1600. It also occurs in the
collection entitled Hispania Illustrata, tom. ii, p. 892. To the first edition
Vasconcellus has prefixed an account of the author's life. This antiquarian work of Resendius, when viewed as a restitution of decayed intelligence,
is of considerable value. He has very diligently resorted to one copious and
genuine source of information, ancient inscriptions. From documents of
this kind, he acquainted mythologists with a Pagan divinity which had entirely escaped their knowledge ; and concerning which a German author of
great erudition has composed an elaborate dissertation. (Reinesius De Deo
Endovellico. Altenb. 1637, 4to.)

ed Belgian, is a poet worthy of being compared
with the ancients.[a] Resendius studied at Alcala
under Nebrissensis, and at Salamanca under his
countryman Barbosa. The esteem and admiration which he has so frequently and so earnestly
testified for Erasmus, may be recorded as a proof
of his intelligence and liberality ; for Erasmus's
free spirit of disquisition was very far from recommending him to the majority of his ecclesiastical brethren.[b] About the same period, Michael
Cabedius, an eminent lawyer, likewise cultivated
Latin poetry with a degree of success which secured him the applause of his countrymen. He
translated the [c]*Plutus* of Aristophanes, and composed some original poems, with considerable felicity.[d]

The family of Govea, so intimately connected
with Buchanan, was remarkable for its talents
and literature. James Govea was principal of the
College of St. Barbe at Paris ; where he superin-

---

[a] Clenardi Epistolæ, p. 244.—He is also mentioned with approbation by
Bembus, in an epistle addressed to Damian de Goes. (Bembi *Epistolæ
Familiares*, lib. vi, p. 741.)

[b] See particularly Resendii Opera, tom. ii, p. 51.

[c] Parisiis, apud Michaelem Vascosanum, 1547, 8vo.

[d] Jacobus Menœtius Vasconcellus was related to Michael, as well as to
Antonius Cabedius ; and the Latin poems of these three authors have, with
sufficient propriety, been associated in one volume. They are appended to
the second edition of Resendius *De Antiquitatibus Lusitaniæ*. Romæ,
1597, 8vo.—Vasconcellus has written an account of his own life ; which
accompanies both this and the former edition. To that work of Resendius
he has added a fifth book, " De Antiquitate Municipii Eborensis." His
Vita Michaelis Cabedii Senatoris Regii occurs among the *Opuscula* appended to the Roman edition of the antiquities.

tended the studies of three promising nephews, who
were educated at the charge of the Portugueze
monarch, King John. They were natives of Be-
ja. Martial, the eldest of these learned brothers,
published a Latin grammar at Paris in the year
1534; and likewise composed various poems,
which are not however known to have been printed. Andrew, who belonged to the ecclesiastical
order, and who, according to Beza, was a doctor
of the Sorbonne, taught grammar, and afterwards
philosophy, in the college over which his uncle
presided. He at length obtained the principality himself: Andrew Govea, principal of St.
Barbe, was chosen rector of the university of
Paris on the twenty-third of June 1533.[e] In the
course of the following year, he was invited to
Bordeaux,[f] where he governed the College of
Guienne with great moderation and address.[g]
He died at Coimbra on the ninth of June 1548,
after having reached the age of about fifty. His
friend Vinetus, in an epistle to Andreas Schottus,
has commemorated him as a man of liberal sen-

* Bulæi Hist. Universitatis Parisiensis, tom. vi, p. 977.
De Lurbe, Chronique Bourdeloise, f. 42.
Montagne has characterised him as "le plus grand principal de France."
(*Essais*, liv. i, chap. xxv.) "Ab avunculo," says Vasconcellus, "Burdi-
galam missi sumus, ad capiendum ingenii cultum, in celebri gymnasio quod
ibi eo tempore florebat sub moderamine Andreæ Goveani Lusitani, ex Pace
Julia oriundi, viri gravissimi." (*Vita Jacobi Menœtii Vasconcelli, ab ipso
conscripta*, p. 3.) "Vir de universa Aquitania et literis, ut si quis alius,
optime meritus, homo pius, doctus, et ad regendam juventutem omnino natus." (Schotti *Bibliotheca Hispanica*, p. 617.)

timents, and as an encourager of learning.[h] He does not however belong to the list of authors.

· Anthony Govea was the youngest and the most renowned of these brothers. While he prosecuted his studies in the College of St Barbe, he made very unusual progress in ancient literature and philosophy; and at Avignon and Toulouse, he afterwards applied to the study of jurisprudence with the same assiduity and · success. He studied at Toulouse about the year 1539; but before that period he had taught humanity in the College of Guienne. In 1542 he was a regent in some Parisian college under his uncle: and in the course of the ensuing year, he was engaged in a dispute with Ramus[i] which occasioned great commotion in that university. Ramus had undertaken to impugn the philosophy of Aristotle; and Govea, notwithstanding his youth, was the first who entered the lists against him.[k] He was seconded by Perionius, and other strenuous advocates of old opinions; and the contest at length rose to such a height that it was determined by

[h] Schotti Bibliotheca Hispanica, p. 475.

[i] A biographical account of Ramus, who certainly was no ordinary character, was published by Nicolaus Nancelius, one of the regents of his college. (*Vita Petri Rami.* Paris. 1599, 8vo.) It is remarked by Dr Reid that Ramus had the spirit of a reformer in philosophy, and force of genius sufficient to shake the Aristotelian fabric in many parts, but insufficient to erect any thing more solid in its place. (*Analysis of Aristotle's Logic,* p. 30, edit. Edinb. 1806, 12mo.)

[k] Antonii Goveani pro Aristotele Responsio, adversus Petri Rami Calumnias. Paris. 1543, 8vo.

F

a royal mandate,[1] Govea, afterwards returned
to the College of Guienne, where he was left by
the colony which departed for Coimbra. He successively taught jurisprudence at Toulouse, Ca-
hors, Valence, and Grenoble, to crowded audito-
ries; but when France began to be annoyed with
the tumults of a civil war, he retired into Italy,
and found an honourable asylum at the court of
Savoy. From the duke he is said to have obtained the offices of counsellor, and master of the requests. He died at Turin at the age of about
sixty. Manfred, one of his sons, was also a man
of learning: he published several works, among
which are Latin poems, and annotations on the
writings of Julius Clarus.[m] Anthony Govea, according to Thuanus, was the only man of that
age who, by the common consent of the learned,
was considered as a very elegant poet, a great
philosopher, and a most able civilian.[n] The purity of his Latin style is highly commended by
the same admirable historian. Besides his juridical writings and his answer to Ramus, he published Latin poems, editions of Virgil, Terence,[o]
and some of the works of Cicero, and a Latin
translation of Porphyry's introduction to Aris-

[1] Launoi de Varia Aristotelis Fortuna in Academia Parisiensi, p. 59,
edit. Hag. Com. 1656, 4to. Wesenfelsii Dissertatio de Logomachiis Eruditorum, p. 56, edit. Amst. 1702, 8vo.

[m] Ghilini Teatro d'Huomini Letterati, vol. ii, p. 189.

[n] Thuani Hist. sui Temporis, tom. ii, p. 468.

[o] See Wasii Senarius, sive de Legibus et Licentia Veterum Poetarum,
p. 243. Oxon. 1687, 4to.

totle's logic. Joseph Scaliger represents him as an excellent French poet.[p] But his chief praise is that of having been deemed the most formidable rival of Cujacius. He is highly extolled by Gravina, the most elegant of the modern civilians;[q] and Cujacius himself had awarded him the superiority over all the interpreters of the Justinian law in ancient or modern times.

Jacobus Tevius, the friend of Buchanan and Govea, was a native of Braga. Having completed his studies in the university of Paris,[r] he obtained a regency at Bordeaux; where, as we have already seen, he was associated with Buchanan. After his removal to Coimbra, he composed an historical work,[s] which has been highly

---

[p] " Goveanus doctus erat vir, et valens dialecticus, optimus poeta Gallicus: nec enim Hispanum judicaveris, adeo bene Gallice loquebatur." (*Prima Scaligerana*, p. 86.) He is likewise mentioned with great respect in Scaliger's *Castigationes in Festum*, p. 11. In Sanderus's *catalogue* of " famous Anthonies," the name of Govea has not been omitted; but the notices of this writer are slight and unsatisfactory. (Sanderus *De Claris Antoniis*, p. 184. Lovanii, 1627, 4to.) Edward Henryson, LL. D. a Scotish civilian who taught in the university of Bourges, published a tract against Govea, entitled " Pro Eg. Barone adversus A. Goveanum de Jurisdictione libri II." Paris. 1555, 8vo. It occurs in Meerman's *Thesaurus Juris Civilis et Canonici*, tom. ii, p. 447. Of the works of Govea there is a recent edition. Roterod. 1766, fol.

[q] " Ingenium habuit varium et velox, ut rerum ab eo tum in philosophia, tum in humanioribus literis, tum in jure civili agitatarum finem ante initium animadverteres. Neque ullum fuit involucrum, unde non se celeriter ac feliciter expediret."[q] (Gravinæ *Origines Juris Civilis*, p. 127.)

[r] Schotti Bibliotheca Hispanica, p. 479.

[s] Commentarius de Rebus a Lusitanis in India apud Dium Gestis, anno salutis nostræ M.D.XLVI. Jacobo Tevio Lusitano autore.—The dedication to King John is dated Coimbra, March the first 1548. This work of Tevius occurs in *Hispania Illustrata*, tom. ii, p. 1347. Dempster has absurdly

commended for the elegance of its Latinity.[t]
Schottus informs us that he also published some
orations, as well as some Portugueze and Latin
poems. It was his intention to compose a general history of his native country; but this plan
he did not live to execute.

Buchanan has repeatedly testified his affection
for this associate of his learned labours. When
Tevius published his historical commentary, Buchanan furnished him with a very happy address
to King John;[u] which is prefixed to the various
editions of that work. In his elegy to Tastæus
and Tævius, he addresses him with all the warmth
of friendship:

> O animæ, Ptolemæe, meæ pars altera, tuque
> Altera pars animæ, Tevi Jacobe, meæ.[x]

In a poem inscribed to Anthony Govea, he has
strongly indicated his regard for each of these
Portugueze scholars.

> Si quicquam, Goveane, fas mihi esset
> Invidere tibive, Teviove,
> Et te nostro ego Tevio inviderem,
> Et nostrum tibi Tevium inviderem.
> Sed cum me nihil invidere sit fas
> Vel tibi, Goveane, Teviove,
> Si fas est quod amor dolorque cogit,

---

affirmed that its real author was Buchanan. (*Hist. Ecclesiast. Gent. Scotor.*
p. 110.)
[t] Vasæi Rerum Hispanicarum Chronicon, cap. iv.
[u] Buchanani Opera, tom. ii, p. 102.
[x] Buchanani Elegiarum liber, iv.

4

Vobis imprecor usque et imprecabor,
Uterque ut mihi sed cito rependat
Hoc pravum ob facinus malumque pœnas :
Te mi Tevius invidere possit,
Tu possis mihi Tevium invidere.
Ambobus mihi si frui licebit,
Cœlum Diis ego non suum invidebo,
Sed sortem mihi Dii meam invidebunt.ᶨ

Hieronymus Osorius, bishop of Sylves, has likewise illustrated a portion of the Portugueze history with more than common elegance.ˢ At the request of King John, he had taught theology in the newly-founded university of Coimbra. Ascham was of opinion that, since the days of Cicero, no author had written with greater purity and eloquence;ᵃ but Lord Bacon, who was however a less competent judge of style, has characterized his vein of composition by the epithet *watery*.ᵇ The most celebrated of his productions seem to be his five books *De Gloria*. This treatise bears the form of a dialogue ; and one of the interlocutors is his very learned friend Antonius Augustinus, archbishop of Tarragona, of whom Spain deservedly boasts as a philologer and civi-

ʲ Buchanani Hendecasyllabon liber, v.

ˢ Osorii de Rebus Emmanuelis Regis Lusitaniæ Invictissimi Virtute et Auspicio Gestis libri duodecim. Olysippone, 1571, fol.—An edition of his works, with the life of the author, was published by his nephew, who bore the same name, and was a canon of Evora. (H. Osor Opera Omnia. Romæ, 1592, 4 tom. fol.)

ᵃ Aschami Epistolæ, p. 268.

ᵇ Bacon of the Advancement of Learning, p. 36.

lian of the first order.[c] Osorius attracted the
particular attention of English scholars by his
epistle to Queen Elizabeth, and his subsequent
altercation with Haddon.[d] This was certainly
no despicable antagonist; though Osorius and
his friend Manuel d'Almada[e] have treated him
with much contempt.

Gyraldus has enumerated several of the Portugueze who had cultivated Latin poetry; but
to Didacus Pyrrhus,[f] who is one of the interlocutors in his second dialogue, he assigns the superiority over all the rest.[g] Hermicus Caiadus,
Georgius Cœlius,[h] and Michael Sylvius,[i] flourished during the earlier part of the sixteenth century; and their poetical attempts were not altogether slighted by the fastidious scholars of Italy.

[c] His edition of Varro *De Lingua Latina*, Fabricius and other writers
have referred to the year 1557. A copy in my possession bears *Romæ apud
Vincentium Luchinum*, 1554, 8vo. Menage styles Augustinus " acutissi-
mi vir ingenii et doctrinæ singularis." (*Juris Civilis Amœnitates*, p. 55.)

[d] Osorii in Gualterum Haddonum libri tres. Olysippone, 1567, 4to.

[e] Epistola Emmanuelis Dalmada, Episcopi Angrensis, adversus Epistolam Gualteri Haddoni contra Osorii Epistolam, nuper editam. Antverp.
1566, 4to.—Haddon's epistle to Osorius, which was published in 1563,
occurs in the collection of his *Lucubrationes*, p. 210. Lond. 1567, 4to. He
afterwards renewed the controversy.

[f] Six epitaphs written by Pyrrhus in Greek and Latin occur in the first
volume of Le Clerc's edition of Erasmus.

[g] Gyraldus de Poetis suorum Temporum, p. 404.

[h] Sadoleti Epistolæ, p. 612. Bembi Epistolæ Familiares, lib. vi, p. 730.
Clenardi Epistolæ, p. 244.

[i] This poet was the son of Diego da Silva, count of Portalegre; and
having been educated for the church, he rose to the dignity of a cardinal.
(A. de Macedo *Lusitania Infulata et Purpurata*, p. 242.) He died at Rome
in the year 1556.

Ignatius Moralis, Ludovicus Crucius, and Manuel Pimenta, who succeeded them, were likewise poets of a temporary reputation. Crucius executed a paraphrase of the psalms;[k] and in the preface, he has treated his predecessor Buchanan with sufficient acrimony. Achilles Statius and Thomas Correa likewise aspired to distinction as writers of Latin verse, but they were more conspicuous for their merit as philologers: the former, in particular, is entitled to a station among the most learned of his countrymen.

Besides Anthony Govea, Portugal produced several other civilians.[l] The name of Amatus Lusitanus is inserted in the catalogue of illustrious physicians;[m] and Hector Pintus, who was a professor at Coimbra, is represented as a learned and eloquent divine.[n] But the most famous of the Portugueze theologians was Franciscus Forerius, who had distinguished himself in the coun-

---

[k] Spain, though Latin poetry was not much cultivated in that country, likewise produced a complete paraphrase of the psalms. It was executed by the famous Benedictus Arias Montanus. Antverp. 1574, 4to. With respect to this learned monk, a late critic has fallen into a very unaccountable mistake. "The language," says Lord Woodhouselee, "of that ludicrous work, *Epistolæ Obscurorum Virorum*, is an imitation, and by no means an exaggerated picture of the style of Arias Montanus's version of the scriptures." (*Principles of Translation*, p. 117.) The *Epistolæ Obscurorum Virorum* were published upwards of fifty years before the work of which they are here said to be an imitation.

[l] Duck de Authoritate Juris Civilis, p. 318.

[m] Castellani Vitæ Illustrium Medicorum, p. 745. Antv. 1617, 8vo.— Gesner however represents him as "homo temerarius et indoctus." (*Epistolæ Medicinales*, f. 105.)

[n] Schotti Bibliotheca Hispanica, p. 524.

cil of Trent, and who presided over the Domi-
nican monastery of Almada-hill.[o]   Manuel Al-
varez, an acute and learned Jesuit born in the
island of Madeira, is regarded as one of the ablest
grammarians of modern times.[p]   Petrus Nonius,
a native of Alcazar do Sal, and a professor in the
university of Coimbra, is denominated by Osorius the prince of mathematicians ;[q]   and the
learned of various nations have assigned him a
conspicuous station among the cultivators of
science.

Such was the general state of learning among
the Portugueze during the century to which
Buchanan belonged.   In science and in literature, that nation had evidently made no inconsiderable advances; and its progress had only
been retarded by the despotism of the state, and
by the more intolerable despotism of the church.
But to a country which regarded the inquisition
as one of its choicest blessings, the generous
frame of his mind was ill adapted.

Buchanan found that his prospect of being
promoted by the Portugueze monarch was somewhat precarious; and he ther fore determined
to abandon a country in which he had experienced such unworthy treatment.   Having embark-
ed in a Candian vessel which he found in the

* Colomesii Italia et Hispania Orientalis, p. 238.   Hamb. 1730, 4to.
[p] Walchii Hist. Crit. Linguæ Latinæ, p. 193.   Lipsiæ, 1716, 8vo.
[q] Osorius de Rebus Gestis Emmanuelis, p. 424.

port of Lisbon, he was safely conveyed to England. Here however he did not long remain, though he might have procured some creditable situation, which he himself has not particularized. The political affairs of that nation bore a very unpromising aspect ; and he was therefore more anxious to visit the accomplished associates whom he had left in France. In France he arrived about the beginning of the year 1553. The siege of Metz was raised about the same period ; and at the earnest request of his friends, he composed a poem on that event.[r] This was a task which he undertook with considerable reluctance : several other poets, most of whom were of his acquaintance, had already exercised their talents upon the same occasion ; and he was unwilling to enter into a competition. On this subject his friend Melin de St Gelais had written a poem, which he commends as erudite and elegant. St Gelais was once a favourite poet at the French court ;[s] and Buchanan has celebrated him in verse as well as in prose.[t] To the French nation Buchanan appears to have

---

[r] Buchanani Miscellaneorum liber, viii. *Ad Henricum II. Franciæ Regem de soluta urbis Mediomatricum Obsidione.*

[s] Melin de St Gelais, says Pasquier, " produisoit de petites fleurs, et non fruicts d'aucune durée, c'estoient des mignardises qui couroient de fois à autres par les mains des courtisans et dames de cour, qui luy estoit une grande prudence. Parce qu' apres sa mort, on fit imprimer un recueil de ses œuvres, qui mourut presque aussi tost qu'il vist le jour." (*Recherches de la France,* p. 613.) His life occurs in Niceron, tom. v, p. 197.

[t] Buchanani Vita, p. 7. Epigram. lib. i, 57.

been strongly attached; and, in return, they
were proud in regarding him as their countryman by adoption.[u] His sentiments on thus revisiting France, he has warmly expressed in a
poem composed on the occasion, and entitled *Ad-
ventus in Galliam.*

Of Buchanan's attainments the French were
more competent judges than the Portugueze.
Before the reign of Francis the first, science and
literature had indeed begun to revive; but under the generous protection of that accomplished
monarch, their progress was rapid and brilliant.[x]
Buchanan's talents were not long permitted to
remain inactive. Soon after his return to Paris,
he was appointed a regent in the College of Boncourt; [y] and in the year 1555, he was called from

---

[u] " In Levinia Scotiæ provincia ad Blanum amnem natus, sed adoptione
nostræ; qualis Antonius Goveanus Lusitanus, 'summus et ipse Buchanani
amicus, dici et existimari volebat." (Thuani *Hist. sui Temporis,* tom. iv,
p. 99.)

[x] " Nam," says Turnebus, " ut hujus optimi post homines natos principis cætera decora, majore concipienda fortassis ore, et nuper concepta, omit-
tam, et de literis potissimum agam, quæ meæ partes sunt, nullus unquam
ex omni memoria omnium ætatum et temporum betignius et prolixius eas
muneratus est. Nemo majora præmia constituit doctrinæ et eruditioni, nemo uberiora : nemo juventutis studia ad discendum acrius inflammavit : cum
æstimatione doctrinæ, non census amplitudine, homines pendere soleret, doctis sacerdotia mandaret, honores deferret, ad res gerendas adhiberet, benefi-
ciis augeret, omni liberalitatis genere complecteretur." (*Oratio habita post
J. Tusani Mortem,* p. 9.)—See Dr Robertson's *Hist. of Charles V,* vol. iii,
p. 127.

[y] His regency in this college, as well as in that of Cardinal le Moine,
Buchanan has himself neglected to mention. That he taught in the Col-
lege of Boncourt is evident from a passage in a letter addressed to him by
Nicolaus Nancelius. " Specimen frequens et nobile jam tum edidisti, cum

that charge by the celebrated count de Brissac, who retained him as the domestic tutor of his son Timoleon de Cossé. To that warlike nobleman he addressed a very poetical ode after the capture of Vercelli,[x] an event which occurred in the month of September 1553; and on the twenty-eighth of July 1554, he dedicated to him the tragedy of *Jephthes*. Of the value of such tributes the count was not insensible: in the dedication, Buchanan acknowledged himself already indebted to his politeness and to his liberality;[a] and their closer connection ensued in the course of the subsequent year. At that period the marshal presided over the French dominions in Italy; whither Buchanan was invited to attend his hopeful pupil.[b]

inde ab annis circiter triginta, tu Lutetiæ in Bœcodiano profitereris, ego eodem tempore in *prælio* [lege *Prælico*] (ubi regii tum juvenes Stuarti vestrates discebant) sub Ramo antesignano, longe ea ætate eloquentissimo et disertissimo Romuli nepotum militarem doceremque." (Buchanani *Epistolæ*, p. 35.) The date of this epistle is March the fifteenth 1583; for Nancelius had not then heard of Buchanan's death. He returned to France in 1553, precisely thirty years antecedent to that date.

[x] Buchanani *Miscell.* xxiii. *Ad Carolum Cosæum Brixiaci Dynastam, post captas Vercellas.*

[a] "Me autem absentem," says Buchanan, "nec ulla alia re quam literarum commendatione tibi cognitum, ita complexus es omnibus humanitatis et liberalitatis officiis, ut si quis ingenii mei sit fructus, si qua vigiliarum velut fœtura, ea merito ad te redire debeat."—One of his odes is entitled *De Amore Cosæi et Aretes (Miscell.* iii.); and he has also written the epitaph of his illustrious friend. (*Epigram.* lib. ii, 25.)

[b] "Inde evocatus in Italiam a Carolo Cosæo Brixiacensi, qui tum secunda fama res in Ligustico et Gallico circa Padum agro gerebat, nunc in Italia, nunc in Gallia, cum filio ejus Timoleonte quinquennium hæsit, usque ad annum millesimum quingentesimum sexagesimum." (*Buchanani*

Marshal de Brissac lived in a state of princely
magnificence.   Though much of his life had
been spent amidst the tumults of war, he appears to have been a man of a liberal mind, and
to have cultivated an acquaintance with eminent
scholars.   During his campaigns, he was accompanied by men of learning;* and the society
which he now enjoyed with Buchanan, must have
been productive of mutual satisfaction.   In the
preceptor of his son he recognized a man capable
of adorning a higher station ; and he accordingly
treated him with the utmost respect and deference.   He was even accustomed to place him at
the council board among the principal officers of
his army.   To this singular honour Buchanan was
not entitled from his actual acquaintance with
the theory or practice of war : he had recommended himself by the intuitive sagacity of his
comprehensive mind ; and his original admission
arose from a circumstance entirely accidental.
He happened to enter an apartment contiguous
to the hall in which the marshal and his officers
were engaged in discussing some measure of
great importance ; and on being arrested by
their debates, he could not refrain from murmur-

Vita, p. 7.)   Mr Ruddiman is apparently mistaken in referring his new en-
gagement to the year 1554.   Buchanan's connection with Brissac continued
five years, and terminated in 1560 ; but between 1554 and 1560, the space
of five complete years intervenes.   His dedication is dated at Paris on the
twenty-eighth of July 1554, and contains no allusion to any domestic connection with the count.

  * Buchanani praef. in Jephthen.

ing his disapprobation of the opinion supported
by the majority. One of the generals smiled at
so unexpected a salutation; but the marshal having invited Buchanan into the council, enjoined
him to deliver his sentiments without restraint.
He accordingly proceeded to discuss the question
with his wonted perspicacity, and to excite the
amazement of Brissac and his officers. In the
issue his suggestions were found to have been
oracular.[d]

Buchanan's pupil neither discredited his father
nor his preceptor: he was afterwards distinguished for his bravery, and for his acquaintance
with military science; and his literary attainments were such as reflected honour on a young
nobleman, destined for the profession of arms.[e]
His career was short and brilliant; at the age of
twenty-six, it was terminated by a musket-ball

[d] H. Stephani Orationes II, p. 163. Franc. 1594. 8vo.—Menage has related an anecdote of another complexion. " Bucanan avoit été precepteur
des enfans de M. de Brissac. Comme il étoit un jour à sa table, il lui arriva dans le temps qu'il mangeoit du potage bien chaud, de laisser aller un
vent qui fit du bruit: mais sans s'étonner, il dit à ce vent qui étoit sorti
comme malgré lui; Tu as bien fait de sortir, car j'allois te brûler tout vif.
Puisque la conversation est sur ce sujet, je diray encore ce qui j'ay sçu de
M. de Racan. Le Cardinal du Perron jouant aux échets avec Henry IV.
dans le temps qu'il plaçoit un cavalier, il lui arriva la même chose qu' à
Bucanan en mangeant sa soup. Le cardinal pour couvrir cette liberté, dit;
Au moins, Sire, il n'est pas parti sans trompette. M. de Racan m'a assuré
qu'il avoit entendu l'un et l'autre. Ces sortes d'inconveniens peuvent arri-
ver à tout le monde dans les meilleurs compagnies, et l'on ne devroit pas s'en
offenser." (*Menagiana*, tom. ii, p. 133.)

[e] Brantome, Vies des Hommes Illustres et Grands Capitaines François
de son temps, tom. iii, p. 409.

at the siege of Mucidan.[f] When committed to
Buchanan's tuition, he was about twelve years of
age. As he was intended for a military life, his
attention was directed to other objects as well as
to literature; and his preceptor, in the mean time,
found sufficient leisure for his favourite pursuits.
Many of his hours were devoted to the study of
theology. At that æra, religious controversy exercised the faculties of a large proportion of mankind; and he was likewise anxious to place his
faith on the solid foundation of reason. His
poetical studies were not however entirely neglected. It was apparently about this period
that he conceived the design of his philosophical
poem *De Sphæra*; which his future avocations
did not suffer him to bring to a conclusion. It
is addressed to his interesting pupil.

During the five years of his connection with
this illustrious family, Buchanan alternately resided in Italy and France. In the mean time, several of his poetical works were published at Paris. In 1556 appeared the earliest specimen of
his poetical paraphrase of the psalms; and his
version of the *Alcestis* of Euripides was printed
in the course of the subsequent year. This tragedy he dedicated to Margaret, the daughter of
Francis the first; a munificent princess, whose
favour he seems to have enjoyed.[g] Nor was it

---

[f] Thuani Hist. sui Temporis, tom. ii, p. 707.

[g] " Quod si audacius," says Buchanan, " a me factum videatur, eam tu

improper to submit a Latin drama to her inspection; for with the principal writers in that language she had contracted a familiar acquaintance.[h] Brantome has extolled her as a prodigy of virtue and wisdom.[i] In the fortunes of accomplished scholars, she interested herself with a generous warmth; and it was to her friendly zeal that the excellent De l'Hôpital was indebted for his elevation. To this princess, who was at length married to the duke of Savoy, many of the chancellor's poems are addressed; and she is likewise celebrated by Salmonius Macrinus, and by various other authors of eminence. Buchanan's ode on the surrender of Calais was published in the year 1558. The same subject exercised the talents of De l'Hôpital, Turnebus, and many other poets.

His connection with the count terminated in the year 1560, when the civil war had already commenced. It was perhaps the alarming state of France that induced Buchanan to hasten his return to his native country. The precise period of his return has not been ascertained: but it is certain that he was at the Scotish court in January 1562; and that, in the month of April, he was officiating as classical tutor to the queen, who was then in the twentieth year of her age.

potissimum culpam præstes oportet; quæ me tua auctoritate ad scribendum impulisti, et in arenam productum omni favoris genere prosequeris et foves."

[h] Hospitalii Carmina, p. 23. Gallandii Vita Castellani, p. 43.

[i] Brantome, Vies des Dames Illustres de France de son temps, p. 323.

Every afternoon she perused with Buchanan a portion of Livy.[k] This author is not commonly recommended to very young scholars; and indeed the study of the Latin language is known to have occupied a considerable share of her previous attention. She had been sent to France in the sixth year of her age, and had acquired every accomplishment that could adorn her station. The charms of her person rendered her conspicuous among the most elegant of her fair contemporaries;[l] and the polish of her mind corresponded to the elegance of her external form. She was acquainted not only with the Scotish and French, but also with the Italian and Spanish languages; and her knowledge of the Latin tongue was likewise considerable.[m] In the fourteenth year of her age, she pronounced before a

---

[k] In a letter from Randolph to Cecil, dated at Edinburgh on the thirtieth of January 1561-2, the following passage occurs. "Ther is with the quene one called Mr George Bowhanan, a Scottishe man, verie well lerned, that was schellemaster unto Monr de Brisack's sone, very godlye and honest." On the seventh of April, Randolph wrote thus from St. Andrews to the same statesman : "The queen readeth daily after her dinner, instructed by a learned man Mr George Bowhanman, somewhat of Lyvie." (Chalmers's Life of Ruddiman, p. 319, 320.)

[l] " Fœmina," says Julius Cæsar Bulenger, " omnium sui sæculi corporis dignitate maxime conspicua, humanitate, prudentia, liberalitate, eximia, sed variis miseriis toto vitæ tempore exercita." (Hist. sui Temporis, p. 352. Lugd. 1619, fol.) On the tragical story of this accomplished and ill-fated princess, a Spanish author famous for his prolific vein has composed a poem in five books. See Lord Holland's Account of the Life and Writings of Lope de Vega, p. 87. Lond. 1806, 8vo.

[m] " In optimis quibusque Europæ linguis perdiscendis," says George Con, " plurimum studii locabat ; tanta autem erat suavitas sermonis Gallici, ut in eo facunda doctissimorum judicio haberetur, nec Hispanicum aut

splendid audience of the French court, a Latin
declamation against the opinion of those who
would debar the female sex from the pursuits of
science and literature. This oration, which she
had herself composed, she afterwards translated
into French; but neither the original nor the
version has ever been published.[a] Some of her
Italian and French verses are however preserved.[o] Mary was unquestionably entitled to the
character of a learned princess; but her subse-

Italicum neglexit, quibus ad usum magis quam ad ostentationem, aut volu-
bilitatem, utebatur; Latinum intelligebat melius quam efferebat; ad poetices leporem plus a natura quam ab arte habuit." (*Vita Mariæ Stuartæ,*
p. 15, apud Jebb.)

[a] La Croix du Maine, Bibliotheque Françoise, tom. ii, p. 90. Brantome, Vies des Dames Illustres de France, p. 114.

[o] Most of them are collected by Mr Laing. (*Hist. of Scotland,* vol. ii, p.
217.) Two of her French poems, which have escaped the notice of this
historian, occur in a work of Bishop Lesley. (*Piæ Afflicti Animi Consola-
tiones,* f. 38, b. Paris. 1574, 8vo.) They are accompanied with Latin
translations; one of which was executed by Adam Blackwood. (Blacvodæi
Opera, p. 478.) An unpublished French sonnet of Mary addressed to her
son, is preserved in the State-Paper Office. From the *Diot. du Vieux Langage,* p. 337, Dr Burney has quoted a *chanson* which she is supposed to
have written on leaving Calais. (*Hist. of Music,* vol. iii, p. 14.) But these
verses seem to be a mere paraphrase of the words recorded by Brantome.
Bishop Montague, in his preface to the works of King James, informs us
that she " wrote a booke of verses in French of the institution of a prince."
The original manuscript, which was in the possession of her son, may still
be preserved. Among the poems of Sir Thomas Chaloner occurs a " Trans-
latio quorundam Carminum quæ Gallico primum sermone conscripta, a
Serenissima Scotiæ Regina in mutuæ amicitiæ pignus, una cum excellentis
operis annulo, in quo insignis adamas prominebat, ad Serenissimam Angliæ
Reginam Elizabetham missa fuerant." (*De Rep. Anglorum Instauranda,*
&c. p. 353. Lond. 1579, 4to.) But it is not evident, at least from this
inscription, that the original verses were composed by the Scotish queen.

G

quent conduct rather serves to confirm than to refute the caustic observation of Muretus.[p]

The æra at which Buchanan finally returned to his native country, was highly important. After a violent struggle between the old and the new religion, the latter had at length prevailed: its fundamental doctrines had received the sanction of parliament in the year 1560. Those bold and ardent characters who accomplished the reformation have bequeathed so many essential benefits to posterity, that we ought to treat with some degree of tenderness even the greatest errors into which their zeal betrayed them. If judged with equity, they must be judged by the maxims of their own age. When they renounced the other errors of Popery, they retained its persecuting spirit; nor do they seem to have entertained any doubt of their having obtained the right, as soon as they had obtained the power, to compel all the world to acquiesce in their opinions. The spirit of the reformed legislature may be very clearly discerned in an act of parliament, passed in 1560, and again con-

---

[p] Mureti Variæ Lectiones, lib. viii, cap. xxi. *Mulieres eruditas plerumque libidinosas esse.* The reason which he assigns ought not to be admitted: " Neque mirum : multæ enim historias legunt, peccare, ut ait Flaccus, docentes." The opinion of Grotius is more liberal, and perhaps more philosophical.

> Crede nihil nostris, sed omnia crede puellis:
> Lectricis mores pagina nulla facit.
> Quæ casta est, totum leget incorrupta Catullum :
> Illi nil tutum est quæ capit, et capitur.
>
> GROTII Poemata, p. 251.

firmed in 1567.[1] By this act, those who either
said or heard mass were liable, for the first offence, to the confiscation of all their property,
and to be further punished in their persons at
the discretion of the competent judge. The second offence subjected them to banishment, and
the third was to be punished with death. We
need not at present enquire whether this iniqui-
tous law was ever executed in its utmost rigour.
The loss of property, corporal punishment, and
banishment from the kingdom, might sufficiently
secure the votaries of the mass from the guilt
of a third offence; but we are certainly authorized to conclude that the legislators who framed
such a law, had no wish to prevent its full and
complete execution.

For the principles of the reformation, Buchanan had always cherished a secret affection; and
his attachment, as he candidly owns, had been
confirmed by the personal malignity of the grey
friars.[r] As he now resided in a country where
he could avow his sentiments without restraint,
he professed himself a member of the reformed
church of Scotland; and this accession to their
cause was duly appreciated by the leaders of the
party. The earl of Murray, who was then rising
towards that summit of power which he after-

[1] Acts of the Parliaments of Scotland, vol. ii, p. 535, vol. iii, p. 23.

[r] " Et dum impotentiæ suæ indulgent, illum sponte sua sacerdotum licentiæ infensum acrius incendunt, et Lutheranæ causæ minus iniquum reddunt." (Buchanani Vita, p. 3.)

wards attained, was one of the few Scotish nobles
of the age who reverenced literature, and pa-
tronised its professors.[s]   His own education had
not been neglected; he had been committed to
the tuition of Ramus,[t] who then presided over
. the College of De Prêle at Paris.   For Buchanan
he soon procured a station of some dignity and
importance.   As commendator of the priory of
St. Andrews, he enjoyed the right of nominating
the principal of St. Leonard's College; and a
vacancy occurring about the year 1566,[u] he placed Buchanan at the head of that seminary.[x]
The masterships of the Scotish colleges are ge-

---

[s] Patrick Cockburn is perhaps the earliest writer who has celebrated his
patronage of literature.   "Accedit etiam generosissimi adolescentis Jacobi
Steuardi, illustrissimi et invictissimi Scotorum quondam regis filii inclyti,
regio plane ingenio et moribus præditi, patroni ac Mæcenatis mei benignis-
simi, seria et pia adhortatio."   (De Vulgari Sacræ Scripturæ Phrasi libri
duo, f. 2.   Paris. 1558, 8vo.)   This work is dedicated to James Stewart. .

[t] Turneri Maria Stuarta Innocens, p. 13, edit. Colon. 1627, 8vo.

[u] Sibbaldi Comment. in Vitam Buchanani, p. 65.

[x] It appears from the original statutes, as quoted by Mr Man, that the
right of nominating the principal of St. Leonard's College was perpetually
vested in the prior of St. Andrews.   (Censure of Ruddiman, p. 94.)   And
at the time of Buchanan's appointment, the priorship was held by his patron
the earl of Murray.   In the act of privy council respecting his resignation
of the principality, and appointment to the office of preceptor to the king,
the subsequent clause occurs.   "Albeit the presentation, nomination, and
admission of the master of the said colledge pertained of old to the prior of
St. Andrews, yet the same right and patronage presently appertains to our
sovereign lord, as well by reason of the laws of the realm, as because the
priory of St. Andrews presently vaiks destitute of a prior or commendatar."
Here the expression is somewhat incorrect; but the sense evidently is, that
the right of presentation then belonged to the king, because the priorship was
vacant.   "By reason of the laws of the realm," that right reverted to the
crown in case of such a vacancy.

nerally conferred on ecclesiastics : this preference
does not however, in each instance, result from
the fundamental statutes, but from the influence
of established usage. It has been asserted that
Buchanan was not a layman, but a doctor and
professor of divinity. In one sense he was indeed
a *doctor* of divinity ; [y] for the tenure of his appointment as principal of the college, seems to
have imposed upon him the task of delivering occasional prelections on theology. Public teachers of divinity, though not ordained, were considered as ecclesiastical persons : and it was in this
capacity that some writers suppose Buchanan to
have sat in the general assembly. He might
however sit as a lay elder. Calderwood relates
that he exhibited proofs of his skill in theology
in " the exercise of prophecying." This term
denoted a weekly meeting of the clergy and
other learned men of a district, who alternately
expounded a passage of scripture. [z] The theological prelections of a gay and satirical poet
must have excited no ordinary curiosity. Buchanan was a man of universal talent ; and the
study of theology had recently occupied a considerable share of his attention.

[y] " Doctores igitur," says the learned Dr Forbes, " scholastici, sive ec-
clesiastici, prout a parochiarum pastoribus distinguuntur, duorum sunt gene-
rum. Alii sunt doctores officio, nempe, publici professores : alii sunt doctores facultate." (Forbesii *Irenicum Amatoribus Veritatis et Pacis in Ecclesia
Scoticana*, p. 305. Aberdoniæ, 1629, 4to.)

[z] M'Crie's Life of Knox, vol. ii, p. 282-5.—The same exercise, and un-

On his return to Scotland, he determined to
publish in a correct manner, the poetical works
which he had composed at many different periods
of his variegated life. In the year 1556, H. Stephanus had printed Buchanan's paraphrase of
eighteen psalms as a specimen; and had placed
it in contrast with the corresponding versions of
Eobanus Hessus, Salmonius Macrinus, Flaminius, and Rapicius. * The first of these poets
translated all the psalms into elegiac verse; the
other three have only versified a select portion.
Stephanus subjoined his own Greek version of
seven psalms, contrasted with that of Paulus Dolscius. This publication is inscribed to Buchanan
in a friendly and familiar style. " You have been
too long concealed, my Buchanan: you must
now, as you perceive, come into public notice:
whether you will or not, I will draw you from
your concealment. Are you angry with me on
this account? and yet I am either deceived, or it

.der the same name, was likewise introduced in England. (Peirce's *Vindication of the Dissenters*, p. 92, 2d edit. Lond. 1718, 8vo.)

* Davidis Psalmi aliquot Latino carmine expressi a quatuor illustribus
Poetis, quos quatuor regiones, Gallia, Italia, Germania, Scotia, genuerunt;
in gratiam studiosorum poetices inter se commissi ab Henrico Stephano:
cujus etiam nonnulli Psalmi Græci cum aliis Græcis itidem comparati in
calce libri habentur. *Ex officina Henrici Stephani*, 1556, 4to.—See Appendix, No. vii. The version of Eobanus Hessus was published at Mar-
purg in 1537. There is a complete version of the psalms, jointly executed
by Flaminius and Spinula: " Psalmi Davidis, a M. Antonio Flaminio et
P. Francisco Spinula, Poetis elegantissimis, Latinis versibus expressi." Antverpiæ, 1559, 8vo. It does not sufficiently appear from Tiraboschi's account whether Spinula, or Spinola, versified all the psalms. (*Storia della
Letteratura Italiana*, tom. vii, p. 1439.)

shall be effected by my services, that hereafter George Buchanan, a Scotchman, above all the French and Italian poets of our age

Laudetur, vigeat, placeat, relegatur, ametur. [b]

For I willingly adopt a verse of Augustus in celebrating so august a poet : and unless I were afraid to commend you to your face, I should advance something much more august. Yet what occasion have you for me to publish your praise, since almost every verse that you have composed proclaims your superior genius? At present therefore I shall only mention one circumstance : as there is nothing more honourable, nothing more splendid, than after excelling all others, at length to excel one's self; so, in my judgment, you have most happily attained to this praise in your version of these psalms. For in translating the other odes of this sacred poet, you have been Buchanan, that is, you have been as conspicuous among the other paraphrasts, as the moon among the smaller luminaries : but when you come to the hundred and fourth psalm, you surpass Buchanan; so that you do not now shine like the moon among the smaller luminaries, but, like the sun, you seem to obscure all the stars by your brilliant rays." Stephanus afterwards introduces a comparison of the different translators who are

---

[b] Laudetur, placeat, vigeat, relegatur, ametur.

AUGUSTI Fragmenta, p. 189.

here placed in competition. " If Flaminius had
previously exerted his talents in composing tragedies or translating them from the Greek (a labour by which you some time ago acquired high
reputation), it might not perhaps have happened,
as it does now, that you should obtain a victory
so easy and almost without a contest. But such
as Flaminius is, I ingenuously confess that when
I pass over Buchanan, I do not find another
whom I can compare with him. My countryman Salmonius (for I am a friend to my country,
but a greater friend to truth) is not only much
inferior to Flaminius in purity of language, but
likewise yields to him in elegance of versification : and as his verses are less polished, so his
style is much more prosaic. These observations
I do not make with a view to anticipate the opinion of the reader, should he apply to the discussion with a nice ear, an acute understanding,
and a still more acute judgment ; but because I
might be considered as a foolish panegyrist and
admirer of your poetry, unless I should point out,
by a comparison with other poets, what chiefly
appears to me worthy of admiration. But some
person may perhaps say, what you admire in Buchanan, but do not meet with in Flaminius, an
Italian, and Salmonius, a Frenchman, may be
found in Eobanus, a German, or in Rapicius,
likewise an Italian. Far from it : for (not to
mention Eobanus, a great part of whose verses
have nothing in common with poetry but the

metre), Rapicius certainly writes without choice or selection."

This famous printer is represented as having long deferred the publication of Buchanan's complete version; and it is at least certain that the manuscript was in his custody so early as the year 1562.[c] Its suppression might be imputed to various causes; but, according to the learned Hadrianus Junius, he had protracted the edition with the secret view of claiming this version as his own, in the event of Buchanan's decease.[d] Many circumstances render this supposition highly improbable; and it must be recollected that Junius regarded with manifest hostility, the man to whom he imputes so flagitious a scheme. The date of this first complete edition is uncertain; for it has been omitted in the book itself.[e] It

[c] Maittaire, Historia Stephanorum, p. 256.[']
[d] Junii Animadvers, p. 390, edit. Roter. 1708, 8vo.
[e] Psalmorum Davidis Paraphrasis Poetica, nunc primum edita, authore Georgio Buchanano, Scoto, poetarum nostri seculi facile principe. Ejusdem Davidis Psalmi aliquot a Th. B. V. versi. Psalmi aliquot in versus item Graecos nuper a diversis translati. *Apud Henricum Stephanum, et ejus fratrem Robertum Stephanum, typographum regium.* Ex privilegio regis. 8vo.—This volume includes a specimen of Beza's Latin version, together with several of the psalms translated into Greek by Stephanus, Chrestien, Jamotius, and an anonymous poet. The editions of Buchanan's version are very numerous; but I shall only mention some of the more remarkable. The earliest commentator on this work was Nathan Chytraeus; who published an edition set to music, and accompanied with scholia adapted to the use of younger students. Francof. 1585, 12mo. That of Alexander Yule, or *Julius*, is illustrated with an ecphrasis, which had been partly sketched by Buchanan himself. Lond. 1620, 8vo. But the best edition of Buchanan's paraphrase is that published by Robert Hunter, professor of Greek at Edinburgh, and John Love, master of the grammar school of Dalkeith. Edinb.

was printed by H. Stephanus and his brother. In the year 1566 they published a second edition, which includes the author's tragedy of *Jephthes.* Buchanan, in the title-page of both impressions, is styled " Poetarum nostri sæculi facile princeps :" and his paraphrase was recommended to the learned world by the poetical encomiums of several respectable scholars ; by the Greek verses of H. Stephanus, Franciscus Portus, and Federicus Jamotius, and by the Latin verses of Stephanus and Castelvetro. Jamotius, whose name is less known, was a native of Bethune in Artois, and by profession a physician. ᶠ Castelvetro, an Italian critic of high reputation, is still regarded as one of the most subtile commentators on Aristotle's poetics. ᵍ Of

1737, 8vo. It is neatly and correctly printed by the Ruddimans ; and beside the notes of the associated editors, it contains the illustrations of Chytræus, Yule, Ruddiman, and Burman. Buchanan's paraphrase was published, along with the Greek version of Duport, by an editor whose preface is subscribed R. R. and dated at Westminster. Lond. 1742, 8vo. Andrew Waddel, A. M. left for publication " G. Buchanan's Paraphrase of the Psalms of David, translated into English prose, as near the original as the different idioms of the Latin and English languages will allow : with the Latin text and order of construction in the same page." Edinb. 1772, 8vo. The best edition for the use of schools was published by Mr Adam Dickinson. Edinb. 1812, 12mo.

ᶠ Andreæ Bibliotheca Belgica, p. 216, edit. Lovan. 1643, 4to.—Among other works, Jamotius published the following. " Varia Poemata Græca et Latina." Antverp. 1593, 4to. " Galeni Paraphrasis in Menodoti Exhortationem ad Liberalium Artium Studia, Annotationibus illustrata." Lutetiæ, 1583, 4to. He also published an edition of Tryphiodorus, accompanied with a poetical translation, and with notes.

ᵍ Castelvetro, says Dr Bentley, " was one of the most ingenious and judicious and learned writers of his age ; and his books have at this present such a mighty reputation, that they are sold for their weight in silver in

Buchanan's genius, Stephanus was a very zealous admirer: it was he who conferred upon him the appellation of first poet of the age; and this honourable title was afterwards recognized by the scholars of France, Italy, Germany, and other countries. [h] Of this celebrated printer, it may safely be affirmed that he was at least as much inclined to censure as to commend: his contemporary Joseph Scaliger, though very willing to applaud his erudition, has characterized him as a man of an arrogant and morose temper; and even his son-in-law, the candid and amiable Casaubon, [i] however anxious he might be to conceal his infirmities, has occasionally mentioned him in terms of similar import. The erudition of Stephanus was however extensive and profound; insomuch that he is regarded as the most learned printer who has yet appeared. He was one of the best Grecians of that laborious age; and was eminently skilled in the Latin as well as in his vernacular language. The Greek tongue he studied before the Latin; and this unusual method he afterwards recom-

---

most countries of Europe." (*Dissertation upon Phalaris*, p. cii.) See the excellent Mr Tyrwhitt's *Animadversiones in Aristotelis librum de Poetica*, p. 167. Oxon. 1794, 8vo. The life of Castelvetro, written by Muratori, is published with the collection of his *Opere Critiche*. Berna, 1727, 4to. It is likewise prefixed to the splendid edition of *Le Rime del Petrarca brevemente esposte per Lodovico Castelvetro*, printed at Venice in 1756 in two volumes quarto.

[h] H. Stephani Orationes II. p. 164. Franc. 1594, 8vo.

[i] Ruhnkenius observes of this very learned man, " quo non fuit lenioris naturæ criticus." (*Opuscula*, p. 23.)

mended as the most eligible.[k] The services
which he rendered to the cause of literature
were such as entitle him to perpetual gratitude:
before his time, Greek books were extremely
rare; and the numerous editions which proceeded from his press, are generally distinguished for
their correctness and elegance. Of his own compositions it is more difficult to speak. By his
Thesaurus Linguæ Græcæ as well as by some of
his philological annotations, he undoubtedly rendered essential service to classical learning; but
his efforts at a higher species of excellence are
for the most part attended with indifferent success. He produced an infinite number of little
works, which certainly display but a slender
share of judgment. Among other critical lucubrations, he published a dissertation *De Criticis
Veteribus Græcis et Latinis*;[l] and on such a subject, a curious and interesting treatise might
have been expected from so learned a man: this
dissertation however is sufficiently trifling and
jejune. Another book he has professedly written on the Latinity of Lipsius;[m] but many pages
of it are occupied with considerations respecting

---

[k] Estienne, Traicté de la Conformité du Langage François avec le Grec,
pref. Paris, 1569, 8vo.—The same method of study is strenuously recommended by Dr Sharpe. *(Origin and Structure of the Greek Tongue*, p. 10,
edit. Lond. 1777, 8vo.)

Parisiis, 1587, 4to.

[m] Francfordii, 1595, 8vo. Pp. 590.—The Latinity of Lipsius was zealously vindicated by a later critic. (Klotzii *Opuscula Varii Argumenti*,
p. 1. Altenb. 1766, 8vo.)

a war with the Turks. This, says Scaliger, appeared so ridiculous, that some person proposed to entitle it " De Lipsii Latinitate *adversus Turcam.*" He was judiciously advised by Thuanus and by P. Pithœus to confine himself to the publication of ancient authors ;[n] a plan by which he would have contributed more effectually to the advancement of learning.

Stephanus, who was ambitious of universal excellence, might perhaps expect to obtain the same preëminence among the Greek, as was due to Buchanan among the Latin paraphrasts of the psalms. A complete Greek translation had formerly been exhibited by Apollinarius ; and at a more recent æra, others were executed with different degrees of success by Paulus Dolscius, Æmilius Portus, Petavius, and Duport. The Latin versions amount to a very large number ; and by competent and impartial judges, the superiority has generally been awarded to Buchanan. In this celebrated work, he has employed no fewer than twenty-nine varieties of metre ; and each of them with the utmost propriety and skill. The adaptation of the measures, the harmony of the verse, the elegance and purity of the diction, the pious and dignified strain of the phraseology, would have been sufficient to secure a high reputation independent of his original compositions. This production indeed displays all the

[a] Vavassor de Epigrammate, p. 201, edit. Paris. 1672, 8vo.

spirit and freedom of an original : the poet seems
unfettered by the necessity of adhering to a prescribed train of thought; and he often rises to
all the enthusiasm and sublimity of his proto-
type. His version of the hundred and fourth
psalm might alone have conferred upon him the
character of a poet.° The next in merit is perhaps the hundred and thirty-seventh; which he
has translated into elegiac verse of uncommon
excellence. His work is professedly a paraphrase; and indeed it would be impossible to
execute a strict translation with any degree of
elegance. That he has frequently dilated the
original thought, is sufficiently evident; but no
translator has been more successful in retaining
the spirit and essence. It is not certain that
Buchanan was intimately acquainted with the
Hebrew language; but he must have consulted
with diligence the principal commentators on
the book of psalms. He is reported to have enjoyed the particular friendship of Franciscus
Vatablus; and to have derived from that famous
professor some more curious elucidations of the
Hebrew text.P

° Several other Scotish poets have attempted to rival this exquisite version. See a collection entitled *Octupla; hoc est octo Paraphrases Poticæ
Psalmi civ. Authoribus totidem Scotis.* Edinb. 1696, 8vo. This collection
also includes the critical tracts of Barclay and Eglisham. Lauder has reprinted the prose as well as the verse, in his *Poetarum Scotorum Musæ Sacræ.* Edinb. 1739, 2 tom. 8vo.

P " Doctissimus poeta," says Dr Barclay, " sequutus Francisci Vatabli
psalmorum interpretationem; quem Parisiis Hebraicæ linguæ professorem

From his admirable version, he has carefully
excluded such expressions as are strictly and
solely applicable to subjects of classical mythology; but as he had adopted a classical language,
it would have been utterly impossible to exclude
every word or phrase, capable of suggesting the
mythological allusions of his Pagan predecessors.
The ancient Pagans often addressed Jupiter,
whom they regarded as the supreme being, in a
strain of phraseology which may reverently be
applied to the true God; a and sometimes perhaps a Christian could not select words more suitable to the devotional ideas that may arise in his
mind. When he writes in a language which
derives its vital principles from a people whose
objects of worship were fictitious, he cannot express himself without employing words originally
appropriated by mythology: the boundaries of
speech are already ascertained, and the only expedient that remains is a happy and judicious
adaptation. Buchanan has however been censured by a late writer. " In the translation of a
psalm," says Lord Woodhouselee, " we are
shocked when we find the almighty addressed
by the epithets of a heathen divinity, and his

habuit summe amicum et familiarem. Itaque consulebat curiose fontes ipsos,
et linguam qua psalmos cecinit *regius propheta.* Unde deducit aliquando
plus sententiæ quam appareat in vulgatis editionibus." (*Judicium de Cer-*
tamine Egilsemnell, p. 14.) Vatablus died in 1547.

a " Et qui Jovem principem volunt," says Minucius Felix, " falluntur
in nomine, sed de una potestate consentiunt." (*Octavius,* p. 145, edit.
Ouzelii, 1672.)

attributes celebrated in the language and allusions proper to the Pagan mythology. . . . In the
entire translation of the psalms by Johnston, we
do not find a single instance of similar impropriety. And in the admirable version by Buchanan, there are, (to my knowledge) only two passages which are censurable on that account. The
one is the beginning of the 4th psalm :

O pater, O hominum *divûmque* æterna potestas

which is the first line of the speech of Venus to
Jupiter, in the 10th Æneid : and the other is
the beginning of psalm 82, where two entire
lines, with the change of one syllable, are borrowed from Horace :

Regum timendorum in proprios greges,
Reges in ipsos imperium est *Jovæ*.

In the latter example the poet probably judged
that the change of *Jovis* into *Jovæ* removed all
objection ; and Ruddiman has attempted to vindicate the *divûm* of the former passage, by applying it to saints or angels :[r] but allowing there
were sufficient apology for both these words, the
impropriety still remains ; for the associated
ideas present themselves immediately to the
mind, and we are justly offended with the literal
adoption of an address to Jupiter in a hymn to

[r] Ruddiman's Vindication of Buchanan, p. 161.

the creator."[r] Whatever may be the general effect of the two passages, it may at least be affirmed that those particular words are employed without any degree of impropriety. In the original scriptures, the angels are repeatedly denominated gods; and *Jova* is the tetragrammaton of the Hebrews.[s] To insert the word Jehovah in the translation of a psalm, certainly cannot be deemed reprehensible.[t]

Some feeble attempts have been made to dispossess Buchanan of his high preëminence in this department. Dr Eglisham had the vanity to suppose himself capable of executing a paraphrase, superior to that of his illustrious countryman; and was even so infatuated as to exhibit a version of the hundred and fourth psalm in

---

[r] Woodhouselee's Essay on the Principles of Translation, p. 268, 3d edit. Edinb. 1813, 8vo.

[s] Drusii Observationes Sacræ, p. 6.

[t] Dr Pitcairne commences his version of the hundred and fourth psalm with the following line.

Dexteram invictam canimus *Jovamque.*

This genuine reading occurs in the *Octupla,* which was published during the lifetime of Dr Pitcairne. Ruddiman and Lauder have very improperly substituted *Jovem.*

The following notice of this distinguished physician occurs in a letter of Bayle, dated 7th March 1697. "Ce médecin philosophe [Bellini] a peu près de la maniere que Pitcarnius, médecin Ecossois, qui a été quelque tems professeur à Leyde, et qui se retira de cette charge sans dire adieu à personne. Ses leçons ne plaisoient pas, quoi qu' elles fussent fort singulieres, et fort relevées; mais il y mêloit trop de mécanique, et trop de géométrie." (*Oeuvres Diverses,* tom. iv, p. 732.) In the Appendix, No. xii, I have inserted an original paper of Dr Pitcairne, explanatory of some obscure allusions in his Latin poems. Several other passages are explained by Lord Hailes, in a communication to the *Edinburgh Magazine and Review,* vol. i, p. 235.

H

contrast with his. On Buchanan's translation of that psalm, he at the same time published a violent criticism; which he concludes very complacently, by submitting his lucubrations to the judgment of the university of Paris. Dr Johnston, who was aware that the reputation of his native land was closely connected with that of Buchanan, exposed the vanity of Eglisham in two galling satires;[u] and Dr Barclay, another learned physician, refuted his captious criticisms, and exposed the puerility of the version which he had exhibited in so hazardous a situation.

Arthur Johnston was one of the best Latin poets of the age in which he flourished. His original compositions are distinguished by a spirit of classical elegance; and he has executed a complete paraphrase of the psalms, which is regarded as superior to that of every other poet

[u] Jonstoni Parerga, p. 3, 12. Aberdoniæ, 1632, 8vo.—Another Aberdeen poet, John Leech, A. M. of King's College, has likewise satirised him under the name of Onopordus. (*Musæ Priores,* epig. p. 13. Lond. 1620, 8vo.) Eglisham's treatment of Buchanan drew from Daniel Heinsius these expressions of poignant indignation: " Quominus est ferendum, esse hominem tam confidentem qui leoni mortuo insultet. Sed et pulices et pedes idem faciunt; animalia quæ e putredine nascuntur." (Burmanni *Sylloge Epistolarum,* tom. ii, p. 451.) In the Appendix, No. xiv, I have mentioned the first edition of his work. He soon published a second, under the title of " Duellum Poeticum, pro Dignitate Paraphraseos Psalmi centesimi quarti, decertantibus G. Eglisemmio, medico regio, G. Buchanano, pædonomo regio. Cui annexa Epigrammata, nec non Astrologicum de causis et effectibus novi Cometæ Judicium." Londini, 1619, 4to. Dempster describes the author as a native of Hamilton; but in 1616, George Eglisham, M. D. was served heir to his father John Eglisham, a burgess of Edinburgh. (*Inquisitionum Abbreviatio,* vol. ii, inq. gen. 632.)

except Buchanan. Of Buchanan's superiority
he professes to have been sufficiently aware; but
some of his admirers have bestowed their praise
with too lavish a hand, and perhaps have rather
diminished than increased his reputation. Lauder, who rendered himself conspicuous by his attack on Milton, was the first writer who endeavoured to establish Johnston's fame on the ruin
of Buchanan's; and he found an ardent supporter
in Mr Benson, an English gentleman respectable
for his love of literature. Several impressions
of Johnston's paraphrase were published at his
expense; one of which is a splendid edition for
the use of the prince of Wales, on the plan of the
French edition of classics for the use of the dau-
phin.[y] But the editors of Buchanan did not
tamely acquiesce in this encroachment: his defence against Lauder was undertaken by Mr
Love;[z] against Benson by Mr Ruddiman, a
more formidable antagonist. Not satisfied with
overwhelming Johnston with hyperbolical praise,
Mr Benson had laboured to prove that Buchan-

---

[y] Arturi Jonstoni Psalmi Davidici Interpretatione, Argumentis, Notisque
illustrati: in usum Serenissimi Principis. Lond. 1741, 4to.—This edition,
which includes a portrait engraved by G. Vertue, was also printed in 8vo
during the same year. Mr Benson published a third impression of Johnston's
paraphrase, accompanied with the Greek metaphrase of Duport. Lond.
1742, 8vo. These editions were all printed by Bowyer. The first edition
of Johnston's work is that of Aberdeen, 1637, 8vo.

[z] The controversy between Lauder and Love produced many pamphlets;
but the only one that I have seen is the first part of Lauder's *Calumny Display'd.* Of that work there are at least other two parts. In the catalogue
subjoined to this volume, I have mentioned Love's comparison of Buchanan
and Johnston on the authority of Mr Chalmers, p. 137.

an's paraphrase is unworthy of the commendation which it has received: but his criticisms
were completely exposed by that excellent gram-
marian; whose elaborate performance, though
perhaps somewhat deficient in compression, may
still be recommended for its intrinsic value.

The elegant and melodious version of Johnston is almost entirely confined to the elegiac
measure, in which he had attained to great proficiency. In the hundred and nineteenth psalm
alone, his metre is varied; and each stanza is exhibited in a new species of verse. Buchanan's
plan of varying the measure according to the
characteristics of the poem, was evidently more
eligible to a writer who possessed such versatility
of talent. His friend Beza has likewise adopted
a variety of metres; but he has not perhaps selected them with equal judgment.

Dr Beattie, who has passed a general condem-
nation on poetical paraphrases of the psalms, is
by no means disposed to exempt Buchanan's from
this sentence. " If we look into Buchanan, what
can we say, but that the learned author, with
great command of Latin expression, has no true
relish for the emphatic conciseness, and unadorn-
ed simplicity, of the inspired poets? Arthur
Johnston is not so verbose, and has of course
more vigour: but his choice of a couplet, which
keeps the reader always in mind of the puerile
epistles of Ovid, was singularly injudicious.—As
psalms may, in prose, as easily as in verse, be
adapted to music, why should we seek to force

those divine strains into the measures of Roman
or of modern song? He who transformed Livy
into iambics, and Virgil into monkish rhime, did.
not in my opinion act more absurdly. In fact,
sentiments of devotion are rather depressed than
elevated by the arts of the European versifier."ᵃ
This censure of Buchanan, when properly understood, is less applicable to the manner than to
the language in which he wrote. The genius of
the Hebrew is essentially different from that of
the Latin tongue; and what is beauty in the one
may be deformity in the other. To this rash
charge of verbosity and want of vigour, it will
be sufficient to oppose the judgment of a learned
writer who had studied the works of Buchanan
with great assiduity. " Of all our modern poets,"
says Mr Ruddiman, " I know of none who have
better preserved that masculine and elegant simplicity, which we so much admire in the ancient
writers, and whose stile is farther removed from
all gaudiness and affectation."

Sir Thomas Hope, who was king's advocate
from 1626 till 1641, and who is well known to
Scotish lawyers, must also be commemorated
among the Scotish poets who have executed Latin paraphrases of this sacred book. His version still remains in manuscript; and its merit is
not perhaps sufficient to render its publication
an object of much solicitude.ᵇ

ᵃ Beattie's Dissertations Moral and Critical, p. 645. Lond. 1783, 4to.
ᵇ Hope's version of the hundred and fourth psalm may be found in Lau-

Buchanan's paraphrase continues to be read in the principal schools of Scotland, and perhaps in those of some other countries. Lauder's attempt to supplant it by that of Johnston proved unsuccessful. During the lifetime of Buchanan, it had begun to be introduced into the schools of Germany; and its various measures had been accommodated to appropriate melodies, for the purpose of being chanted by academical students.[c] Pope Urban the eighth, himself a poet of no mean talents, is said to have averred that " 'twas pity it was written by so great a heretic, for otherwise it should have been sung in all churches under his authority."[d] The famous Bishop Bedell " loved it beyond all other Latin poetry;"[e] and Nicolas Bourbon, who was himself a poet of considerable celebrity, declared that he would rather have been the author of this paraphrase than archbishop of Paris.[f]

When Buchanan consigned his psalms to the printer, he was probably engaged in superintending the classical studies of Queen Mary; and to that most accomplished and hopeful princess, he

der's *Poetarum Scotorum Musæ Sacræ,* tom. ii, p. xxvi. To this famous lawyer Johnston has addressed one of his epigrams. (Jonstoni *Poemata,* p. 374. Middelb. 1642, 16to.)

[c] Chytræi præf. in Collectanea in Buchanani Paraphrasin Psalmorum.

[d] Sir John Denham's preface to his Version of the Psalms. Lond. 1714, 8vo.—Cowley, speaking of the writers who have versified the psalms, denominates Buchanan " much the best of them all, and indeed a great person." (*Pref. to Pindarique Odes.*)

[e] Burnet's Life of Bishop Bedell, p. 77. Lond. 1685, 8vo.

[f] Menage, Observations sur les Poësies de M. de Malherbe, p. 395.

gratefully inscribed a work destined for immortality. His dedication has received, and indeed is entitled to the highest commendation for its terseness, compression, and delicacy.

> Nympha, Caledoniæ quæ nunc feliciter oræ
>   Missa per innumeros sceptra tueris avos;
> Quæ sortem antevenis meritis, virtutibus annos,
>   Sexum animis, morum nobilitate genus,
> Accipe (sed facilis) cultu donata Latino
>   Carmina, fatidici nobile regis opus.
> Illa quidem Cirrha procul et Permesside lympha,
>   Pene sub Arctoi sidere nata poli:
> Non tamen ausus eram male natum exponere fœtum,[f]
>   Ne mihi displiceant quæ placuere tibi.[h]
> Nam quod ab ingenio domini sperare nequibant,
>   Debebunt genio forsitan illa tuo.[i]

Instead of this conclusion, other four verses, not destitute of elegance, have been substituted by Dr Atterbury, the well-known bishop of Ro-

---

[f] This verse is sometimes misunderstood. It is thus explained by Lancelot: "Non ausus essem in publicum edere fœtum, non faventibus Musis editum." (*Epigrammatum Delectus*, p. 383, edit. Lond. 1686, 8vo.) But the poet evidently alludes to the practice of *exposing* deformed or sickly infants. "I durst not however expose my unpromising offspring."

[h] Invideo Pisis, Laurenti, nec tamen odi,
  Ne mihi displiceat quæ tibi terra placet.
    POLITIANI Opera, sig. gg. 5. Venet. 1498, fol.

[i] This famous epigram is imitated by Johnston in the dedication of his psalms, and by Dempster in that of his Latin version of Montgomery's *Cherrie and Slae.* "Quod tamen epigramma," says Vavasseur, "fere epigramma non sit, cum exitu subtili nullo concludatur." (*De Epigrammate,* p. 263.) This point it seems unnecessary to dispute with the learned Jesuit; for however these verses are to be described, no person will deny their excellence.

chester. They certainly partake more of the spirit of a modern dedication, but do not sufficiently correspond with the majestic simplicity of Buchanan's sentiments.

> Quod si culta parum, si sint incondita, nostri
> Scilicet ingenii est, non ea culpa loci.
> Posse etiam hic nasci quæ sunt pulcherrima, spondet
> E vultu et genio Scotica terra tuo.

Buchanan recommended himself to the queen by other poetical tributes. One of his most beautiful productions is the epithalamium which he composed on her first nuptials.[k] This attractive subject had also excited the poetical talents of De l'Hôpital and Turnebus; but the rival composition of Buchanan displays a fertility of fancy, and a felicity of diction, which preclude all comparison. His encomium on his native land it would be unpardonable to overlook.

> Illa 'pharetratis est propria gloria Scotis,
> Cingere venatu saltus, superare natando
> Flumina, ferre famem, contemnere frigora et æstus;
> Nec fossa et muris patriam, sed Marte tueri,
> Et spreta incolumem vita defendere famam;
> Polliciti servare fidem, sanctumque vereri

---

[k] Buchanani Silva, iv.

[l] " Nostra autem ætate," says Crinitus, " [Scotorum] complures cum Carolo Francorum rege Italiam invaserunt, qui sub ejus signis militarent: sunt enim in dirigendis maxime sagittis viri acres atque egregii." (De Honesta Disciplina, p. 56, edit. Lugd. 1554, 8vo.) It was however a general characteristic of our ancestors to place very little reliance on missile weapons.

Numen amicitiæ, mores, non munus amare.[m]
Artibus his, totum fremerent cum bella per orbem,
Nullaque non leges tellus mutaret avitas
Externo subjecta jugo, gens una vetustis-
Sedibus antiqua sub libertate resedit.
Substitit hic Gothi furor, hic gravis impetus hæsit
Saxonis, hic Cimber superato Saxone, et acri

---

[m] One of the most learned of Buchanan's friends had bestowed similar praise.

Si cui simplicitas, et priscæ sæcula vitæ,
   Sors sine dissidiis, mens sine fraude placet,
Ne Scotiæ dextras, hirsutaque pectora spernat :
   Haud bene junguntur hamus et arma simul.
            JUL. SCALIGERI Poemata, tom. i, p. 533.

" Est vero," says another Italian of great celebrity, " inter amicitiæ fœdera non vulgare, hospitii jus, quod invidia vacet, quale apud Scotos : nam apud nos rarius est, et omnes jam ad cauponas divertunt." (Cardanus *De Utilitate ex Adversis capienda*, p. 41, edit. Amst. 1672, 8vo.) Cardan had himself visited Scotland; where he remained seventy-five days with Arch-bishop Hamilton. (*De Propria Vita*, p. 193, edit. Naudæi. Paris. 1643, 8vo.) See Robertson, vol. i, p. 353. In his works he has scattered various remarks on the climate, soil, and productions of Britain. In one passage, he mentions the excellence of the British wool; but he adds that the country produces no serpents. (*De Subtilitate*, p. 310, edit. Basil. 1553, fol.) His antagonist Scaliger, who does not dispute the fact, has however rejected the causes which he assigns for it. (*De Subtilitate, ad H. Cardanum*, f. 269.) The fuel used in this country seems to have excited the surprise of Cardan as much as it did that of Æneas Sylvius. (*Commentarii Rerum Memorabilium*, p. 4, edit. Francof. 1614, fol.) " Britannia adeo bituminosa est, ut non solum lapides ardeant, sed et terra, cum erica deram : ultra Novocastrum civitatem in cuniculos eruerunt. Hæc utuntur, et pro alendis ignibus, et pro domorum tectoriis, tegularum loco. Adjuvant ad concipiendos ignes ericæ radices. Tremit etiam terra ipsa Britanniæ non parum superequitantibus nobis, ut cum ex Amulthone Lifconem [*from Hamilton to Linlithgow* ?] veniremus. Causam esse animadverti, non quod cavernæ subessent, sed quod terra illa nigra quasi fungus inanis esset. Ardet enim et ibi terra, et lapidum qui uruntur tanta copia in Scotia est, ut pretio viliori vendantur longe quam apud nos ligna" (Cardanus *De Rerum Varietate*, p. 54, edit. Basil. 1557, 8vo.)

Perdomito Neuster Cimbro. Si volvere priscos
Non piget annales, hic et victoria fixit
Præcipitem Romana gradum : quem non gravis Auster
Reppulit, incultis non squalens Parthia campis,
Non æstu Meroe, non frigore Rhenus et Albis
Tardavit, Latium remorata est Scotia cursum :
Solaque gens mundi est, cum qua non culmine montis,
Non rapidi ripis amnis, non objice silvæ,
Non vasti spatiis campi Romana potestas,
Sed muris fossaque sui confinia regni
Munivit : gentesque alias cum pelleret armis
Sedibus, aut victas vilem servaret in usum
Servitii, hic contenta suos defendere fines
Roma securigeris prætendit mœnia Scotis: ·
Hic spe progressus posita, Carronis ad undam
Terminus Ausonii signat divortia regni.
Neve putes duri studiis assueta Gradivi
Pectora mansuetas non emollescere ad artes,
Hæc quoque, cum Latium quateret Mars barbarus orbem, ·
Sola prope expulsis fuit hospita terra Camœnis.ª

The elegant poem which he composed on the
birth of his future pupil King James, affords an
interesting proof of the early solicitude with
which he regarded his destiny, as connected with
the welfare of his native country.

Vos quoque felices felici prole parentes,
Jam tenerum teneris puerum consuescite ab annis
Justitiæ, sanctumque bibat virtutis amorem
Cum lacte ; et primis pietas comes addita cunis

ª Archbishop Usher has remarked that this part of the ·poet's encomium
belongs to Ireland, the Scotia of the ancients. " Quod de sua cecinit poeta
optimus, de nostra Scotia multo rectius possit usurpari." (Veterum Epistolarum Hibernicarum Sylloge, præf. Dublin. 1632, 4to.)

Conformetque animum, et pariter cum corpore crescat.
Non ita conversi puppis moderamine clavi
Flectitur, ut populi pendent a principe mores.
Non carcer, legumque minæ, torvæque secures
Sic animos terrent trepidos formidine pœnæ,
Ut veræ virtutis honos, moresque modesti
Regis, et innocui decus et reverentia sceptri
Convertunt mentes ad honesta exempla sequaces.[o]

Several of his miscellaneous poems of less importance relate to the same accomplished princess; who was not insensible of his powerful claims upon the protection of his country. In the year 1564, she had rewarded his literary merit by conferring upon him the temporalities of Crossragwell abbey; which amounted in annual valuation to the sum of five hundred pounds in Scotish currency.[p] The abbacy was at that time vacant by the decease of Quintin Kennedy; who was a man of learning, and the brother of Buchanan's former pupil the earl of Cassillis.

But while he thus enjoyed the favour of the queen, he did not neglect his powerful friend the earl of Murray. To that nobleman he inscribed his *Franciscanus* during the same year. The date of the earliest edition is uncertain; but the dedication was written at St Andrews on the fifth of June 1564, when he was perhaps residing in the earl's house.[q]

[o] Buchanani Silvæ, vii. [p] See Appendix, No. v.

[q] This poem has lately been translated by George Provand; whose publication bears the title of "The Franciscan Friar, a Satire; and the Marriage

He at the same time prepared for the press his miscellany entitled *Fratres Fraterrimi ;*[r] a collection of satires, almost entirely directed against the impurities of the Popish church. The absurdity of its doctrines, and the immoral lives of its priests, afforded him an ample field for the exercise of his formidable talents ; and he has alternately employed the weapons of sarcastic irony and vehement indignation. His admirable wit and address must have contributed to promote the cause which Luther had so ardently espoused ; and Buchanan ought also to be classed with the most illustrious of the reformers. Guy Patin was so fascinated with his satirical powers, that he committed to memory all his epigrams, his *Franciscanus,* and his *Fratres Fraterrimi.* After having particularized some of Buchanan's verses, he subjoins, Virgil never produced better, but it has required fifteen centuries to produce a poet like Virgil.[s] This lively and intelligent physician was evidently no bigot : many decided Papists have however mentioned the heretical poet with enthusiasm ; though such indeed as expect-

Ode of Francis of Valois and Mary, Sovereigns of France and Scotland ; translated into English Verse from the Latin of George Buchanan," Glasgow, 1809, 8vo.

[r] Robert Monteith, A. M. published " The very learned Scotsman Mr George Buchanan's Fratres Fraterrimi, three books of Epigrams, and book of Miscellanies, in English Verse : with the illustration of the proper names and mythologies therein mentioned." Edinburgh, 1708, 8vo.

[s] Lettres de Guy Patin, tom. i, p. 592.

ed preferment, have constantly interposed a formal caution relative to his heresy.[t]

To these satires, which seem to have been
composed in Scotland, Portugal, and France, he
prefixed a poetical dedication to his friend Utenhovius. Buchanan and Utenhovius apparently
maintained a particular intimacy, and they have
repeatedly interchanged poetical compliments.
Carolus Utenhovius was born at Ghent in the
year 1536; and prosecuted his studies at Paris
with more than common success. His birth seems
to have been superior to his fortune; for he engaged himself as preceptor to the daughters of
Jean de Morel, so highly celebrated for their literature. He afterwards visited England in the
train of Paul de Foix, the French ambassador;
and his poetical incense recommended him to the
notice of Queen Elizabeth. Having entered into
the matrimonial state, he settled at Cologne;
where he died of an apoplexy in the year 1600.
His works chiefly consist of miscellaneous verses,

---

[t] " Eorum nemo est," says Scioppius, " cui idem quod Buchanano con-
tigerit, ut in quovis carminum genere summam obtineret : cujus quidem rei
laude omnem etiam antiquitatem provocat ; ut tanta illa ingenii, vere unici
et incomparabilis, ornamenta ad impietatem conversa fuisse, vehementer non
ipsius magis quam reipublicæ causa dolendum sit." (De Rhetoricarum Exercitationum Generibus, p. 26.) Gaddius characterizes him as " historicus,
poeta maximæ famæ, propter hæresin non nisi cum venia memorandus, ingenio vere unico et incomparabili ornatus." (De Scriptoribus non Ecclesiasticis, tom. i, p. 87.) " Tantus in Latinitate nitor et puritas," says Morhoff
in allusion to the former passage, " ut nil in illo præter hæresin ille inter
grammaticos Momos omnes Argus et Lynceus Scioppius reprehendat." (De
Patavinitate Liviana, p. 116. Kilonii, 1685, 4to.)

composed in seven different languages. He was
long understood to be engaged in preparing an
edition of the Dionysiacs of Nonnus, together
with a Latin translation ; and, in the opinion of
Falkenburgius, he was excellently qualified for
the task.[u]   This edition however did not make
its appearance.[x]

.   In the year 1567, Buchanan published another
collection, consisting of *Elegiæ, Silvæ, Hendeca-
syllabi.*[y] To· this miscellany was prefixed an
epistle to his friend Peter Daniel; a learned
man who is still remembered for his edition of
Virgil with the commentary·of· Servius. This
epistle contains several hints relative to the history of the author's poetical works. " Between
the occupations of a court," says Buchanan,
" and the annoyance of disease, I have hardly
been ·able to steal any portion of time, which I
could either devote to my friends or to myself;
and I have therefore been prevented from maintaining a frequent correspondence with my
friends, and from collecting my poems which lie
so widely dispersed. For my own part, I was
not extremely solicitous to recal them from per-
dition ; for the subjects are generally of a trivial
nature, and such as at this period of life are at

---

[u] Falkenburgii Epist. ante Nonnum. Antverp. 1569, 4to.

[x] Thuani Hist. sui Temporis, tom. v, p. 847. Andreæ Bibliotheca Belgica, p. 129. Du Verdier, tom. i, p. 310. La Croix du Maine, tom. i;
p. 119.

[y] Parisiis, apud Robertum Stephanum, 1567, 12mo.

once calculated to inspire me with disgust and shame. But as Pierre Mondoré and some other friends, to whom I neither can nor ought to refuse any request, demanded them with such earnestness, I have employed some of my leisure hours in collecting a portion, and placing it in a state of arrangement. With this specimen, which consists of one book of elegies, another of miscellanies, and a third of hendecasyllables, I in the mean time present you. When it shall suit your convenience, I beg you will communicate them to Mondoré, De Mesmes, and other philological friends, without whose advice I trust you will not adopt any measure relative to their publication. In a short time, I hope to send you a book of iambics, another of epigrams, another of odes, and perhaps some other pieces of a similar denomination: all these I wish to be at the disposal of my friends, as I have finally determined to rely more on their judgment than on my own. In my paraphrase of the psalms, I have corrected many typographical errors, and have likewise made various alterations: I must therefore request you to advise Stephanus not to publish a new edition without my knowledge. Hitherto I have not found leisure to finish the second book of my poem *De Sphæra*; and therefore I have not made a transcript of the first: as soon as the other is completed, I shall transmit them to you. Salute in my name all our friends at Orleans, and such others as it may be convenient.

Farewell. Edinburgh, July the twenty-fourth
1566."[a]   The two friends whom Buchanan par-
ticularises in this letter, were men of no inconsiderable distinction. Pierre Mondoré, who has
been commemorated by Thuanus as a man of
excellent talents, was master of the requests, a
counsellor in the great council, and keeper of the
royal library. He composed Latin verses with
uncommon felicity, and was profoundly skilled in
the mathematical sciences.[a]   His attachment to
the cause of rational religion involved him in mis-
fortune: having been driven from Orleans, the
place of his nativity, he retired to Sancerre sur
Loire, where his unmerited exile was soon terminated by death. He died on the nineteenth of
August 1570; and his intimate friend De l'Hôpital composed his epitaph in affectionate and
indignant terms.[b]   His library, which was uncommonly rich in mathematical manuscripts,
was pillaged during the subsequent tumults of
St Bartholomew.[c]   Henry de Mesmes, who was
master of the requests, and enjoyed other offices of

[a] Buchanani Epistolæ, p. 5.

[a] Sammarthani Elogia Gallorum Doctrina Illustrium, p. 46, edit. Paris.
1630, 4to.—See likewise M. Bernardi's "Essai sur la Vie, les Ecrits et
les Lois de Michel de l'Hôpital, Chancelier de France," p. 88, 222. Paris,
1807, 8vo. Mondoré's commentary on the tenth book of Euclid was published in 1551. (Vossius De Scientiis Mathematicis, p. 335.) Three of
his Latin poems occur in the Delitiæ Poetarum Gallorum, tom. ii, p. 711.

[b] Hospitalii Carmina, p. 385, edit. Amst. 1732, 8vo.—One of the epistles
of De l'Hôpital is addressed "Ad Petr. Montaureum, elegantissimum poetam,
et mathematicum præstantissimum." (P. 81.)

[c] Thuana, p. 197.

dignity, descended from a family that derived its remote lineage from the native country of Buchanan.[d] Although he did not court the fame of authorship, few individuals have been more generally known among their learned contemporaries.[e] He was not only a generous encourager of literature, but was himself a man of erudition. He was possessed of a noble library, which was always accessible to the learned; and his illustrious family continued to be distinguished by the same liberality of conduct.[f] The name was long afterwards commemorated as dear to letters.[g] Buchanan was not the only poet who confided in the critical judgment of De Mesmes; his decisions seem to have been very generally regarded with the utmost deference.[h]

His promise relative to the three books of iambics, epigrams, and odes, Buchanan seems to have forgotten : after an interval of nearly ten years, Daniel strongly urged its performance. It

[d] Sammarthani Elogia Gallorum Doctrina Illustrium, p. 121.

[e] Turnebus dedicated to him the second volume of his *Adversaria;* and Gruchius, another learned friend of Buchanan, inscribed to the same respectable character his *Responsio ad binas Caroli Sigonii Reprehensiones.* Passerat, who resided many years in the family of De Mesmes, has written a poem in celebration of his library (*Del Poet. Gall.* tom. iii, p. 2.); and has likewise devoted many other effusions to the praise of his munificent patron.

[f] Le Gallois, Traité des Bibliotheques, p. 152.—See likewise the dedication of Henninius's edition of Juvenal. Ultraj. 1685, 4to.

[g] D'Alembert, Hist. des Membres de l'Academie Françoise, tom. iv, p. 339.

[h] Sammarthani Poemata, p. 190, edit. Lutet. 1629, 4to. Bonefonii Carmina, p. 48, edit. Lond. 1720, 12mo.

is not certain whether most of those poems were published before the author's decease. His *Miscellanea* were not printed till the year 1615.[i] Of his short and miscellaneous pieces, the subjects are sometimes indeed of a trivial nature; but even those lighter efforts serve to evince the wonderful versatility of his mind. His epigrams, which consist of three books, are not the least remarkable of his compositions: the terseness of the diction, the ingenuity and pungency of the thought, have deservedly placed them in a very high class. Every nation, says a learned critic, has its writers of epigrams; but if a selection of them were to be formed, they would scarcely equal in number the gates of Thebes or the mouths of the Nile.[k] The estimation in which Buchanan's epigrams have generally been held, may be inferred from the frequency with which they are translated and imitated by poets of various countries. The pointed epigram has always been a favourite mode of intellectual exer-

---

[i] They first appeared in Andrew Hart's edition of Buchanani *Poemata Omnia*. Edinb. 1615, 24to.

[k] Morhofius de Arguta Dictione, p. 190, edit. Lubec. 1731, 8vo.—Ten of Buchanan's epigrams are quoted in the work of Nicolaus Mercerius *De Conscribendo Epigrommate*. Paris. 1653, 8vo. The same number is inserted in the *Epigrommatum Delectus*. Paris. 1659, 12mo. This collection, afterwards reprinted for the use of Eton school, was edited by Lancelot; but the preliminary dissertation was written by Nicole. (Barbier, *Dictionnaire des Ouvrages Anonymes et Pseudonymes*, tom. iii, p. 386.) It is on this publication that Vavasseur has made so many animadversions, in his elegant book *De Epigrammate*. He had himself composed an immense number of epigrams; not one of which was selected by Lancelot.

cise with the French; and several accomplished scholars of that nation have sufficiently testified their approbation of Buchanan's epigrammatic wit. Menage, who has pronounced all his verses to be excellent, was particularly delighted with the felicity of the subsequent lines.[1]

> Illa mihi semper præsenti dura Neæra,
>   Me, quoties absum, semper abesse dolet.
> Non desiderio nostri, non mœret amore,
>   Sed se non nostro posse dolore frui.[m]

That accomplished philologer has imitated them in one of his Italian madrigals.

> Chi creduto l'avrebbe ?
> L'empia, la cruda Iole
> Del mio partir si duole.
> A quel finto dolore
> Non ti fidar, mio core.
> Non è vera pietade
> Quella che monstra, nò; ma crudeltade.
> Dell' aspro mio martire
> La cruda vuol gioire ;
> Udir la cruda i miei sospiri ardenti,
> E mirar vuole i duri miei tormenti.[n]

M. de la Monnoye, a man of extensive and accurate literature, translated the same epigram into French.

> Philis, qui tête à tête insensible à mes feux,
> Comte pour rien mes pleurs, mes soupirs, et mes vœux,

[1] Menagiana, tom. ii, p. 133.
[m] Buchanani Epigram. lib. i, 31.
[n] Menagii Poemata, p. 267, edit. Paris. 1668, 8vo.

Quand je suis éloigné regrette ma présence.
Ah ! dois-je là-dessus me flater vainement ?
Non, non, le déplaisir qu'elle a de mon absence
Lui vient de ne pouvoir jouïr de mon tourment.[q]

Buchanan's epigram *In Zoilum* has frequently
been repeated with much relish, and frequently
translated.

Frustra ego te laudo, frustra me, Zoïle, lædis :
Nemo mihi credit, Zoïle, nemo tibi.[r]

Menage, who has written another in the very
same strain, avers that Buchanan, as well as himself, was indebted to the prose of Libanius.[s]

Μὰψ ἐμὶ λοιδορέεις, μὰψ, Ζωῖλε, καί σε ἐπαινῶ·
Οὐ γὰρ ἐμοῖς, ἐ σοῖς πίστις ὕπεστι λόγοις.[t]

The following verses of M. de la Monnoye are
professedly a translation of Buchanan's distich.

Tu dis par tout du mal de moi,
Je dis par tout du bien de toi ;
Quel malheur est le nôtre !
L'on ne nous croit ni l'un ni l'autre.[v]

His epigrammatic epitaph on Jacobus Silvius, a
famous professor of physic in the university of
Paris, shall close these motley transcripts.

[q] Poesies de M. de la Monnoye, p. 47. Haye, 1716, 8vo.
[r] Buchanani Epigram. lib. i, 12.
[s] Menage, Anti-Baillet, tom. ii, p. 277.
[t] Menagii Poemata, p. 110.
[v] Poesies de M. de la Monnoye, p. 242.

Silvius hic situs est, gratis qui nil dedit unquam :
Mortuus et gratis quod legis ista, dolet.[x]

Silvius was famous for his learning, and infamous
for the most sordid avarice. Buchanan's indignation had been provoked by the indecent rage
·which he publicly testified against two poor stu-
·dents, who had occasionally attended his preleo-
tions without paying their fees. He died in the
year 1555; and so little was his memory revered
among his pupils, that during his funeral service,
some of them exhibited Buchanan's epigram on
the door of the church.[y] H. Stephanus has trans-
·lated this distich into French.

Ici gist Sylvius, auquel onc en sa vie
De donner rien gratis ne prit aucune envie:
Et ores qu'il est mort et tout rongé de vers,
Encores a despit qu'on lit gratis ces vers.[z]

The editors of Buchanan have uniformly inserted among his works, and without any suggestion of its spuriousness, an epigram on Julius
the second,[a] which was perhaps written before
Buchanan was born, and certainly before he had
exceeded the seventh year of his age. It was
composed and circulated during the lifetime of
that pontiff, who died on the twenty-second of

---

[x] Buchanani Epigram. lib. ii, 10.
[y] Sammarthani Elogia, p. 24. Bulæi Hist. Univ. Paris. tom. vi, p. 933.
[z] Estienne, Apologic pour Herodote, p. 181.
[a] Buchanani Miscell. xxi.

February 1513; and Janus Lascaris had obtained his favour by repelling it in another epigram, where the same topics are converted to his praise.[b] In one collection,[c] the satirical lines are ascribed to C. Gr. supposed to be Conradus Grebelius of Zurich.[d]

In the present arrangement of Buchanan's poetry, no separate book of odes is to be found; but a great proportion of his *Miscellanea* is of the lyric species. In his paraphrase of the psalms, lyric measures are chiefly employed; and

---

[b] Ferronus de Rebus Gestis Gallorum, f. 60, b, edit. Lutet. 1554, fol. —An account of Lascaris may be found in the learned work of Dr Hody, " De Græcis Illustribus Linguæ Græcæ Literarumque Humaniorum Instauratoribus," p. 247. Lond. 1742, 8vo.

[c] Pasquillorum tomi duo, p. 91. *Eleutheropoli*, 1544, 8vo.—This very rare book is supposed to have been edited by Cœlius Secundus Curio. It was printed by Joannes Oporinus of Basil. (Gesneri *Partitiones Universales*, f. 40.)

[d] Menagiana, tom. iii, p. 57.—To the curious remarks of M. de la Monnoye it may be added, that the two epigrams are printed among those of Janus Lascaris. In the edition published by Jacobus Tusanus, they stand thus:

Ἀδήλου de quodam Pontifice.

Patria cui Genua est, genitricem Græcia, partum
  Pontus et unda dedit, qui bonus esse potest?
Sunt vani Ligures, mendax est Græcia, ponto
  Nulla fides: malus est hæc tria quisquis habet.

Lascaris.

Est Venus orta mari, Graium sapientia, solers
  Ingenium est Ligurum: qui malus esse potest
Cui genus ut Veneri, a Graiis sapientia, solers
  Ingenium a Genua est? Mome proterve tace.

Lascaris Epigrammata, sig. c, edit. Paris. 1527, 8vo.

The former epigram, as it occurs among the posthumous poems of Buchanan, is more pointed; and in this improved form it may have been found in his hand-writing.

many odes occur among his other productions.
In this department of composition, as well as in
various others, he deservedly holds the first rank
among the modern · Latinists.ᵉ His diction is
terse and elegant, his numbers are harmonious;
and as his genius possessed a native elevation, he
did not find it requisite to invest his thoughts
with a perpetual pomp of words. Several of the
moderns, and even Casimir himself, seem to have
entertained an opinion that the dignity of lyric
poetry cannot be supported without a perpetual
straining after brilliant metaphors : from an adherence to this notion, their productions are often
removed to an equal distance from classical elegance, and from genuine sublimity. Buchanan's
diction is lofty when the subject requires it; but
the practice of Horace had taught him that every
ode need not aim at sublimity, and that every
sublime ode need not be darkened by a cloud of
metaphors. His ode on the first of May has
been very honourably distinguished by a late ingenious and elegant writer. " I know not," says
Mr Alison, " any instance where the effect of association is so remarkable in bestowing sublimity
on objects ‘to which it does not naturally belong,
as in the following inimitable poem of Buchanan's, on the month of May. This season is, in
general, fitted to excite emotions very different
from sublimity, and the numerous poems which

* Morhofii Polyhistor, tom. i, p. 1067.

have been written in celebration of it, dwell uniformly on its circumstances of ' vernal joy.' In
this ode, however, the circumstances which the
poet has selected, are of a kind which, to me,
appear inexpressibly sublime, and distinguish the
poem itself by a degree and character of gran-
deur which I have seldom found equalled in any
other composition."[f]

His book of elegies, nine in number, is composed with his usual felicity. Some of them
however which relate to the ladies are not the
most pleasing of his performances. The most
beautiful of these poems is the elegy on the first
of May; a season which awoke in Buchanan the
finest emotions of a truly poetical mind. The
whole is exquisite, and breathes the genuine spirit
of the ancient elegy.

In the sportive effusions of his youth, Buchanan
has occasionally indulged a vein of pruriency,
from which some authors have rashly drawn con-
clusions respecting the morality of his conduct.
" His life," says Dr Stuart, " was liberal like his
opinions. From the uncertain condition of his
fortune, or from his attachment to study, he kept
himself free from the restraint of marriage; but
if a judgment may be formed from the vivacity
of his temper and the wantonness of his verses,
he was no enemy to beauty and to love, and

[f] Alison's Essays on the Nature and Principles of Taste, p. 21. Edinb.
1790, 4to.

must have known the tumults and the languors of voluptuousness."[g]   The necessity of this inference is very questionable. Dr Blacklock has frequently descanted with enthusiasm on the beauties of external nature ; and yet he was absolutely blind from his infancy. Buchanan might allude to raptures which he never felt. His friend Beza had indulged his youthful fancy in the utmost freedom of description; yet he afterwards protested with solemnity, that although his verses were lascivious, his conduct was chaste.[h] The manners of that age, when com-

---

[g] Stuart's Hist. of Scotland, vol. ii, p. 243.

[h] The ancient Latin poets, and even Ovid himself, adopted the same excuse.

> Nam castum esse decet pium poetam
> Ipsum ; versiculos nihil necesse est.
>
> CATULLUS.

> Crede mihi ; mores distant a carmine nostro:
> Vita verecunda est, Musa jocosa mihi.
>
> OVID.

> Innocuos censura potest permittere lusus :
> Lasciva est nobis pagina, vita proba.
>
> MARTIAL.

> Est jocus in Nostris, sunt seria multa libellis:
> Stoicus has partes, has Epicurus agit.
> Salva mihi veterum maneat dum regula morum,
> Ludat permissis sobria Musa jocis.
>
> AUSONIUS.

Muretus, whose juvenile poems are not altogether unexceptionable, has however insinuated the futility of such allegations.

> Nil immundius est tuis libellis,
> Nil obscenius, impudiciusque ;
> Et vis te tamen ut putemus esse
> Numa Fabricioque sanctiorem.

pared with those of the present, will appear extremely coarse and indelicate.   National manners may frequently be improved and refined by
works of literature; but works of literature are
more commonly and more deeply influenced by
national manners.   " Horace," says Lord Kames,
" is extremely obscene, and Martial no less.   But
I censure neither of them, and as little the queen
of Navarre for her tales; for they wrote according to the manners of the times : and it is the
manners I censure, not the writers." [i]   The contemporaries of Buchanan, even in the most refined nations of Europe, were only emerging from
barbarism : and a familiar acquaintance with the
ancient classics, however it might contribute to
the improvement of taste, could contribute but
little to the improvement of manners.   The ancient poets, both Greek and Roman, had indeed
bequeathed for their use abundant examples of
elegant obscenity.   The modern Italians, whether
laymen or priests, did not hesitate to follow ancient precedents: some of the productions of Antonius Panormita,[k] Pontanus, and Bembus, verge

> At sententia nostra ea est, Noalli,
> Quisquis versibus exprimit Catullum,
> Raro moribus exprimit Catonem.
>
>   MURETI Opera, tom. i, p. 705.

[i] Kames's Sketches of the Hist. of Man, vol. i, p. 377.

[k] For the benefit of studious youth, a complete edition of the *Herma-phroditus* of Antonius Beccatellus of Palermo has at length been published, in a collection entitled *Quinque Illustrium Poetarum Lusus in Venerem.* Paris. 1791, 8vo.   It is no disparagement to Mr Roscoe that he was un-acquainted with this precious collection.   (*Life of Lorenzo de' Medici*, vol. i, p. 71, 4th edit.)

upon the very extremity of wantonness and im-
purity. These examples passed to other nations;
Secundus, Bonefonius, and many eminent poets
beside, vied with each other in the elegance of
their language, and the grossness of their ideas.
And, what may perhaps be regarded as still
more extraordinary, in the scholastic compila-
tions published during that period for the use of
Latin versifiers, this department is very seldom
neglected: the *Epithetorum Opus* of Jo. Ravisius
Textor exhibits the most obscene words in the
Latin language, studiously illustrated by accurate quotations from ancient and modern poets.
Joseph Scaliger, who was anxious to be regarded
as a man of piety, exerted much industry and
learning in elucidating ancient reliques of the
most impure denomination.[1] A long train of Catholic priests have expatiated on the languors of
love and the ecstacies of enjoyment: as they were
doomed to perpetual celibacy, they must either
have entertained a hardy contempt of moral reputation, or supposed that such productions
would be regarded as mere efforts of a poetical
fancy. Even the queen of Navarre, who is represented as a woman of consummate virtue, did
not blush to write what few modern ladies would
profess to read.[m] There are some poets, says

[1] Deinde," says Scaliger, " quare non licebit mihi, quod omnibus licuit
etiam sanctissimis et doctissimis viris?" (*Virgilii Appendix*, p. 448. Lugd.
1573, 8vo.)

[m] The poems of Queen Margaret, the well known sister of Francis the
first, are chiefly of a serious cast, and some of them are very pious; but in

Bayle, who are equally chaste in their verses and in
their conduct; others who are neither chaste in
their conduct nor in their verses: some there are
unchaste in their verses, and yet chaste in their
conduct; and whose fire is entirely confined to
the head. All their wanton liberties are sports
of fancy; their Candidas and their Lesbias mis-
tresses of fiction.[n] Dr Stuart's suggestion ought
therefore to have been delivered in more cautious
terms; and Mr Warton has likewise mentioned
Buchanan's amatory verses in a manner which betrays some degree of precipitancy.[o] These ob-

her novels, composed in imitation of Boccaccio, she indulges herself in the
utmost freedom of description. Many of these novels are apparently founded on real incidents. To omit other instances, she has given a circum-
stantial account of the assassination of Alessandro de' Medici. See " L'Hep-
tameron des Nouvelles de tresillustre et tresexcellent princesse, Marguerite de
Valois, Royne de Navarre," f. 44, b, edit. de Paris, 1560, 4to. The collection of her poems bear the title of " Marguerites de la Marguerite des Prin-
cesses, tresillustre Royne de Navarre." Lyons, 1547, 8vo. To this accomplished princess, who was equally conspicuous for her beauty and for her
virtue, Buchanan has addressed one of his epigrams. (Lib. i, 11.)

[n] Bayle, Eclaircissement sur les Obscénitez, § iv.

[o] " Milton here, at an early period of life, renounces the levities of love
and gallantry. This was not the case with Buchanan, who unbecomingly
prolonged his *amorous descant* to graver years, and who is therefore obliquely
censured by Milton in the following passage of *Lycidas*, hitherto not exactly
understood, v. 67.

> Were it not better done, *as others use,*
> To sport with *Amaryllis* in the shade,
> Or with the tangles of *Neæra's hair* ?

The *Amaryllis* to whom Milton alludes, is the *Amaryllis* of Buchanan the
subject of a poem called *Desiderium Lutetiæ,* a fond address of considerable
length from an importunate lover....It is allowed that the common poetical
name, *Amaryllis,* might have been naturally and accidentally adopted by
both poets ; nor does it at first sight appear, that Milton used it with any re-
strictive or implicit meaning. But Buchanan had another mistress whom

4

servations, which are merely historical, do not insinuate the expediency of following a bad example, however prevalent. Buchanan has repeatedly expressed his compunction for having been guilty of such levity;[p] nor is it incumbent on his biographer to commend the youthful sallies which he himself condemned in his graver years. By some authors, and particularly by Mr Benson,[q] his delinquency has however been described in terms of unnecessary exaggeration. If compared with most of the contemporary poets, Buchanan will be regarded as a chaste and scrupulous writer.

While he presided over St Leonard's College, he appears to have enjoyed the esteem and confidence of the university. The public register

he calls *Nexra*, whose golden hair makes a very splendid figure in his verses, and which he has complimented more than once in the most hyperbolical style." (Warton's *Notes on Milton*, p. 474, 2d edit.) That Buchanan prolonged his amorous descant to graver years than Milton, cannot be denied; but the opinion which he entertained of his love verses during a more advanced period of life, ought not to be overlooked. These notions Mr Warton seems to have adopted too rashly. The Amaryllis of Buchanan is not his mistress, but the city of Paris; and Nexra was the mistress of Tibullus, Marullus, Secundus, Bonefonius, and five hundred poets beside. The allusion of Milton, with due deference to his commentator, is more simple and obvious. Amaryllis and Nexra are names very generally adopted by pastoral and elegiac poets: the question which Milton asks therefore is, whether it were not better to apply himself to the composition of amatory pastorals or of love elegies.

[p] " Argumenta enim fere levia sunt, et quorum hanc ætatem nescio pigeat magis an pudeat." (Buchanani *Epistolæ*, p. 5.) " Elegias, Silvas, ac plersque Epigrammata amicis poscentibus dedi, quorum nomina hic subjice', re non est necesse. Hæc omnia, si per amicos licuisset, sempiternæ oblivioni consecrassem." (*Ibid.* p. 25.)

[q] Benson's Comparison betwixt Johnston and Buchanan, p. 42.

bestows upon him the honourable title for which
he was indebted to Stephanus. In 1566 and the
two ensuing years, he was one of the four electors of the rector; and was nominated a preroc-
tor by each of the three officers who were successively chosen. For several years, he was likewise dean of the faculty of arts.[r]

Of the general assembly of the national church,
convened at Edinburgh on the twenty-fifth of
December 1563, Buchanan had sat as a member;
and had even been appointed one of the commissioners for revising the book of discipline. In
that commission he had been associated with the
Earl Marischal, Lord Ruthven, the secretary of
state, the commendator of Kilwinning, the bishop
of Orkney, the clerk register, the justice clerk,
and Henry Balnaves. He sat in the June assemblies of 1564 and the three following years,
and likewise in that of December 1567. In 1564
Buchanan, Knox, John Rutherford, the superin-
tendents of Lothian, Fife, Angus, and the West,
together with various other members, were named
as a committee " to confer about the causes ap-
pertaining to the jurisdiction of the kirk, and to
report their judgment to the next convention."
During the same assembly, Buchanan belonged
to a committee of less importance, appointed to
consider the expediency of removing Andrew
Simson from the church of Dunning to the school

---

[r] Sibbaldi Comment. in Vitam Buchanani, p. 16, 65.

of Dunbar. In 1565, the bishop of Orkney, John Craig, Christopher Goodman, John Row, George Buchanan, and Robert Pont, " were ordained to convene and sit from six till eight in the morning, to decide questions propounded or to be propounded, and to report their decision to the assembly." Their report, which was inserted in the records, contains some curious matter. In 1566, we find Buchanan joined in a similar commission with John Douglas, rector of the university of St. Andrews, George Hay, Robert Pont, and Robert Hamilton. He had the honour of being chosen moderator of the assembly which met at Edinburgh on the twenty-fifth of June 1567.[*]

The nation was now in a state of anarchy; and Buchanan was soon to assume the character of a politician. The late conduct of Queen Mary, whom he once regarded in so favourable a light, had offered such flagrant insults to virtue and decorum, that his attachment was at length converted into the strongest antipathy. The ingratitude and misconduct of her husband having speedily alienated her affections, she transferred them to the earl of Bothwell, a nobleman of the most profligate character. The king and queen separated from each other with every demonstration of mutual aversion and disgust; and Henry retired to Glasgow, in order to escape from the neglect and indignities to which he was daily ex-

[*] Wodrow's MS. Life of Buchanan.

posed. Before his arrival he was seized with an
alarming distemper, which has been ascribed to
different causes. The treatment which he had
uniformly experienced for several months, was
not such as could lead him to expect a visit from
his consort. Having exhibited no appearance of
sympathy or concern while his life was in the
utmost danger, she set out for Glasgow after he
had begun to recover from his illness. Here she
bestowed upon him every mark of tenderness
and affection; nor did this weak prince perceive
that such a change was too sudden and too violent to be regarded as sincere. He had formerly
adopted the resolution of quitting the kingdom ;
but he now suffered himself to be conducted to
Edinburgh, where he was lodged in a solitary
house situated in an open field. This retired and
airy situation was sufficiently adapted to the lan-
guishing state of his health ; but the event which
ensued seemed too clearly to evince that it had
been selected with a different view. Mary continued to treat him with every mark of confidence and attachment. She attended him with
much assiduity ; and she slept two nights in the
chamber under his apartment. But on the ninth
of February 1567, she took leave of him about
eleven o'clock at night, under the pretext of attending a masque to be given at the palace, on
account of the marriage of one of her servants.
During their interview she had redoubled her ca-
resses, and had presented him with a ring in token

of her affection. About two in the morning, the house in which the king lay was blown up with gunpowder; and his dead body was found in an adjacent garden. The queen was immediately suspected of being accessory to this crime; and the nation indignantly pointed to the earl of Bothwell as the actual murderer; but she protected him from the vengeance of the law, and distinguished him by many unequivocal marks of her favour. On the nineteenth of March, she appointed him governor of Edinburgh castle, which was then a fortress of great importance. A public trial could not with any appearance of decency be avoided; but it was conducted with the utmost precipitation, and with a palpable disregard for the ordinary forms of justice. It was one remarkable feature of this trial, that the indictment was laid against Bothwell for murdering the king on the ninth of February, though it was well known that the crime was committed on the tenth. This error, which can scarcely be considered as accidental, would have enabled him to escape the sentence of the law, even if the court could have ventured to enter into the investigation. Bothwell had attended that meeting of the privy council which regulated the time and manner of his own trial; and two days after an acquittal which rather strengthened than removed the imputation of guilt, the queen appointed him to carry the sceptre before her at the opening of parliament. On the twenty-fourth of April, he seized the person of his sovereign, and conducted her as a prisoner to the castle of Dunbar. This act of apparent violence, which at first seemed to be so unnecessary, had evidently been devised with the entire approbation of the queen, who exhibited no symptoms of reluctance or constraint. The ultimate object of such an expedient did not long remain doubtful. In the course of a few days, she granted him a pardon for this treasonable act, and for all other crimes with which he could be charged. By this general clause, inserted in the common form, she pardoned the murder of her own husband, and yet avoided the scandal of mentioning it in direct terms. Soon afterwards she created him duke of Orkney. Having hastily procured a divorce from his wife, his infamous nuptials with the queen were solemnized on the fifteenth of May, about three months after he had assassinated her former husband. A series of actions so unprecedented and so atrocious could not fail of producing the utmost indignation and alarm. But the schemes of Bothwell were not yet completed; his extreme solicitude to secure the person of the young prince, excited new apprehensions; and a powerful confederacy was at length formed for the purpose of defeating the design which he had evidently conceived. Both parties had recourse to arms, and Mary followed her new husband to the field. But when the hostile armies

encountered each other, he found his followers so
little disposed to engage, that he abandoned the
queen in the midst of her parley with the con-
federates, and quitted the field with precipitation. She found herself in the power of her indignant subjects, and was exposed to treatment
more suited to her degraded character than to
her hereditary dignity. As her undiminished
passion for this unworthy favourite would not
permit her to yield to their proposal of dissolving
so indecent a marriage, they readily perceived
the consequences of suffering her to retain the
sovereign power. They formed the resolution of
securing her person; and she was committed to
strict custody in the castle of Lochlevin. Her
policy induced her to accede to the proposition of
resigning her crown, and to invest her natural
brother the earl of Murray with the regency. On
the second of May 1568, she escaped from her
prison, and soon afterwards found herself at the
head of a numerous army. The defeat at Lang-
side terminated her prospects of being speedily
reinstated in her authority. She now retired
into England, where she hoped to find an asylum;
but she soon discovered that she had reposed her
confidence in a cruel rival. Having incautiously
offered to submit her cause to the cognisance of the
English queen, she thus furnished a pretext for
degrading her to the level of an English subject;
and in the mean time she was detained in a state
of captivity. Elizabeth required the regent to

empower delegates to appear before her commissioners; but as his principal adherents declined
so hazardous an office, he was reduced to the
necessity of attending in person.   His associates
in this commission were the earl of Morton,
Bothwell bishop of ¡Orkney, Lord Lindsay, and
Pitcairne commendator of Dunfermline.   He was
also accompanied by Buchanan, Maitland, Balnaves, Macgill, and some other individuals of inferior attainments.   Balnaves and Macgill bore
the character of able civilians; and the abilities of
Maitland were of the first order.   The delegates
nominated by the unfortunate queen were Dr
Lesley, bishop of Ross, a prelate distinguished
by his talents and learning, Lord Livingston,
Lord Boyd, Lord Herries, Sir John Gordon of
Lochinvar, Sir James Cockburn of Skirling, and
Gavin Hamilton, commendator of Kilwinning.
On the fourth of October 1568, the conference
was opened at York before the commissioners
of Elizabeth, but in the course of the ensuing
month it was transferred to Westminster.   This
singular transaction was managed with great address on both sides.   Nor was Buchanan the least
powerful of Murray's coadjutors : he composed in
Latin a detection of Queen Mary's actions, which
was produced to the commissioners at Westminster,[t] and was afterwards circulated with great
industry by the English court.   His engaging in

---

[t] Laing's Hist. of Scotland, vol. i, p. 161, 241, 2d edit.

a task of this kind, as well as his mode of executing it, has frequently been urged as a proof of his moral depravity; and, to augment his delinquency, the benefits conferred upon him by the queen have been multiplied with much ingenuity." It is certain that she granted him the temporalities of Crossragwell abbey; and beyond this single point the evidence cannot be extended. Nor was this reward bestowed on a man who had performed no correspondent services. He had officiated as her classical tutor, and had composed various poems for the entertainment of the

---

" " On the head," says Dr Stuart, " of his ingratitude to Mary, the evidences, I fear, admit not of any doubt or palliation. Mary invited him from France to Scotland with a view that he should take the charge of the education of her son; and till James should be of a proper age to receive instruction, she appointed him to be chief master of St. Leonard's College in the university of St. Andrews." (*Hist. of Scotland*, vol. ii, p. 246.) These assertions are well combined, and are only liable to one material objection. That Mary invited him from France, nominated him preceptor to her son, and appointed him principal of St Leonard's College, are bold surmises totally unsupported by evidence. In the common editions of Buchanan's life, he is said to have been appointed the preceptor of King James "anno millesimo quingentesimo sexagesimo quinto." These words however are most evidently an interpolation; and in some of the earlier editions, for example those printed at Herborn in 1616 and 1624, they do not occur. James was not born till the nineteenth of June 1666; nor was Buchanan appointed his preceptor till after Mary had been expelled from the kingdom. Mr. Chalmers has employed what he deems a conclusive argument of his having nevertheless been indebted to the queen for his original nomination. " Buchanan says expressly in his history [p. 386.], ' Ut ex iis, quos *mater*, antequam se regno abdicarat, filio tutores nominaverat." (Chalmers, p. 329.) This writer evidently supposes the Latin word *tutor* to signify a preceptor. By referring a few pages back, he might have discovered that the *tutores*, or guardians, nominated by the queen were the duke of Chatelherault, and the earls of Murray, Lennox, Argyle, Athole, Morton, Glencairn, and Mar. (Buchanan. *Rerum Scotic. Hist.* p. 365.)

Scotish court; but the dedication of his psalms
might almost be considered as alone equivalent
to any reward which she conferred. If Buchanan celebrated her in his poetical capacity, and
before she ceased to be an object of praise, it certainly was not incumbent upon him to approve
the atrocious actions which she afterwards performed. The duty which he owed to his country was a prior consideration; and with that
duty, his further adherence to the infatuated
princess was utterly incompatible.

Another accusation of a still more serious nature has been brought against Buchanan by the
defenders of Queen Mary's innocence. They represent him as a principal agent in forging the
letters and sonnets, which were produced before
the commissioners in evidence of her criminal
connection with Bothwell, and participation in
the murder of her husband. On this subject so
much has already been written, that it would occupy too large a space to enter into a full discussion of the controversy; nor does it seem in-
dispensibly requisite, after the very satisfactory
investigations of our ablest historians.[x] It is sufficiently evident that her most zealous adherents
could not withstand the overwhelming proofs of
her guilt; and the defence which her advocates
have been compelled to adopt, imputes to the

[x] Hume's Hist. of England, vol. v, p. 467. Robertson's Dissertation on
the Murder of King Henry. Laing's Dissertation on the Participation of
Queen Mary in the Murder of Darnley.

earl of Murray and to Buchanan a degree of deep depravity, totally irreconcileable with the general tenor of their conduct. The simple and uncontroverted history of Mary's proceedings, from the period of her pretended reconciliation with Darnley to that of her marriage with Bothwell, exhibits such strong moral evidence of her criminality as it seems impossible for an unprejudiced mind to resist. " There are, indeed," as Mr Hume has remarked, " three events in our history, which may be regarded as touchstones of party-men. An English Whig, who asserts the reality of the Popish plot, an Irish Catholic, who denies the massacre of 1641, and a Scotch Jacobite, who maintains the innocence of Queen Mary, must be considered as men beyond the reach of argument or reason, and must be left to their prejudices."

The earl of Murray and his associates returned to Scotland in the beginning of the ensuing year. Buchanan's Detection,[y] which was not

---

[y] De Maria Scotorum Regina, totaque ejus contra Regem conjuratione, fœdo cum Bothuelio adulterio, nefaria in maritum crudelitate et rabie, horrendo insuper et deterrimo ejusdem parricidio, plena, et tragica plane Historia. 8vo.—This unclassical title, as Mr Laing suggests, must have been fabricated by the editor. A translation, with the following title, soon afterwards made its appearance. " Ane Detectioun of the Duinges of Marie Quene of Scottes, touchand the murder of hir husband, and hir conspiracie, adulterie, and pretensed mariage with the Erle Bothwell : and ane Defence of the trew Lordis, maintenaris of the Kingis Graces ctioun and auchaoritie. Translated out of the Latine quhilke was written by G. B." 8vo, black letter. These two publications are without date, place, or printer's name ; but they are supposed to have issued from the press of John Day. The first of them appears to have been circulated at London before the first of No-

published till 1571, seems to have been intrusted
to Dr Thomas Wilson; who is supposed, with
great plausibility, to have added the "Actio
contra Mariam Scotorum-Reginam," and the Latin translation of Mary's first three letters to the
earl of Bothwell.[2]   From a manuscript notice inserted in a copy which belonged to Mr Herbert,
it appears that the *Actio* was by some ascribed to
Sir Thomas Smith, but by the annotator himself
to Wilson,[3] of whom he may be supposed to have
had some personal knowledge.   Wilson was at
that time master of the requests, and afterwards
secretary of state.   Some of the sentiments, and
the general texture of the composition, are such
as cannot easily be supposed to have proceeded
from Buchanan; and, in the present enquiry, it
is of more consequence to ascertain that it was
not written by him, than who was its real author.
" It resumes," says Mr Laing, " the detail of the

---

vember 1571; the second before the close of the same month.   (Laing, vol.
i, p. 242, 243.)   This translation was unskilfully executed by some Eng-
lishman, in imitation of the Scotish idiom and orthography.   It was afterwards transformed into the genuine Scotish language, and reprinted at St
Andrews. " Ane Detectioun of the Doingis of Marie Quene of Scottis,"
&c.   *Imprentit at Sanctandrois be Robert Lekprevick*, 1572, black letter.
The Scotish version occurs in Anderson's *Collections*, vol. ii : but with respect to the history of the publication, this editor has committed more than
one mistake.   Other three editions of the English detection, but in a modern-
ized style, appeared at London in 1651, 1689, and 1721.   A French translation bears, in the title page, " A Edimbourg par Thomas Waltem, 1572."
It appears to have been printed by the Huguenots at Rochelle.   (Robertson, vol. iii, p. 249.   Laing, vol. i, p. 256, 259.)

  [2] Laing's Hist. of Scotland, vol. i, p. 243.

  [3] Herbert's Typographical Antiquities, vol. iii, p. 1629.

same facts contained in the Detection, with the tedious repetition natural to one author, when retracing the footsteps of another, whom he strives only to surpass in violence: superadding such local description, and vulgar reports as a keen enquirer, who had visited Scotland in person, might collect from Lesley, and other Scots, whom he examined on the subject. The Detection is a concise historical deduction of facts; a rapid narrative, written with that chaste and classical precision of thought and language, from which each sentence acquires an appropriate idea, distinct from the preceding, neither anticipated, repeated, nor intermixed with others; and the style is so strictly historical, that the work is incorporated in Buchanan's history almost without alteration. But the Action against Mary is a dull declamation, and a malignant invective, written in professed imitation of the ancient orators, whom Buchanan has never imitated; without arrangement of parts, coherence, or a regular train of ideas; and without a single passage which Buchanan in his history has deigned to transcribe. A man inured to extemporary eloquence, whose mind is accustomed only to popular arguments, and his tongue to prompt, and loose declamation, never writes with such lucid arrangement, with such accuracy of thought, or compression of style, as a professed author, who thinks no labour too great for what is bequeathed to posterity; and

the virulent Action against Mary no more resembles Buchanan's Detection, than the coarse and
verbose ribaldry of Whitaker, or the elegant yet
diffuse rhapsodies of Burke and Bolingbroke, to
the correct and classical precision of Junius or
Hume."[b]

The regent, to whom Buchanan was so cor-
dially attached, did not long survive those transactions. On the twenty-third of January 1570,
he was shot in the street of Linlithgow by Hamilton of Bothwellhaugh, whom his clemency had
formerly rescued from an ignominious death.[c]
The assassin had been confirmed in his enter-
prize by the approbation of his powerful kins-
men. The indignation of Buchanan was naturally roused against the house of Hamilton; and
he had sufficient cause to suspect that their purposes were not yet completely effected. Under
these impressions, he addressed an admonition to
the faithful peers;[d] in which he earnestly adjured

[b] Laing's Hist. of Scotland, vol. i, p. 347.

[c] Buchanan has written the earl's eulogium and epitaph in very affectionate terms. (Rerum Scotic. Hist. p. 385. Epigram. lib. ii, 29.)

[d] Ane Admonitioun direct to the trew Lordis, Maintenaris of the Kingis
Graces Authoritie. M. G. B. Imprentit at Striviling be Robert Lekprevick, 1571, 8vo.——Another edition was printed by Lekprevick in the course
of the same year; and a third was " imprinted at London by Iohn Daye,
according to the Scottish copie," 1571, 8vo. This tract is inserted in The
Harleian Miscellany, vol. iii, p. 395. It is a curious anecdote, for which I
am indebted to Sir William Hamilton, Bart. that the Admonitioun was actually printed for Ruddiman's edition, and, from some penitential considerations on the part of the editor or publisher, was afterwards suppressed. A
copy of the first volume of that edition which belonged to Ruddiman himself, and which is now in the possession of Charles Kirkpatrick Sharpe, Esq.

them to protect the young king, and the children
of the late regent, from the perils which seemed
to await them. It was apparently in the course
of the same year, 1570, that he composed another
Scotish tract, entitled *Chamæleon.*[e] In this satirical production, he very successfully exposes the
wavering politics of the famous secretary Maitland. The secretary, who was justly alarmed at
the prospect of being publicly exhibited in such
glaring colours, entertained a suspicion that the
work was to issue from the press of Robert Lekprevick; and on the fourteenth of April 1571,
his emissary Captain Melvin searched, for the
third time, that printer's house in Edinburgh.
This search took place about eleven o'clock on a
Saturday night; but Lekprevick being warned
of his danger, had previously disappeared with
such papers as seemed to threaten disagreeable
consequences.[f] The *Chamæleon,* if it was actually delivered to the printer, seems to have been

has the *Admonition* inserted before the *Chamæleon.* It is reprinted from the
first edition, collated with a transcript of the Cotton manuscript dated 1570;
and the editor has subjoined an advertisement respecting the various readings.
This tract occupies ten pages; and the *Chamæleon,* as it now appears in the
edition, begins at the eleventh page. In the Advocates' Library there is
likewise a copy which includes the *Admonition.* I have seen a copy containing another edition, printed on five pages with double columns. See
Appendix, No. ii.

[e] Of Buchanan's *Chamæleon,* the copy preserved among the Cotton MSS.
bears the date of 1570. This tract was first printed in the *Miscellanea Scotica.* Lond. 1710, 8vo. It occurs in both editions of the author's works. A
separate edition was printed in 8vo in the year 1741.

[f] Bannatyne's Journal, p. 130. Edinb. 1806, 8vo.

suppressed by Maitland's vigilance; for it remained in manuscript till the beginning of last
century. The style of these two productions is
at least equal in vigour and elegance to that of
most compositions in the ancient Scotish language; though it is sufficiently obvious that the
happy genius of the author cannot there appear
in its genuine splendour. " When we read,"
says an accomplished and able writer, " the compositions of Buchanan in his native tongue, how
completely are his genius and taste obscured by
those homely manners which the coarseness of
his dialect recals; and how difficult is it to believe that they express the ideas and sentiments
of the same writer, whose Latin productions vie
with the best models of antiquity!"[g]

Soon after the assassination of his illustrious
friend, Buchanan was removed to a situation of
no inconsiderable importance; he was appointed
one of the preceptors of the young king. For
this preferment he was apparently indebted to
the privy council, and others of the nobility and
gentry, who assembled in consequence of that
disastrous event, for the purpose of regulating
the affairs of the nation.[h] Having appeared be-

[g] Stewart's Life of Robertson, p. 43. Edinb. 1801, 8vo.

[h] The act of privy council, which Mr Ruddiman has inserted in his notes
on Buchanan's life, commences thus: " The Lords of Secret Council and
others of the Nobility and Estates, being conveened for taking order in the
affairs of this common-wealth, among other matters being carefull of the
King's Majestie's preservation and good education, and considering how necessary the attendance of Mr George Buchanan, Master of St Leonard's

fore the council, he resigned his office of principal in favour of his friend Patrick Adamson, probably the famous poet who was afterwards archbishop of St Andrews. The privy council now
admitted Adamson to the principality; but it
does not appear from the university records that
he ever exercised his new functions.

The prince had been committed during his infancy to the charge of the earl of Mar, a nobleman of the most unblemished integrity. In 1570,
when Buchanan entered upon his office, he was
only four years of age. The chief superintend-
ence of his education was intrusted to the earl's
brother Alexander Erskine, " a gallant well-
natured gentleman, loved and honoured by all
men." The preceptors associated with Buchanan
were Peter Young and the two abbots of Cambuskenneth and Dryburgh, both related to the
noble family of Mar. Young was respectable
for his capacity and learning. His disposition
was naturally mild; and his attention to his future interest rendered him cautious of offending
a pupil, who was soon to be the dispenser of public favours. He was afterwards employed in se-

---

Colledge within the university of St Andrews, upon his Highness shall be,
and that it behoves the said Mr George to withdraw himself from his charge
of the said colledge," &c. This record afterwards mentions the priory of
St Andrews as being without a commendator. The arrangement must
therefore have taken place soon after the regent's death. " As to its date,"
says Mr Ruddiman, " I found none at the act itself; only at the top of
the page is marked 1569." (Animadversions, p. 67.) According to the
computation of that period, the year ended on the twenty-fourth of March.

veral political transactions of importance, obtained the honour of knighthood, and received an
annual pension of considerable amount.[i]   The
lofty and independent spirit of Buchanan was
not to be controlled by the mere suggestions of
cold caution : the honourable task which the voice
of his country had assigned to his old age, he discharged with simple integrity, and was little solicitous what impression the strictness of his discipline might leave on the mind of his royal pupil.[k]   James, who was of a timid nature, long
remembered the commanding aspect which his
illustrious preceptor had assumed.   He was ac-

[i] An account of the life of Sir Peter, and likewise of his learned son Patrick Young, may be found in Dr Thomas Smith's *Vitæ quorundam Eru-
ditissimorum et Illustrium Virorum.* Lond. 1707, 4to.

[k] " Now the young king," says Sir James Melvil, " was brought up
in Sterling by Alexander Areskine and my Lady Mar. He had four
principal masters, Mr George Buchanan, Mr Peter Young, the abbots of
Cambuskenneth and Dryburgh, descended from the house of Areskine.
The laird of Drumwhassel was master of his household. Alexander Areskine
was a gallant well natur'd gentleman, loved and honoured by all men, for
his good qualities and great discretion, no ways factious nor envious, a
lover of all honest men, and desired ever to see men of good conversation
about the prince, rather than his own nearer friends, if he found them not so
meet. The laird of Drumwhassel again was ambitious and greedy, his greatest
care was to advance himself and his friends. The two abbots were wise and
modest. My Lady Mar was wise and sharp, and held the king in great
awe; and so did Mr George Buchanan. Mr Peter Young was more gentle,
and was loath to offend the king at any time, carrying himself warily, as a
man who had a mind to his own weal, by keeping of his majesty's favour :
but Mr George was a Stoick philosopher, who looked not far before him.
A man of notable endowments for his learning and knowlege of Latin
poesia, much honoured in other countries, pleasant in conversation, rehearsing
at all occasions moralities short and instructive, whereof he had abundance,
inventing where he wanted." (Melvil's *Memoires*, p. 125. Lond. 1683, fol.)

customed to say of some person high in office about
him, " that he ever trembled at his approach, it
minded him so of his pedagogue."[1] Of the un-
courtly discipline to which he was subjected, two
instances have been recorded. The king having
coveted a tame sparrow which belonged to his
play-fellow the [m]*master* of Mar, solicited him
without effect to transfer his right; and in attempting to wrest it out of his hand, he deprived
the poor little animal of life. Erskine loudly lamented its fate, and the circumstances were reported to Buchanan; who lent his young lover,
reign a box on the ear, and admonished him that
he was himself a true bird of the bloody nest to
which he belonged. A theme which had one
day been prescribed to the royal pupil, was the
conspiracy of the earl of Angus and other noblemen during the reign of James the third. After
dinner, he was diverting himself with the master
of Mar : and as Buchanan, who in the mean time
was intent on reading, found himself annoyed by
their obstreperous mirth, he requested the king
to desist; but as no attention was paid to the
suggestion, he threatened to accompany his next
injunction with something more forcible than
words. James, whose ear had been tickled by

[1] Osborne's Advice to a Son, p. 19.—" The severity of the excellent Buchanan" is likewise mentioned by John Hall, *Grounds and Reasons of Monarchy*, p. 30; reprinted in Toland's edition of Harrington's Works. Lond.
1700, fol.

[m] See Wallace on Ancient Peerages, p. 424.

the quaint application of the apologue mentioned
in his theme, replied that he should be glad to
see who would *bell the cat*. His venerable preceptor, who might have pardoned the remark,
was perhaps offended with the mode in which it
was uttered : he threw aside his book with indignation, and bestowed upon the delinquent that
species of discipline which is deemed most ignominious. The countess of Mar, being attracted
by the wailing which ensued, hastened to the
scene of his disgrace ; and taking the precious
deposit in her arms, she demanded of Buchanan
how he presumed to lay his hand upon " the
Lord's anointed?" To this interrogation he is
said to have returned an answer, that contained
a very unceremonious antithesis relative to the
part which had received the chastisement.[a]

A brief sketch of the method prescribed to the
royal pupil at some particular period of his
studies, was preserved among the papers of Sir
Peter Young. After morning prayers his attention was devoted to the Greek] authors ; and he
read a portion of the New Testament, Isocrates,
or the *Apophthegmata* of Plutarch, and was exercised in the grammar rules. After breakfast he
read Cicero, Livy, Justin, or modern history.
In the afternoon he applied himself to composition, and when his leisure would permit, to arith-
metic or cosmography, which included geogra-

[a] Mackenzie's Lives of Scots Writers, vol. iii, p. 180.—" Madam, I
have whipt his....; you may kiss it if you please."

phy and the doctrine of the sphere, or to logic or rhetoric.[o]

The young monarch's proficiency in letters was such as reflected no discredit on his early instructors. He undoubtedly acquired a very considerable portion of scholastic knowledge, and attained to the command of a fluent and not inelegant style. By some of the most illustrious of his contemporaries, he has even been extolled as a prodigy of erudition: but the commendations bestowed upon a living potentate are generally to be received with the utmost caution. His literary attainments are however commemorated in terms of respect by several eminent writers, who cannot be suspected of the same partiality of judgment. The very learned Dr Parr admits that he was possessed of no contemptible share of erudition;[p] and an admirable historian mentions his Βασιλικὸν Δῶρον with appropriate praise. " Notwithstanding," says Dr Robertson, " the great alterations and refinements in national taste since that time, we must allow this to be no contemptible performance, and not to be inferior to the works of most contemporary writers, either in purity of style or justness of composition."[q] His works are numerous, and of various denominations.

o Smithi Vita Petri Junii, p. 6.

p Parr, præf. in Bellendenum, p. lxiii.

q Robertson's Hist. of Scotland, vol. iii, p. 137.

On some occasions, when his own reputation was concerned, he seems to have been sufficiently disposed to connect it with that of Buchanan. At the disputation which was held by the Edinburgh professors before his majesty in the royal chapel of Stirling, one of the English doctors expressed his admiration at the fluency and elegance of his Latinity. " All the world," replied the king, " knows that my master, George Buchanan, was a great master in that faculty. I follow his pronunciation both of the Latin and Greek, and am sorry that my people of England do not the like : for certainly their pronunciation utterly spoils the grace of these two learned languages. But you see all the university and learned men of Scotland, express the true and native pronunciation of both." [r] That the Scotish is the true and native pronunciation must not be considered as quite so certain : but we may at least aver with confidence, that it bears a much closer resemblance to the standard of those countries of modern Europe, where the ancient pronunciation may reasonably be supposed to be preserved with the greatest degree of accuracy. The English, when they pronounce Greek or Latin in their own peculiar manner, are only intelligible to each other; [s] whereas the Scotch

---

[r] Crawford's Hist. of the University of Edinburgh, p. 86. Edinb. 1808, 8vo.

[s] " Anglorum vero etiam doctissimi," says Joseph Scaliger, " tam prave Latina efferunt, ut in hac urbe, quum quidam ex ea gente per quadrantem horæ integrum apud me verba fecisset, neque ego magis eum intelligerem

are readily understood by the scholars of any nation on the continent.

That he should regard the memory of his preceptor with any unusual degree of affection, could not reasonably be expected. The character of his mother Buchanan had discussed in a very unceremonious style; and, in return, James has repeatedly mentioned the name of Buchanan with very little reverence.[t] The royal author condemns his history of Scotland as an infamous invective; and admonishes his heir apparent to punish such of his future subjects as should be guilty of retaining it in their custody. James is to be considered as one of Buchanan's most formidable enemies. The only son of an ill-fated princess was naturally solicitous to wash away the

---

quam si Turcice loquutus fuisset, hominem rogaverim, ut excusatum me haberet, quod Anglice non bene intelligerem." (*Epistolæ*, p. 700.)—With respect to the pronunciation of the Greek language, there is a very recent discussion in Reuvens's *Collectanea Litteraria*, p. 151. Lugd. Bat. 1815, 8vo.

[t] K. James's Works, p. 176, 480. Lond. 1616, fol.—Buchanan seems to have been a favourite author of a much greater monarch. The subsequent anecdote of Gustavus Adolphus it would be improper to overlook. "Some days afterwards he invested Elbingen, where the defendants were almost equal in number to those that assailed them. And here the king gave a fresh proof, both of his good nature and contempt of danger; for whilst the commander and burgomaster were signing a capitulation in the royal tent, he walked up to the town-gates, and desired to be admitted within the walls upon courteous terms. He then asked pardon of the inhabitants for not making his appearance in a better suit of apparel, and conveying himself from the crowd, in the midst of their admiration, stepped unnoticed into a bookseller's shop, and desired the honest man to supply him with an edition of Buchanan's poems." (Harte's *Hist. of the Life of Gustavus Adolphus*, vol. i, p. 81. Lond. 1759, 2 vols. 4to.)

foul spots of her reputation; and, with this view,
he exerted all the powerful influence attached to
his sceptre. Men of letters who courted his favour, were too easily induced to consider his mother's fame as immaculate; and as her reputation was incompatible with that of her principal
accuser, the next step was to convict Buchanan
in the most summary manner. " I cannot fail
to represent to your majesty," said the most illustrious of his courtiers, " the unworthiness of
the history of England in the main continuance
thereof, and the partiality and obliquity of that
of Scotland, in the latest and largest author that
I have seen."[u] The monarch's strong antipathy
cannot indeed excite much surprize; but it would
perhaps have been more magnanimous to sup-
press his indignation against a preceptor, who
had discharged his duty with the most conscien-
tious solicitude. Of the future glory of his pupil, and the attendant felicity of his country,
Buchanan seems to have cherished many a fond
and anxious hope; but all his labours proved
abortive, and his expectations deceitful. The
understanding of James, which had presented no
unfavourable dawn, was naturally opaque; and
the influence of courtly adulation speedily coun-
teracted the effect of those maxims of virtue and
polity, with which it was the perpetual solicitude of Buchanan to fortify his tender mind.

[u] Bacon of the Advancement of Learning, p. 114.

From the mature wisdom of his instructor, he might have imbibed the durable principles of a legitimate sovereignty ; he might have learned to secure his own glory, to provide for the future peace of his race, and to consider the happiness of his people as the most splendid object of regal ambition. But his notions of prerogative, after having been fostered by a more genial atmosphere, became at length so extravagant as to approach the borders of phrensy. In his native country, he was frequently treated with much contempt ; but England had long been habituated to the tyranny of the house of Tudor. His son inherited his political errors as well as his crown. Though the royal family scorned improvement, the rest of the nation had begun to sicken at perpetual encroachment and submission ; and the ensuing struggle, which was followed by remote consequences of a salutary nature, involved the death of a monarch whose faults, though of great magnitude, were faults of education. If the pupil of Buchanan had been worthy of such a preceptor, the royal house of Stewart might still have swayed the sceptre of their ancestors.

One of the earliest propensities which he discovered, was an excessive attachment to favourites ; and this weakness, which ought to have been abandoned with the other characteristics of childhood, continued to retain its ascendency during every stage of his life. His facility in

complying with every request alarmed the sagacity of Buchanan.   On the authority of the
poet's nephew, Chytræus has recorded a ludicrous expedient which he adopted for the purpose of correcting his pupil's conduct.   He presented the young king with two papers, which
he requested him to sign ; and James, after having slightly interrogated him respecting their
contents, readily affixed his signature to each,
without the precaution of even a cursory perusal.   One of them was a formal transfer of the
regal authority for the space of fifteen days.
Having quitted the royal presence, one of the
courtiers accosted him with his usual salutation ;
but he announced himself in the new character of
a sovereign, and with that humour for which he
was distinguished, began to assume the demean-
our of royalty.   He afterwards preserved the
same deportment towards the king himself; and
when James expressed his amazement at such
extraordinary conduct, Buchanan reminded him
of his having resigned the crown.   This reply
did not tend to lessen the monarch's surprize;
and he began to suspect his preceptor of de-
rangement.   Buchanan then produced the instrument by which he was formally invested ; and,
with the authority of a tutor, proceeded to re-
mind him of the absurdity of assenting to peti-
tions in so rash a manner.

An incident which occurred ten years after the
death of Buchanan, will at once serve to illus-

trate the sentiments of his pupil and the manners of that age. It is recorded by the industrious and zealous Calderwood. A deputation from the general assembly having waited on the king in May 1592, he expressed his indignation against the clergy, for speaking with so much freedom from the pulpit against him and his nobility, and defending the conduct of the earl of Murray, Buchanan, and Knox; who, said his majesty, could only be defended by traitors and seditious *theologues*. They seem at first to have replied with some degree of caution; but when the audience was renewed in the afternoon, Andrew Melvin was so vehement in his defence of those distinguished characters, that the chancellor reminded him this was not the " errand he came for." Melvin undauntedly replied that he would not be silenced by him, or any other subject. The king renewed his censure of the good regent and his two adherents, and particularly objected to Buchanan's book *De Jure Regni*. Those men, said Melvin, placed the crown upon your majesty's head. No, replied James; the crown came to me by succession, and not through the favour of any man. Melvin rejoined, they were however the instruments; and whoever has prejudiced your mind against them, is neither true to your majesty nor to the commonwealth. The king afterwards remarked that Knox had called his mother a whore, and had approved of the " slaughter of David" in her pre-

sence. If a king or a queen, said Patrick Galloway, be a murderer, why should they not be
called so?

About the period when Buchanan was appointed preceptor to the king, he seems to have entertained some apprehensions for his personal
safety, as well as his pension from the temporalities of Crossragwell abbey. The abbacy had
been granted to Allan Stewart *in commendam;*
but a most daring and barbarous attempt was
made to deprive him of its principal emoluments.
In defiance of all law and justice, the earl of
Cassillis, son to Buchanan's former pupil, continued to levy the abbey rents for the space of
three years; and in order to obtain a more permanent possession, he had recourse to an expedient of singular atrocity. Having enticed
the abbot into the castle of Dunure, he treacher-
ously detained him as a prisoner, and insisted on
his signing a *feu,* or perpetual lease, of all the
abbey lands, together with two leases of nineteen and five years of the fruits, tithes, and duties of the whole churches and parsonages belonging to the abbey. On his refusing to accede
to this unreasonable proposition, the earl commanded some of his dependents to carry him to
a place called the black vault of Dunure; where
they stripped him to the shirt and doublet, and
having bound him before a fire by the feet and
wrists, kept him in that excruciating situation
till his strength was nearly exhausted. In order

to be relieved from his tortures, the unfortunate abbot consented to sign the deeds; and Lord Cassillis made his emissaries swear on a bible that they would never reveal this transaction. *" Benedicite Jesu Maria,"* said the earl, " you are the most obstinate man that ever I saw: if I had known that you had been so stubborn, I would not for a thousand crowns have handled you so." But after an interval of six days, he required his prisoner to confirm the writings before a notary and witnesses; and on his refusal, he was subjected to the same inhuman treatment. On hearing his cries, this feudal lord commanded one of his servants to thrust a handkerchief into his mouth; nor did they desist from their cruelties till they had nearly burnt the flesh from his bones. Stewart afterwards obtained a mandate, charging Lord Cassillis upon pain of treason to release him from his confinement; but the earl disregarded this denunciation, and was accordingly declared a traitor. When the abbot was at length restored to his liberty by force of arms, he presented a petition to the regent in council, praying for the redress of his wrongs, and the protection of his person and property. At Stirling on the twenty-seventh of April 1571, the regent, with the advice of his council, commanded the earl of Cassillis to find security for two thousand pounds, that he would neither injure Allan Stewart in his person, nor interfere with his living of Crossragwell.

He also ordained " the said earl to find the like caution and security, and under the same pain, to Mr George Buchanan, pensioner of Crossragwell, being personally present, who craved the same as well for his own person as his pension." It appears that the earl was then in custody for different offences, and that he was committed to the castle of Dunbarton. [x]

Before this period, Buchanan had obtained considerable preferment. His first civil appointment, which he seems to have retained but a short time, was that of director of the chancery. [y] The keeper of the privy seal, John afterwards Lord Maitland, [z] having been deprived of his office on account of his adherence to the unfortunate queen, it was very laudably conferred on Buchanan, in the year 1570. [a] The earl

---

[a] Bannatyne's Journal, p. 55, 142.—Lord Cassillis having submitted to the regent's authority, was relieved from the penalties of the law by an act of the parliament which met at Stirling on the 28th of August 1571. (*Acts of the Parliaments of Scotland*, vol. iii, p. 63.)

[y] Scot's Staggering State of the Scots Statesmen, p. 109.—As Sir John Scot soon afterwards held the same office, it is not to be supposed that he could easily be mistaken in an assertion of this kind. Mr Chalmers has however convinced himself that Buchanan never was director of the chancery, because his admission to the office cannot be traced in the records. This writer must have forgotten that " the most diligent search could not find the appointment of Buchanan to" another high situation, which he most unquestionably enjoyed.

[z] Lord Maitland of Thirlstane, chancellor of Scotland, was the son of Sir Richard Maitland, and the brother of Buchanan's friend Thomas Maitland; all of whom are still remembered as poets.

[a] Crawfurd's Peerage of Scotland, p. 252. Edinb. 1716, fol. Douglas's Peerage of Scotland, p. 394. Edinb. 1764, fol.—The confirmation of the master of Glencairn's infeftment in the lands of Boghall and Myln-

of Lennox was at that time regent. His situation as lord privy seal was undoubtedly honourable, and probably lucrative. It entitled him to a seat in parliament.[b] This office he retained for the space of several years. On the thirtieth of April 1578, soon after the earl of Morton's temporary retirement from power, his nephew Thomas, the son of Alexander Buchanan of Ibbert, was appointed keeper of the privy seal. But the uncle certainly continued, at least for some time, to act in that capacity. In the month of June, he voted in parliament for the abbot of Dunfermline's being sent as ambassador to the English court; and in July, he is described as voting there, in the character of lord privy seal, for the earl of Morton's being excluded from the king's council.[c] He seems to be represented in the same character at a much later period. In November 1579, he is enumerated among the ordinary officers of state, entitled to a seat in the council.[d] It is neither very easy nor very important to determine whether we are to consider Thomas Buchanan as his deputy and

town was attested, among other witnesses, by " Magistro Georgio Buchanname, pensionario de Corsraguell, nostri secreti sigilli costode," at Glasgow on the 16th of March 1570_1. (*Acts of the Parliaments of Scotland*, vol. iii, p. 108.)

[b] Wight on Elections, p. 66.

[c] Chalmers's Life of Ruddiman, p. 338, 339, 340.

[d] The act of parliament does not indeed describe him as keeper of the seal, but as " pensionar of Corsraguell, preceptor to the kingis Maiestie." This character could not however entitle him to be classed with " his hienes ordiner officiaris of the estate." (Vol. iii, p. 150.)

successor, or to impute this appearance of irreg.
gularity to the general irregularity of the times.

With the three former agents he was cordial-
ly connected; but the conduct of Morton had deservedly excited his indignation.   It was by the
seasonable counsel of Buchanan and Alexander Erskine, that the king had been induced to
depose him from his office.[e]   On the twenty-
third of March 1578, Buchanan was associated,
with other officers of state, in the privy council
appointed for directing the young monarch in
the management of affairs.[f]   But the earl's in-
trigues speedily enabled him to resume his authority.   The situation of Scotland during that
unhappy period is sufficiently known.   It was
the policy of Elizabeth to exert over this country a very unwarrantable influence; and the an-
ticipation of a speedy union might perhaps have
considerable tendency to reconcile many upright
men to her views.   A list of twenty-four persons
in Scotland whom she proposed to attach by pen-
sions is still preserved.[g]   One hundred pounds
was the gratuity intended for Buchanan; and
several noble earls are not there valued at a
higher price.   But it is far from being certain
that this pension was ever conferred; nor is any
material inference to be rashly deduced from the

[e] Melvil's Memoires, p. 126.
[f] Acts of the Parliaments of Scotland, vol. iii, p. 119.
[g] Chalmers's Life of Ruddiman, p. 343.

insertion of his name in the scrolls of a political projector, residing in a different kingdom.

Buchanan was equally consulted as a politician and as a scholar. The general assembly which met in August 1574, appointed the Right Hon. George Buchanan, keeper of the privy seal, Peter Young, Andrew Melvin, and James Lawson, to peruse Adamson's history of Job in Latin verse; and if it should be found " by them agreeable to the truth of God's word, to authorize the same by the testimony of their hand and subscription."[h] This anecdote serves to illustrate the state of the Scotish press at that period. The nature of their report is not mentioned; but Archbishop Adamson's paraphrase of Job was not printed till after the author's death.[i]—We have already seen that at an earlier period, the assembly appointed Buchanan one of the commissioners for revising the book of discipline. And in the year 1578, the parliament associated him in a commission for examining " a book of the policy of the kirk."[k]

[h] Wodrow's MS. Life of Buchanan.

[i] Adamsoni Poemata Sacra. Lond. 1619, 4to.—His paraphrase of the fourth chapter had formerly been printed as a specimen. It is subjoined to the " Confessio Fidei et Doctrinæ per Ecclesiam Reformatam Regni Scotiæ professæ." Andreapoli, excudebat R. Lekprevik, 1572, 8vo. The title-page of his earliest publication ascertains the fact that Adamson was not his original name: " De Papistarum Superstitiosis Ineptiis, Patricii Adamsonii, *alias Constantini*, Carmen." Impressum Edinburgi, per R. Lekprevik, 1564, 8vo. The running title is, *Ad Papistas Abirdonenses*. The preface is dated at St Andrews, " ex Pædagogio."

[k] Acts of the Parliaments of Scotland, vol. iii, p. 105.—See Calderwood's Hist. of the Church of Scotland, p. 83.

The same parliament revived a plan which had
been recommended and approved in the year
1567. It had then been proposed that a commission should be granted to competent persons
to form a body of the municipal law, digested in
imitation of that of the Romans; and that the
different heads should be successively submitted
to parliament, in order to receive a legislative
sanction.[1] The preamble of the act of 1578 re-
cites, that there are certain constitutions and
laws devised and ordained to be made and authorized, which should be universally observed
by the subjects of this realm, but which as yet
are not thoroughly consulted and advised upon;
so that the same cannot at this time be declared
by our sovereign lord and the estates of parliament to be established as laws. And a numerous commission, including the earls of Morton
and Buchan, Archbishop Adamson, Craig, Buchanan, Arbuthnot,[m] and other persons of distinction, was appointed to examine and consider

---

[1] " Item, that ane comissioun be gevin to sufficient personis to mak ane
body of the ciuile and municipale lawis, deuidit in heidis conforme to the
fassone of the law Romane; and the heidis, as thai ar reddy, tobe brocht to
the parliament tobe confirmit." (*Acts of the Parliaments of Scotland*,
vol. iii, p. 40.)

[m] Alexander Arbuthnot, principal of King's College, Aberdeen, having
been originally destined for the bar, had studied the civil law under Cujacius, and had taken the degree of licentiate. Spotswood commends him as
a good lawyer. (*Hist. of the Church of Scotland*, p. 335.) He is the author of a work entitled *Orationes de Origine et Dignitate Juris*. Edinb,
1572, 4to. Adamson was educated for the same profession, and had practised as an advocate.

the said laws, and to reason and confer upon them; with that view, to convene at Stirling on a day appointed; and to report their proceedings to the king and parliament.[n] This plan of forming the municipal law into a regular digest was never carried into execution; and even in a country like Scotland, where the statutes had not accumulated to an enormous mass, it must have been attended with considerable difficulties. It is however worthy of remark, that those early legislators proceeded on rational principles. In this commission they associated noblemen, prelates, and burgesses, with professional lawyers and men of letters; nor do they seem to have been prepared to give their sanction to such a body of laws, without considering each of them in detail. The immense accumulation of the British statutes, which in modern times are so remarkable for their verbosity, will at length render some scheme of reduction expedient and even necessary. Such a scheme was a considerable time ago recommended by a learned lawyer; whose proposal only extended to repealing obsolete laws, and reducing into one consistent statute the different acts of parliament which relate to the same subject. A similar plan had been agitated in the reign of Elizabeth; and in that of her successor, Lord Bacon and other

[n] Acts of the Parliaments of Scotland, vol. iii, p. 105.

eminent lawyers were actually employed in di-
gesting the penal statutes. *

Buchanan was included in another commission.
of less importance. The inconveniences which
were found to result from the use of a multiplicity of Latin grammars in the different schools
of the kingdom, having been represented to the
young monarch, a committee of learned men
was appointed to deliberate respecting a competent remedy. Buchanan presided, and his coadjutors were Peter Young, Andrew Simson, and
James Carmichael. They assembled in the royal
palace of Stirling; and while they continued
to exercise their commission, were suitably entertained at the charge of the king. Having
found the grammars commonly in use to be extremely defective, it was resolved that three of
their number should attempt to establish a more
rational standard. Simson, [p] who was schoolmaster and afterwards minister of Dunbar, undertook the rudiments; Carmichael, who was likewise a schoolmaster, what is termed etymology;
and to Buchanan was assigned the department
of prosody.[q] The respective tracts of these
grammarians were in due time committed to the
press;[r] but they did not long continue to be re-

---

* Barrington's Observations on the Statutes, p. 500.
p David Hume of Godscroft inscribes his elegies " Ad Andream Symo-
nidem ludimagistrum Dumbarensem præceptorem suum."
q Sibbaldi Comment. in Vitam Buchanani, p. 16.
r Ruddimanni Bibliotheca Romana, p. 61. Edinb. 1757, 8vo.

ceived as the standard introduction to the Latin
language. The expediency of the legislature
interfering in a case of this kind, may very
safely be called in question. From the promis-
cuous use of different elementary treatises, some
inconveniences undoubtedly may arise: but if
certain grammars, recommended by public authority, were to be intruded on all the schools of
a kingdom, no future opportunity would be left
for that gradual improvement, which may be expected in every department of human art. If
King James's regulations, which were probably
authorized by an order of council, had continued
to be enforced with any degree of rigour, the
grammatical works of Ruddiman might never
have been undertaken. If the Scotish geometers
had been compelled to adhere to a particular
text-book, Euclid might never have been illustrated by the labours of Dr Simson and Mr
Playfair.

The parliament held at Edinburgh on the
fourth of June 1563, had granted a commission
to the earl of Murray, the president of the college of justice, the secretary of state, the clerk
register, the justice clerk, the queen's advocate,
George Buchanan, John Winram, prior of Port-
moak, and John Erskine of Dun, empowering
them to enquire into the revenues of the different colleges in the university of St Andrews;
to consider in what manner, and with what
emoluments, " men of cunning and understand-

M

ing" might be established in these and other col-·
leges; and to offer· their opinion and advice
with respect to the mode of instruction which
might appear to them most advantageous.*
They were enjoined to prepare their report for
the next session of parliament; but they do not
appear to have executed their important trust.
There is however a paper ascribed to Buchanan,
which may be supposed to have been drawn up
in consequence of this parliamentary commission. † Besides some minute details respecting
the revenues and commons of the colleges, it
contains the outline of a plan for new-modelling
the university of St Andrews; a plan which
seems to have been well adapted to the state of
Scotland at that early period of our literary history. The university then consisted of three
colleges; one of which he allotted to the study
of humanity, another to the study of philosophy,
and the third to the study of divinity. His regulations for the college of humanity place it in
a great measure on the footing of a grammar

---

* Acts of the Parliaments of Scotland, vol. ii, p. 544.

† This paper, which I have printed in the Appendix, No. iii, is entitled
a " Copie of Mr George Buchannan's Opinion anent the Reformation of
the Universitie of St Androis, written with his owne hand in anno 1579 ut
intus." The date which the transcriber has thus assigned, is evidently erroneous; for as the author refers to the authority of the queen, he must have
written before the 24th of July 1567, when Mary was compelled to resign
her crown. The hand is much more recent than the age of Buchanan; and
the transcriber has executed his task in a very incompetent manner. His
copy abounds with manifest errors; some of which cannot easily be corrected.

school. One part of this plan for the subdivision of the faculties was afterwards carried into execution; and New College is still appropriated to theological studies.

Those who consider the difficulty of effecting any material change in old institutions, will not be surprised that this first attempt should have failed of success. The plan was however revived in the year 1578. The parliament which met at Stirling on the twenty-fifth of July, authorized certain right honourable and reverend persons to inspect and consider the foundations and erections of the universities and colleges within this realm; to reform such things as savoured of superstition, idolatry, and popery; to displace unqualified and unfit persons from the discharge of their offices in the said universities; and to establish such qualified and worthy persons therein as they should find good and sufficient for the education of youth.[u] These commissioners having failed to convene at the time specified, the business was consequently delayed; but it was afterwards expedited by a remonstrance from the general assembly. The delegates of the church particularized the university of St Andrews as a proper subject for the first experiment of reformation: and the privy council enjoined the heads of that university to repair to Edinburgh on a certain day, and to submit their charters to the

[u] Acts of the Parliaments of Scotland, vol. iii, p. 98.

inspection of a commission which was now appointed. The commissioners who acted upon this occasion were the earl of Lennox, Robert commendator of Dunfermline, George Buchanan, James Haliburton, and Peter Young. Having found much to alter and redress, they subscribed a memorial, dated on the eighth of November 1579; and their scheme of reformation was ratified by the parliament held at Edinburgh on the eleventh of the same month.[x] This memorial, which is recited in the act of parliament, has likewise been ascribed, though without any external evidence, to the pen of Buchanan. Whatever share he might have in the composition, it cannot reasonably be doubted that his opinion had the greatest weight with the other commissioners. The general plan is very skilfully delineated; and it evidently proceeds on the supposition that the nation then abounded with men of learning. The reformation, among many other advantages, had produced an ardour of study and investigation, unknown to former ages; and many learned men had now returned from the continent, to profess a purer religion, and to instruct their countrymen in ancient literature. By this plan, the students were not only to enter more fully into the study of the Greek language, but were even to be initiated into Hebrew, Chaldee, and Syriac. In each of

---

[x] Acts of the Parliaments of Scotland, vol. iii, p. 178.

the two colleges appropriated to the study of
humanity and philosophy, they were to read, in
the Greek text, the most important parts of
Aristotle's logic, physics, ethics, and politics,
and were to declaim in Greek as well as in Latin.   The principal of St Leonard's College was
to teach the philosophy of Plato.   Buchanan appears to have been very anxious to promote the
study of Grecian literature.   He made a valuable present of Greek books to the university of
Glasgow: all of which have been carefully pre-
served.ʸ

. The act of parliament which ratified this plan
of reformation was afterwards repealed, in consequence of the confusion and uncertainty which
the members of the university pretended had
arisen from the introduction of such material alterations. . But they may fairly be suspected of
having been unwilling to pursue the arduous
path of erudition which had been prescribed.
It was more easy to observe the old formalities
of the schools, than to embrace so large a plan
of discipline.   The former act was repealed on
the fourth of August 1621; and the general
principles of the repealing statute are such as
might have been expected.   To these legislators it seemed " most equitable that the will of
the founders should take effect, except where
the same is repugnant to the true religion pre-

ʸ See Appendix, No. viii.

sently professed within this kingdom." But it was certainly as far remote from the will of the founders, that their colleges should ever become seminaries of any new religion, as that the plan of scholastic discipline originally prescribed should be subjected to salutary innovations. If in one instance it was absolute sacrilege to violate the tenor of their bequest, it must in all other instances have been the same. But as it had been found expedient to supersede their regulations with respect to the very essential article of religion, it ought likewise to have occurred to the legislature, that to banish unprofitable modes of study was a measure not less consistent with equity. Whatever may be their genuine origin, it is always proper to consider foundations of this kind as having originated in the pure motives of benevolence and public spirit; and to promote their correspondence with the progressive nature of man, must be deemed perfectly consistent with the general principles which their authors ostensibly entertain.

The merit of Buchanan, as must already have appeared, was not overlooked by his countrymen; and his consequence abroad had been increased by the respect which he secured at home. From the general state of religious opinions in the nation, as well as from the conspicuous character of the royal instructor, the Protestants on the continent seem to have conceived early hopes of finding in the Scotish monarch a powerful accession to the common cause. So considerable was the influence of this illustrious scholar, that his favour was even solicited by the king of Navarre, afterwards so famous by the name of Henry the Great. In a letter addressed to Buchanan in the year 1577, that accomplished prince requested him to instil into the tender mind of his pupil, such sentiments as might conduce to their future attachment. This letter he intrusted to his faithful adherent Philip de Mornay, a man distinguished by his literary and political talents. In the progress of his voyage to England, Mornay fell into the hands of pirates, and it was carried off with the rest of the plunder ; but upon his arrival in London, he apprized Buchanan of his master's wishes.[a] The French Protestants were extremely solicitous for a matrimonial alliance between James and the king of Navarre's sister ; and at the suggestion of several persons of that class, R. Lemacon de la Fontaine requested Buchanan to promote a scheme which might essentially contribute to the advancement of the reformed religion. Two of his letters relative to this sub-

---

[a] Colomesii Gallia Orientalis, p. 247.—Mornay is one of the principal characters in the *Henriade.* Voltaire, in his notes on the first canto, characterizes him as " le plus vertueux et le plus grand homme du parti protestant. Il savait le Latin et le Grec parfaitement, et l'Hébreu autant qu'on le peut savoir ; ce qui était un prodige alors dans un gentilhomme. Il servit sa religion et son maitre de sa plume et de son épée."

[b] Buchanani Epistolæ, p. 15.

ject have been preserved; but what encouragement the project received, is not known.[b]

Beza, the friend of Buchanan, and the terror of the Papists, addressed himself to the young king with similar views. In the year 1580 he dedicated to James one of his publications, in a strain sufficiently calculated to engage his attachment to the Protestant interests.[c] On this occasion, he wrote a short epistle to his early friend. " Behold, my dear Buchanan, a notable instance of double extravagance in a single act; affording an illustration of the characteristic phrensy of poets—provided you admit me to a participation of that title. I have been guilty of trifling with a serious subject, and have dedicated my trifles to a king. If with your usual politeness, and in consideration of our ancient friendship, you should undertake to excuse both these circumstances to the king, I trust the matter will have a fortunate issue: but if you refuse, I shall be disappointed in my expectations. The scope of this little work, such as it is, you will learn from the preface; namely that the king, when he shall be aware of the high expectations which he has excited in all the churches, may at the same time, delighted with those various and excellent examples, become more and more familiar with his duty. Of this work I likewise

---

[b] Buchanani Epistolæ, p. 27, 28.

[c] Bezæ Icones Virorum Doctrina simul et Pietate Illustrium: quibus adjectæ sunt nonnullæ picturæ quas Emblemata vocant. Genevæ, 1580, 4to.

send a copy to you, that is, owls to Athens; and request you to accept it as a token of my regard. My late paraphrase of the psalms, if it has reached your country, will I hope inspire you with the design of reprinting your own, to the great advantage of the church; and, believe me, it is not so much myself as the whole church that entreats you to accelerate this scheme. Farewell, excellent man. May the Lord Jesus bless your hoary hairs more and more, and long preserve you for our sake. Geneva, March the sixteenth 1580."[d]

In a former letter, Beza had congratulated him on the promising disposition of his royal pupil. "I could not suffer this trusty messenger to depart without a letter, at once to convince you that, during your absence, I have carefully preserved and continually cherished your remembrance, and to offer you, or rather the whole nation, my congratulations in reference to what you have signified to our friend Scrimger;[e] namely

---

[d] Buchanani Epistolæ, p. 28.

[e] Henry Scrimger, a native of Dundee, was the first professor of the civil law in the university of Geneva; and is still known to civilians as the editor of the Greek Novels. *Impp. Justiniani, Justini, Leonis Novellæ Constitutiones: Justiniani Edicta.* Excudebat H. Stephanus, 1558, fol. With respect to this publication, Brunquellus has committed two mistakes: he speaks of an edition printed at Basil in 1541, and of a Latin version by the editor. (*Hist. Juris Romani,* p 388-5.) The two regents Lennox and Mar, probably at the suggestion of Buchanan, invited Scrimger to return to Scotland, and accept of some public employment: but he was then advanced in years, and was besides alarmed at the tumults and assassinations which at that period disgraced his native country. (Buchanani *Epistolæ*, p. 7, 8, 10, 12.) He was eminently skilled in the Greek language; and had prepared

that you are blest with a king whose childhood
has already afforded such indications of piety and
every virtue, as have excited in the public mind
the hope and expectation of all that is desirable.
God forbid that the same mischance which not
long ago befell a neighbouring nation, should befall you : but may he rather grant that Scotland,
being thus possessed of a king endowed with every
accomplishment of body and mind, may at length
repose from the domestic wars and assassinations
with which it has so long been annoyed, and enjoy the blessings of holy peace.   May the same
merciful father rid you of your Medea, or Atha-
lia ; for I cannot find a name suitable to her
misdeeds.   With respect to our affairs, you will
I hope receive complete information from our
friend Young.   From the perusal of your psalms
I have derived incredible delight : although they
are such as could only have proceeded from
yourself, yet I wish, what to you will by no
means be difficult, that from being good you
would render them the best, or, if you please,
better than the best.   Farewell, excellent man,
together with all the good and pious.   May the

editions of Demosthenes, Strabo, Athenæus, the ecclesiastical history of Eu-
sebius, and various other works both Greek and Latin.   After his death,
which happened in 1572, his library and papers became the property of his
nephew Sir Peter Young; from whom Casaubon solicited his manuscript
notes on Strabo.   (*Epistolæ*, p. 182, 306, edit. Almeloveen.   Roterod. 1709;
fol.)

Lord Jesus preserve you in health and safety. Geneva, April the twelfth 1572."[f]

These illustrious friends displayed a strong congeniality of disposition: they were animated with the same ardent spirit of independence, and were equally attached to the principles of the reformation. From the same warmth of zeal that prompted them to the pursuit of excellence, they were sometimes betrayed into a violent and intemperate style. The terms which Buchanan has applied to Queen Mary and s Archbishop Hamilton are such as can hardly be justified; and Beza has often treated his literary antagonists in a very reprehensible manner. Beza, like his admirable correspondent, evinced an early predilection for poetry; and he likewise executed a complete paraphrase of the psalms.[h] Their respective versions have repeatedly been associated together.[i]

Theodorus Beza was many years younger than Buchanan: he was born on the twenty-fourth of June 1519, at Vezelay a city of Burgundy. Both his parents were noble, and he received an education suitable to his birth. Under the tuition of Melchior Wolmar, first at Or-

[f] Buchanani Epistolæ, p. 11, collated with Bezæ Epistolæ Theologicæ, p. 343. The variations are considerable.

[g] Buchanani Epigram. lib. ii, 30, 31.—The archbishop, it ought however to be recollected, was a profligate priest who had been privy to the murder of King Henry, and to that of Buchanan's patron the earl of Murray.

[h] Genevæ, 1579, 8vo. [i] Morgiis, 1581, 8vo. Genevæ, 1594, 8vo.

leans, and afterwards at Bourges, he not only
made uncommon progress in classical learning,
but was also initiated into the principles of
the reformed religion. Besa continued under
his roof till the year 1535, when Wolmar returned to Germany. He was then sent back to
Orleans for the purpose of studying jurisprudence; but this was a pursuit for which he entertained no affection. Here he composed several Latin poems, which being distributed in manuscript, procured him a high reputation in that
seminary. Having taken the degree of licentiate
in 1569, he returned to Paris with very flattering
prospects of ecclesiastical promotion. It was
about this time that he became acquainted with
Buchanan; for whom he seems to have cherished
the highest regard. He also enjoyed the society
of Turnebus, Ant. Govea, Tevius, and other distinguished members of the university; and his
Latin poems obtained the most flattering marks
of their approbation.[i] The first edition was
printed in the year 1548. This collection, along
with some effusions of piety, includes some very
lascivious verses, which, although he rejected
them in the next impression, his Popish adversaries were extremely solicitous to preserve from
oblivion.[k] These wanton prolusions he after-

[i] Bezæ Epist. ad Dudithium, p. 6, ante Poematum edit. secund. Excudebat H. Stephanus, 1569, 8vo. In this edition are inserted some of the
poems of Buchanan.

[k] Theodori Bezæ Vezelii Poemata. Lutetiæ, ex officina Conradi Badii,
1548, 8vo. Pp. 100.—This very rare volume has the following colophon:

wards classed among the sins of his youth; and
he was destined to employ his powerful talents
for much nobler purposes. Beza had completely imbibed the principles of the reformation;
and although the gaiety of youth, and the allurements of wealth, rendered him somewhat irreso-
lute, yet he was too honest to acquiesce in cor-
ruptions which were so palpable to his senses.
Having adopted the resolution of entering into
the open profession of the reformed faith, he bade
adieu to his native country, and arrived at Geneva on the twenty-fourth of October 1548. In
the course of the ensuing year, he accepted the
Greek professorship at Lausanne. This charge
he retained for the space of nine or ten years;
and at the expiration of that period removed
to Geneva, where he was ordained a minister,
and continued to exercise his clerical functions
till the time of his death. He was also associated with his illustrious friend Calvin as a profes-

"Lutetiæ, Roberto Stephano regio typographo, et sibi Conradus Badius excudebat, idibus Julii 1548." On the back of the title-page there is a portrait of the author. The juvenile poems of Beza, Muretus, and Secundus,
with other compositions of the same kind, were reprinted by Barbou in a collection entitled *Amœnitates Poeticæ.* Paris. 1779, 12mo. His editor seems
to have been unacquainted with the original edition of Beza's poems, which,
according to his account, bears the title of "Adeodati Sebæ Juvenilia."
They occur under that title, in the *Deliciæ Poetarum Gallorum,* tom. iii,
p. 578. The posthumous fame of this reformer was vindicated by an anonymous author, in a work entitled "De Juvenilibus Theodori Bezæ Poema-
tis Epistola ad N. C. qua Maimburgius, aliique Bezæ nominis obtrectatores
accurate confutantur." Amst. 1683, 12mo. This defence indicates sufficient zeal, but is not always very judicious. It was written by Jean
Graverol. (Bayle, *Oeuvres Diverses,* tom. iv, p. 606.)

sor of divinity. After having long enjoyed a
very splendid reputation, he died at Geneva on
the thirteenth of October 1605.[1] The zeal and
talents which Beza displayed in the cause of religion, rendered him one of the most conspicuous characters of the age. He has always been
enumerated among the chief pillars of the reformed church; and his proficiency in polite literature must likewise have contributed to insure
Buchanan's attachment. His works are numerous and miscellaneous; and he generally writes
with uncommon force and elegance. His reputation as a biblical critic was very high among
his contemporaries; but a more unfavourable
estimate of his labours has been formed by some
of his ablest successors, particularly by Wetstein,
Griesbach, and Campbell. " Of all the faults,"
says Dr Campbell, " with which Beza is charge-
able as a translator, the greatest is, undoubtedly,
that he was too violent a party-man to possess
that impartiality, without which it is impossible
to succeed as an interpreter of holy writ. It requires but a very little of a critical eye to dis-
cern in him a constant effort to accommodate
the style of the sacred writers to that of his sect."[m]

---

[1] An account of his life was soon afterwards published by Antonius Fayus.
It is entitled, *De Vita et Obitu Clariss. Viri D. Theodori Bezæ Vezelii.*
Geneva, 1606, 4to. Many curious particulars respecting Beza may be
found in the dictionary of Bayle. See likewise Senebier, *Histoire Littéraire
de Geneve,* tom. i, p. 266. Geneve, 1786, 3 tom. 8vo.

[m] See the prolegomena of Wetstein, cap. xiii, of Griesbach, p. xxxi, and
Campbell's tenth dissertation, part v.—After expressing a more favourable

In his controversial writings, and his controversies were numerous, Beza has commonly exes
pressed himself in too intemperate a style. His
treatment of Sebastian Castalio, an able scholar
and a worthy though unfortunate man, cannot
easily be justified. With this elegant writer he
was engaged in different controversies, and certainly did not hesitate to retail some of the most
gross calumnies which had been propagated
against him. Castalio, with a degree of wisdom and humanity of which that age did not
furnish many examples, had exerted his talents
to inculcate the maxims of religious toleration;
and this laudable conduct ought to endear his
memory to a more enlightened posterity. Calvin
and Beza however entertained a different opinion; they evinced themselves as hostile to liberty of conscience as the most furious bigots of
the Popish party. If their notions had evapora-
ted in mere speculation, such wonderful incon-
sistency might have excited less regret; but
they produced effects of a most deplorable kind.
Michael Servetus, a Spanish physician, having
published several books which contained hete-
rodox opinions, was, at the instigation of Calvin,
arrested by the magistrates of Geneva, and in-
humanly committed to the flames. The lumi-

---

opinion, Ernesti subjoins, " in sententiis autem indulget opinionibus suis, et
saepe a veritate aberrat." (*Institutio Interpretis Novi Testamenti*, p. 196.)
Wetstein justly condemns his treatment of Castalio. See also Porson's *Letters to Travis*, p. 96.

naries of that church ought to have paused for a
moment upon the obvious reflection, that their
doctrine respecting the punishment of heretics
was an indirect vindication of all the butcheries
perpetrated by another church, which they regarded with the most sincere detestation.. Heretic
is a very vague, and therefore a very convenient
term; it will equally suit each party in its turn;
for what human tribunal shall finally judge of
mere opinions? After having applied this term to
Calvin, the Romish inquisition might have doomed him to a cruel death, with as much equity as the
Genevan inquisition extended to the unfortunate
Servetus. The fate of this ingenious man must
leave an indelible stigma on the memory of those
who were accessory to his murder;[n] and yet,·
such is the natural obliquity of the human mind,
many considerations must be admitted in palliation of so atrocious an action.[o]. The genuine
spirit of toleration is but imperfectly diffused,

[n] See Dr Benson's Tracts, p. 161, 3d edit. Lond. 1748, 8vo.

[o] It is Calvin's best apology that he adopted a hideous error from which
very few of his contemporaries were exempted. The execution of Servetus
was approved even by Melanchthon, so highly, and indeed so justly, extolled for his comparative moderation. In one of his epistles to Calvin, the
subsequent passage occurs. " Affirmo etiam vestros magistratus juste fecisse, quod hominem blasphemum, re ordine judicata, interfecerunt." (Calvini *Epistolæ*, p. 306.) Every age has its peculiar deformities; and some of
our present maxims will not fail to excite the utter astonishment of the more
enlightened tribes who are yet to people the earth.—Among other proofs of
intelligence and liberality which occur in an old book with a very unpromising title, I find the following sentiment: " Magistratus hæreticos non
debet occidere." (Acontii *Stratagemata Satanæ*, p. 53, edit. Basil. 1610,
8vo.) This book was first printed at Basil in 1565.

even in a country which has long been accustomed to boast of its illumination.

The history of·persecution may receive a striking illustration from the doctrines and catastrophe of an eminent civilian, contemporary with Beza and Buchanan. A famous doctor, says Corasius, contends that the practice of punishing heresy with fire was only introduced by custom, and not formally sanctioned by any law; and that it might therefore be sufficient to punish it with the sword. But, subjoins this learned author with much coolness, since what has been confirmed by long custom is not of less force than written law; since we ought not rashly to depart from what has long been considered as equitable; and since that may be endured which is recommended by ancient usage; I leave the determination of this question to the judgment of the church. With respect to those heretics however who deny the being and attributes of God, he is decidedly of opinion that they should not merely be burnt alive, but should be subjected to more exquisite tortures, if more exquisite could be devised.[p] Such was the deliberate decision of this humane expounder of the laws. Corasius afterwards embraced the doctrines of Calvin, and was butchered as a heretic in 1572.[q]

---

[p] Corasii Miscellanea Juris Civilis, p. 177, edit. Franc. 1614, 8vo.

[q] Terrasson, Hist. de la Jurisprudence Romaine, p. 460.—" We must conclude," says the excellent Bishop Burnet, " that under what form soever of religion such things are set on foot in the world, such a doctrine is so far

N

Effera tantum igitur potuit suadere malorum
Impietas, non Relligio ; quæ prava coercens
Corda metu, spe recta fovet ; cunctisque suum jus
Spondet, et humanas vetat obbrutescere mentes.[r]

Beza has addressed one of his Latin poems to
Buchanan,[s] and on various other occasions has
mentioned him with high respect. One of Buchanan's hendecasyllables, inscribed to Beza,
seems to have been transmitted with a present of
the author's poetical works. Calvin has likewise
been enumerated among the eminent characters
with whom he maintained a literary intercourse:
but of their personal acquaintance, or epistolary
correspondence, no evidence occurs   Buchanan
has indeed written a poem entitled *Joannis Calvini Epicedium ;*[t] which is quoted with satisfaction by one of Calvin's most eloquent apologists.[u]

Another of the French Protestants who courted the favour of Buchanan's pupil was Jean de
Serres, better known by the name of Joannes
Serranus. His splendid edition of Plato, consisting of three volumes in folio, was printed by H.

from improving and exalting the nature of man, that really it makes him
worse than he would otherwise be, if he were left to the softness of his own
nature : and certainly it were better there were no revealed religion in the
world, than that mankind should become worse, more cruel, and more barbarous by its means, than it would be if it were governed by nature or a
little philosophy." (*Letter of the Clergy of France to the Protestants, Translated into English, and Examined*, p. 156. Lond. 1683, 8vo.)

  [r] Polignac, Anti-Lucretius, lib. i, v. 894.
  [s] Bezæ Poemata Varia, p. 18. [*Exc. H. Stephanus*], 1597, 4to.
  [t] Buchanani Miscell. xxiv.
  [u] Alexandri Mori Calvinus, p. 4. Genevæ, 1648, 4to.

Stephanus in the year 1578. The first volume
he dedicated to Queen Elizabeth, the second to
King ˙James,ʷ and ˙the third to the senate of
Berne. After the completion of his laborious
task, he wrote to Buchanan from Lausanne on the
twenty-ninth of February 1578. " Sir, although
I have not had the happiness to know you except by your learned writings, I have honoured
you for a long time, as do all those who love letters. In the course of last year, with the view
of alleviating the misery incident to our condition, and even after the remarkable ˑcalamity of
St Bartholomew, I have endeavoured to follow
your footsteps by teaching David to speak Greek;
though I acknowledge that my first attemptˣ
does not afford me any encouragement to prosecute the undertaking; as in reality I did not
commence it from the hope of praise, but con-
tented myself with the salutary effects which I
experienced from it as a remedy against my inquietudes. At all events, it furnished me with a
pretext for soliciting your correspondence; and
I then wrote to you, without receiving any answer. Another occasion now presents itself:
having, by the advice of my friends, dedicated a
portion of my labour to the majesty of your king,

---

* In the year 1581, H. Stephanus dedicated to King James his second
edition of Xenophon.

ˣ Psalmorum Davidis aliquot Metaphrasis Græca, Joannis Serrani. Ad-
juncta eregione Paraphrasi Latina G. Buchanani. *Excudebat H. Stephanus,*
1575, 8vo.

I have been inclined thus to address you, with the view of entreating you to love one who loves and honours you; and to do me the honour of presenting these volumes to his majesty, with such a recommendation as your erudition and goodness shall deem suitable. You may thus oblige a man who will not forget this favour, but who will pray to God for your prosperity. I might find many subjects to discuss with you; but in the expectation of receiving an answer that may encourage me to familiarity, I shall pray God to bless your happy old age, and to permit you to see in your most noble pupil the accomplishment of your good desires. Recommending myself very humbly, Sir, to your good graces, I entreat you to preserve me in those of the king....I send you a copy of Plato as a testmony, if you please, of the love and honour which I bear you."y]

Serranus's version of Plato, though deficient in elegance, is commended for its fidelity and perspicuity.[z] Dr Duport regarded him as an excellent Greek poet, and adjudged him a decided superiority over most of those who had versified the psalms.[a] His edition of Plato, and version of select psalms, he published at an early period of life; and high expectations were entertained of his future eminence in the department of phi-

---

[y] Buchanani Epistolæ, p. 17.
[z] Huetius de Interpretatione, p. 172.
[a] Duport, præf. in Metaph. Psalmorum. Cantab. 1666, 4to.

lology.[b] But he was induced to apply his talents to other subjects, connected with his views as a Protestant. He is the reputed author of several anonymous works relative to the history of France;[c] and he engaged in a pertinacious controversy with John Hay, a Scotish Jesuit of considerable note among his brethren.[d] Though thus involved in ecclesiastical warfare, he indulged the hope of a general and lasting union of the great divisions in the Christian church: he was led to adopt a plan[e] which had been entertained by Erasmus, and which was afterwards revived by the piety and learning of Grotius;[f] a plan which has never been attended with the slightest degree of success, and has only procured general odium to the excellent men by whom it was so fondly cherished. The intentions of Serranus seem to have been strangely misrepresented;[g] and even the memory of Grotius was per-

[b] " Si diu fuerit superstes," says Languet, " meo judicio, habebitur inter clarissimos viros in re literaria ; nam est adhuc juvenis, et insigniter doctus." (Epistolæ ad Sydnæium, p. 238, edit. Hailes.)

[c] Placcii Theatrum Anonymorum et Pseudonymorum, tom. i, p. 282. Deckheri de Scriptis Adespotis, Pseudepigraphis, et Supposititiis, Conjecturæ, p. 262, 378, edit. Amst. 1686, 12mo.—Serranus acknowledges himself to be the author of the commentaries " De Statu Religionis et Reipublicæ in Regno Galliæ." (Epistolæ Selectiores, p. 780.)

[d] Sotvelli Bibliotheca Scriptorum S. Jesu, p. 459, Romæ, 1676, fol.

[e] Serranus de Fide Catholica, sive Principiis Religionis Christianæ, communi omnium Christianorum consensu semper et ubique ratis. Paris. 1597, fol. Ibid. 1607, 8vo.

[f] Erasmus de Sarcienda Ecclesiæ Concordia. Grotii Opera Theologica, tom. iii.

[g] Casauboni Epistolæ, p. 474, edit. Almeloveen. Roterod. 1709, fol.—

secuted with deplorable malignity. Such a project indeed is evidently wild and impracticable:
an infallible church can never acknowledge itself
guilty of error;[h] and it is to be hoped that a reformed church will never be induced to reform
backwards. "As there were many reformers,"
says Sir Thomas Browne, "so likewise many
reformations; every country proceeding in a particular way and method, according as their national interest, together with their constitution
and clime, inclined them; some angrily, and with
extremity; others calmly, and with mediocrity,
not rending but easily dividing the community,
and leaving an honest possibility of a reconciliation; which though peaceable spirits do desire,
and may conceive that revolution of time and
the mercies of God may effect, yet that judgment
that shall consider the present antipathies between the two extreams, their contrarieties in

What is stated by Cardinal du Perron with respect to his abjuration of the
Protestant faith, seems to be totally destitute of foundation. (*Perroniana*,
p. 299.)

[h] Every church indeed that imposes its articles as the only true interpretation of the scriptures, must necessarily be understood as asserting an arrogant claim to infallibility; and the church of Rome only differs from some
other churches in advancing this claim without any reserve or circumlocu-
tion. The reformed churches are certainly more cautious and bashful; but
whether they are in reality more modest, is another question. They all profess to regard the scriptures as the only standard of faith; yet not one of
them will permit its members to interpret the scriptures for themselves.
Without the exercise of this privilege, the scriptures are no standard to us;
our belief is nothing better than a blind and bigoted reliance on the infallibility of the original imposers of articles. And whence did these article-mong-
ers derive their authority to interpret the scriptures for all posterity?

condition, affection and opinion, may with the same hopes expect an union in the poles of heaven."[i]

The personal history of Serranus, who was a native of Viviers or the adjacent district, is involved in obscurity.[k] It however appears that soon after the publication of his edition of Plato, he returned to France,[l] and there exercised the functions of a minister. In the respective dedications of his Greek psalms, and of the second volume of Plato, he mentions Buchanan with high commendation. " I have been wonderfully charmed," he remarks, " with the erudite felicity of George Buchanan, a man indeed not only to be equalled to the greatest poets of our own age, but even of all learned antiquity."

Rodolphus Gualtherus, an eminent minister of the reformed church of Zurich in Switzerland, addressed himself to Buchanan on a similar occasion. Having inscribed to the young monarch his homilies on the epistle of St Paul to the Galatians, which were printed in the year 1576, he transmitted two copies to Buchanan; requesting him to present one to his hopeful pupil, and to retain the other as a token of the author's regard. Relative to this subject, four of their letters are extant ;[m] and they tend to exhibit our illustrious

---

[i] Browne's Religio Medici, p. 7, 8th edit. Lond. 1682, 8vo.

[k] Oeuvres Diverses de Bayle, tom. iv, p. 648. Niceron, tom. iv, p. 316. Senebier, Hist. Litteraire de Geneve, tom. ii, p. 101.

[l] Epistolæ Selectiores, p. 778. Lugd. Bat. 1617, 8vo.

[m] Buchanani Epistolæ, p. 16, 17, 20, 26.

countryman in no unamiable point of view. His
correspondent Gualtherus, the author of various
works,[n] was a native of Zurich. In his youth he
had applied himself to the study of polite literature; he had discovered some talent for poetry,
and had executed a Latin version of the *Onomasticon* of Julius Pollux.[o] He afterwards acquired
distinction as a theologian; and for the space of
more than forty years, he exercised with great
fidelity and diligence the pastoral care in his native city.[p]

Buchanan, about this period of his life, corresponded with many other characters of distinction: with some of them he was personally acquainted; the rest he attracted by the splendour
of his reputation. Tycho Brahe having published his tract *De Nova Stella* in the year 1573, did
not neglect to present it to a man who, like himself, had essentially contributed to advance the
intellectual fame of the northern nations. Buchanan was for some time prevented from ac-
knowledging this gratifying mark of attention;
but he at length addressed a very elegant and po-

[n] Teissier, Eloges des Hommes Savans, tom. ii, p. 55.
[o] Gualtherus is a contributor to the *Delitiæ Poetarum Germanorum*. His
translation of Pollux was published without the Greek text, accompanied
however with annotations. Basil. 1541, 4to. It is mentioned in disparaging
terms by Jos. Scaliger. (*Epistolæ*, p. 528.) Beza has written the epitaph
of Gualtherus, and that of his son. (*Poemata Varia*, p. 120, 121.)
[p] Verheiden, Præstantium aliquot Theologorum Elogia, p. 200. Hag.
Com. 1602. fol. Boissardi Icones, tom. iv, p. 154. Adami Vitæ Germanorum Theologorum, p. 592.

lite letter to that renowned astronomer.[q] When King James, in the year 1590, visited Tycho Brahe at his castle of Uranienburg, he observed Buchanan's picture hanging in the library, and immediately recognized the lineaments of his deceased preceptor. This picture had been presented by Sir Peter Young, during one of his embassies to the court of Denmark.[r]

Although Buchanan did not professedly devote himself to the illustration of ancient authors, yet he bore a high reputation for critical sagacity. He was consulted by scholars of different nations; and some of his emendations have been published by Turnebus and Lambinus.[s] It cannot indeed be regretted that a man capable of producing original works of such excellence, should not have devoted a larger portion of his life to illustrate the reliques of ancient genius : but his sagacity and erudition would have enabled him to secure a very high station in that department, preoccupied as it then was by scholars of the first order. Whatever may be the fashionable estimate of our contemporaries, the manly and robust age of Buchanan entertained no contemptu-

---

[q] Buchanani Epistolæ, p. 14.

[r] Gassendi Vita Tychonis Brahei, p. 123. Paris. 1654, 4to.

[s] These emendations are reprinted in Ruddiman's edition of Buchanan, tom. i, p. xx, tom. ii, p. 103. Lambinus characterizes him as " vir omni doctrina præstans." " Neminem esse," says Turnebus, " existimo in Gallia paulo humaniorem, cui Georgius Buchananus non sit notus, non solum exingius poeta, verum etiam vir omni liberali eruditione non leviter tinctus, sed penitus imbutus." (*Adversaria*, lib. i, cap. ii.)

ous opinion of the character or occupation of those learned men, who contributed to restore the Greek and Roman authors to their original purity. To acquire distinction as a classical commentator was one of the principal objects of youthful ambition. The splendid talents of Calvin were first exercised in illustrating a treatise of Seneca.[t] The useful labours of verbal criticism have employed some of the most powerful intellects of which modern Europe can boast. That eminent philologers have written with pedantic prolixity, or judged with precipitation, or have attached an inordinate value to trifles,[u] it would

---

[t] Calvini Opera, tom. viii, edit. Amst.

[u] Joseph Castalio shall supply us with an illustration. " *Incredibili* me nuper *voluptate* perfudit Vergiliorum nomen in marmore pervetusto inscalptum," &c. To settle the mighty contention between *e* and *i*, he has written a tract entitled " De Recta Scribendi Vergili Nominis Ratione Commentarius :" and his exultation seems not so much to arise from his ascertaining the orthography of the name, as from his ascertaining it to be Vergilius instead of Virgilius. (*Variæ Lectiones et Opuscula.* Romæ, 1594, 4to.) Klotzius has written a very entertaining epistle " De Minutiarum Studio et Rixandi Libidine Grammaticorum quorundam." (*Opuscula Varii Argumenti*, p. 191.)

With respect to conjectural criticism, it would have been fortunate if some scholars of eminence had formed the same estimate as J. M. Gesner. " Conjecturas ingeniosas," says Ernesti, " laudabat magis quam probabat : et nihil magis quam dulces illecebras in judicando cavendum monebat. Nec tamen ingenio, literis et doctrina diu subacto, nihil tribuebat : quo et ipse non pauca feliciter correxit." (*Opuscula Oratoria*, p. 331. Lugd. Bat. 1762, 8vo.) " Nec semper, meo judicio," says the elegant Gravina, " vera lectio erit ea quæ melior : scriptores enim, varia distracti scriptionis cura, industriam aliquando remittunt. Neque humanum ingenium contendere ubique potest omnibus nervis : ideo ut in acie milites, etsi minus fortes, tamen, quia fessis integri succedunt, pugnant aliquantisper alacrius ; ita evenit, ut acutius aliquando comminiscantur interpretes, quam ipsimet auctores invenerunt." (*Origines Juris Civilis*, præf.)

not indeed be safe to dispute : but those who
deny that they have contributed to the advancement of solid learning, ought to be superseded
as incompetent judges.   To treat with derision
the memory of scholars, whose exertions have at
once been so strenuous and so useful, must either
be regarded as a proof of ignorance or ingratitude.[x]

It was remarked by an early writer of a singular character, that " most of the Scotish nation never having astricted themselves so much
to the propriety of words, as to the knowledge
of things, where there was one preceptor of languages amongst them, there were above forty
professors of philosophy." During the age of
Buchanan, and the earlier part of the following
century, Scotland produced many authors who
wrote in Latin with a very considerable degree
of purity and elegance.   On comparing the style
of Fordun and Mair with that of Boyce and
Lesley, the progress of taste is very conspicuous ;
but a more classical vein may be distinguished
in the dialogue on tranquillity of mind, written

---

[x] " Ingratissimi certe fuerimus," says Henricus Valesius, " nisi tantis hominibus plurimum a nobis deberi profiteamur, qui labore suo et industria perfe-
cerunt, ut jam nobis expeditior sit via studiorum, minusque sit in literis
postea laborandum, adeo nobis fere omnia complanata et facilia præstiterunt."
(*De Critica*, p. 151.   Amst. 1740, 4to.)   " Non defuturos, scio," says
Markland, " qui totam hanc doctrinæ partem, ut levem, nec aut ad utilitatem
aut oblectationem vitæ aliquid conferentem, calumniaturi sunt : nulli enim
liberius judicant, quam qui aut non legunt, aut non intelligunt."   (*Epistola
Critica*, p. 3,   Cantab. 1723, 8vo.)

by Florence Wilson, a scholar whom Buchanan
has celebrated as dear to the Muses.[y] But the
disposition of our countrymen did not lead them
very strongly to the study of verbal criticism,
even at a period when it was prosecuted with astonishing ardour in the rest of Europe. A few
names may however be traced in this department. Scrimger was highly celebrated for his
skill in the Greek tongue, and prepared editions
of many ancient authors. His contemporary
Henryson likewise united the study of philology
with that of the civil law ; and the same union
was afterwards preserved by Dempster, and a
few others. Among other works of erudition,
this learned professor published editions of Claudian and Corippus, which entitled him to a place
among the critics of the age. Balfour distinguished himself by his edition of Cleomedes, and
his commentaries on the logic and ethics of Aristotle. Cameron, who flourished about the same

---

[y] De Animi Tranquillitate Dialogus, Florentio Voluseno autore. Lugduni, apud Gryphium, 1543, 4to.—Florence Wilson prosecuted his studies at Aberdeen, and afterwards at Paris ; where he was intrusted with
the tuition of Cardinal Wolsey's nephew. After the uncle's death, he was
patronized by other two cardinals, Jean de Lorraine and Jean du Bellay.
As he was proceeding with the latter towards Rome in the year 1536, he was
seized with an indisposition which detained him at Carpentras. Here he
waited on Cardinal Sadolet, then bishop of the see ; and this excellent prelate was so delighted with his literary accomplishments and elegant manners,
that he placed him at the head of a classical seminary in that city. (Sadoleti
Epistolæ, p. 227, 639, 687, edit. Lugd. 1554, 8vo.) Wilson afterwards
intended to revisit his native country, but death overtook him at Vienne in
the year 1546.

period, was celebrated for his knowledge of the Greek[s] and Hebrew languages; and his annotations on the New Testament have procured him a respéctable rank among biblical critics. [a] These and other scholars maintained the credit of our national literature till the approach of the solemn league and covenant, when times of greater ignorance and barbarism ensued; and it was not till after a long and gloomy interval that Scotland could boast, in Alexander Cunningham,[b] of a critic distinguished by uncommon sagacity and erudition.[c]

In the library of the university of Edinburgh, there is a manuscript ascribed to Buchanan, containing a commentary on the eclogues, georgics, and first seven books of the Æneid of Virgil. This commentary appears to have been dictated, without much effort, to younger students; and as many phrases are explained in the Scotish language, it may be supposed to have been dictated

---

[a] " Græce enim," says Ludovicus Capellus, " tam expedite et eleganter quam quivis alius Latine extempore loquebatur; ita ut doctissimis viris quos ubique convenit, adeoque et ipsi magno Casaubono (cui paulo post fuit notissimus) admirationi esset, fueritque charissimus." See the account of John Cameron, prefixed to his *Myrothecium Evangelicum.* Genevæ, 1632, 4to.

[a] Simon, Hist. Critique des Principaux Commentateurs du N. Testament, p. 791.

[b] See Appendix, No. xi.

[c] This subject may be very properly concluded in the words of Daniel Heinsius. " Sane, quemadmodum qui priscos vel contemnunt, vel ne tangunt quidem, stolidi aut imperiti sunt: ita qui eodem loco omnes habent, aut in uno aliquo mirantur omnia aut imitanda arbitrantur, miseratione dignos arbitror." (*Aristarchus Sacer*, p. 5.)

at St Andrews.   The manuscript was presented
to the library by Andrew Fletcher.

Among other scholars who solicited his contributions was Obertus Gifanius, a civilian and philologer of no inconsiderable reputation.   One of
his letters to Buchanan has been preserved: it
is dated at Orleans on the sixteenth of January
1567.   " Relying on your candour and good nature," says Gifanius, " I repeatedly wrote to you
some months ago.   Supposing my former letters
to have miscarried, I now address you a third
time; and that more confidently through the encouragement of your countrymen Gordon, Cunningham, Guthrie, and other youths whom I understand to be very dear to you, and with whom,
much to my satisfaction and improvement, I here
live upon terms of intimacy.   If therefore my
correspondence should prove irksome to you,
which I should very much regret, recollect what
vouchers I have it in my power to allege; vouchers who will never disown their having insti-
gated me; such is their candour, such their sin-
cerity, and such their regard for me, unworthy of
it as I am.   In those my former letters, I wrote
I know not what respecting certain passages
of Cæsar, in my opinion somewhat obscure, with
the view of obtaining from you their elucidation.
If you have made any remarks upon his commentaries, as I doubt not you have, it is now my request that you will communicate them to me.   I
shall take care to convince both yourself and the

public that I do not, as that fellow Dionysius has with abundant impudence objected to me,[d] pro-duce the emendations of others as my own, but most gratefully recognize every man's claims; and to you, should you liberally condescend to favour me, an obscure individual and a foreigner, with such a communication, I shall be particular-ly studious to mark my obligations.   Although I am aware of your being eminently versed in writers of every denomination, yet I am chiefly anxious to procure your assistance with respect to Cæsar, as I have determined speedily to pub-lish an edition of that author accompanied with notes.   If you should however subjoin by way of ἐπιλλὴν and corollary, any remarks on Livy, Ovid, or other authors, you will thus strengthen the at-tachment of one firmly attached before; and having already been bound to you by many obli-gations, I shall then acknowledge them to be much increased.   There is another circumstance of which I wish you to be apprized, and which has furnished me with almost the only reason for addressing you at this time.   Plantin, a Flemish printer who, if I am not deceived, is known to you, and who always wishes to publish works of the greatest value, is very solicitous to edit with

---

[d] Gifanius published an edition of Lucretius (Antv. 1565, 8vo.) soon af-ter that of Dionysius Lambinus had made its appearance; and Lambi-nus, in his preface to the third impression, has in strong terms accused him of appropriating his labours. This charge is confirmed by Thomasius and Bayle.

a Latin version, all or the greater part of the
Greek epigrams contained in the Anthology.
Having learned from those countrymen of yours
that you have translated much from the Greek
into the Latin language, and being habitually
eager to procure for my friend Plantin all the
assistance within my compass, it was extremely
fortunate that I should meet with this Scotish
merchant, who is well acquainted with you, and
who was then hastening directly homeward : for
I am persuaded that when you shall have received this account of Plantin's scheme, you will
approve of it, and will also promote it by sending him, as soon as possible, your versions of
some of the epigrams. It is a favour which I entreat of you, but with due regard to your own
convenience ; for I would not be guilty of importunity.   This person is both worthy of being intrusted with your verses, and encouraged by your
good offices : he has already printed a very elegant edition of your psalms,[e] and is hardly ambitious of undertaking the impression of any productions except your own. With respect to other
matters, although you receive abundant information from many correspondents, yet it will not I
trust be disagreeable if I add my contribution.
Your *Jephthes* and *Franciscanus*, translated into
French by your friend Chrestien, are printing in

---

[e] Antverpiæ, 1566, 12mo.

this city.[f] An edition of Lycophron by my friend Canterus has very lately been published at Basil, together with the younger Scaliger's translation, replete with antiquity, and in the style of Pacuvius.[g] Your astronomical poem is expected with the utmost avidity. Auratus having lately been presented with the title of *Poeta Regius*, and with a pension sufficiently ample, will, if I am not deceived, discontinue his professorial functions. Ramus is said to have published some very learned mathematical prolegomena."[h] Among the poetical works of Buchanan several translations from the Greek occur; but Plantin's project was never carried into execution. Nor did Gifanius publish his intended edition of Cæsar.

Obertus Gifanius was a native of Buren in Guelderland. Having taught jurisprudence and philosophy at Strasburg and Altdorf, and juris-

[f] Le Cordelier de Buchanan, fait en François. *Genève*, 1567, 4to. The reason for substituting Geneva instead of Orleans is sufficiently obvious.

[g] Basileæ, 1566, 4to.—This very obscure poet was illustrated by Canterus at the age of twenty-four. · Even at an earlier age, he produced a philological work of no vulgar erudition. (*Novæ Lectiones*. Basil. 1564, 8vo.) Guilielmus Canterus was born at Utrecht in 1542, and died at Louvain in 1575. His portrait may be found in Miræi *Elogia Belgica*, p. 127, and an ample account of his life in Suffridus Petrus *De Scriptoribus Frisiæ*, p. 111. Colon. Agrip. 1593, 8vo. His brother Theodorus Canterus wrote his *Variæ Lectiones* at the age of twenty. (Colomesii *Opuscula*, p. 231.) Meursius published an edition of Lycophron at the age of eighteen. Lugd. Bat. 1597, 8vo. Potter published his edition about the same age. The task of illustrating so obscure and difficult a writer would require the most mature earning and judgment.

[h] Buchanani Epistolæ, p. 6.

prudence at Ingolstad, his literary fame procured him the patronage of the emperor Rodolph; who conferred upon him the honourable title of imperial counsellor, accompanied with considerable emolument. He was undoubtedly a man of no vulgar erudition; but his moral qualities seem to have been of a more dubious nature.[i] In his youth, he had embraced the doctrines of the reformation; but as his new creed was not sufficiently adapted to the meridian of Vienna, he reverted to Popery. His sordid love of money exposed him to the derision of Joseph Scaliger; who informs us that although Gifanius was master of twenty-five thousand ducats, he lived in a garret, and, to avoid the expense of company, sent his wife to live at Nuremberg.

Florent Chrestien, whom he mentions as the friend of Buchanan and the translator of some of his writings, was born at Orleans in 1540. His father, whose name was William, and who descended from a noble family of Bretagne, was a favourite physician of Henry the second; and was likewise the author or translator of several

[i] Zeidleri Vitæ Professorum Juris in Academia Altdorffina, p. 37, Norimb. 1770, 4to.—A list of books which Gifanius left for publication occurs in the *Amœnitates Literariæ*, tom. xii, p. 589. Bayle, who has given a short account of this scholar, was not aware of the publication of his posthumous production, entitled *Observationes Singulares in Linguam Latinam*. Franc. 1624, 8vo. This work had been pilfered by Scioppius. It is reprinted in the collection of Ketelius, *De Elegantiori Latinitate comparanda Scriptores Selecti*. Amst. 1713, 4to. " Gifanius," says Christopher Wase, " rei antiquariæ peritia ultra statem eminuit." (*De Legibus et Licentia Veterum Poetarum*, p. 244.)

works. Florent was his mother's fifth child, and was born in the seventh month: in allusion to these circumstances, he assumed, when he wrote in Latin, the name of Quintus Septimius Florens Christianus.[k] His royal pupil, afterwards so conspicuous by the name of Henry the Great, is said to have regarded him with little kindness, and to have bestowed upon him with considerable reluctance the office of keeper of the royal library. Chrestien, like his friend Buchanan, had perhaps enforced subordination. At Orleans he was invested with some military command, which he discharged with bravery. Having afterwards retired to Vendôme, he fell into the power of the Leaguers upon the capture of that town; but his pupil soon delivered him by paying his ransom. He was one of the duke of Vendôme's counsellors. His character was that of an excellent scholar and a worthy man. He was regarded as one of the best Grecians of the age; and Jos. Scaliger was of opinion that France could not boast of another person who composed in Greek, Latin, and French, with equal felicity. He wrote many poems upon occasional subjects, but only an inconsiderable portion has been printed.[l]

---

[k] Jos. Scaligeri Poemata, p. 40. Lugd. Bat. 1615, 16to.

[l] Janus Gruterus, or, according to his anagram, *Ranutius Gherus*, has inserted some of Chrestien's Latin verses in the *Deliciæ Poetarum Gallorum*; but many of them had escaped his notice, and many more were never printed. Nine poems written by Chrestien in Greek, Latin, and French, occur in the collection entitled *Christophori Thuani Tumulus*. Lutetiæ, 1583, 4to. He translated the Cynegetics of Oppian into French, and various other

His translating those works of Buchanan must
have afforded the author no trivial gratification;
for Chrestien was both respected and feared by
his brother poets. In the year 1596, his life was
terminated at Vendôme by a rapid fever.[m] The
only stain which affixes itself to his memory is
that of apostasy. His attachment to the reformed religion had been marked by no inconsiderable
zeal; and yet Fronto Ducæus, a learned and honest Jesuit who flourished soon afterwards, alludes to his reconversion as a circumstance well
known.[n] If such conduct admits of palliation, it
was certainly excusable in France after the massacre of St. Bartholomew; and the conversion of
Petrus Pithœus, a man equally revered for his
probity and learning, had been effected by the
same process of reasoning.

Lucas Fruterius, the friend of Gifanius, is likewise entitled to a place among the more remarkable correspondents of Buchanan; to whom he
has repeatedly addressed himself in affectionate
terms. In an epistle, written, it must be confess-
ed, with sufficient pedantry, he reminds Bucha-

poems into Latin.   His version of the Cyclops of Euripides is subjoined to
Casaubon *De Satyrica Græcorum Poesi, et Romanorum Satira.* Paris. 1605,
8vo. He likewise translated some of the dramas of Æschylus, Sophocles,
and Aristophanes. His version of Musæus is reprinted in Röver's edition
of that poet. Lugd. Bat. 1737, 8vo. Some of his epistles occur in the collections of Gabbema and Burman. See also *Epistres Françoises à M. de la
Scala,* p. 58, 229, 386.

[m] Thuani Hist. sui Temporis, tom. v, p. 643. Sammarthani Elogia,
p. 124. Niceron, Memoires des Hommes Illustres, tom. xxxiv, p. 132.
[n] Burmanni Sylloge Epistolarum, tom. i, p. 647.

nan of a promise to aid him with his *Verisimilia,*
a critical work in which he was then engaged.[o]
From the same letter it appears that they had
been personally acquainted at Paris, subsequently
to the nuptials of the Scotish queen.   Her marriage was celebrated on the twenty-ninth of July 1565, and the letter of Fruterius was written
on the first of February 1566.[p] A tradition formerly prevailed that Buchanan stole away from
St. Andrews, and, without having communicated
the project to any of his friends, made a voyage
to France.[q] This rumour has been supposed to
derive considerable probability from the allusion
of his correspondent.   Fruterius, a native of
Bruges in Flanders, was regarded by his contemporaries as a young man of the highest promise;[r] but a fatal accident soon terminated his
career.   After having heated himself by playing
at tennis, he imprudently swallowed a draught
of cold water, and was immediately seized with
a distemper which his constitution could not resist.   He died at Paris in the month of March
1566.[s] Although he had scarcely entered the

[o] Buchanani Epistolæ, p. 4.

[p] Ruddiman's Animadversions, p. 65.

[q] " I have heard it related an hundred times," says Mr Ruddiman, " that
Buchanan, when principal of St Leonard's College at St Andrews, without
acquainting any of his friends of it, did make such a voyage to France."
(*Anticrisis,* p. 139.)

[r] Thuani Hist. sui Temporis, tom. ii, p. 479., Miræi Elogia Belgica,
p. 202. Antv. 1608, 4to. Andreæ Bibliotheca Belgica, p. 628. Sweertii
Athenæ Belgicæ, p. 517. Antv. 1628, fol.

[s] Gabbemæ Epistolæ, p. 650.

twenty-fifth year of his age, he had made uncommon progress in the study of philology.[t]

The name of Peter Daniel is frequently mentioned with that of Buchanan; with whom he appears to have been intimately connected. At the suggestion of several of their common friends, he addressed a letter to Buchanan for the purpose of urging the impression of those poetical works which had been promised many years before. This letter is short, and indicates the general respect in which his correspondent was held. "Several learned men," says Daniel, "by whom you are very much esteemed, have requested me to stimulate you, by a letter, to the publication of those iambics, epigrams, and odes, which we have now been expecting for the space of nearly ten years. This commission I certainly undertake with cheerfulness; and I adjure you by the sacred rites of the Muses, not to withhold from your friends what will so much conduce to the common advantage of men of letters, but to pro-

[t] Janus Dousa published a collection of his writings 'under the title of "Lucæ Fruterii Brugensis Librorum qui recuperari potuerunt Reliquiæ." Antverpiæ, 1584, 8vo. Prefixed is an epistle from Lipsius to the editor, which begins thus: "Vere mihi sæpe adfirmasti: inter prima ingenia Belgii nostri, imo Galliæ, Lucas Fruterius fuit." Gruterus afterwards published a third book of the *Verisimilia* of Fruterius, and some of his philological epistles. (*Thesaurus Criticus*, tom. v, p. 832, 884.) A long epistle from this young Belgian occurs among those of Muretus. (Lib. i, epist. xxvi.) Two of his letters to Guilielmus Canterus may be found in the collection of Simon Abbes Gabbema, entitled "Epistolarum ab Illustribus et Claris Viris scriptarum Centuriæ tres," p. 614, 639. Harlingæ Frisiorum, 1664, 8vo. Some of his unpublished poems are mentioned by Saxius. (*Onomasticon Literarium*, tom. iii, p. 390.)

ceed, when your leisure shall permit, with the plan of collecting your scattered productions. Their impression will be carefully managed by my countryman Mamert Patisson, who has married the widow of Stephanus, and whom you will find extremely disposed to comply with your wishes. Your books *De Sphæra* are also expected with anxiety; and if you likewise transmit to me any other work which you have recently finished, you will at once fulfil both your promises, and preserve your writings from perishing. By this plan, they who ascribe your productions to themselves will be put to the blush; and they will be derided who, under your name, either publish other men's works or their own; as we readily supposed to have been done of late with respect to the verses on the admiral. Farewell, distinguished man. All the learned and pious salute you, especially Scaliger, La Hatte,[a] and Chrestien. Cujacius is in town, and it is rumoured that he is speedily to open a school of the civil law. If you have made any alterations in your paraphrase of the psalms, let me request you to send them."[x]

[a] " Nicolai Hattei Aurelii, regis et Aureliorum ducis secretarii, Carmen ad P. Danielem civem suum," is prefixed to Daniel's edition of the *Querolus.* Thuanus mentions " Nic. Hata actuarius publicus" as a violant partisan of the League in the year 1567. (*Hist. sui Temporis,* tom. iv, p. 441, 465.)

[x] Buchanani Epistolæ, p. 12.—This letter is without a date; but Mr Ruddiman rightly conjectures that it must have been written at the end of 1575 or the beginning of 1576. Terrasson has printed an *arrest* of the par-

Daniel was a native of St Benoist sur Loire,[y] but the principal part of his life was spent at Orleans. His profession was that of an advocate, and he held the office of *bailli* of the abbey of Fleuri. But he was zealously attached to critical studies, and attained to uncommon familiarity with ancient manuscripts.[z] Scioppius characterizes him as a storehouse of every species of antiquities.[a] He lived on terms of intimacy with some of the most distinguished scholars of the age: Scaliger and Turnebus acknowledge themselves indebted to him for the communication of his manuscript treasures. After his death, which happened in the year 1603, his manuscript library was purchased by Bongars and Paul Petau, for the sum of fifteen hundred livres.[b] His only publications were editions of Petronius,[c] Virgil and Servius,[d] and of the curious relique entitled *Querolus, sive Aulularia.*[e] To this comedy, which

---

liament, dated 2 April 1576, which authorizes Cujacius to give lectures on the civil law in the university of Paris. (*Hist. de la Jurisprudence Romaine.* Paris, 1750, fol.)

[y] Baillet, Jugemens des Sçavans, tom. ii, par. ii, p. 251.

[z] " Egregius est adolescens Petrus Daniel Aurelianus, et bonis literis ita deditus, ut nihil aliud in delitiis habere videatur : librorum autem veterum tam cupidus, ut bibliothecas omnes pervestiget, et aliquid semper in lucem proferat, et libros vetustate sepultos velut redivivos hominum lectioni reddat." (Turnebi *Adversaria*, lib. xxvi, cap. xxi.)

[a] Scioppius de Arte Critica, p. 13, edit. Amst. 1662, 8vo.

[b] Mabillon de Liturgia Gallicana, præf. Paris. 1685, 4to.

[c] Daniel's preface is reprinted in Burman's edition of Petronius Arbiter, p. 256. Traj. ad Rhen. 1709, 4to.

[d] Parisiis, 1600, fol.

[e] Paris. 1564, 8vo. This is the *Aulularia* of Plautus transprosed. An-

had not formerly been printed, he prefixed the commendatory verses of Buchanan.[f]

Hubert Languet seems likewise to claim a share of our attention. His letter to Buchanan, dated at Delft on the twentieth of February 1581, will illustrate the nature of their connection. " By your virtue, and by the various and noble monuments of your genius, you have rendered yourself so conspicuous in the Christian world, that hardly a single lover of science and literature can be found, who does not regard you with the utmost reverence and admiration. I consider it as an instance of no common felicity, that about twenty years ago, it was my lot not only to see you at Paris, and to enjoy your most pleasant and most learned conversation, but also to entertain you as my guest, together with those distinguished men, Turnebus, Auratus,[g] Balduinus the civilian,[h] Sambucus the Hungarian,[i] Carolus Clu-

---

other edition was afterwards published by Rittershusius; who has subjoined the same comedy transformed into elegiac verse by Vitalis Blesensis. *Ex typographeio H. Commelini*, 1595, 8vo. The notes of Daniel, and his dissertation respecting the author, are likewise retained. Pareus has inserted the prose *Aulularia* in his edition of Plautus, and has strangely enough imputed it to Gildas.

[f] Buchanani Opera, tom. ii, p. 102.

[g] Bayle, Dictionaire Historique et Critique, art. *Daurat.* Niceron, Memoires des Hommes Illustres, tom. xxvi, p. 109.—His real name seems to have been Dorat.

[h] Bayle, art. *Baudouin.* Niceron, tom. xxviii, p. 255.

[i] Thuanus, tom. iv, p. 252. Boissardus, tom. iii, p. 44. Pope Blount, Censura Celebriorum Authorum, p. 551. Lond. 1690, fol. Bullart, Academie des Sciences, tom. ii, p. 184. J. Fabricii Hist. Bibliothecæ Fabricianæ, tom. iii, p. 465. Bezæ Poemata Varia, p. 100.

sius,[k] and some others. We then heard you discuss various subjects in a manner which tended
very much to our edification and delight.   To
these circumstances I now allude, for the purpose
of trying whether I can suggest to your recollection who I am : but whoever I am, assure yourself of my being a very warm admirer of your
virtue.   For several years, I lived with Philip
Melanchthon, and I then seemed to myself to
live happily.[l] Having after his decease been exposed to various chances, I have at length betaken
myself to these regions, as to a haven more secure
than any other that I could find, notwithstanding their having been agitated for many years by
the storms of civil war.   Even amidst these warlike tumults, the light of the gospel shines forth ;
to us is announced the doctrine which points out
the true path of salvation ; and while the Spaniards threaten destruction, the superstition which
infects their minds is expelled from the churches.
It was the prince of Orange, the great ornament
of our age, who commanded me to accompany
him to this place.   Supported by the vigour and
acuteness of his mind, he has hitherto maintained such a contest with the formidable power of
the Spaniards as has procured him immortal glory. After having under his auspices severed their

---

[k] Meursius, p. 196.   Andreas, p. 118.   Sweertius, p. 116.   Boissardus,
tom. ii, p. 3.   Bullart, tom. ii, p. 114.   Adami Vitæ Germanorum Medicorum, p. 407.

[l] Camerarii Vita Melanchthonis, p. 341.   Lipsiæ, 1666, 8vo.

tyrannical empire, these provinces have happily constituted various republics and churches, which being closely leagued together, have hitherto resisted the attacks of the enemy. The king of Spain having for several years endeavoured without success to overwhelm him by force, has at length resorted to arms which do not seem altogether suitable to so great a monarch; he has issued an edict in which he pronounces sentence of prescription, and endeavours, by proposing rewards, to impel assassins to accomplish his murder.[m] Since many falsehoods are there alleged against him, he has been advised by his friends to publish an apology, for the purpose of vindicating his innocence against the calumnies of the Spaniards. This apology I transmit to you.[n] During the winter, I have lived in these puddles of the Dutch, which nature seems rather to have intended for the habitation of frogs and eels than of men. This town is however very handsome; and at the distance of three hours journey stands Leyden, or *Lugdunum Batavorum*, as they now speak, the residence of Justus Lipsius, Janus Dousa the poet, and Donellus the French civilian,[o] men of learning and celebrity. From the

---

[m] See Dr Watson's Hist. of Philip II, vol. ii, p. 355, 416.

[n] Apologie ou Defense de tresillustre Prince, Guillaume par la Grace de Dieu Prince d'Orange. Delft, 1581, 4to. Pp. 104.—This apology, which was translated into various languages, is supposed to have been drawn up by Languet. (Niceron, tom. iii, p. 305.) Grotius ascribes it to Pierre de Villiers. Dr Watson mentions it as " one of the most precious monuments in history."

[o] Zeidleri Vitæ Professorum Juris in Acad. Altdorf. p. 63.

vicinity of this town, we have a prospect of Ro-
terdam; a prospect which not only recalls to my
memory the great Erasmus, in whom it glories
as a citizen, but also you: for I cannot sufficiently express my astonishment, that such horrid
places should produce men to whose talents neither our own age, nor that of our fathers or
grandfathers, has exhibited a parallel.   Erasmus
was invited to instruct the youth of Ferdinand
brother to the emperor Charles, but he declined
this employment.   I account you more fortunate
and virtuous in not having refused to aid your
country, when it called you to imbue the king's
tender mind with those precepts which being observed in his riper years, will secure the happiness and prosperity of himself, and of all those to
whom his dominion extends.   Daniel Rogers,
our common friend, who regards you with singular esteem, was four months ago seized by
the Germans serving under the king of Spain;
nor has the queen of England, who had sent him
upon an embassy to the emperor and some other
German princes, hitherto been able to obtain his
release.p   He was lately reported to have made
his escape through the assistance of some woman;
but we have heard of his being retaken and committed to more rigorous confinement.   I am extremely concerned that such an accident should
have befallen a worthy man, with whom I have

---

p Langueti Epistolæ ad Sydneium, p. 287.

cultivated a particular intimacy for many years. I am very anxious to learn, provided it should not be disagreeable to you, when you shall publish your Scotish history. From Melville, an excellent man, you may know the state of my affairs. Farewell."q

This letter must have been highly grateful to Buchanan's feelings : it expressed the warm admiration of a distinguished and truly honest man, whose applause was not rashly bestowed ; and it recalled to his memory some of the learned associates of his earlier years. Languet himself was equally conspicuous for his talents and for his virtues. He was the son of Germain Languet, governor of Viteaux in Burgundy; and was born at that place in the year 1518. He prosecuted his studies at Leipzig under the excellent Camerarius, for whom he maintained the highest regard. At an early period of life he had begun to entertain serious doubts respecting the doctrines of Popery ; and after having consulted the theologians of that city, he openly embraced the reformed religion. He studied the laws in the university of Padua, where he took the degree of doctor, and afterwards removed to that of Bologna. Prompted by the innate curiosity of a philosophical mind, he determined to visit several other countries, and he even penetrated so far as Lapland. His profession of heretical

q Buchanani Epistolæ, p. 31. *Clarissimo et Præstantissimo Viro, Domino Georgio Buchanano, domino suo et amico observando.*

opinions rendered his return to France less desirable : the best part of his life was spent among
the honest Germans ; and for a long time he exercised the charge of counsellor to the elector of
Saxony, by whom he was likewise employed in
different embassies.   It was apparently during
one of his embassies to the court of France, that
he became acquainted with Buchanan.   Being
suspected of having encouraged Gaspar Peucer
to publish a [r]Calvinistic exposition of the eucharist, he found it expedient to withdraw himself
from the elector's service ; and he now retired to
Holland, where he was intrusted by the prince
of Orange with the management of some important affairs. He died at Antwerp on the thirtieth
of September 1581.[s]   During his last moments,
he was very affectionately attended by the wife
of his excellent and accomplished friend Mornay ;
and he expressed an earnest wish that her illustrious spouse should, in the next work which he
published, commemorate their mutual attachment
and regard.[t]   This dying request Mornay executed in the preface to a Latin translation of his

[r] See Moshemii Institutiones Historiæ Ecclesiasticæ, p. 745. Helmsta-
dii, 1755, 4to.

[s] Beza has written his epitaph.   (*Poemata Varia*, p. 111.)

[t] Vie de Philippes de Mornay, Seigneur du Plessis Marlay, p. 57.
Leyde, 1647, 4to.   Vita Huberti Langueti, p. 151.   Halæ, 1700, 12mo.—
This account of Languet was written by Philibert de la Mare, a counsellor
of Dijon ; who appears from one of his epistles to N. Heinsius, to have
been occupied in its composition about the year 1660.   (Burmanni *Sylloge
Epistolarum*, tom. v, p. 662.)   It was edited by J. P. Ludovicus, or Lude-
wig ; who has not mentioned the name of the author.

treatise " De la Verité de la Religion Chres-
tienne."[u] To his natural endowments, Languet
had united much variegated and accurate knowledge; he was well· acquainted with books, and
still better with the dispositions and manners of
mankind. His long experience of public affairs
had rendered him a very able politician, without
diminishing the candour and probity of his mind.
His admirable sagacity was accompanied with
the utmost modesty and benevolence. His literary performances exhibit sufficient proofs of a
cultivated and elegant mind; and if his active
life had been devoted to letters, he might have
arrived at high celebrity as a polite writer.[x]

· A translation of this work, begun by Sir Philip Sidney, and at his re-
quest completed by Arthur Golding, was published in 1587. See Dr.
Zouch's " Memoirs of the Life and Writings of Sir Philip Sidney," p. 365.
York, 1808, 4to.

Among the great men who have cultivated poetry, Sidney enumerates " so
piercing wits as George Buchanan; so grave counsellors, as besides many,
but before all, that Hospital of France; than whom, I think, that realm never brought forth a more accomplished judgment, more firmly builded upon
virtue." (*Defence of Poesy*, p. 81, edit. Glasg. 1752, 8vo.)

x The following is a list of the principal works of which Languet is the
undisputed author. " Historica Descriptio susceptæ a Cæsarea Majestate
Executionis contra S. Rom. Imperii Rebelles." Sine loci indicio, 1566,
1569, 4to. Bremæ, 1735, 4to. The last edition was published by E. G.
Coldwey. " Epistolæ Politicæ et Historicæ ad Philippum Sydneium."
Franc. 1633, 12mo. " Epistolæ ad Joachimum Camerarium P. et Joachimum Camerarium F." Groningæ, 1646, 12mo. " Epistolæ Secretæ ad
Augustum Saxoniæ Ducem." Halæ, 1699, 4to. Of the epistles to Sir Philip Sidney a valuable edition was published by the late Lord Hailes. Edinb.
1776, 8vo.

Languet is the reputed author of other two publications. " De Furori-
bus Gallicis Vera et Simplex Narratio, Ernesto Varamundo Frisio auctore."
Edimburgi, 1573, 4to. " Vindiciæ contra Tyrannos: sive de Principis in
Populum, Populique in Principem, Legitima Potestate, Stephano Junio

Besides the continental scholars who have already been enumerated, there were various others who regarded Buchanan with particular affection: and whatever may be the notion of some, writers of the present age, certain it is that his character excited the respect, and even the veneration, of contemporaries highly distinguished by their moral virtues, and by their intellectual endowments. Daniel Rogers informed him that in Holland he had many zealous admirers, and, among the chief of them, Janus Dousa, and Philippe de Marnix de Ste. Aldegonde; men equally illustrious by the nobility of their birth, and by the superiority of their attainments. " The former of these," he subjoins, " I introduced to your acquaintance while you were residing in Paris; and I now at his particular request transmit to you a copy of his poems, which have recently been published. The latter, whose intrinsic merit has rendered him the favourite of a most excellent prince,[y] you also knew at Paris. When I lately returned from my embassy to that prince, he addressed to you the letter which accompanies this."[z] Janus Dousa was, like Buchanan, a poet and a states-

---

Bruto Celta auctore." *Edinburgi,* 1579, 8vo. His biographer contends that the first of these compositions could not proceed from the pen of Languet, because it betrays great ignorance of French affairs. (*Vita Huberti Langueti,* p. 68.) But this reasoning is fallacious; for if Languet had undertaken so hazardous a work, it must have been a principal object of his care to preserve the assumed character of a foreigner.

[y] The prince of Orange.

[z] Buchanani Epistolæ, p. 13.

man. He enjoyed some of the highest civil honours which his country could bestow; and having been appointed governor of Leyden, he defended it during a memorable siege with distinguished bravery. He was one of the first cura-
tors of the university founded in that city in
1575. His moral character seems to have been
blameless; and he held a very respectable station
among the scholars of that learned age. His merits are highly celebrated in the poems of Jos.
Scaliger, Grotius, Heinsius, and Baudius. His
reading, according to Meursius, was multifarious,
his memory almost incredible: he was the Varro
of Holland, and the common oracle of the university. Nor was he more conspicuous for his
learning than for his humanity, candour, urbanity, and modesty.[a] His amiable family was singularly attached to letters: five of his sons,
namely, Janus, Francis, George, Stephen, and
Theodore, were known as authors; and the Latin poems of the first, who died before he had
completed his twenty-sixth year, have been preferred by Grotius to those of his father.[b] Ste.
Aldegonde, another of Buchanan's friends, has
also been classed among the illustrious characters
of that age.[c] He was of French lineage, but was
a native of Brussels; and after having distinguish-

---

[a] Meursii Athenæ Batavæ, p. 89. Lugd. Bat. 1625, 4to.
[b] Grotius de Rebus Belgicis, p. 267. Amst. 1657, fol.
[c] Bayle, art. Sainte-Aldegonde.

P

ed himself as a politician and a man of letters, he
died at Leyden in 1598. He was well acquainted with jurisprudence and theology, with the
Hebrew, Greek, and Latin, as well as with several of the living languages. At the time of
his death, he was engaged in a Flemish translation of the scriptures. Grotius has repeatedly
mentioned him in very respectful terms; and his
epitaph was written by Heinsius in a strain of
high admiration.[d] These were individuals entitled to Buchanan's esteem, and he certainly was
not unworthy of theirs. In the same epistle,
which bears the date of August the thirtieth
1576, Rogers alludes to his friendship with another scholar of distinction. "Joannes Sturmius,
in a letter which I lately received, earnestly entreats me to send him some intelligence respecting you. I now forward a letter of his, which
however is of an old date." Sturmius was at the
period of that correspondence rector of the College of Strasburg; which under his auspices became the most flourishing in Germany. He was
equally distinguished by his skill in ancient literature, and by his familiarity with the political
affairs of his own times. Such was the benevolence of his disposition, that his house was regarded as a common asylum for exiles, and a retreat for poor strangers: those in particular who
had abandoned their country from motives of

[d] Heinsii Auriacus, sive Libertas Saucia: accedunt ejusdem Iambi, p. 121.
Lugd. Bat. 1602, 4to.

conscience, he entertained with unbounded generosity.[e] As an elegant writer, he has received very high commendation.[f] His intercourse with Buchanan and Ascham contributed to render his name familiar to the scholars of this island. Among the epigrams of Buchanan are three inscriptions for the portrait of Sturmius.[g]

Roger Ascham, the accomplished friend of Sturmius, must not be excluded from the present enumeration. Buchanan and he were personally acquainted,[h] and they have celebrated each other in their respective writings. One of Buchanan's epigrams is addressed " Ad Rogerum Aschamum Anglum, qui librum[i] cum honorifico elogio, et

* An account of Sturmius may be found in the curious work of Bayle, and in many other biographical collections. Lord Monboddo speaks of " one Sturmius, a German." *(Origin and Progress of Language*, vol. iii, p. 390.) His illustrations of the rhetorical productions of Aristotle, Hermogenes, and Cicero, might alone have recommended him to his lordship's acquaintance. Among other original works, he published treatises " De Periodis," " De Imitatione Oratoria," and " De Amissa Dicendi Genere." Beza has written his epitaph in terms of high respect. *(Poemata Varia*, p. 135.)

f Sambucus de Imitatione Ciceroniana, f. 47, b. Paris. 1561, 8vo. Bergerus de Naturali Pulchritudine Orationis. p. 707. Lipsiæ, 1720, 4to.

g Buchanani Icones, p. 91.   h Buchanani Epistolæ, p. 30.

i This book I have accidentally discovered in Williams's Library. It is a copy of the work of Fulvius Ursinus, entitled *Virgilius Collatione Scriptorum Græcorum Illustratus.* Antv. 1567, 8vo. The title-page is confronted with the subsequent inscription. " Rogerus Aschamus Georgio Buchanano, Anglus Scoto, amicus amico, hunc poetam omnis veteris memoriæ optimum, poetæ hujus nostræ ætatis optimæ, amoris ergo, dono dat : cum hoc monosticho :

" Φίλον φίλω μνημόσυνον εὐμενῶς ἔχω."

This inscription is dated at Hampton Court, on the twentieth of November 1568. Ascham died on the thirtieth of the following month. Buchanan's epigram, written with his own hand, occurs at the end of this precious volume.

sui amoris significatione miserat."[k] Ascham, the
preceptor, and afterwards the Latin secretary of
Queen Elizabeth, appears to have been a very
amiable, though not a very prudent character.
Notwithstanding the elegance of his taste, he
was immoderately addicted to the degrading
amusements of dice and cock-fighting ; and as he
was an honest man, his losses were so considerable, that he lived and died in poverty, or at
least not in affluence.[l] A German critic of various erudition pronounced him the only English-
man who had caught any considerable portion of
the genuine diction of antiquity.[m] The elegance
of his English productions is much superior to
the common standard of the age : his *Schole
Master* is equally valuable as a specimen of style,
and as a treatise of practical application. In the
composition of Latin verse he attained to less
proficiency.[n]

[k] Buchanani Epigram, lib. i, 39.

[l] Camdeni Annales, vol. i, p. 177, edit. Hearnii.

[m] Morhofius de Pura Dictione Latina, p. 41. Hanov. 1725, 8vo.—" In
Sexta gente," says Morhoff, " plures fuere, qui linguae Latinae studiosiores
fuere, quam in Anglia." I subjoin the testimony of his countryman Pufen-
dorf: " Est quoque Scotorum gens ingeniorum praestantissimerum ferax, et
maxime Latinae linguae cognitione illustrium. Nam cum in reliquis Eu-
ropae partibus bonarum artium disciplina barbarie oppressa jaceret, diu in
Scotia viguit: quippe quae reliquis gentibus complures doctores et magistros
eruditione conspicuos suppeditavit dicam an commodavit." (*Introductio ad
Historiam Europaeam*, p. 201.)

[n] The Latin epistles and poems of Ascham were published by Dr Edward Grant, master of Westminster school, who has prefixed an account
of the author's life. Lond. 1576, 8vo. The collection has frequently been
reprinted. The best edition of the epistles is that of Mr Elstob, who has
however omitted Ascham's verses. Oxon. 1703, 8vo. Dr Johnson's life

Walter Haddon, LL. D. was another English scholar of reputation with whom Buchanan seems to have maintained a familiar intercourse. To that learned man he addressed the first of his iambics, when he was verging towards the sixtieth year of his age. Haddon, who descended from a genteel family in Buckinghamshire, had contributed with Ascham, Cheke, and Smith, to reform the university of Cambridge from monkish barbarism. He was master of Trinity Hall at Cambridge, and afterwards president of Magdalen College at Oxford; and on the accession of Elizabeth, he was appointed one of the masters of the court of requests.[o] The style of his Latin prose is not inelegant; but he was much less successful as a versifier.—Dr Jewel, the famous bishop of Salisbury, has also been enumerated among the learned men with whom he maintained a literary correspondence;[p] but this sugges-

---

of Ascham was prefixed to the collection of his English works, published by James Bennet. Lond. 1761, 4to. One of his productions has escaped the researches of this biographer. It is entitled "Apologia doctissimi viri Rogeri Aschami, Angli, pro Cœna Dominica, contra Missam et ejus Præstigias." Lond. 1577, 8vo. This work was likewise edited by Dr Grant.

[o] Biographia Britannica, vol. iv, p. 2458.—The court of requests was instituted about the ninth of Henry VII, and was dissolved by statute 16 Car. I. c. 10. Of this court, which professed to distribute justice gratuitously, the lord privy seal was chief judge; and was assisted by the two masters of the requests, who in general seem to have been civilians. "Therein for the most part," says Sir Thomas Ridley, "are handled poor miserable persons causes, as widdows and orphans, and other distressed people, whose cases wholly rely on piety and conscience." (View of the Civile and Ecclesiasticall Law, p. 395, 4th edit. Oxford, 1675, 8vo.)

[p] Sibbaldi Comment. in Vitam Buchanani, p. 60.—One of Buchanan's English friends was Edward Bulkeley, D. D. a clergyman of Shrewsbury.

tion seems merely to have originated from Buchanan's having celebrated him in two funeral
inscriptions. These inscriptions were first published by his biographer Dr Humphrey; who
has exhibited the similar contributions of many
other scholars.[q]

Sir Anthony Cooke and his learned daughters
are highly extolled in the poems of Buchanan.[r]
Cooke had been associated with Sir John Cheke
as one of the preceptors of Edward the sixth;[s]
and his virtue and erudition entitled him to so
important a trust. With this most accomplished
family,[t] Buchanan perhaps became acquainted
during his political visit to London in the year
1568. Mildred Cooke, the eldest daughter, was
the second wife of the famous Lord Burleigh.[u]

(Buchanani *Epistolæ*, p. 30.) The Bodleian catalogue ascribes to him two
controversial works in English. I have a curious collection edited by Dr
Bulkeley under the title of *Speculum Ecclesiæ Pontificiæ*. Lond. 1606, 8vo.
The principal tract in the volume is that of Nicolaus Clemangis *De Corrup-
to Ecclesiæ Statu*.

[q] Humfredi Vita Joannis Juelli. Lond. 1573, 4to.—Dr Laurence
Humphrey is the author of several works. The most remarkable of them is
entitled *Interpretatio Linguarum: seu de Ratione Convertendi et Explicandi
Autores tam Sacros quam Profanos, libri tres*. Basil. 1559, 8vo. This production displays considerable learning, but not much precision of thought, or
elegance of diction. He was regius professor of divinity, and president of
Magdalen College, at Oxford: he likewise enjoyed the deanery of Gloucester,
and afterwards that of Winchester. His portrait may be found in Holland's
Herωlogia Anglica, p. 207. Lond. 1620, fol.

[r] Buchanani Epigram. lib. i, 53, lib. iii, 12, 13, 14, 17.

[s] Strype's Life of Sir John Cheke, p. 28. Lond. 1705, 8vo.

[t] Ballard's Memoirs of Learned Ladies, p. 182, 198, 194. Oxford,
1752, 4to.

[u] " Praetereo filias," says Dr Humphrey, " Antonii Coki equestris ordi-
nis dignitate clari, linguarum ornamentis clarioris, religionis fideique laude

Buchanan congratulates her on having produced
a poem more precious than gold; and her proficiency in the Greek language was so considerable, that she translated a work of Chrysostom
into English.[x]   The poet, who seems to have
been repeatedly indebted to her munificence, has
addressed her in several epigrams.   Anne the
second daughter, who was married to Sir Nicholas
Bacon, is likewise celebrated for her uncommon
skill in the classical languages.[y]   She translated
from the Italian twenty-five sermons of Ochino,
and from the Latin the famous apology of Bishop Jewel for the church of England.   Both her
versions were published.   When she communicated her manuscript to the learned prelate, she
accompanied it with an epistle written in Greek.[z]
But it is her highest praise that she was the mo-

---

clarissimi, Joannis Cheki in Edovardi sexti pueritia informanda collegæ:
quæ parentem suum vere referunt, Latinis Græcisque literis eruditæ, quarum
Gulielmi Cicilii electissimi viri uxor Græcam linguam perbene exacteque
callere dicitur." *(De Ratione Interpretandi,* præf.)   The father is mentioned by Sleidan, *De Statu Religionis et Reipublicæ,* f. 461, edit. Argent. 1557,
8vo.   An epistle to Cooke from Cœlius Secundus Curio is præfixed to the
work of his colleague Cheke, *De Pronunciatione Græcæ potissimum Linguæ.*
Basil. 1555, 8vo.   See also Aschami *Epistolæ,* p. 395, 414, 418, 427, 439,
edit. Elstob, Fuller's *Hist. of the Worthies of England,* p. 327, and Tan-
neri *Bibliotheca Britannico-Hibernica,* p. 197.   Lond. 1748, fol.   Cooke is
by some writers supposed to be the author of a work published at Strasburg,
under the title of " Diallacticon dè Veritate, Natura, atque Substantia Corporis et Sanguinis Christi in Eucharistia." (Placcii *Theatrum Anon. et
Pseudon.* tom. i, p. 107.   Blackburne's *Memoirs of Thomas Hollis, Esq.*
vol. ii, p. 565.)

   [x] Peck's *Desiderata Curiosa,* vol. i, p. 7.
   [y] Caius de Libris suis, f. 12, b.   Lond. 1570, 8vo.
   [z] Strype's *Life of Archbishop Parker,* p. 178.   Lond. 1711, fol.

ther and early instructer of the great Lord
Bacon.

Daniel Rogers, whom the English court employed in various embassies, appears to have been
one of Buchanan's particular friends. A greater
number of the letters which passed between
them has been preserved, than of those between
Buchanan and any other of his correspondents.
He was the son of John Rogers, a Protestant
clergyman, and of Adriana de Weyden. His father had conducted him to Frankfort at an early
age; and he there obtained a familiar acquaintance with the classical languages. Returning to
his native country at the commencement of Queen
Elizabeth's reign, he prosecuted his studies at
Oxford. He married the daughter of Nicasius
Yetswiert, French secretary to the queen, and
one of the clerks of the signet; and by means of
this connection was introduced to the notice of
the court. He was appointed one of the clerks
of the privy council.[a] Rogers is represented as
a man of an excellent character, and he was undoubtedly possessed of talents and learning.[b]

[a] Wood's Athenæ Oxonienses, vol. i, col. 199.

[b] Three Latin poems by Rogers are inserted in Ortelius's *Theatrum Orbis Terrarum*, edit. Antv. 1579, fol.: nine in Latin, and one in Greek, are
published in Humphrey's *Vita Joannis Juelli*. Many of his occasional
verses occur in other books. See Dousæ *Poemata*, p. 470, *Epistolæ Selectiores*, p. 667, Meursii *Athenæ Batavæ*, p. 28, Hearnii *Præf. in Camdeni Annales*, p. cxxxix, and Lundorpius's continuation of Sleidan, tom. ii.
" De veterum Britannorum moribus et legibus," says Ortelius, " scripsit
commentarium Daniel Rogersius cognatus meus. Idem de Romanorum in
Britannia imperio præ manibus habet." (*Theatrum Orbis Terrarum*, f. 10.)

Sir Thomas Randolph, LL. D. whose name is familiar to the readers of Scotish history, was also a warm admirer of Buchanan's genius and virtues. He was the son of Avery Randolph of Badlesmere in Kent; prosecuted his studies in Christ Church, Oxford; and about the period when he took the degree of bachelor of laws, was made a notary public. In 1549, he was appointed principal of Broadgate Hall, which was afterwards transformed into Pembroke College; and he retained the office till 1553. In the reign of Elizabeth, he was employed in various embassies to Scotland, France, and Russia,[c] Nor were his faithful services unrewarded; he received the honour of knighthood, and enjoyed the office of chamberlain of the exchequer, and that of comptroller general of the post-horses.[d] Of the epistles of Buchanan and Randolph, only two have been preserved. Buchanan's is written in the Scotish,[e]

In the Cotton Library is a quarto MS. entitled " Danielis Rogersii Angli Antiquæ Britanniæ Observationes [manu propria]." At p. 89, occurs a a division of the work, entitled " Politia, seu Documenta Administrationis Romanæ in Britanniis." These observations, which merely consist of digest-ed extracts from ancient and modern writers, were apparently never intended for publication. Rogers was a very intimate friend of Janus Dousa; who has dedicated to him his Præcidanea pro Satyrico Petronii Arbitri, and addressed him in several of his poems. (Dousæ Poemata, p. 5, 18, 174, 185, 604.)

[e] Some papers of Randolph may be found in Hakluyt's Voyages and Discoveries of the English Nation, p. 399. Lond. 1589, fol. Buchanan has addressed to him his verses on the character of a good king, and has written the epitaph of his lady, Anne Walsingham. (Icones, p. 89. Miscell. xxvii.)

[d] Wood's Athenæ Oxonienses, vol. i, col. 195.

[e] Buchanan's letter, which occurs in Mr Ruddiman's preface, p. xix,

and Randolph's in the English language. In the collection there is a French letter of Buchanan, addressed to M. de Sigongues, who had been governor, while Buchanan was preceptor, to Timoleon de Cossé,[f] and who was afterwards governor of the city and castle of Dieppe. These two are the only epistles of his which are not written in Latin. The correspondence of Buchanan[g] forms a very inconsiderable volume ; nor can it be sufficiently regretted that there is little probability of its ever being augmented.

· Though so small a portion of his correspondence has been preserved, it is certain that his

is not unworthy of attention. " To Maister Randolf Squier, Maister of Postes to the Quenes Grace of Ingland. Maister, I haif resavit diverse letters frome you, and yit I have ansourit to naine of thayme : of the quhylke albeit I haif mony excusis, as age, forgetfulnes, besines, and disease, yit I wyl use nane as now, eccept my sweirness and your gentilnes ; and geif ye thynk nane of theise sufficient, content you with ane confession of the falt w'out fear of punition to follow on my onkindnes. As for the present, I am occupiit in writyng of our historie, being assurit to content few, and to displease mony tharthrow. As to the end of it, yf ye gett it not or thys winter be passit, lippin not for it, nor nane other writyngs from me. The rest of my occupation is wyth the gout, quhilk haldis me besy both day and ny'. And quhair ye say ye haif not lang to lyif, I traist to God to go before yow, albeit I be on fut, and ye ryd *the post :* praying you als not to *dispost* my hoste at Newwerk, Jone of Kelsterne. Thys I pray you, partly for his awyne sake, quhame I tho' ane gud fellow, and partly at request of syk as I dar no' refuse. And thus I tak my leif shortly at you now, and my lang leif quhen God pleasis, committing you to the protection of the almy'ty. At Sterling xxv. day of August, 1577.
          Yours to command w' service,

                                        G. BUCHANAN."

f Brantome, Vies des Hommes Illustres, tom. iii, p. 409.

g His correspondence was originally collected by Dr Oliphant, and published under the title of " Georgii Buchanani Scoti ad Viros sui seculi Clarissimos, eorumque ad eundem, Epistolæ." Lond. 1711, 8vo.

intercourse with learned foreigners was very extensive : and he may be supposed to have been acquainted with most of the remarkable scholars of whom his country could then boast, with the exception however of such as were separated from him by theological and political prejudices. The celebrated John Knox, who had likewise been a pupil of Mair at St Andrews,[h] seems to have belonged to the number of his friends.[i] The talents of Knox, if we may judge from their effects, were powerful and commanding: his share of acquired knowledge was far from being inconsiderable ; his eloquence was vehement and impressive ; his vernacular style is copious, forcible, and, for the age in which he lived, not inelegant.[k] He died at Edinburgh in the month

[h] See Dr M'Crie's Life of Knox, vol. i, p. 7.

[i] Buchanani Epistolæ, p. 8. Bezæ Epistolæ Theologicæ, p. 336.

[k] King James, if we may rely on John Barclay, regarded Knox as a *warlock.* " Ut de cæteris sileam, Knoxium (quem Beza Apostolum Scotiæ vocat) non impium modo fuisse, sed magum, serenissimus Britanniarum rex sæpe magnis argumentis asseruit." (*Parænesis ad Sectarios,* p. 38. Romæ, 1617, 8vo.) Calvin and Beza seem to have regarded him in a very different light. Two epistles from Calvin to Knox, and one from Knox to Calvin, are preserved. (Calvini *Epistolæ,* p. 460, 461, 503, edit. Lausan. 1576, 8vo.) Two of the epistles of Beza are addressed to this Scotish apostle. (Bezæ *Epistolæ Theologicæ,* p. 333, 344. Genevæ, 1573, 8vo.) One of them opens in an elegant strain of affection. " Etsi tanto terrarum et maris ipsius intervallo disjuncti corporibus sumus, mi Cnoxe, tamen minime dubito quin inter nos semper viguerit et ad extremum vigeat summa illa animorum conjunctio, unius ejusdemque spiritus fideique vinculo sancita." A high eulogium of Knox occurs in Beza's *Icones Virorum Illustrium,* sig. Ee. iij. Genevæ, 1580, 4to. Of this work a French version was published under the title of *Les Vrais Pourtraits des Hommes Illustres en Piété et Doctrine.* Geneve, 1581, 4to. In the translation, which Senebier ascribes to Simon Goulart, are inserted original verses on Knox, Patrick Hamilton,

of November 1572, and the Papists immediately began to revile his memory in a most indecent manner. Archibald Hamilton, one of their most bitter revilers, attempted to involve Buchanan in the same infamy.[1] His work was formally refuted by Thomas Smeton, principal of the university of Glasgow; who has vindicated the character of Knox with great zeal and success. Smeton has incidentally extolled Buchanan as the glory of the age, as a miracle of erudition, as the prince and parent of all learning and of all the learned, as an exemplar of ancient virtue and piety, as an ornament to Scotland and to human nature.[m]

Andrew Melvin, principal of New College, St Andrews, is entitled to a place among the accomplished friends of Buchanan. He was himself a Latin poet of no mean character; and he composed many verses in celebration of Buchanan, whom he addresses as his preceptor, and the parent of the Muses. Melvin was a stern and undaunted presbyter. When cited before the king and privy council, to answer to the charge of sedition, he deported himself with a degree of

Adam Wallace, and Alexander Aless. A remarkable passage respecting Knox occurs in Milton's *Areopagitica.* Lond. 1644, 4to.

[1] Hamiltonius de Confusione Calvinianæ Sectæ apud Scotos. Paris. 1577, 8vo.

[m] Smetonii ad Virulentum Hamiltonii Dialogum Orthodoxa Responsio, p. 44, 89. Edinb. 1579, 4to.—Hamilton replied in a work entitled "Calvinianæ Confusionis Demonstratio, contra maledicam Ministrorum Scotiæ Responsionem." Paris. 1581, 8vo.

resolution which bordered on extreme insolence.[n]
It was his duty to teach theology to the students
of his college; but he was apt to discuss some of
the great topics of political science, with a freedom of sentiment which he had perhaps imbibed
from his illustrious friend. It was alleged by
Archbishop Spotswood that his pupils bestowed
more attention on Buchanan's political dialogue,
than on Calvin's theological institution.[o] This
poetical and political divine was a man of powerful talents; profoundly skilled in the Hebrew,
Greek, and Latin languages.[p] But his fervent admiration of a particular form of ecclesiastical polity betrayed him into considerable excesses.
Buchanan seems to have entertained no mean
opinion of his literature; and Melvin's attachment to his preceptor was filial and enthusiastic.[q]
One of Melvin's literary friends has related an
anecdote which exhibits the character of the illustrious historian in a very favourable point of
view. Thomas Jack, who for some time was a

[n] Stuart's Hist. of Scotland, vol. ii, p. 258.

[o] Spotswood, Refutatio Libelli de Regimine Ecclesiæ Scoticanæ, p. 67,
Lond. 1620, 8vo.

[p] Archbishop Spotswood, who cannot be suspected of any undue prejudice
in his favour, speaks of him in the following terms. " Redit in patriam
Andreas Melvinus bonis literis excultus, et trium linguarum, quarum eo se-
culo ignorantia, illi famam et tantum non admirationem apud omnes peperit,
callentissimus." (Ibid. p. 31.)

[q] I have much pleasure in announcing that a copious and elaborate life of
Andrew Melvin will soon be published by the Rev. Dr M'Crie; to whom,
I must also add, I am indebted for the most obliging communication of va-
rious notices.

schoolmaster at Glasgow, informs us that he waited upon Buchanan to request he would re-vise the manuscript of his *Onomasticon Poeticum*;ᵠ and that he then experienced his friendly dispo-sition, as he had frequently done on former occa-sions. " I found him," says Jack, " in the royal palace of Stirling, diligently engaged in writing his history of Scotland. He was so far from be-ing displeased with my interruption, that he cheerfully took my work into his hands, and af-ter continuing to read two or three pages of it, he collected together his own papers, which were scattered on the table, and said, I will desist from my undertaking till I have done what you wish. This promise he accurately performed; and, with-in a few days, gave me a paper written with his own hand, and containing such corrections as he thought necessary."ʳ

Buchanan's benevolence and urbanity, united to his unrivalled intelligence, seem to have ren-dered his familiarity highly grateful to ingenu-ous and aspiring youth ; and it unquestionably

---

ᵠ Onomasticon Poeticum : sive Propriorum quibus in suis Monumentis usi sunt Veteres Poetæ, Brevis Descriptio Poetica, Thoma Jacchæo Cale-donio authore. Edinburgi, excudebat Robertus Waldegrave, 1592, 4to.

ʳ " Cujus amicum in me animum," says Jack in his dedication, " cum sæpius ante, tum eo præsertim tempore expertus sum. Rerum enim Scoti-carum historiam Sterlini in regiis ædibus diligenter scribentem interpellavi. Tantum abest, meam interpellationem ægre tulerit, ut libellum hilariter amplexus, duabus aut tribus paginis sine intermissione perlectis, ac omnibus sui operis chartis, quæ tunc temporis dissolutæ in mensa jacebant, illico col-lectis : ego meis, inquit, desistam cœptis, donec quod tu velis, tibi effectum reddam."

afforded him a generous pleasure to mark and
accelerate the progress of the tender mind.[1]
The premature death of Alexander Cockburn he
has commemorated in terms so remote from vulgar regret, that it would be unpardonable in his
biographer to leave unnoticed what was apparently so interesting to his feelings.

> Omnia quæ longa indulget mortalibus ætas,
>   Hæc tibi, Alexander, prima juventa dedit.,
> Cum genere et forma generoso stemmate digna,
>   Ingenium velox, ingenuumque animum.
> Excoluit virtus animum, ingeniumque Camœnæ
>   Successu, studio, consilioque pari.
> His ducibus primum peragrata Britannia, deinde
>   Gallia ad armiferos qua patet Helvetios:[2]
> Doctus ibi linguas, quas Roma, Sion, et Athenæ,
>   Quas cum Germano Gallia docta sonat.
> Te licet in prima rapuerunt fata juventa,
>   Non immaturo funere raptus obis.
> Omnibus officiis vitæ qui functus obivit,
>   Non fas est vitæ de brevitate queri.[3]

Not satisfied with this enviable tribute, he has

---

[1] " Erat enim vir ille," says Alexander Yule, who in his youth had been
personally acquainted with Buchanan, " ea ingenii dexteritate, ut cum
pueris repuerascere, et ad omnes omnium ætatum usus modeste et sapienter
sese accommodare et posset et vellet." (Julii Ecphrasis Paraphraseos G.
Buchanani in Psalmos Davidis, epist. nunc. Lond. 1620, 8vo.)

[2] On the subject of closing a pentameter verse with a polysyllable, consult
the younger Burman's preface to Lotichii Poemata Omnia. Amst. 1754,
2 tom. 4to.

[3] Buchanani Epigram. lib. ii, 26.—In this conclusion there is an obvious
coincidence with a verse of Lotichius, Elegiarum lib. iv, el. v, v. 64.

> Si tamen exactæ considero facta juventæ,
>   Nil potes hac vitæ de brevitate queri.

anxiously devoted another elegant little poem to
the commemoration of talents and virtues, which
might otherwise have remained without a lasting
memorial.ˣ Some of his expressions seem to elevate this youthful prodigy to a competition with
the admirable Crichton ; nor can it fail to excite the most poignant regret, that intellectual
splendour capable of attracting the admiration of
Buchanan, should thus have been extinguished
in its earliest dawn. Alexander Cockburn, for
the subject cannot be dismissed but with reluctance, is said to have died in the year 1572, at
the age of twenty-five.ʸ Dempster, the suspicious
author of this report, likewise affirms that he
composed various works, and that some of them
had fallen under his own inspection. Hume of
Godscroft commemorates the premature death of
an Alexander Cockburn, son to Cockburn of
Langton.ᶻ

The admirable Crichton is mentioned by Aldus
Manutius as a pupil of Buchanan ; but the history of this extraordinary character is involved
in so much obscurity, that it is not easy to verify
the assertion. Buchanan must have resigned his
office at St Andrews when Crichton was only
about ten years of age. But from the dedication

ˣ Buchanani Miscell. xii.
ʸ Dempsteri Hist. Ecclesiast. Gent. Scotor. p. 183.
ᶻ Humii Poemata, p. 110. Paris. 1639, 8vo.—Daniel Rogers mentions a Captain Cockburn, who seems to have been one of Buchanan's
friends. See the epistle inserted in Mr Ruddiman's preface, p. xx.

of Manutius's edition of Cicero's *Paradoxa*, it may be inferred that Crichton had induced his Italian friend to believe he was educated along with the young king of Scotland;[a] nor does this seem to have been the only misrepresentation into which his vanity betrayed him.

The infirmities of age, and a multiplicity of engagements, did not render Buchanan unmindful of his literary character. Having prepared his tragedy of *Baptistes* for the press, he dedicated it to the young king in the year 1576. The dedication, dated at Stirling on the first of November, is characterized by a manly freedom of sentiment which has never been surpassed on a similar occasion. " Since I have been employed in your education, all my compositions approach you with familiarity, salute you, converse with you, and repose under the shade of your protection; and, for many reasons, this my *Baptistes* seems more confidently to demand the patronage of your name. Although an abortive one, it is yet my first production; and it called the youth from the vulgar strains of dramatic poetry to the imitation of antiquity, and strenuously endeavoured to excite in their minds a regard for piety, which at that time was almost every where banished. But this circumstance may seem to bear a more peculiar reference to you, that it clearly

---

[a] Manutius's dedication to Crichton, together with four Latin poems by the latter, may be found in Grævius's edition of Cicero *De Officiis*, &c. Amst. 1688, 8vo. See Appendix, No. x.

Q

discloses the punishment of tyrants, and the misery which awaits them even when their prosperity seems at the height. That you should now acquire such knowledge, I consider as not only expedient but even necessary ; in order that you may early begin to hate what you ought ever to shun. I therefore wish this work to remain as a witness to posterity, that, if impelled by evil counsellors, or suffering the licentiousness of royalty to prevail over a virtuous education, you should hereafter be guilty of any improper conduct, the fault may be imputed, not to your preceptors, but to you, who have not obeyed their salutary admonitions. May the Lord grant a more favourable issue ; and, according to the expression of Sallust, convert your virtuous habits into nature. This is what I, along with many others, both hope and wish. Farewell."

The precarious state of Buchanan's health did not permit him to complete his poem *De Sphæra*, which he had begun several years before. In the month of September 1576, he informed Tycho Brahe that during the two preceding years he had been so severely afflicted with violent diseases, as hardly to be able to devote a single hour to composition ; so that besides other projects of less moment, he was compelled to relinquish his astronomical poem in an unfinished state, and even to abandon the hope of renewing his poetical efforts.[b] At the distance of three years,

---

[b] Buchanani Epistolæ, p. 14.

he again alludes to the frustration of this plan with some degree of regret.[c] A fragment of the poem was inserted in an edition of his poetical works which appeared after his decease;[d] and in 1586, as much as the author had completed was published by Robert Howie, who was then a student at Herborn, and was afterwards principal of New College, St Andrews.[e] Another edition was published in the course of the following year by his learned preceptor Pincier, who has added supplements to the fourth and fifth books.[f] The

[c] " Astronomica," says Buchanan, " non tam abjeci, quam extorqueri invitus tuli ; neque enim aut nunc libet nugari, aut si maxime vellem, per ætatem licet." (*Epistolæ*, p. 25.)

[d] Genevæ, 1584, 8vo.

[e] Sphæra Georgii Buchanani Scoti, Poetarum nostri seculi facile Principis, quinque libris descripta : nunc primum e tenebris eruta et luce donata. Herbornæ, apud Christophorum Corvinum, 1586, 8vo.—The dedication to John count of Nassau is subscribed Robertus Hovæus Scotus. Howie is the author of a work entitled " De Reconciliatione Hominis cum Deo, seu de Humani Generis Redemptione, Tractatio Theologica." Basil. 1591, 4to. His name occurs in Tomasini's *Parnassus Euganeus, sive de Scriptoribus ac Literatis hujus Ævi Claris*, p. 8. Patavii, 1647, 4to.

[f] Sphæra, a Georgio Buchanano Scoto, Poetarum nostri seculi facile Principe, quinque libris descripta, multisque in locis ex collatione aliorum exemplorum integritati restituta : cui accessere libri quarti et quinti quos autor non absolverat, Supplementa, autore Johanne Pinciero, Aulæ Dillebergensis Medico. Herbornæ, 1587, 8vo.—Pincier published a corrected edition of his arguments and supplements, at the end of his *Parerga Otii Marpurgensis Philologica*. Herb. 1617, 8vo. This philological work includes many occasional remarks on Buchanan. He is the author of several other publications, and among the rest, of a curious poem which bears the title of " Otium Marpurgense, in sex libros digestum : quibus fabrica corporis humani, insertis passim disputationibus, historiis, et fabulis ad rem pertinentibus, facili ac perspicuo carmine describitur." Herb. 1614, 8vo. In one of the epigrams prefixed, he records some particulars of his own history. Pincier was born at Wettera in the year 1556, but the time of his

same deficiencies were afterwards supplied by
Adam King, a Scotish advocate, who has composed several other poems in the Latin language.[g]
Though the efforts of these two poets are not
despicable, they evidently serve as a foil to the
more happy effusions of Buchanan. That he
did not himself complete so remarkable a production, must excite considerable regret. To invest so intricate a subject with the precision of
science, and with the allurements of poetry, certainly required talents of no ordinary denomination. His versification is elegant and lofty. In
illustrating some of the abstruser parts of astronomy, he evinces a happy dexterity peculiar to
himself. His acquaintance with the dogmas of
ancient philosophy was familiar; and if he has
occasionally been betrayed into a radical error in
science, it must be remembered that he wrote in

death is uncertain. (Freheri *Theatrum Virorum Eruditione Clarorum*,
p. 1305.)

[g] King likewise illustrated this poem of Buchanan, with a commentary,
which Mr Ruddiman has characterized as " luculentum admodum om-
nigenæque eruditionis copia refertum." Though he certainly intended it
for publication, it never made its appearance; but the manuscript is preserved in the library of the university of Edinburgh. His poems occur in
the *Deliciæ Poetarum Scotorum*, tom. ii, p. 201. He published a Scotish
translation of the catechism of Canisius. Dempster, who imputes to him
other works, has extolled him as a miracle of learning. " Adamus Regius,
vulgo *Kyng*, Edimburgensis, bonis artibus instructissimus, ad miraculum
usque ductus, maximo auditorum concursu philosophiam Parisiis docuit, et
[disciplinas] mathematicas, in quibus facile eo sæculo princeps habebatur."
(*Hist. Ecclesiast. Gent. Scotor.* p. 576.) David Chalmers denominates him
" vir doctissimus, *historiographus* clarissimus." (*De Scotorum Fortitudine,*
p. 46.)

the sixteenth century. When he maintains that the earth does not revolve round the sun, he supports his opinion by arguments which must at least be allowed to be poetical.[h] The difficulties of his subject, which might seem almost insuperable, afforded him an opportunity of displaying that singular combination of talents for which he was so preëminent; but he might easily have selected some theme of a more popular nature. Poetical astronomy cannot hope to allure a very numerous class of readers. The principal object indeed of poetry is not profit but pleasure:[i] if however a scientific poem be intended for solid instruction, the endless progression of human knowledge will speedily abridge the importance of almost every precept which it may contain; and when the scientific part is completely obsolete, the poetry will no longer be found attractive. Aratus, Germanicus,[k] and Manilius, among the ancient poets, had applied their talents to the embellishment of astronomical subjects; and perhaps the most remarkable of Buchanan's successors in the same department is Boscovich, who has written a Latin poem on the solar and lunar eclipses. Manilius, from whom the Scotish author apparently derived considerable aid, has evinced an elegant and copious fancy; but, in the judgment of Sca-

[h] Buchanan's reasoning on this subject is cursorily noticed by La Lande, *Astronomie*, tom. i, p. 402.

[i] See Le Clerc, *Parrhasiana*, tom. i, p. 55, and Dr Beattie's *Essay on Poetry and Musick*, p. 9.

[k] See Grotii *Syntagma Arateorum*. Lugd. Bat. 1600, 4to.

liger, his science was not sufficiently accurate or
profound.[1] Some of the digressive parts of his
work are extremely beautiful, but the whole cannot be perused with uninterrupted pleasure. Buchanan's poem, though less generally relished
than most of his other productions, contains passages of superlative excellence: without anxious
research, 'the opening of the fifth book may be
particularized as an adequate specimen. The
hexameters of this poet are not the least perfect
of his various measures. His pauses are distributed with eminent skill; his verses are sonor-
ous and magnificent. The constitution of his
mind did not lead him to entertain the sole ambition of transfusing the characteristic beauties
of some particular poet. Of the majestic suavity
of Virgil he has caught no inconsiderable portion; but his genius was original,[m] and the Vir-
gilian graces would often have been incompatible
with the subjects which he had chosen. He was
familiarly acquainted with every poet of the
purer ages of antiquity; and had even profited
by the perusal of Claudian, whom he mentions
in terms of high respect.[n] Claudian, who appeared long after the decline of Roman literature,
succeeded in reviving it with some degree of an-

[1] Jos. Scaliger ad Manilium, p. 10, edit. Lugd. Bat. 1600, 4to.

[m] Dr Johnson was of opinion that " Buchanan has fewer centos than any
modern Latin poet. He not only had great knowledge of the Latin language, but was a great poetical genius." (Boswell's *Life of Johnson*, vol. ii,
p. 88.)

[n] Buchanan. de Jure Regni apud Scotos, p. 18.

cient splendour; and although his writings partake of the general deterioration of the age, yet his genius was elegant, vivid, and lofty.

Notwithstanding the precarious state of his health, and the number of his avocations, Buchanan had found leisure to compose a most profound and masterly compendium of political philosophy.° Its professed subject are the rights of the crown of Scotland; but the work comprehends a subtile and eloquent delineation of the general principles of government. The origin of this production is sufficiently detailed in the author's manly dedication to his royal pupil. " Several years ago," says Buchanan, " when our af-

° De Jure Regni apud Scotos Dialogus, authore Georgio Buchanano Scoto. Edinburgi, apud Johannem Reissum pro Henrico Charteris. Cum privilegio regali. 1579, 4to.—The second edition has the following title. " De Jure Regni apud Scotos Dialogus, auctore Georgio Buchanano Scoto. Ad Jacobum VI. Scotorum Regem. Editio secunda. M.D.LXXX. Ad exemplar Joannis Rossei Edinburgi, cum privilegio Scotorum Regis." 8vo. The dialogue was printed in 4to during the same year. There are several other editions in a separate form. Edinb. 1581, 4to. Glasg. 1750, 12mo. Lond. 1765, 8vo. This work is printed with all the editions of the history except the first. It has repeatedly been translated into English. In the archiepiscopal library at Lambeth, the Rev. Mr Todd pointed out to me a MS. version which bears the following title. " A Dialogue made by George Buchanan, Sobottishman, of the Prerogative and Right of the Kingly Governement in Scotlande." It has this colophon: " Finis, Maii 4, 1607. Labour no burden to love." (No. 509.) In the year 1680, a translation was published in 12mo, but the place of printing is concealed. The dialogue has been exhibited in an English dress at several other times. Lond. 1689, 4to. Edinb. 1691, 8vo. Lond. 1721, 8vo. The last translation that appeared was executed by Mr Macfarlan. Lond. 1799, 8vo. To this work Buchanan has subjoined a poetical extract, under the title of " Rex Stoicus, ex Seneca." In a recent publication, it is alleged that he only borrowed the sentiments from the ancient writer, and exhibited them in their present dress. But the whole passage occurs in Seneca's *Thyestes*, v. 343,

fairs were in a most turbulent condition, I composed a dialogue on the prerogatives of the Scotish crown; in which I endeavoured to explain
from their very cradle, if I may adopt that expression, the reciprocal rights and privileges of
kings and their subjects. Although the work
seemed to be of some immediate utility, by si-
lencing certain individuals who with importunate
clamours rather inveighed against the existing
state of things, than examined what was conformable to the standard of reason, yet in consequence of returning tranquillity, I willingly consecrated my arms to public concord. But having
lately met with this disputation among my papers, and supposed it to contain many precepts
necessary to your tender age (especially as it is
so conspicuously elevated in the scale of human
affairs), I have deemed its publication expedient,
that it may at once testify my zeal for your service, and admonish you of your duty to the community. Many circumstances tend to convince
me that my present exertions will not prove
fruitless; especially your age, yet uncorrupted by
perverse opinions; a disposition above your years,
spontaneously urging you to every noble pursuit;
a facility in obeying not only your preceptors,
but all prudent monitors; a judgment and dexterity in disquisition, which prevent you from
paying much regard to authority, unless it be
confirmed by solid argument. I likewise perceive that by a kind of natural instinct you so

abhor flattery, the nurse of tyranny, and the most grievous pest of a legitimate monarchy, that you as heartily hate the courtly solecisms and barbarisms as they are relished and affected by those who consider themselves as the arbiters of every elegance, and who, by way of seasoning their conversation, are perpetually sprinkling it with majesties, lordships, excellencies, and, if possible, with other expressions still more nauseous. Although the bounty of nature and the instruction of your governors may at present secure you against this error, yet am I compelled to entertain some slight degree of suspicion lest evil communication, the alluring nurse of the vices, should lend an unhappy impulse to your still-tender mind; especially as I am not ignorant with what facility the external senses yield to seduction. I have therefore sent you this treatise, not only as a monitor, but even as an importunate and sometimes impudent dun, who in this turn of life may convoy you beyond the rocks of adulation; and may not merely offer you advice, but confine you to the path which you have entered; and, if you should chance to deviate, may reprehend you, and recall your steps. If you obey this monitor, you will insure tranquillity to yourself and your family, and will transmit your glory to the most remote posterity."

This dedication, which is dated at Stirling on the tenth of January 1579, affords another proof of his solicitude to form the character of a patriot

1

king; and it is only to be regretted that his favourable prognostications should have proved so
fallacious. The work itself is exhibited in the
form of a dialogue between the author, and Thomas the son of Sir Richard Maitland of Lething-
ton. This interlocutor was likewise a votary of
the Latian Muses; and his illustrious friend
seems to have entertained a favourable opinion of
his juvenile efforts.[p] He was a younger brother
of William Maitland, whom Buchanan has so
keenly satirized in the *Chamæleon*. The exor-
dium of this political dialogue is not uninteresting. " When Thomas Maitland lately returned
from France, and I had carefully interrogated
him with regard to the state of affairs in that
kingdom, I began, from a motive of personal attachment, to exhort him to persevere in that
course of glory which he had commenced, and to
inspire him with the best hopes respecting the
progress of his studies. For if I, with moderate
talents, with hardly any pecuniary resources, and
in an unlearned age, have yet maintained such a
conflict with the iniquity of the times as to be

---

[p] Between these interlocutors some family connection must have subsisted. One of the daughters of Sir Richard Maitland was married to James
Heriot of Trabroun, probably the cousin of Buchanan. (Crawfurd, p. 252.
Douglas, p. 393.) Mr Innes mentions a letter of T. Maitland to Queen
Mary, " in which he protests to her majesty, that his being brought interlocutor into that dialogue, to say whatever Buchanan thought proper for his
purpose, was wholly Buchanan's own invention." (*Critical Essay*, vol. i,
p. 359.) Maitland composed some verses in commendation of Buchanan's
paraphrase of the psalms. (*Delitiæ Poetarum Scotorum*, tom. ii, p. 178.)

thought to have effected something, assuredly they who, born in a happier age, are abundantly blest with youth, wealth, and genius, should neither be deterred by labour from so honourable a pursuit, nor, when aided by so many supports, can yield to despair. They ought therefore to persist with strenuousness in advancing the glory of letters, and in recommending themselves and their countrymen to the regard of posterity. A little perseverance in their literary efforts would serve to banish from the minds of men an opinion, that those who inhabit the frigid regions of the globe are as remote from literature, politeness, and every species of intellectual cultivation, as they are distant from the sun. For although nature may have favoured the Africans, Egyptians, and various other nations, with more prompt conceptions, and greater keenness of intellect, yet to no people has she been so unpropitious as to preclude them from all access to virtue and glory.[q]

" After he had, according to his wonted modesty, spoken of himself with reserve, but of me with more affection than truth, the course of conversation at length conducted us so far, that when he had interrogated me concerning the turbulent state of our native country, and I had returned such an answer as I then deemed suitable, I began in my turn to question him respecting

[q] Bartholinus, a learned Dane, has not neglected to enforce the same doctrine. (*De Libris Legendis*, p. 46. Hafniæ, 1676, 8vo.)

the opinion generally entertained of our transactions, either by the French, or by such strangers as he had met in France. For I was sufficiently aware that the novelty of the events, as is usually the case, must have furnished occasion and materials for universal discussion."

Buchanan's dialogue excited a degree of attention which will not appear surprising, when we consider the high reputation of the author, and the boldness of the precepts which he inculcated. " Your dialogue *De Jure Regni*," says his correspondent Rogers, " which you transmitted to me by Zolcher the letter-carrier of our friend Sturmius, I have received; a present which would be extremely agreeable to me, if the importunate entreaties of some persons did not prevent me from enjoying it: for the moment it was delivered into my hand, Dr Wilson requested the loan of it: he yielded it to the importunity of the chancellor; from whom the treasurer procured a perusal of it, and has not yet returned it: so that to this day it has never been in my custody. The work is commended by those who possess ingenuity, directed by judgment, and improved by an acquaintance with public business, and who remark the present aspect of political affairs; but it is rejected by those who study to conciliate by means of flattery the favour of princes, and who wish the reins of law to be relaxed according to their pleasure: almost all admire the genius of a man who in the declining winter of age, is capable of imitating with such dexterity the Platonic mode of composition. I have laid my injunctions on Vautrollier,[r] a very honest man who is the bearer of this letter, to procure some copies which I intend to communicate to our friends. For Sturmius, Metellus,[s] Hotman, Dousa, and

[r] "Thomas Vautrollier, a Frenchman," says Mr Herbert, "was a scholar and printer, as is said, from Paris or Rouen, who came into England about the beginning of Q. Elizabeth's reign, and was admitted a brother of the stationer's company, Oct. 2, 1564, for which he paid ijs. vjd. He set up his press in Black-friars, where it appears to have continued all his lifetime, notwithstanding his residence for some time in Scotland." (*Typographical Antiquities*, vol. ii, p. 1065.)

[s] Joannes Metellus, a native of Franche Comté, was closely connected with some of the eminent scholars of the age. While he prosecuted his studies at Bologna, he contracted an intimacy with Augustinus and Osorius: Augustinus and Metellus are the interlocutors in the dialogue of Osorius *De Gloria*. Metellus afterwards attended Augustinus during his nunciate to England; and he there became acquainted with Roger Ascham. He resided a long time at Cologne. Though he wished for a reformation in the Catholic church, he did not secede. His contemporaries have frequently mentioned him as a man of learning; but his literary productions are inconsiderable. He laid the foundation of a work which was completed after his decease: it bears the title of *Asia Tabulis Æneis secundum rationes geographicas Delineata*. Ursellis, 1600, fol. The Bodleian catalogue ascribes to him an *Epistola de Lusitanorum Navigationibus in utramque Indiam*. Col. Agrip. 1576, 8vo. Ten of his epistles occur in the collection entitled " Illustrium et Clarorum Virorum Epistolæ Selectiores, superiore sæculo scriptæ vel a Belgis, vel ad Belgas." Lugd. Bat. 1617, 8vo. See also Aschami *Epistolæ*, p. 424, edit. Elstob, and Burmanni *Sylloge Epistolarum*, tom. i, p. 60, tom. ii, p. 288. Verses by Metellus are prefixed to Stewechius's edition of Vegetius, Antv. 1585, 4to, and to Suffridus Petrus *De Scriptoribus Frisiæ*. Col. Agrip. 1593, 8vo. He reëdited two productions of his elegant friend Osorius. (*De Rebus Gestis Emmanuelis*. Col. Agrip. 1574, 8vo. *De Regis Institutione et Disciplina*. *Ibid.* 1588, 8vo.) To these editions he has prefixed long dedications, which are chiefly remarkable for the singularity of the punctuation. He denominates himself Jo. Matalius Metellus, J. C. Sequanus. He is mentioned in *La Vie de Philippes de Mornay*, p. 15, 17. The suavity of his disposition and the multiplicity of his erudi-

other friends, expect your dialogue with eagerness."—Of Hotman's connection with Buchanan no other document occurs; but his talents and
erudition entitled him to Buchanan's particular
regard.[u] He is the author of a famous political
work,[x] which bears some affinity to that of our
countryman.   Another work of a similar complexion exhibits in its title-page, the same time
and place of printing as the dialogue of Buchanan.   This production bears the title of *Vindiciæ
contra Tyrannos;* a title which alone was sufficient in those days to excite a general alarm
among the advocates of hereditary tyranny.[y] It
has been imputed to Buchanan,[z] Hotman, Beza,

tion, are commemorated by Osorius. (*In Gualterum Haddonum,* f. 2.
Olysippone, 1567, 4to.)

[t] Buchanani Epistolæ, p. 22.

[u] Hotman mentions him in very respectful terms. "Animadverti præ-
terea Dionys. Lambinum in suis scholiis in Orat. Ciceron. pro Cæcina,
scripsisse Georgium Buchananum singulari doctrina virum, &c. Buchanani
judicio nemo plus tribuit, quam ego." (*Observationes,* lib. ii, cap. xix.)

[x] Hotomani Francogallia. [Genevæ], 1573, 8vo.—A translation of this
work was published by Lord Molesworth in 1711. To the second edition
his lordship added a long and spirited preface. Lond. 1721, 8vo.

[y] Another remarkable work of the same class, and of the same age, is that
of the famous Jesuit Mariana, *De Rege et Regis Institutione.* Toleti, 1599,
4to. This composition is distinguished by the very uncommon boldness of
its sentiments; but it is not a little deformed by the author's professional
bias. He proceeds upon the Jesuitical principle of depressing the civil, and
exalting the ecclesiastical authority.

[z] This production has only been imputed to Buchanan by the inadvertency of Placcius. (*Theatrum Anon. et Pseudon.* tom. ii, p. 143.) In the
work which he quotes as his authority, Buchanan is clearly distinguished
from the author of the *Vindiciæ contra Tyrannos.* See the *Acta Eruditorum
anno 1684 publicata,* p. 22, or the book which is there quoted, Jurieu's *Histoire du Calvinisme et celle du Papisme mises en Parallele,* tom. ii, p. 386.

Mornay, and to various other authors; but it appears with a high degree of certainty that its real author was Hubert Languet.[a]

That Buchanan's political principles rendered him extremely odious to the more zealous of the Popish party, may, without offering any insult to their memory, be recorded as highly honourable to his. Between the Catholics of those and of the present times, every Protestant of common intelligence and candour will readily acknowledge a wide and glaring distinction : he will not be more inclined to compare them together, than to assimilate himself to the bigoted and persecuting Protestants of the sixteenth, or even of the seventeenth century.[b] In point of liberality, the two denominations will not now be found so essentially different as some individuals may be inclined to suppose : and in a country like this, where they are blended with each other, Protestants and Catholics who have enjoyed similar advantages of education, may almost be placed on the same level. Nor ought it here to be forgotten that, from the age of Erasmus to that of Dr

---

[a] See Bayle's *Dissertation concernant le livre d'Etienne Junius Brutus*, subjoined to the last volume of his dictionary ; and Blackburne's *Memoirs of Thomas Hollis, Esq.* vol. i, p. 129, vol. ii, p. 545.

[b] In the reign of Edward the sixth, a poor creature called Joan Bocher, or Joan of Kent, was condemned to the flames for professing to believe " that the word was made flesh in the virgin's belly, but not that he took flesh of the virgin." (Peirce's *Vindication of the Dissenters*, p. 33, 2d edit. Lond. 1718, 8vo.) The inquisition was never guilty of a more atrocious murder. Many other instances of Protestant persecution are collected by the same zealous and well-informed writer.

Geddes, the Catholic church has produced writers
who, in genuine liberality and benevolence, of
sentiment, do not yield to many of their Protestant brethren. If religion could be extricated
from politics, which so frequently absorb its vital
essence, the animosities of Christian sects might
at length subside ; and as every man is persuaded
that his own religion is the best, he might quiet-
ly enjoy his felicity without endeavouring to dis-
turb the religious meditations of his neighbour.
During the age of Buchanan however, and especially in those countries where the reformation
had newly reared its standard, the Popish writers
inculcated many pernicious doctrines, and generally conducted their enquiries with great fero-
city.

In the course of a few years, his tenets were
formally attacked by his learned countrymen
Blackwood, Winzet,[c] and Barclay, all of whom
were zealous Catholics. Some of Barclay's arguments were long afterwards refuted by Locke.[d]
Buchanan was also attacked, though in an indirect manner, by Sir Thomas Craig,[e] and by Sir

[c] " Intercessit etiam mihi," says Winzet addressing himself to Buchanan,
" cum Patricio fratre tuo, viro, ut humanis disciplinis, ita et modestia atque
humanitate satis perspicuo, non ingrata, neque omnino inutilis, opinor, ipsi
consuetudo. Teipsum præsenti colloquio nunquam nisi semel sum affatus."
(Velitatio in G. Buchananum, p. 156.)

[d] Locke's Two Treatises on Government, p. 406, edit. Lond. 1764, 8vo.

[e] Cragii de Jure Successionis Regni Angliæ libri duo. MS. penes D.I.—
Of this work the original has never been printed ; but a translation of it was
published by Bishop Gatherer, under the title of The Right of Succession to
the Kingdom of England. Lond. 1703, fol.

John Wemyss,[f] who were both of the reformed religion. Craig was a lawyer of much learning and ability; and his treatise on the feudal law still continues to be held in great estimation. Sir George Mackenzie, the servile tool of a most profligate court, undertook to defend against Buchanan the same maxims of polity; and it must be acknowledged that he lived at a period when it was expedient enough to persuade his fellow subjects, that the persons of good and bad kings are equally sacred and inviolable. " The right divine of kings to govern wrong," was a very suitable doctrine for the ministers of Charles and James. In another work, Mackenzie has exhibited a further specimen of his talent for historical and political investigation. The learned Bishop Lloyd having rationally rejected the fabulous catalogue of our ancient kings, his majesty's advocate maintained that he who denies the antiquity of the royal line is guilty of *lese-majesty*. In the course of the seventeenth century, the leading principles of Buchanan were also oppugned by Sir Lewis Stewart, a lawyer, and by Sir James Turner, a soldier. The former wrote in Latin,[g] the latter in English;[h] but nei-

---

[f] Wemii Βασιλέως Ὑπεροχὴ, sive de Regis Primatu Libellus. Edinb. 1623, 4to.

[g] Ruddiman's Answer to Logan's Treatise on Government, p. 186. Edinb. 1747, 8vo.—Mr Ruddiman afterwards prosecuted his controversy with Logan, in an elaborate " Dissertation concerning the Competition for the Crown of Scotland, betwixt Bruce and Baliol, in the year 1291." Edinb. 1748, 8vo.

[h] Nicolson's Scottish Historical Library, p. 15.

R

ther of their productions has been printed; and
the republic of letters has probably sustained no
very heavy detriment by their long suppression.
He was incidentally assailed by many foreign authors; who seem in general to have been bewil-
dered by the current doctrine of the divine and
indefeasible right of kings, and the passive obedience of subjects. This was indeed the doctrine
of Protestants and Catholics, of civilians and
divines. Grotius, though born under a free republic, and certainly a man of a great and liberal
mind, did not entirely escape the contamination
of those slavish maxims that were so prevalent
during the age in which he lived. The right of
resisting any superior power which happens to be
established, he has discussed in a manner that
could hardly offend the completest despot in Europe.[i] There is perhaps too much justice in the
remark of Rousseau, that it is his most common
method of reasoning, always to establish the
right by the fact.[k] It is one general fault of those
writers, to found their theories on passages of
scripture which are not didactic or exegetical, but
merely historical. This obsolete perversion they
seem to have derived from the authority of those
early theologians who are commonly styled the
fathers of the Christian church;[l] and who, if not
always very safe guides in morality and in bibli-

[i] Grotius de Jure Belli ac Pacis, lib. i, cap. iv.

[k] Rousseau du Contract Social, p. 4.   Amst. 1762, 12mo.

[l] Gibbon's Hist. of the Roman Empire, vol. iii, p. 246.

cal criticism,[m] are certainly exceptionable guides
in political science. The degrading doctrine of
divine right and passive obedience was inculcated
by Salmasius,[n] Bochart,[o] Usher,[p] and indeed by
several very able men who approached much
nearer to our own times: it was even inculcated
by the famous Dr Berkeley, in some metaphysical discourses preached before the university of
Dublin in the year 1712.[q] It is however a doctrine which no Briton, capable of reflection, will
now hesitate a single moment in rejecting with
the utmost indignation. So slow, and yet so
certain, is the progress of reason; which, though
sometimes retarded in its course, or partially ab-
sorbed by the quicksands of ambition, avarice,
and superstition, will never fail to roll onward
with one irresistible tide, till it at length reach
the ocean of eternity. " Methinks," to adopt the
language of Milton, " I see in my mind a noble

* See Barbeyrac, Traité de la Morale des Peres de l'Eglise, Amst. 1728,
4to, and Dr Whitby's Dissertatio de Scripturarum Interpretatione secundum
Patrum Commentarios. ' Lond. 1714, 8vo.—But with respect to the treatise of Barbeyrac, consult Lord Hailes's ", Inquiry, into the Secondary
Causes which Mr Gibbon has assigned for the Rapid Growth of Christiani-
ty," p. 176. Edinb. 1786, 4to.

ª Salmasii Defensio Regia: Sumptibus regiis, 1649, fol. et 12mo.

º Bocharti Opera, tom. i, col. 988.

ᵖ Usher's Power communicated by God to the Prince, and Obedience required of the Subject. Lond. 1661, 4to.—The best specimen of this doctrine was furnished by Dr Sanderson, the learned bishop of Lincoln; " who
declared, it was not lawful to resist the prince upon the throne, even to save
all the souls in the whole world." (Blackburne's 'Confessional, p. 347, 3d
edit. Lond. 1770, 8vo.)

ᵠ Berkeley's Works, vol. ii, p. 1. Dublin, 1784, 2 vols 4to.

and puissant nation rousing herself like a strong
man after sleep, and shaking her invincible locks:
methinks I see her as an eagle muing her mighty
youth, and kindling her undazl'd eyes at the full
midday beam ; purging and unscaling her long
abused sight at the fountain it self of heav'nly
radiance; while the whole noise of timorous and
flocking birds, and those also that love the
twilight, flutter about, amaz'd at what she
means."[r]

But the full measure of Buchanan's ignominy
has not yet been related.   In the year 1584, the
parliament condemned his dialogue and history
as unfit to remain for records of. truth to posterity ; and, under a penalty of two hundred
pounds, commanded every person who possessed copies, to surrender them within forty days,
in order that they might be purged of " the of-
fensive and extraordinary matters" which they
contained.[s] In 1664, the privy council of Scotland issued a proclamation prohibiting all subjects of whatever degree, quality, or rank, from
transcribing or circulating any copies of a ma-

---

[r] Milton's Areopagitica, p. 345.—An edition of this tract was published
by Thomson, an ardent lover of liberty. Lond. 1738, 8vo. The title-page
bears, " with a Preface by another hand." In the copy belonging to Williams's Library, the words by Mr Thomson are inserted in a contemporary,
hand at the beginning of the preface. The tract and the preface are reprinted with Blackburne's Remarks on Johnson's Life of Milton. Lond. 1780,
8vo.

[s] Acts of the Parliaments of Scotland, vol. iii, p. 296.

nuscript translation of the dialogue.[t] And
in 1683, the loyal and orthodox university of
Oxford doomed to the flames the political works
of Buchanan, Milton, Languet, and several
other heretics.[u] This university, says a contemporary historian, debauched the minds of the
youth with its slavish doctrines, and pronounced
a severe judgment against Buchanan for his book
in vindication of the rights of the kingdom.[v] The
Scotish legislature, the English university, and
the Popish tribunal of the inquisition, seem to

---

[t] Wodrow's Hist. of the Sufferings of the Church of Scotland, vol. i,
p. 218. Edinb. 1721-2, 2 vols. fol.—This proclamation, as my excellent
friend Mr Ninian Little suggests, is likewise mentioned by Dr Parker, the
apostate bishop of Oxford. *(De Rebus sui Temporis Commentarii*, p. 77.
Lond. 1726, 8vo.) To the same gentleman these memoirs have many other
obligations.

[u] Smithi Vita R. Huntingtoni, p. xxv. Birch's Life of Tillotson, p. 188.
Lond. 1752, 8vo.—" The Judgment and Decree of the University of Ox-
ford, passed in their Convocation, July 21, 1683, against certain pernicious
Books, and damnable Doctrines, destructive to the sacred Persons of Princes,
their State and Government, and of all human Society," may be found in
Lord Somers's Tracts, vol. iii, p. 223. The first of these damnable doc-
trines is, that " all civil authority is derived originally from the people."
This notable decree found a panegyrist in some nameless member of Christ
Church. The subsequent passage of his *Decretum Oxoniense* relates to Bu-
chanan.

> Ille etiam Scotica qui quondam turbidus aula
> Jus regum angusti contraxit limite gyri,
> Qui toties populos immisit in arma furentes,
> Multaque subjecit gliscenti incendia bello,
> Nunc ignem subit, et flammis ultricibus ardet.
>   Musarum Anglicanarum Analecta, vol. ii, p. 181.

The Oxford decree was dutifully presented to Charles the second; and in
1710, the house of lords ordered it to be publicly burnt with Sacheverel's
foolish sermon. (Burnet's *Hist. of his own Time*, vol. ii, p. 545.)

[v] Cunningham's Hist. of Great Britain, vol. i, p. 54.

have regarded this unfortunate speculator with equal abhorrence. All the arts of ignorance, superstition, and sycophancy, have not however been able to quench the vital principle of his immortal productions, but, like oil added to a rising flame, have only served to augment their splendour.[x]

Other individuals, and those too of high reputation, have viewed him in a different light. He has found enthusiastic admirers among the most enlightened of modern scholars ; and the effects of his bold and manly speculations have been widely felt. It was objected to Milton that he had stolen his celebrated defence of the people of England from the eloquent work of Buchanan.[y]

[x] " Libros per ædiles cremandos censuere patres ; sed manserunt occultati, et editi. Quo magis socordiam eorum inridere libet, qui præsenti potentia credunt extingui posse etiam sequentis ævi memoriam. Nam contra, punitis ingeniis gliscit auctoritas : neque aliud externi reges, aut qui eadem sævitia usi sunt, nisi dedecus sibi, atque illis gloriam peperere." (Taciti *Annales*, lib. iv, § 35.)

[y] Dryden's Epistle to the Whigs, prefixed to the Medal.—The political work of Buchanan seems to have been read and approved by a patriot of a high order. A copy of the dialogue, formerly in the possession of Mr Hollis, exhibited the following sentence, subscribed with the respectable name of Chatham. "Ἥμισυ γάρ τ᾽ ἀρετῆς ἀποαίνυται δύλιον ἧμαρ. (Blackburne's *Memoirs of Thomas Hollis, Esq.* vol. ii, p. 550.) These remarkable expressions, which had likewise been adopted by Longinus (*De Sublimitate*, p. 152, edit. Weiske), are derived from the subsequent verses of Homer.

"Ἥμισυ γάρ τ᾽ ἀρετῆς ἀποαίνυται εὐρύοπα Ζεὺς
Ἀνέρος, εὖτ᾽ ἄν μιν κατὰ δύλιον ἧμαρ ἕλησιν.
                                        Odyss. xvii, 322.

Dr Brown has well remarked that " liberty and human nature are inseparable ; to destroy the former, is to annihilate the latter—is to annihilate every notion of duty, and virtue, and happiness, beyond what is merely sensual and brutish." (*Essay on the Natural Equality of Men,* p. 123, 2d edit.

And what are the terrible doctrines which once excited so violent an alarm? Buchanan maintains that all power is derived from the people; that it is more safe to intrust our liberties to the definite protection of the laws, than to the precarious discretion of the king; that the king is bound by those conditions under which the supreme power was originally committed to his hands; that it is lawful to resist, and even to punish tyrants. Those who maintain the contrary, must have recourse to the absurd and exploded doctrine of divine and indefeasible right. When he speaks of the people as opposed to the king, he evidently includes every individual of the nation except one.[2] And is a race of intelligent beings to be assimilated to a tract of land; or to a litter of pigs; to be considered, absolutely and unconditionally, as the lawful patrimony of a family which either merit, accident, or crime, may originally have elevated to the summit of power? In this country and this age it certainly is not necessary to remark, that man can neither

Lond. 1794, 8vo.) As a further commentary on these verses, I subjoin the emphatic words of Lord Molesworth. · " Slavery, like a sickly constitution, grows in time so habitual, that it seems no burden nor disease; it creates a kind of laziness, and idle despondency, which puts men beyond hopes and fears: it mortifies ambition, emulation, and other troublesome, as well as active qualities, which liberty and freedom beget; and instead of them affords only a dull kind of pleasure of being careless and insensible." (*Account of Denmark*, p. 75. Lond. 1694, 8vo.)

" Nam appellatione populi," says Justinian, " universi cives significantur, connumeratis etiam patriciis et senatoribus." (*Institutiones*, lib. i, tit. ii, § 4.)

inherit nor possess a right of property in his fellow creatures. What is termed loyalty, may,
according to the circumstances of the case, be
either a virtue or a vice. Loyalty to Antoninus
and to Nero must assuredly have flowed from
different sources. If the Roman people had endeavoured to compass the death of Nero, would
this have been foul and unnatural rebellion?
The doctrine of punishing tyrants in their persons, either by a private arm, or by the public
forms of law, is indeed of a delicate and dangerous nature;* and it may be considered as amply
sufficient, to ascertain the previous right of forcible resistance. It will always be extremely
difficult, if not impossible, to find a competent
tribunal and impartial judges. But that tyrants
ought to be punished, is an abstract proposition
which cannot easily be controverted : for under
the word tyranny, is generally included all that
is most odious and intolerable in human delinquency. If mankind are at length roused to the
redress of enormous wrongs, the prince who has
either committed or sanctioned an habitual vio-
lation of the best rights of the people, will seldom fail to meet with his adequate reward ; and
in spite of all the slavish theories of his priests
and lawyers, mankind will not long be reasoned
out of the strongest feelings of their nature.
Divine right and passive obedience were never

* See Dr Ferguson's Hist. of the Roman Republic, vol. iii, p. 37, 4to,
and Mr Fox's Hist. of James the Second, p. 13.

more strenuously inculcated, than in the reign of
Charles the first.   That Buchanan endeavoured
to undermine the very foundations of monarchi-
cal government, is an assertion utterly destitute
of candour.   He has indeed affirmed, that it is
of little importance whether the supreme ma-
gistrate be denominated king, duke, emperor, or
consul; but with regard to the distinguishing
qualities of a good king, no writer has expressed
himself with higher enthusiasm.   His general
principles seem to be incontrovertible; though it
must certainly be admitted that some of his illustrations are not introduced with sufficient
caution.   That his chief scope was to prepare
the nation for receiving Murray as their lawful
sovereign, is another calumny which party zeal
has frequently propagated: it is a calumny totally unsupported by any degree of probable evidence that could satisfy an unprejudiced mind.
Buchanan, like other men who have attained to
high distinction, had his personal and political
enemies; and for every action of his life the
worst motives have too often been assigned.   He
was animated with an ardent and disinterested
love of mankind; and it was upon the most enlarged principles that he undertook to instruct
them in their political rights.   The best commentary on his work is the revolution of 1688.
   That memorable event, which produced so
many important consequences, was not without
its effects on the reputation of Buchanan.   From

the very acrimonious terms in which he is frequently mentioned by the Jacobites, it may justly
be inferred that they supposed his political doctrines to have had considerable influence : and
this influence they endeavoured to destroy by depressing his moral and literary ' character.   Of
the treatment to which he was thus exposed,
it may not be superfluous to produce a single
example, selected from the writings of a non-
juring divine, respectable for his learning, and
entitled to commiseration for his prejudices.
According to his averment, " the disciples and
followers of Buchanan, Hobbes, and Milton, have
exceeded their masters in downright impudence,
scurrility, and lying."[b]   On the indecency of these
expressions it is not necessary to offer any animadversions ; nor does it seem requisite to point
out the dexterity with which Buchanan and Milton are here associated with Hobbes, from whom
they differed so widely in their political as well
as their religious opinions.   The name of this philosopher had an alarming sound to pious ears ;
and the learned divine was doubtless aware of
the popular effect of such a classification.

An ardent love of freedom was long a characteristic of the Scotish nation.   Mair and Boyce
had, in their historical productions, vindicated
with becoming zeal the unalienable rights of the

Dr Smith's preface to Sir Philip Warwick's Discourse of Government.
Lond. 1694, 8vo.

people ;[c] but to Buchanan must unquestionably be awarded the high praise of having been the earliest writer who established political science on its genuine basis. The southern part of this island had likewise produced political speculators: Sir John Fortescue had endeavoured to trace the line of distinction between an absolute and a limited monarchy; and Sir Thomas More had engrafted his novel theories on the description of an imaginary commonwealth. More afterwards forgot the liberal speculations of his youth : in his

* These two writers had completely imbibed the maxims of a free government. Boyce is commemorated by Paulus Jovius as " moderatæ libertatis nusquam oblitus." (*Elogia Virorum Literis Illustrium,* p. 212.) Mair inculcates some of the leading doctrines that were afterwards methodised and embellished by his pupil Buchanan. " Populus liber primo regi dat robur, cujus potestas a toto populo dependet; quia aliud jus Fergusius primus rex Scotiæ non habuit : et ita est ubilibet, et ab orbe condito erat communiter. Hoc propter reges Judææ a Deo institutos dico. Si dicas mihi ab Henrico septimo Henricus octavus jus habet, ad primum Anglorum regem ascendam, quærendo a quo ille jus regni habuit; et ita ubivis gentium procedam. Et quod jus a populo habuit dicere necesse est, quia aliud dare non potes: sed sic est quod totus populus in Robertum Bruseum consensit, de republica Scotica optime meritum. Tertio arguitur ad eandem conclusionem probandam : Regem et posteros pro demeritis populus potest exauthorare sicut et primo instituere." (Major *De Gestis Scotorum,* f. 76, b. Ex officina Ascensiana, 1521, 4to.) The whole of the passage from which I have extracted this specimen is extremely curious.

During the minority of King James, several coins were struck with a remarkable inscription, borrowed from the emperor Trajan. One side presents a naked sword, supporting a crown on its point, and surrounded with this legend : PRO. ME. SI. MEREOR. IN. ME. " Hoc lemma," says Ruddiman, " (quo et suum adversus reges ingenium prodit) Georgium Buchananum Jacobi VI. præceptorem subministrasse omnes consentiunt." (Andersoni *Selectus Diplomatum et Numismatum Scotiæ Thesaurus,* p. 103. Edinb. 1739, fol.)

Utopia,[d] he inculcates the doctrine of religious toleration, and yet he lived to assume the odious character of a persecutor. That he was himself a victim of divine retribution, it would be indecent to affirm :[e] but it is an historical fact that he was wantonly sacrificed by the execrable tyrant whom he had served with too much zeal. On the solid foundation which had been laid by Buchanan, a spacious edifice was afterwards reared by Milton, Sidney, and Locke; names which every enlightened Briton will always recollect with peculiar veneration.[f] That two of them were republicans, need not alarm the most zealous friends of a legitimate monarchy :[g] if the same individuals had flourished at a more recent period, they would undoubtedly have entertained different sentiments. The principles which prompted stern resistance to the wide encroachments of the house of Stewart, are perfectly com-

[d] Basil. 1518, 4to.

[e] Κρίνειν οὐκ ἐπίσταμαι θεῖα ἔργα βροτοῖσι.

BION. IdyL vi, v. 9.

[f] Among the distinguished authors who have defended the liberties of their country, we must not neglect to enumerate Bishop Hoadley ; in reference to whom it has been remarked, that " civil liberty perhaps owes more to one great man of the clerical profession, than to any other single writer of any denomination." (Sturges's *Considerations on the Present State of the Church-Establishment,* p. 165. Lond. 1779, 8vo.) The political works of this eminent prelate are of a controversial nature, and chiefly relate to the questions which occupied the particular attention of his contemporaries. Though they appear less brilliant to posterity, they were of great importance to his own age.

[g] See Dr Symmons's *Life* of Milton, p. 519.

patible with those which recommend a cordial attachment to the house of Hanover.

~ This political work of Buchanan is highly commended by an able and eloquent writer of our own time. " The science," says Sir James Mackintosh, " which teaches the rights of man, the eloquence that kindles the spirit of freedom, had for ages been buried with the other monuments of the wisdom and relics of the genius of antiquity. But the revival of letters first unlocked only to a few, the sacred fountain. The necessary labours of criticism and lexicography occupied the earlier scholars, and some time elapsed before the spirit of antiquity was transfused into its admirers. The first man of that period who united elegant learning to original and masculine thought was Buchanan, and he too seems to have been the first scholar who caught from the ancients the noble flame of republican enthusiasm. This praise is merited by his neglected, though incomparable tract, *De Jure Regni*, · in which the principles of popular politics, and the maxims of a free government, are delivered with a precision, and enforced with an energy, which no former age had equalled, and no succeeding has surpassed."[h]

Mr Stewart's suffrage is also important. " The dialogue of our illustrious countryman Buchanan, *De Jure Regni apud Scotos*, though occasionally

<hr/>

[p] Mackintosh's Defence of the French Revolution, p. 309.

disfigured by the keen and indignant temper of
the writer, and by a predilection (pardonable in
a scholar warm from the schools of ancient
Greece and Rome) for forms of policy unsuitable
to the circumstances of modern Europe, bears,
nevertheless, in its general spirit, a closer resemblance to the political philosophy of the eighteenth century, than any composition which had
previously appeared. The ethical paradoxes afterwards inculcated by Hobbes as the ground-
work of his slavish theory of government, are
anticipated and refuted; and a powerful argument is urged against the doctrine of utility
which has attracted so much notice in our times.
The political reflections, too, incidentally introduced by the same author in his history of Scotland, bear marks of a mind worthy of a better
age than fell to his lot. Of this kind are the remarks with which he closes his narrative of the
wanton cruelties exercised in punishing the mur-
derers of James the first. In reading them, one
would almost imagine, that one is listening to
the voice of Beccaria or of Montesquieu."[i]

In the seventy-fourth year of his age,[k] Buchan-

_____

[i] Stewart's Dissertation on the Progress of Metaphysical, Ethical, and
Political Philosophy, p. 47.

[k] " Ruddiman," says his biographer, " gives a sceptical note, which seems
to discover his doubts of an assertion, which has never been supported by
proof. Yet he saw only part of the truth. He did not perceive, what appears to have been *the fact*, that of this life Sir Peter Young was the author."
(*Life of Ruddiman*, p. 68.) Ruddiman's note, the first on Buchanan's life,
is far from being sceptical. The reasons which have here convinced Mr

an composed a brief sketch of his own life. To this task he was urged by some of his numerous friends;[1] and the annals of literature supplied

Chalmers, seem to be very inadequate, and will probably convince no other person. His first reason is, that on the fifteenth of March 1579-80, Randolph advised Young to write Buchanan's life. But the biographical tract in question, as appears from the concluding sentence, was written when Buchanan was in the seventy-fourth year of his age: it was therefore written before the beginning of February 1580, that is, at least a month before Randolph's letter. His second and last reason is, that " Dr Thomas Smith says expressly, That Peter Young wrote briefly the life of Buchanan." " Cujus vitam compendio descripsit," says Dr Smith in one passage; but in another, he only mentions as a probable conjecture what he had before asserted in positive terms. (*Vita Petri Junii*, p. 17, 29.) But if Young actually wrote a life of Buchanan, are we under the necessity of concluding that he must have written the identical life which has uniformly been ascribed to Buchanan himself? This tract is written in a strain of dignified simplicity, highly becoming an illustrious character who had undertaken to be his own historian; but if the same events and circumstances had been related by a friend, they would undoubtedly have been related in a different manner.

" This writer, whoever he were, talks of John Major as being *in extrema senectute*, in 1524, when he was only fifty-five." The period of Mair's birth is by no means ascertained; for Dr Mackenzie's date is a mere figment. George Crawfurd, the most industrious of his biographers, could discover no better *datum* than this incidental notice of Buchanan: he accordingly refers the birth of Mair to the year 1446.—" He speaks of Henry VIII. as *jam seniore*, in 1539, when he was but *forty-eight*." And therefore he speaks as any man of learning might do without hesitation. Consult Aulus Gellius, *Noctes Atticæ*, lib. x, cap. xxviii.—" He makes Buchanan meet Cardinal Beaton at Paris, in 1539, a twelve-month after he had returned to Scotland: I am thence led to suspect, that Buchanan made his escape *from St Andrew's*, by the way of London, to Paris, not in 1539, but in 1538, when he might have met the cardinal." The dates on the margin are not those of the author, but of the editor. In his history, Buchanan however informs us that he did not leave his native country till 1539. Because Cardinal Beaton was at Paris in 1538, he could not also be at Paris in 1539, is the next proposition.—" I could run through the whole life, and shew similar fooleries, and some malignity, in every page of it." Αὐτῷ ταῦτά σοι δίδωμ' ἔχειν.

[1] " Hæc de se Buchananus, amicorum rogatu," is the colophon of some of the early editions.

him with abundant instances of autobiography.
The practice, as we learn from Tacitus, was not
unusual among the ancient Romans,[m] though
not a single specimen has descended to our
times.   Augustus wrote an account of his own
life, consisting of thirteen books;[n] but it has pe-
rished with the other literary monuments of that
prince.   The two works of Josephus and Libanius are almost the only specimens of this mode
of composition which antiquity has bequeathed.
More recent examples are exhibited by Erasmus
and Cardan; who have likewise been followed
in the same tract by Thuanus, Clarendon, Herbert, Le Clerc, Huet, Holberg, Hume, Gibbon,
Franklin, Rousseau, and five hundred others. In
Cardan and Rousseau it might perhaps have been
more prudent to leave the task unperformed;
for, even according to their own representation,
their genius must have been accompanied with
at least an equal portion of folly. Buchanan's
little work is composed with his usual elegance,
and with a degree of modesty and candour worthy of so illustrious a character.   It has been
commended by Huet, a most learned writer, who
entertained very different opinions relative to
some of the leading topics of speculation. " More
sparing and modest in his biographical narrative
was George Buchanan, as well as brief and con-

---

[m] Taciti Vita Agricolæ, p. 4, edit. Boxhornii. Lugd. Bat. 1642, 12mo.
[n] Augusti Temporum Notatio, Genus, et Scriptorum Fragmenta, curante
J. A. Fabricio, p. 190.   Hamb. 1727, 4to.

cise in his style, and so candid in laying open
his mind, that he does not well dissemble his sentiments concerning the new and depraved modes
of religion which had infected many in that age."[o]

Buchanan still continued his epistolary correspondence with some of the surviving friends
of his earlier days. By the Scotish merchants
who resorted to Bordeaux for the purpose of
procuring wine, he annually transmitted a letter to his former colleague Vinetus.[p] But of
those letters, only one has been preserved : it is
dated at Edinburgh on the sixteenth of March
1581. " Upon receiving accounts of you by the
merchants who return from your coasts, I am filled with delight, and seem to enjoy a kind of second youth ; for I am then apprized that some
remnants of the Portugueze peregrination still
exist. As I have now attained to the seventy-fifth
year of my age, I sometimes call to remembrance
through what toils and inquietudes I have sailed
past all those objects which men commonly regard as pleasing, and have at length struck upon
that rock, beyond which (as the ninetieth psalm

[o] Huetii Commentarius de Rebus ad eum pertinentibus, p. 424. Eng.
Com. 1718, 12mo.—This interesting work of Huet has been well translated by Dr Aikin ; who has added copious notes, biographical and critical.
The notes do not display any very curious research, but they are replete with
judgment and good sense. His publication is entitled " Memoirs of the
Life of Peter Daniel Huet, Bishop of Avranches." Lond. 1810, 2 vols.
8vo.
[p] Thuanus de Vita sua, p. 39, edit. Buckley.

s

very truly avers) nothing remains but labour
and sorrow. The only consolation which now
awaits me, is to pause with delight on the recollection of my coëval friends, of whom you are almost the only one who still survives. Although
you are not, as I presume, inferior to me in years,
you are yet capable of benefiting your country
by your exertion and counsel, and even of pro-
longing, by your learned compositions, your life
to a future age. But I have long bade adieu to
letters. It is now the only object of my solicitude, that I may remove with as little noise as
possible from the society of my ill-assorted com-
panions; that I who am already dead, may relinquish the fellowship of the living. In the mean
time, I transmit to you the youngest of my literary offspring, in order that when you discover it
to be the driveling child of age, you may be less
anxious about its brothers. I understand that
Henry Wardlaw, or Νομοφύλαξ, a young man of our
nation, and the descendant of a good family, is
prosecuting his studies in your seminary with no
inconsiderable application. Although I am aware
of your habitual politeness, and you are not ignorant that foreigners are peculiarly entitled to your
attention, yet I am desirous he should find that
our ancient familiarity recommends him to your
favour."q

This epistle, says the illustrious Thuanus, was
written with a tremulous hand, but in a generous

q Buchanani Epistolæ, p. 32.

style. He had seen it in the possession of the amiable old man to whom it is addressed; and his high admiration of Buchanan's genius and virtue induced him to record that little circumstance in the interesting memoirs of his own life.[r] The answer of Vinetus is dated at Bordeaux on the ninth of June 1581. "Your letter of the sixteenth of March was delivered to me on the third of June: and from its being written at such an age, and at such an interval of time and place, and from its mention of our Portugueze peregrination, and of far happier times than the present, nothing could afford me higher delight. I have read it again and again, and read it still; together with the book which you sent as its companion. This book, if I may rely upon my own judgment, and upon that of many friends who were formerly your pupils, and to whom I have lent it, is by no means the production of a driveling author. A certain countryman of yours,[s] a counsellor of the parliament of Poitiers, is however, I understand, of a different opinion; and he has written a book which I shall transmit to you as soon as it is published in that

---

[r] An English life of Thuanus, chiefly compiled from his tract *De Vita sua*, was lately published by Mr Collinson. Lond. 1807, 8vo.

[s] He alludes to Adam Blackwood; whom Mr Ruddiman styles " professor of law in the university of Poictiers." (*Vindication of Buchanan*, p. 124.) But it does not appear that he ever taught in that university. See the eulogium which Gabriel Naudé has prefixed to " Blacvodæi Opera Omnia." Paris. 1644, 4to. Blackwood lived to publish a second edition of his *Apologia pro Regibus*. Paris. 1588, 8vo.

city. What brothers of your literary offspring
you allude to that I have not already seen, I
know not: for the tragedies, psalms, elegies, and
epigrams of George Buchanan are sold here. . It
is your sphere only, which you are understood to
have composed at an earlier period, that many
persons, and I among the first, are now anxiously expecting: but perhaps that poem has not yet
been prepared for the press by your final correction. The works of mine which you mention
are of a puerile kind, and composed for the benefit of the youth whom I educate in this seminary. If you doubt my assertion, you may convince yourself of its accuracy by inspecting my
commentary on the *Somnium Scipionis*; which I
now present to you, with the epistles of Gelida.[1]
With respect to your particular recommendation
of Henry Wardlaw, I beg leave to assure you that
from the time when I here became acquainted
with you, with your personal character and your
erudition, I for your sake love and respect all your
countrymen, and render them every service in
my power, which indeed is very limited. This
school is rarely without a Scotchman: it has two
at present; one of them is professor of philosophy, the other[a] of the Greek language and of

---

[1] J. Gelidæ Valentini Epistolæ. Rupellæ, 1571, 4to.

[a] This was probably Robert Balfour, the learned editor of Cleomedes
and commentator on Aristotle. He was afterwards principal of the college.
There is a letter from Balfour among the *Epistres Françoises à M. de la*
Scala, p. 13. Harderwyck, 1624, 8vo. He is repeatedly mentioned in the

mathematics: both are good, honest, and learned men, and enjoy the favourable opinion of their auditors. Farewell, and expect to hear from me frequently, provided I can find a conveyance for my letters."[x]

Elias Vinetus must have interested those who are sufficiently interested in Buchanan; and it may not therefore be superfluous to devote a digressive page to his commemoration. Descended of humble parents, he was born in the village of Vinet, situated in the *châtellénie* of Barbesieux in Saintonge. He received the rudiments of education at Barbesieux, and afterwards studied four years at Poitiers. Having returned to the former place, he there amassed a small sum of money by engaging in the tuition of youth, and was thus enabled to gratify his literary curiosity by paying a visit to Paris. He began to teach humanity in the College of Guienne at Bordeaux in the year 1539, which was the period when Buchanan likewise became a member of that famous seminary. Having fallen into an infirm state of health, he retired for some time to his native province; and, in 1542, he again betook himself to Paris, where he became acquainted with Anthony Govea.[y] The elder Govea hav-

epistles of Scaliger and Casaubon. He is highly extolled in a work entitled " Epigrammaton Joannis Dunbari Megalo-Britanni centuriæ sex, decades totidem," p. 52. Lond. 1616, 8vo.

[x] Buchanai Epistolæ, p. 83.

[y] These two dates, 1539 and 1542, are copied from an epistle of Vinetus which Schottus has inserted in his *Bibliotheca Hispanica*, p. 475.

ing invited him back to Bordeaux, he there continued to discharge his academical functions till the year 1547, when he emigrated with Buchanan and other learned men to the university of Coimbra. What treatment he experienced among the Portugueze, is uncertain; but soon after the death of Govea, he returned to Bordeaux, and taught humanity and mathematics. After the decease of his friend Gelida, which happened in the year 1556,[z] he succeeded him as principal of the college; which he continued for many years to govern with great credit to himself, and with great utility to the public. Having exceeded the age of seventy-eight, he died on the fourteenth of May 1587.[a] His character seems to have been that of a modest and worthy man. If not entitled to rank with scholars of the first order, he was at least furnished with a very considerable share of erudition. He published some original works,[b] and editions of several ancient writers; and has evinced an ac-

[z] In one part of his extensive work, Niceron refers the death of Gelida to the nineteenth of February, in another to the nineteenth of June, 1556. (*Memoires des Hommes Illustres*, tom. xxii, p. 107, tom. xxx, p. 224.) Both these dates are erroneous: Gelida died on the nineteenth of February 1556.

[a] Niceron, Memoires des Hommes Illustres, tom. xxx, p. 224.

[b] One of them is entitled *De Logistica libri tres.* Burd. 1573, 8vo. Vinetus remarks that this art, originally denominated algorism, was derived from the Arabians; and that Joannes de Sacrobosco, who composed a treatise *De Algorismo* about the year 1250, was the earliest writer on the subject with whom he was acquainted. "L'algorismo," says Menage, "propriamente è una aritmetica logica." (*Origini della Lingua Italiana*, p. 43, fol.)

quaintance with science as well as literature. His editions of Pomponius Mela and Ausonius were once held in no common estimation : Vossius was of opinion that after Hermolaus Barbarus,[c] no editor had contributed so much to the illustration of the former author.[d]

Buchanan's last epistle is addressed to his early friend Beza. " Although my attention is divided by various occupations, and the state of my health is so desperate as to leave me no leisure for the common duties of life, yet the departure of Jerome Groslot has banished all my excuses. For as the father, who was a man of distinction, loaded me, during my residence in France, with every species of kindness, and the son has honoured me here as another parent, I was aware that among you I could not escape the heavy charge of ingratitude, if I should now overlook the kindness which I experienced from the one, the pleasant intercourse which I have enjoyed with the other, and the polite attention which you have uniformly paid me. Yet among those who are not unacquainted with my present condition, such a fault would readily find its apology. It is my best apology, that all my senses dying before me, what now remains of the image of the former man testifies, not that I am, but

---

[c] This learned writer's corrections of Pomponius Mela are printed with his *Castigationes Plinianæ.* Romæ, 1492–3, fol.

[d] Vossius de Scientiis Mathematicis, p. 258.

that I have been, alive ; especially as I can neither cherish the hope of contracting new intimacies, nor of continuing the old.   These circumstances I now mention with greater confidence,
as the present occasion affords you an opportunity of learning my condition from Groslot; whom
it appears superfluous to recommend to your attention. The dispositions of youth disclose themselves without our aid. I have however furnished him with a recommendation, rather to comply
with the common practice, than because it is requisite. With regard to myself, since I cannot
continue my former mode of life by the recipro-
cation of friendly offices, I shall refrain from those
exertions to which I have long been unequal, and
indulge in silence. Farewell. Edinburgh, July
the fifteenth, 1581." This interesting letter is
followed by a more formal testimonial in favour
of the young and accomplished emigrant. " Jerome Groslot, a young man of Orleans who is
the bearer of this, although born in a distinguished city of most distinguished parents, is however
best known in consequence of his calamities. In
that universal tumult, and universal phrensy,
which prevailed in France, he lost his father and
his patrimony, and was himself exposed to jeopardy. As he could not remain at home in safety, he chose to fix his residence in Scotland till
the violence of that storm should a little subside.
As the state of national affairs is now somewhat
more tranquil, and his domestic concerns require

his return, he is determined to travel through
England, that, like Ulysses, he may become acquainted with the manners and cities of many
men, and, as far as the shortness of his time will
permit, may familiarize himself with a branch of
civil knowledge which is of no trivial importance.
This journey I trust he will not perform without
reaping some benefit, such as he has derived from
his late peregrination. During his residence in
Scotland, he has not lived like a stranger in a
foreign land, but like a citizen among his fellows.
The study of letters he has prosecuted so successfully, as not only to be able to sooth by their
suavity the sorrows incident to his disastrous
condition, but also to have provided for himself
and his family a resource against the future con-
tingencies of life. Here it is not necessary for
me to persuade, or even to admonish you, to
treat this excellent youth with kindness; for
that the uniform course of your life, and the bond
of the same faith, demand of you, nay, even compel you to do, for the sake of maintaining your
own character."[e] This young stranger, in whom
he seems to have been so much interested, was
the son of Jerome Groslot, *bailli* of Orleans; who
was assassinated at Paris during the infamous
massacre of St. Bartholomew.[f] The father likewise appears to have been attached to letters.[g]

---

* Buchanani Epistolæ, p. 33.
f Thuani Hist. sui Temporis, tom. ii, p. 42, 44, tom. iii, p. 132.
g Saxius supposes him to be the author of two juridical tracts, written in

The son, though he did not himself publish any
work, was well known to the scholars of the age:
he was one of the intimate friends of Dousa, and
enjoyed the acquaintance of Cujacius, Casaubon,
and Lipsius.[h]

The last production which Buchanan lived to
complete was his history of Scotland.[i] In the

Latin, and published at Paris in 1538. *(Onomasticon Literarium*, tom. iii,
p. 193, 554.) These tracts occur in Otto's *Thesaurus Juris Civilis*, tom. v,
p. 1, 48.

[h] Colomiés mentions a volume of Latin and Italian letters from Father
Paul to M. de l'Isle Groslot and M. Gillot, printed at Geneva in 1673.
Several philological epistles of Groslot may be found in the collections of
Goldastus and Burman. In the latter collection occur his annotations on
Tacitus. (Burmanni *Sylloge Epistolarum*, tom. i, p. 348.) Casaubon styles
him " nobilissimus doctissimusque vir." *(Animadversiones ad Suetonium*,
p. 2.) Josias Mercerus, the father-in-law of Salmasius, inscribed to Groslot his edition of Dictys Cretensis and Dares Phrygius, published at Paris in
1618.

[i] Rerum Scoticarum Historia, auctore Georgio Buchanano Scoto. Edimburgi, apud Alexandrum Arbuthnetum typographum regium. Cum privilegio regali. 1582, fol.—This edition contains many typographical errors; a
list of which may be found appended to Crawford's *Notes on Buchanan.* Of
the history of Scotland there are seventeen editions. The two last are those
of Alexander Finlater and James Man. Edinb. 1727, 8vo. Aberd. 1762,
8vo. Finlater is mentioned by Ruddiman as " a gentleman well versed in
classical learning." *(Further Vindication*, p. 7.) Archbishop Nicolson remarks that Buchanan's history was " epitomized in a good Latin style by
Mr Alexander Hume; who was sometime chief master of the grammar
school at Edinburgh." *(Scottish Historical Library*, p. 43.) This epitome
was never printed. The history was translated into the Scotish language by
John Reid, or Read; who, according to Calderwood's MS. was " servitur
and writer to Mr George Buchanan." In the library of the university of
Glasgow, I have inspected a MS. of this unpublished version, which bears
the following inscription. " The Historie of Scotland, first written in the
Latine tungue by that famous and learned man George Buchanan, and after-
ward translated into the Scottishe tungue by John Read, Esquyar, brother
to James Read, person of Banchory Ternam whyle he liued. They both ly
interred in the parishe church of that towne, seated not farre from the banke

year 1582, it issued from the office of Alexander Arbuthnot, printer to the king. It bears the royal privilege, and, like other works of the same author, is dedicated to the young monarch. The dedication is not unworthy of our attention. " When after a peregrination of twenty-four years,[k] I had at length returned to my native country, the first object of my care was to collect

of the riuer of Dee, expecting the general resurrection, and the glorious appeering of Jesus Christ there redimer." This transcript appears from the colophon to have been completed on the twelfth of December 1634. Another unpublished version belongs to the British Museum : " An History of the State of Scotland, by George Buchquhanane a Scotchman." (*Bib. Har.* N°. 7539.) This MS. is imperfect; it commences with the twelfth, and ends in the nineteenth book. The idiom is English, and the hand apparently of the seventeenth century. An English translation of Buchanan's history and dialogue was printing in London about the æra of the restoration : but on the seventh of June 1660, the publication was prohibited by an order of council. (Chalmers, p. 350.) In 1690, an English translation of Buchanan's history was published at London in folio. Prefixed is a good portrait of the author, engraved by R. White from an original painting in the possession of Sir Thomas Povey. In 1722, the same version was reprinted at London in two volumes octavo. This edition professes to be " revised and corrected from the Latin original, by Mr Bond :" but it is remarked by Ruddiman that although the first abounds with errors, yet he has not made the least alteration. (*Answer to Logan*, p. 315.) Of this translation there are other five editions, each consisting of two volumes octavo. Lond. 1733. Edinb. 1751-2. Edinb. 1762. Edinb. 1766. Glasg. 1799. There is an Aberdeen edition, 1799, consisting of two volumes in one. An English version of several books of Buchanan's history was published as an original work, under the title of " An Impartial Account of the Affairs of Scotland, from the death of King James V. to the tragical Exit of the Earl of Murray : by an eminent hand." Lond. 1705, 8vo.

[k] " Post viginti *quatuor* annorum peregrinationem." This reading must be erroneous. Buchanan left his native country in 1539 ; and he was at the Scotish court in the month of January 1562. Mr Love is inclined to suppose that he returned with the prior of St. Andrews in May 1561. (*Vindication of Buchanan*, p. 61.)

my papers, dispersed by the malignity of former
times, and in many respects exposed to improper
treatment.   For partly by the undue partiality
of my friends, by whom they were prematurely
published, partly by the immoderate licence
which printers, assuming the character of censors,
exercise with respect to other men's works, I
find many passages changed, chiefly according to
their respective fancies, and some vilely cor-
rupted.

" While I was attempting to remedy these in-
conveniencies, the sudden entreaties of my friends
disordered all my plans.   For all of them, as if
they had conspired with each other, exhorted me
to relinquish those performances of a more trivial
nature, which rather sooth the ear than inform
the mind, and to occupy myself in writing the
history of our nation.   This occupation, they
urged, was worthy of my age, and of the expectations concerning me which my countrymen had
formed; and no other subject presented stronger
incentives of praise, or promised to confer a more
lasting reputation.   To omit other considerations,
as Britain is the most renowned island in the
world, and its history involves transactions highly memorable in every respect, you will hardly
discover in the course of ages an individual who
has ventured to undertake so important a subject, and has evinced himself equal to the undertaking.

" It was likewise no slight incentive to me,

that I concluded my labour would neither be undue nor unacceptable to you. For it appeared
absurd and shameful that you, who at this early
age have perused the histories of almost every
nation, and have committed many of them to
memory, should in some measure be a stranger
at home. Besides as the incurable state of my
health will not permit me to discharge the office
intrusted to me of cultivating your genius,[1] I
have deemed it my next duty to betake myself
to that species of composition which is calculated
for improving the mind. With the view of exte-
nuating as far as lies in my power this fault of
cessation, I have therefore determined to send
you faithful monitors drawn from history, that
you may adopt their counsel in your deliberations,
and imitate their virtue in your actions. For
there are among your ancestors men distinguished by every species of excellence, and of whom
their posterity will never be ashamed. To omit
other instances, the records of human affairs will
not supply you with a character whom you can
compare to our king David. If to him divine
benignity has vouchsafed this preëminence, not
only in most miserable, but even in most flagitious times, we may reasonably hope that you (as
the royal prophet has expressed himself)[m] may

---

[1] " Partes ingenii tui. *excolendas*." This passage is evidently inaccurate.
The genuine reading, *excolendi*, is given in the edition of Finlater.

[m] " Ut sit *vates regius*." The purity of this phrase, as it is here applied,
has been called in question; and perhaps with sufficient reason. (Ruddiman's

likewise become to mothers the standard of their request whenever they pray for the prosperity of their offspring; that this commonwealth, now hastening to universal destruction and ruin, may even be regulated in its course, till it at length approach those times when human affairs having fulfilled the decree fixed from eternity, are to reach their destined close."

Between the original formation of his plan, and the publication of the history itself, nearly twenty years must have elapsed: but it is to be supposed that he long.revolved the subject in his mind, and had proceeded to amass the greater part of his materials, before he applied himself to its composition; and during that interval, his attention had been distracted by various pursuits, political as well as literary. His progress seems also to have been interrupted by another accident which cannot easily be defined.[n] Notwithstand-

---

Antichristi, p. 77.) *Vates regius* seems rather to denote a king's prophet, than a person who was at once a prophet and a king. To this very pure and correct writer, a few other improprieties have been imputed, but some of them without any competent foundation. Charges of solecism are more easily advanced than refuted; and many writers have advanced them with great temerity. Dr Johnson, for example, objects to Dryden's using a word of most unquestionable authority. " The *Threnodia*, which, by a term I am afraid neither authorized nor analogical, he calls *Augustalis*." (*Lives of English Poets*, vol. ii, p. 153.) The word *Augustalis* is used by Columella, Suetonius, Tacitus, and other ancient authors. It is sufficiently familiar to the ears of a civilian, for it repeatedly occurs in the Theodosian Code, and in the Code and Pandects of Justinian. " De Officio Praefecti *Augustalis*," is one of the rubrics in each of the two last collections.

[*] The following passage occurs in a letter from Sir Robert Bowes to Lord Burleigh, dated at Stirling on the eighteenth of September 1578.

ing the manifest disadvantages of divided attention, of infirm health, and of a languid old age,
he has produced one of the most eloquent and
masterly performances that have ever been submitted to the inspection of the learned world.
It is very justly remarked by the excellent
Thuanus, that although much of Buchanan's
time had been spent in scholastic occupations,
yet his history might be supposed the production of a man whose whole life had been exercised in the political transactions of the state;
the felicity of his genius, and the greatness of his
mind, having enabled him so completely to remove every impediment incident to an obscure
and humble lot.[o]

Buchanan has divided his history into twenty
books. The first three ought rather to have been
exhibited in the form of an introductory dissertation; for the historical narrative properly commences with the fourth book. His preliminary

---

" Buchanan hath ended his story wrytten to the death of the Erle of
Murrey. He proposith to command it to print shortly; *but one thing of
late hath been withdrawen from him*, which he trusteth to recover, or else to
supply of new with soer travell. He accepteth your lordships commendations with great comfort, and returneth to your lordship his humble duty and
thanks." (Murdin's *Collection of State Papers*, p. 316. Lond. 1759, fol.)

[o] " In senili otio patriam historiam aggressus est; quam tanta puritate,
prudentia, et acumine scripsit, quamvis interdum libertate genti innata,
contra regium fastigium acerbior, ut ea scriptio non hominem in pulvere
literario versatum, sed in media hominum luce et in tractandis reipublicæ
negotiis tota vita exercitatum redoleat: adeo ingenii felicitas et animi mag-
nitudo omnia obscuræ et humilis fortanæ impedimenta ab eo removerant, ut
propterea non minus recte de maximis rebus judicare et scribere prudenter
posset." (Thuani *Hist. sui Temporis*, vol. iv, p. 99.)

enquiries are directed to the geographical situation, the nature of the soil and climate, the ancient names and manners, and the primitive inhabitants of the British islands. The third book
consists of a series of quotations from the Greek
and Latin authors. The whole of this introductory part displays his usual erudition and sagacity; and, in the opinion of Archbishop Usher,
no writer had investigated the antiquities of his
country with superior diligence.[p] In these disquisitions he evinces his knowledge of the Celtic
as well as of the classical languages. He has manifested an unnecessary degree of solicitude and
warmth in exposing some of the antiquarian re-
veries of Humphrey Lhuyd, a Cambro-Briton
who published an historical fragment in the year
1572.[q] This was only ten years before the ap-

---

[p] Usserii Britannic. Eccles. Antiq. p. 733. Dublin. 1639, 4to.

[q] Commentarioli Britannicæ Descriptionis Fragmentum; auctore Hum-
fredo Lhuyd, Denbyghiense, Cambro-Britanno. Hujus auctoris diligen-
tiam et judicium lector admirabitur. Col. Agrip. 1572, 8vo. Mr Herbert
mentions an earlier edition; but I do not suppose that it ever existed. This
fragment is dedicated to Abraham Ortelius, who in his Theatrum Orbis Terrarum has inserted Lhuyd's Epistola de Mona Druidum Insula. A correct
edition of these two tracts of Lhuyd was published by his countryman
Moses Williams, A. M. Lond. 1731, 4to. A translation of the fragment had formerly appeared under the title of " The Breviary of Britayne,
&c. by Thomas Twyne, Gentleman." Lond. 1573, 8vo. A third production of the same author is entitled The Historie of Cambria, now called
Wales. Lond. 1584, 4to. This work was augmented, and published after
his death, by David Powell, D. D. " It pleased God," says Powell, " to
take him awaie in the floure of his time." He had been educated at Oxford, and his profession was that of physic. " Afterwards retiring to his
own country, lived mostly within the walls of Denbigh castle, practised
his faculty, and sometimes that of musick for diversion sake, being then

pearance of Buchanan's work: but the three books which first occur in the present arrangement do not seem to have been first composed; and it is only in those books that he refers to Lhuyd's production.

In the earlier part of his narration, he has reposed too much confidence on his predecessor Hector Boyce. Many of the fables of that romantic writer he has indeed rejected; but he was not sufficiently aware of the extreme hazard of relying on such an authority. Boyce had not yet begun to be generally regarded as a notable fabulist. " Hector," says Bishop Lloyd with

esteemed a well bred gentleman. He was a passing right antiquary, and a person of great skill and knowledge in British affairs." (Wood's *Athenæ Oxonienses*, vol. i, col. 129.) Mr Barrington, a more competent judge, acknowledges that Lhuyd " is generally very accurate in what relates to the history of Wales, or its antiquities." (*Observations on the Statutes*, p. 383.) But many of his notions are sufficiently absurd. Of his antiquarian theories, Languet did not entertain a more favourable opinion than Buchanan. (Langueti *Epistolæ ad Sydneium*, p. 29, 41.)

ʳ Ruddiman, Anticrisis, p. 6, Answer to Logan, p. 80.

ˢ Hector Boyce, D. D. was the first principal of King's College, Aberdeen, and was besides a canon of the cathedral. He was a native of Dundee, and completed his studies at Paris; where he was for some time a professor of philosophy. His first publication is entitled, " Episcoporum Murthlacensium et Aberdonensium per Hectorem Boetium Vitæ." Paris. 1522, 4to. He afterwards published " Scotorum Historiæ a prima Gentis Origine, cum aliarum et Rerum et Gentium Illustratione non vulgari, [libri xvii]." This work was printed in folio by Badius Ascensius, probably in the year 1527. The dedication to King James is dated in 1526; but the commendatory epistle by Alexander Lyon, in the following year. An edition, containing the eighteenth book and a fragment of the nineteenth, was published by Ferrerius; who added an appendix of thirty-five pages. Paris. 1574, fol. Though published at Paris, this edition appears from the colophon to have been printed at Lausanne. Gaddius styles the Scotish

T

some degree of pleasantry, " put this monk's tales into the form of an history ; and pieced them out with a very good invention, that part in which he chiefly excelled. Buchanan put them into excellent Latin : he could have put them into as good verse, if he had pleased ; and that perhaps had been better, for then they would have looked more like a poem.''[1] Buchanan has appealed to several other Scotish historians ; and he unquestionably had access to historical documents which are no longer extant. He has occasionally availed himself of the collateral aid of the English and French writers.[u] His sketch of the earlier reigns is brief and rapid ; nor has he attempted to establish any chronological notation till he descends to the four hundred and fourth year of the Christian æra. It must indeed be acknowledged that he has repeated the fabul-

historian " magister Latino eloquio." (*De Scriptoribus non Ecclesiasticis*, tom. i, p. 75.) And Buchanan describes him as " non solum artium liberalium cognitione, supra quam illa ferebant tempora, insignem, sed et humanitate et comitate singulari præditum." (*Rerum Scotic. Hist.* p. 44.) At the command of King James the fifth, a Scotish translation of Boyce's history was executed by John Bellenden, archdeacon of Murray, and canon of Ross. It was published in folio and in black letter, with the following title : *Heir beginnis the Hystory and Croniklis of Scotland*. This edition, which seems to be the only one, has no date ; but it was " imprentit in Edinburgh be me Thomas Dauidson, prenter to the kyngis nobyll grace." In the library of the university of Edinburgh there is a splendid copy, printed on vellum.

[t] Lloyd's Historical Account of Church-Government in Great Britain and Ireland, pref.

[u] In his history, Buchanan refers to Fordun, Winton, Mair, Boyce, Matthew Paris, William of Newbury, Thomas Walsingham, Polydore Virgil, Caxton, Hall, Grafton, Froissart, and Monstrellet.

the line of our ancient kings; but that continued till a much later period to be regarded as an article of national faith. The erudition and judgment of Lloyd and Stillingfleet, of Innes and Pinkerton, had not then been applied to the intricate investigation. Like most of the classical historians, Buchanan is too remiss in marking the chronology of the different facts which he records. His narrative, from the reign of the great King Robert, becomes much more copious and interesting; but the history of his own times, which were pregnant with remarkable events, occupies far the largest proportion of his twenty books. In some of the transactions which he relates, his own affections and passions were deeply concerned, and might not unreasonably be expected to impart some tincture to his style. "His bitterness in writing of the queen", says Archbishop Spotswood, " and troubles of the time, all wise men have disliked. But otherwise no man did merit better of his nation for learning, nor thereby did bring to it more glory."[1] This is the remark of a candid and enlightened man who enjoyed the particular favour of the queen's son and grandson : he has not however hazarded the slightest insinuation of Buchanan's having asserted what he did not himself believe. It was manifestly the interest as well as the inclination of this prelate, to exhibit the character of Mary in

---

[1] Spotswood's Hist. of the Church of Scotland, p. 325.

the most favourable point of view; and yet his
love of truth, and the force of contemporary
evidence, have compelled him to sanction the
general tenor of his predecessor's narrative. So
great indeed is the archbishop's deference for his
authority, that, in the opinion at least of a noble
author, " he is every where a retailer of Buchanan's prejudices."[y] His indignation against
that deluded princess, Buchanan shared with a
very large proportion of his fellow subjects; and
many of her actions were such as could not fail
of exciting the antipathy of every well-regulated
mind.[z] He believed that the misdeeds of the
ill-fated queen were such as dissolved every tie
by which he might once be bound; and that her
conduct had not only superseded her hereditary
claims of allegiance, but had even reflected disgrace on her country and sex. That some of the
circumstances which he relates are not consistent
with complete accuracy, is only what may be
affirmed with respect to any other historian. He
was not himself an eye-witness of every transaction of his own age; and amidst the animosities of that turbulent period, he must chiefly have
derived his information from the adherents of
one party. That Bishop Lesley has exhibited a

· [y] Elibank's Letter to Lord Hailes, on his Remarks on the History of
Scotland, p. 17. Edinb. 1773, 8vo.

[z] Thuanus to Camden. " Acerbius hæc fortasse a Buchanano scripta,
et audio discipulum præceptori ob id succensere; et tamen quia gesta sunt,
citra flagitium dissimulari non possunt." (Camdeni *Epistolæ*, p. 68. Lond.
1691, 4to.)

more faithful detail of the singular events of
that crisis, is an assertion which has indeed been
hazarded, but which it would be extremely easy
to refute. Lesley has generally evinced as much
candour as could have been expected from a
writer placed in such circumstances; but he was
a Papist, and one of the queen's chief agents; he
had been deprived of a bishopric and other high
preferments; and his work was printed at Rome.[a]
The veracity of Buchanan with respect to the
most controverted facts recorded in his history,
has been confirmed by a very recent examination
of original documents: some of the darkest transactions of that period have been placed in a
clear and steady light by the able disquisitions of
Mr Laing, to whom Buchanan has many obligations.

The style of his history betrays no symptoms
of the author's old age and infirmities: it is not

---

[a] John Lesley, LL. D. bishop of Ross, and president of the court of
session, was born on the 29th of September 1527. He took the degree of
A. M. in King's College, Aberdeen; and afterwards prosecuted his juridical studies in several of the French universities. He was for some time
professor of the canon law at Aberdeen. (Orem's *Description of King's
College*, p. 156.) After a long exile, he died at Brussels on the 31st of
May 1596. See an account of his life in Anderson's *Collections relating to
the Hist. of Q. Mary*, vol. i. Lesley is the author of various works; most
of which may be found in the collections of Anderson and Jebb. His history is entitled "De Origine, Moribus, et Rebus Gestis Scotorum libri
decem." Romæ, 1578, 4to. His "temper and way of writing," says J.
Crawford, "are excellent, only his style, though in the main strokes it be
good, yet in many places wants finishing, and is not altogether free from
errours." (*Hist. of the House of Esté*, pref. Lond. 1681, 8vo.) To
Lesley's history Muretus has prefixed some complimentary verses.

merely distinguished by its correctness and elegance, it breathes all the fervent animation of youthful genius.   The noble ideas which so frequently rise in his mind, he always expresses in language of correspondent dignity.   His narrative is extremely perspicuous, variegated, and interesting : it is seldom deficient, and never redundant.   Notwithstanding his long habits of poetical composition, he has carefully refrained from interspersing this work with phraseologies unsuitable to the diction of prose ; and in the whole course of his narrative he has only introduced a single quotation from a poet.   His moral and political reflections are profound and masterly.   It is with the utmost propriety that he has been characterized as a man of exquisite judgment.[b]   He is ready upon all occasions to vindicate the unalienable rights of mankind ; and he uniformly delivers his sentiments with a nòble freedom and energy.   His zeal in branding vice is only equalled by his zeal in commending virtue.   The martial exploits of his valiant countrymen he has often recited with all the enthusiasm of a young warrior.

To some of his principal characters he has assigned formal speeches.   This was the common practice of the ancient historians, and it has likewise been adopted by several of the moderns.

---

[b] Conringius de Antiquitatibus Academicis, p. 79, edit. Heumanni. Gottingæ, 1739, 4to.

But it has at length been generally exploded; and however it may contribute to diversity or interest, it may safely be stigmatized as unsuitable in a composition which professes to record events and circumstances as they actually occurred.[c] Buchanan's orators are uncommonly eloquent. The most admired of his harangues is that which he imputes to Archbishop Kennedy after the death of James the second. Its principal position is, that the sovereign power ought not to be intrusted to the hands of a woman; a position which had been maintained with equal strenuousness by John Knox, and with equal zeal controverted by Bishop Lesley.[d] Some of the speeches which he ascribes to contemporary characters,

[c] " I hold," says Lord Monboddo, " that in every history well composed, there ought to be *speeches*, without which, I think, a history hardly deserves that name, but should be called a *chronicle or annals*." (*Origin and Progress of Language*, vol. v, p. 280.) That is to say, a history ought not to be called a history unless it assume the appearance of a romance. Vossius likewise contends for the introduction of orations (*Ars Historica*, p. 98, edit. Lugd. Bat. 1653, 4to.); but the opinion of Perizonius appears more solid and judicious: " Eas ego in veteribus, si non sint immodicæ aut nimis crebræ, ferre possum et excusare, at in nostris scriptoribus minus probaverim. Alia enim illorum, alia horum est ratio." (*Q. Curtius Vindicatus*, p. 94. Lugd. Bat. 1703, 8vo.)

[d] Knox published " The First Blast of the Trumpet against the Monstrvovs Regiment of Women." 1558, 8vo. Lesley is the author of a tract entitled " De Illustrium Foeminarum in Repub: administranda et ferendis Legibus Authoritate, Libellus." Rhemis, 1580, 4to. Montesquieu's general opinion coincides with that of Lesley. (*De l'Esprit des Loix*, liv. vii, chap. xvii.)

In the year 1567, the Scotish legislature thought it " expedient that in no tymes cuming ony wemen salbe admittit to the publict autoritie of the realme, or functioun in publict gouernment within the same." (*Acts of the Parliaments of Scotland*, vol. iii, p. 38.)

are such as may be supposed to have been really delivered; for the author must have been present on the occasions to which they are referred. But it is one of the inconveniences attending factitious harangues, that their introduction renders it impossible to distinguish those which are genuine.

Buchanan may be compared to the ancient historians in another respect : with regard to prodigies, he has betrayed some degree of credulity. But this was a defect incident to the age, rather than the individual; nor must it be forgotten that he records some of those preternatural circumstances without professing to consider them as entitled to credit. The national rumour concerning them appears to have been strong; and he might deem it incumbent upon him to submit them to the discussion of his readers. During the age of Buchanan, even the most intelligent were credulous; and many of the opinions revered by the present age may possibly excite the pity or derision of the more enlightened ages which are yet to come. The intellectual slumber of a thousand years had recently been shaken off: but so extremely slow is the progress of good sense, that even now it can only be considered as proceeding towards a distant maturity. Every age is however disposed to rest satisfied with its own attainments; and this is at once the effect and the cause of ignorance.

What particular historian among the ancients Buchanan had selected as his model, is a question which some learned men have not been able to determine. As a preparation for his task, he is said to have perused all the remaining books of Livy not fewer than twenty times.[e] Rapin the Jesuit represents him as a servile imitator of Livy;[f] but this servile imitation is far from being evident to more candid critics. It was an opinion of the celebrated Andrew Fletcher that his diction bears a nearer resemblance to that of Cæsar.[g] Buchanan, says Le Clerc, has united the brevity of Sallust with the elegance and terseness of Livy; for those are the two authors whom he proposed chiefly to imitate; as they who have perused them with attention, will easily recognize when they come to read the Scotish historian.[h] These various assertions are manifestly irreconcilable with each other; nor do they serve to evince that Buchanan has selected any particular model, but rather that he has singly rivalled the characteristic excellencies of several historians of the greatest name. The style of his history is not a borrowed style: he had formed his diction by a long familiarity with the best writers of antiquity; and his manly and delicate taste enabled him to exhibit an admirable model of his own.

[e] Fabricii Bibliotheca Latina, vol. ii, p. 205.
[f] Rapin, Reflexions sur l'Histoire, p. 252.
[g] Ruddimanni præf. in Buchananum, p. x.
[h] Bibliotheque Choisie, tom. viii, p. 174.

It is not his chief praise that he writes like a diligent imitator of the ancients, but that he writes as if he himself were one of the ancients.

Bishop Burnet has remarked that "his stile is so natural and nervous, and his reflections on things are so solid, that he is justly reckoned the greatest and best of our modern authors."[i] Notwithstanding his political prejudices, Dryden likewise mentions him in terms of high commendation. "Buchanan indeed for the purity of his Latin, and for his learning, and for all other endowments belonging to an historian, might be plac'd amongst the greatest, if he had not too much lean'd to prejudice, and too manifestly declar'd himself a party of a cause, rather than an historian of it. Excepting only that, (which I desire not to urge too far on so great a man, but only to give caution to his readers concerning it,) our isle may justly boast in him, a writer comparable to any of the moderns, and excell'd by few of the ancients."[j] Lord Monboddo, whose opi-

[i] Burnet's Hist. of the Reformation, vol. i, p. 311.

[j] Dryden's Life of Plutarch, p. 56.—Buchanan's Latinity is highly commended by Sir William Temple, another very popular writer of that period. "Thus began the restoration of learning in these parts, with that of the Greek tongue; and soon after, Reuchlyn and Erasmus began that of the purer and ancient Latin. After them Buchanan carried it, I think, to the greatest heighth of any of the moderns before or since." (*Essay upon the Ancient and Modern Learning*, p. 161.) Reuchlin has found an industrious biographer in his countryman J. H. Maius; whose publication is entitled "Vita Jo. Reuchlini Phorcensis, primi in Germania Hebraicarum Graecarumque, et aliarum bonarum Literarum Instauratoris." Durlaci, 1697, 8vo.

nion on this subject coincides with Wicquefort's,[k] prefers his history to that of Livy. " I will begin with my countryman Buchanan, who has written the history of his own country in Latin, and in such Latin, that I am not afraid to compare his stile with that of any Roman historian. He lived in an age when the Latin language was very much cultivated; and among the learned it was not only the only language in which they wrote, but a living language; for they spoke no other when they conversed together, at least upon learned subjects..... In such an age, and with all the advantages of a learned education, did George Buchanan write the history of Scotland from the earliest times down to his own time: and I hesitate not to pronounce that the stile of his narrative is better than that of Livy; for it is as pure and elegant, is better composed in periods not intricate and involved like those of Livy, and without that affected brevity which makes Livy's stile so obscure. Even in speeches, in which Livy is supposed to excel so much, I think his composition is better; and he has none of those short pointed sentences, the *vibrantes sententiolæ*, which Livy learned in the school of declamation."[1]

The motives which impel men to arduous undertakings, may be scrutinized with too much

[k] Wicquefort, Memoires touchant les Ambassadeurs et les Ministres Publics, p. 442. Haye, 1677, 8vo.

[1] Monboddo's Origin and Progress of Language, vol. v, p. 229.

nicety. In his dedication, Buchanan has sufficiently revealed the motives which induced him
to write the history of his native country: but
some of his enemies persuade themselves that
they have discovered another powerful motive,
which he has excluded from his enumeration.
The earl of Murray, they imagine, had formed a
secret plan of usurping the crown; and the sole
or at least the principal object of that history
was, to prepare the nation for receiving him as
their legitimate monarch. That Murray ever
entertained such a project, is to be regarded as a
mere fiction;[m] nor must it be forgotten that he
died twelve years before the history was published. If such therefore was the ambition of the
one, and the obsequiousness of the other, they
might certainly have embraced a more direct
method of accomplishing their purpose. Buchanan is accused of having frequently employed, in
his account of the regal succession, such terms as
insinuate popular election, rather than hereditary
right; with the oblique view of reminding the
nation of its inherent power to elevate the good
regent to the permanent dignity of a king. But;

---

[m] " Nam demus," says the impartial Thuanus, " quod ab diversa traden-
tibus jactatur, Moravium ambitione ardentem scelerate regnum appetiisse:
quod tamen constanter negant omnes fide digni Scoti, quaecunque mihi allo-
qui contigit; etiam ii quibus alioqui Moravius ob religionis causam summe
invisus erat; nam virum fuisse aiebant extra religionis causam ab omni ambitione, avaritia, et in quenquam injuria alienum; virtute, comitate, bene-
ficentia vitaeque innocentia praestantem; et qui nisi fuisset, eos qui tanto-
pere mortuum exagitant, hodie minime rerum potituros fuisse." (Camdeni
Epistolae, p. 73.)

unfortunately for this hypothesis, the very same phrases had been adopted by his predecessor Boyce, and even by Lesley, the faithful adherent of the exiled queen. This conduct is in Lesley ascribed to accident, but in Buchanan to treasonable intentions:[a] and the actions of the latter have generally been estimated by the same variable standard. The reason of such phrases being adopted by those authors is simple and obvious. Although they had undertaken to unfold the progress of an hereditary monarchy, they had formed their style by a long and careful perusal of the historians of an ancient republic. To the succession of the Scotish kings they applied the phrases by which Livy had described the succession of the Roman consuls. This practice of accommodating classical terms to modern subjects which they only explain by a faint analogy, is well known to every man of learning; and by some historians, particularly by Bembus, it has been carried to a ridiculous excess.

As Buchanan is supposed to have commenced his great undertaking from motives of treason, so he is charitably represented as having terminated it from motives of revenge. " His history," it has been remarked, " comes no farther than the end of the year 1572, in which the earl of Lennox was slain ; and though he lived ten years af-

---

[a] " The other (Lesley) *inconsiderately*, and contrary to his own principle, following his leader Boece, sometimes *stumbles on that phrase.*" (Ruddiman's *Answer to Logan*, p. 71.)

ter, yet, because he hated (as Sir James Melvil
informs us) the earl of Morton, he would not continue the history through his regency."° To
some men the motives of the living and of the
dead are wonderfully transparent. To dislike
the earl of Morton was not in itself reprehensible ; for, according to Melvil's own account, he
was haughty, avaricious, and cruel. Buchanan
however has frequently mentioned him in his
history, without any invidious insinuations; and
this circumstance, if he actually hated him, must
at least be regarded as a proof of his magnani-
mity.ᴾ   But it was not sufficient to remark that

---

* Ruddiman's Answer to Logan, p. 80.

ᴾ " He was also religious," says Sir James Melvil, " but was easily abused,
and so facile, that he was led by every company that he haunted, which made
him factious in his old days, for he spoke and wrote as those who were about
him informed him: for he was become careless, following in many things
the vulgar opinion : for he was naturally popular, and extreamly revengeful
against any man who had offended him, which was his greatest fault. For
he did write despightful invectives against the earl of Monteeth, for some
particulars that were between him and the laird of Buchanan. He became
the earl of Mortoun's great enemy for that a nagg of his chanced to be taken
from his servant during the civil troubles, and was bought by the regent,
who had no will to part with the said horse, he was so ' sure' footed and so
easie, that albeit Mr George had oft-times required him again, he could not
get him. And therefore though he had been the regent's great friend before,
he became his mortal enemy, and from that time forth spoke evil of him in
all places, and at all occasions." (Memoires, p. 125.)   Here Melvil must
have written " as those who were about him informed him ;" nor must it be
forgotten that his politics were in direct opposition to those of Buchanan.
The best refutation of these assertions is that Buchanan's history, which was
published after the earl's execution, contains not a single insinuation to his
prejudice: on the contrary, he is repeatedly mentioned in very respectful
terms ; for it was not till after he became regent, that his conduct was so obnoxious.

Nisbet's story of Buchanan's enmity towards William Earl Marischal is

he survived the earl of Lennox ten years; it
ought likewise to have been ascertained, whether
he desisted from his task ten years before his
own decease.⁹ . Human actions were never estimated in a more perverse manner; for the completion of his history, and the termination of his
life, took place about the very same period.

In the month of September 1581, some of his
learned friends, namely Andrew Melvin, James
Melvin, and his own cousin Thomas Buchanan,
provost of the collegiate church of Kirkheugh,
having heard that the work was in the press and
the author indisposed, hastened to Edinburgh to
pay him a visit. James, who was the nephew
of Andrew Melvin, and professor of divinity at
St Andrews, has in simple terms recorded the
principal circumstances which occurred during
their interview. On entering his apartment, they
found one of the greatest characters of the age ʳ

of a similar complexion. " Buchanan being by the earl refused the purchase
of a piece of land, said to have of old belonged to some of his relations, as is
vulgarly reported in the family, threatened revenge, which he seems to have
performed by his profound silence through all his history of this noble family, and their heroic actions." (System of Heraldry, vol. ii, app. p. 7.) In
his history, Buchanan has frequently mentioned the noble family of Keith.

" Accessit eo historiæ scribendæ labor," said Buchanan on the ninth of
November 1579,' " in ætate integra permolestus, nunc vero in hac medita-
tione mortis, inter mortalitatis metum, et desinendi pudorem, non potest non
lentus esse et ingratus, quando nec cessare licet, nec progredi lubet." (Epistolæ, p. 25.) He was then in the seventy-fourth year of his age.

. ʳ Salmasius has characterized Buchanan as " summum ætatis suæ
virum." (Epistola ad Menagium, p. 54.) Heinsius, who differed so widely from Salmasius on other subjects, denominates him " virum suo sæculo
majorem." (Burmanni Sylloge Epistolarum, tom. ii, p. 451.)

employed in the humble though benevolent task
of teaching the hornbook to a young man in his
service. After the usual salutations, " I perceive,
Sir," said Andrew Melvin, " you are not idle."
" Better this," replied Buchanan, " than stealing
sheep, or sitting idle, which is as bad." He afterwards shewed them his dedication to the young
king; and Melvin having perused it, remarked
that it seemed in some passages obscure, and required certain words to complete the sense.
" I can do nothing more," said Buchanan, " for
thinking of another matter." " What is that ?"
rejoined Melvin.—" To die. But I leave that,
and many other things to your care." Melvin
likewise alluded to the publication of Blackwood's answer to his treatise *De Jure Regni apud
Scotos*. These visitors afterwards proceeded to
Arbuthnot's printing-office, to inspect a work
which had excited such high expectation. They
found the impression had advanced so far as the
passage relative to the interment of David Rizzio;
and being alarmed at the unguarded boldness
with which the historian had there expressed
himself, they requested the printer to desist.
Having returned to Buchanan's house, they
found him in bed. In answer to their friendly
enquiries, he informed them that he was " even
going the way of welfare." His kinsman then proceeded to mention their fears respecting the consequence of publishing so unpalatable a statement,
and to suggest the probability of its inducing the

king to prohibit the entire work. " Tell me, man," said Buchanan, " if I have told the truth." " Yes Sir," replied his cousin, " I think so." " Then," rejoined the dying historian, " I will abide his feud, and all his kin's. Pray to God for me, and let him direct all." So, subjoins the original narrative, " by the printing of his chronicle was ended, that most learned, wise, and godly man ended this mortal life."•

Such is the substance, and nearly the form, of James Melvin's relation ; which is sufficiently probable in itself, and is sanctioned by the authority of a clergyman and professor of divinity. It furnishes a complete refutation of a story recorded by Camden, that, upon the approach of death, Buchanan testified the utmost compunction for having wielded his pen against Queen Mary.† This story could indeed have been ex-

---

• Life of James Melvin, written by Himself, p. 107. MS. in the Library of the Writers to the Signet.—The visit to Buchanan is very distinctly placed among the occurrences of 1581. Love, Man, and other writers, have, without any hint of such a change, introduced the date of 1582. They may have supposed that Melvin intended to refer this visit to the same year with the publication of Buchanan's history.

† Camdeni Annales, vol. i, p. 130, edit. Hearnii.—The story of Buchanan's repentance is repeated by Strada, *De Bello Belgico*, dec. ii, lib. viii, p. 481, and by Dr Robert Johnston, *Rerum Britannicarum Historia*, p. 81. Amst. 1655, fol. Strada, with more than Jesuitical impudence, asserts that he was " partim spe inductus a Moravió, si hic regnum potiretur, se in Scotiæ patriarcham assumendum ;" that he hoped to be rewarded with the archbishopric of St Andrews. To the vague report of Camden, Mr Sage added an old woman's tale which sufficiently confutes itself. His letter is subjoined to Bishop Gillan's *Life of the Reverend and Learned Mr John Sage*, p. 70. Lond. 1714, 8vo. See also Hearne's preface to Camden,

U

ploded without the aid of such a document: Camden was undoubtedly a man of virtue; and although his Latinity is somewhat barbarous, he was possessed of no contemptible share of learning. But he wrote under the immediate control of King James; who was extremely anxious to prejudice his mind against the character of an historian, who had treated that of his royal mother with so little ceremony. He was employed, along with Casaubon, in transmitting to Thuanus such counterstatements as suited his majesty's views; but this enlightened and impartial foreigner preferred the authority of Buchanan to that of his royal pupil.* Thuanus was one of the most valuable characters whom the world has yet seen. His testimony in favour of the Scotish historian was uniform; nor ought it to be overlooked by those who prefer truth to sophistry. If Buchanan had asserted what he knew to be false, it would be charitable to sup-

---

p. cv, Love's *Vindication of Buchanan*, p. 18, and Laing's *Hist. of Scotland*, vol. ii, p. 139.—A very false and absurd account of Buchanan's death may be found in Garasse's *Doctrine Curieuse des Beaux Esprits de ce Temps*, p. 748. Paris, 1623, 4to. This work is very justly represented by Ogier, a writer of his own communion, as " un cloaque d'impieté, une sentine de profanations, un ramas de beufonneries." (*Jugement et Censure du livre de la Doctrine Curieuse de François Garasse.* Paris, 1623, 8vo.)

* A curious collection of papers, " De Thuani Historiæ Successu apud Jacobum I. Magnæ Britanniæ Regem," may be found in Buckley's noble edition of the works of Thuanus, tom. vii.—" Rem," says Thuanus to Camden, " ut ex Scotorum qui interfuerant sermonibus didici, ita literis mandavi; et ad eorum fidem scripta a Buchanano expendi. De cætero, nigrum in candidum in cujusquam gratiam convertere, neque animus ab initio fuit, neque nunc esse debuit." (Camdeni *Epistolæ*, p. 74.)

pose his subsequent repentance; but the simple and authentic narrative of Melvin leaves no room for suppositions.

Thuanus informs us that a short time before his death, Buchanan was required by his royal pupil to retract what he had written with so much freedom respecting the queen his mother, and to leave to posterity some formal testimony of his compunction. He at first returned an evasive answer; but being afterwards importuned by repeated messages, he made this final declaration; that he could not recall what he had written in the firm conviction of its truth; but that after his decease, it would be in the king's power to adopt such measures with regard to his writings as he might judge expedient. He however admonished him to proceed with mature deliberation; and to reflect that although God has intrusted supreme power to kings, yet that truth, which derives its strength from God, is as superior to their control as God is superior to man.[x] About a month before Buchanan's death, the young monarch, who was then in the seventeenth year of his age, had been seized and forcibly detained by the earl of Gowrie and his accomplices. These conspirators were anxious to

[x] Thuani Hist. sui Temporis, tom. iv, p. 100, var. lect.—Bayle, Mackenzie, and Wodrow, have each preserved a traditionary account of Buchanan's answer. Though these accounts vary the expression, they may all be considered as tending to confirm the essential particulars of Thuanus's narrative. See Mr Laing's *Hist. of Scotland*, vol. ii, p. 138.

obtain the countenance of his preceptor; but they could not prevail upon him to express any approbation of so violent a proceeding.[y]

His usual vein of pleasantry did not entirely desert him on his death-bed; a circumstance which seemed to bespeak a mind free from agony or alarm. When visited by John Davidson, a clergyman, he devoutly expressed his reliance on the blood of Christ; but he could not refrain from introducing some facetious reflections on the absurdities of the mass.[z] One of Buchanan's biographers relates that when he felt the approach of death, he questioned his servant Young respecting the state of his funds; and finding that all the money in his possession was not sufficient to defray the expenses of his funeral, he ordered it to be distributed among the poor. When the servant enquired who was to undertake the charge of his interment, he replied, that was a matter concerning which he was very indifferent; and if they did not chuse to bury him, they might either suffer him to lie where he was, or throw his corpse where they pleased. He was accordingly buried at the expense of the city of Edinburgh.[a] This anecdote may seem to be ren-

[y] Camdeni Annales, vol. ii, p. 386.

[z] Wodrow's MS. Life of Buchanan.

[a] Mackenzie's Lives of Scots Writers, vol. iii, p. 172.—This anecdote he professes to relate from the information of the old earl of Cromarty, who received it from his grandfather Lord Invertyle; who had been placed under Buchanan's tuition along with the king. The two anecdotes introduced above, p. 159, Dr Mackenzie has stated on the same authority.

dered more probable by an authentic document, from which it appears that his only funds at the time of his decease consisted of an arrear of one hundred pounds, due upon his pension arising from the temporalities of Crossragwell abbey.[b] He expired a short while after five o'clock in the morning of Friday the twenty-eighth of September 1582, at the age of seventy-six years and nearly eight months. His remains were interred in the cemetery of the Grey-friars : Calderwood informs us that the funeral took place on Saturday, and was attended by " a great company of the faithful." His ungrateful country never afforded his grave the common tribute of a monumental stone.[c]

---

[b] See Appendix, No. ix.

[c] A late writer has bestowed heavy castigation on Mr Callender for asserting, in the book called " Lord Gardenstone's Miscellanies," p. 252, that Buchanan's grave was never distinguished by a tomb-stone. " Yet," he remarks, " is this positive assertion, of confident ignorance, contradicted by the following record : ' At Edinburgh, the 3d day of December 1701 ; the same day the council being informed, that the through stone [tomb-stone] of the deceast George Buchanan lyes sunk under the ground of the Grey-friars : therefore, they appoint the chamberlain to raise the same, and clear the inscription thereupon ; so as the same may be legible.' The inscription, which was thus restored to the eye of the passenger, by the piety of Edinburgh, was written by John Adamson. From these facts, we may learn, what an easy task it is to write memoirs, without research ; to praise, without knowledge ; and to censure, without proof." (Chalmers, p. 348.) The record certainly proves that the town-council had been assured of the existence of such a stone ; but, like other councils, it may often have been assured of what was absolutely false. The supposed tomb-stone, being sunk under ground, was confessedly invisible. Adamson's epigram, which is not of the monumental kind, unfortunately evinces that Buchanan's tomb was totally undecorated by the art of the sculptor.

> Marmoreæ eur stant hic omni ex parte columnæ,
> Signaque ab artificum dædala facta manu ?

The museum at Edinburgh contains a skull which has long been supposed to be that of Buchanan, and which in its general aspect certainly corresponds with the best portraits. The traditionary history of this venerable relique is, that it was procured by the irregular zeal of John Adamson, and after his decease became the property of the university. To render this account more credible, it may be necessary to mention that Adamson was about six years of age at the period of Buchanan's death, and that he himself survived beyond the middle of the following century. Within little more than forty years after his decease, when the tradition may be supposed to have been sufficiently recent, we find it recorded by a public officer of the university. This skull, which is so thin as to be trans-

Ut spectent oculis monumenta insignia vivi,
    Per quæ defunctis concilietur honos.
Talia nonne etiam debet Buchananus habere,
    Doctius aut melius quo nihil orbis habet ?
Gloriolas vivus qui contemnebat inanes,
    An cupiet divus se decorent lapides ?
Illis fas pulchro nomen debere sepulchro,
    Qui nil quo melius nobilitentur habent.
Per te olim tellus est nobilitata Britanna,
    Et decus es tumulo jam, Buchanane, tuo.

As an inscription actually engraved on Buchanan's tomb-stone, Mr Chalmers quotes an epigram which clearly proves that no such tomb-stone existed. For this epigram he refers to Sir Robert Sibbald's commentary, p. 61, where it is thus introduced : " Joannes Adamsonus de *cespitio Georgii Bu-* " *chanani tumulo* in cœmeterio Edinensi, multorum aliorum marmoreis monumentis affabre exstructis septo et circundato, cecinit." Ninian Paterson, who flourished at a later period than Adamson, has repeatedly upbraided the native country of Buchanan with neglecting to testify its gratitude by the erection of a funeral monument. (*Epigrammata*, p. 66, 142, Edinb. 1678, 8vo.)

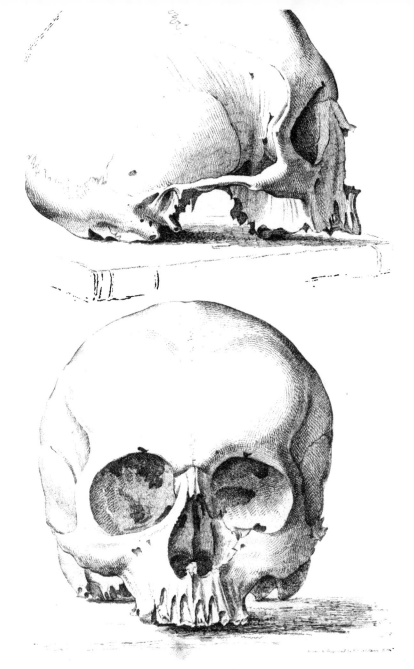

Edinburgh Published by Wm Blackwood 1826

parent, is commonly shewn in contrast with that of an idiot, which is of prodigious thickness.[d]

The death of this illustrious man was less commemorated by the surviving poets than might reasonably have been expected. Some poetical tributes were however produced on the occasion. Melvin, who had frequently celebrated him while alive, did not fail to discharge the last debt of lettered friendship;[e] and Scaliger composed his epitaph in terms of liberal and appropriate praise.

Postquam laude tua patriam, meritisque beasti,
    Buchanane, tuis solis utrumque latus,
Contemptis opibus, spretis popularibus auris,
    Ventosæque fugax ambitionis, obis;
Præmia quina quater Pisææ functus olivæ,
    Et linquens animi pignora rara tui:
In quibus haud tibi se anteferent quos Itala vates
    Terra dedit: nec quos Gallia mater alit,

[a] In a MS. catalogue drawn up about the year 1697, by Robert Henderson, A. M. librarian to the university, I find the subsequent entry. " A very thin skull (said to be Mr George Buchanan's) with a copy of Latine verses affixt, writ by Mr John Adamson, primare prof. of our colledge 1636. It's storied of him that being at Buchanan's burial, he bargained for the skull; which having got from the graveman within the year or so, he carefully kept in his life-time; and being found in his study so inscribed after his removal, was handed down to us." This tradition, like many others, seems to contain a mixture of truth and falsehood. From the dedication which Adamson has prefixed to the posthumous work of Charles Ferme, it appears that he was born in the year 1576. (Fermæi *Analysis Logica in Epistolam Apostoli Pauli ad Romanos.* Edinburgi, 1651, 8vo.) It cannot therefore be supposed that he attended Buchanan's funeral in 1582. He took the degree of A. M. in 1597, was appointed one of the regents in the following year, and was admitted principal on the 21st of November 1623. (Crawford's *Hist. of the University of Edinburgh,* p. 42, 97.) " Ejus cura," says Sibbald, p. 62, " Buchanani cranium de sepulchro erutum, in bibliotheca academiæ Edinburgenæ asservatur." The skull has lately been removed to the museum.

[e] Melvini Musæ, p. 6. 1620, 4to.

Æquabunt genium felicis carminis, et quæ
Orbis habet famæ conscia signa tuæ.
Namque ad supremum perducta poetica calmen
In te stat, nec quo progrediatur habet.
Imperii fuerat Romani Scotia limes:
Romani eloquii Scotia finis erit.[f]

Buchanan had consecrated a monument of his own fame, composed of materials more permanent than brass or marble; but his country has at length afforded him one of those memorials which are of least value when most merited, and which contribute more to the honour of the living than of the dead. An obelisk, nineteen feet square at the base, and rising to the height of one hundred and three feet, was lately erected to his memory at the village of Killearn. The plan was suggested by the late Robert Dunmore, Esq. to a very numerous company assembled in the house of a gentleman in that vicinity. A subscription was immediately opened, and nearly completed; and one of their number, the late Mr Craig, a nephew of Thomson, furnished the architectural design as his contribution.

Buchanan had experienced many of the vicissitudes of human life, and had been tried by prosperity as well as adversity. His moral and his intellectual character procured him the same high respect from the most enlightened of his contemporaries; and it ought to excite some degree of surprise, that notwithstanding the rigid

[f] Jos. Scaligeri Opuscula, p. 286. Paris. 1610, 4to.

scrutiny of a long succession of enemies, political
and theological, his lengthened and variegated
life has been found to betray so few of the frail-
ties inseparable from our nature. His stern integrity, his love of his country and of mankind,
cannot fail of endearing his memory to those
who possess congenial qualities; and such errors
as he actually committed, will not perhaps be
deemed unpardonable by those who recollect the
condition of humanity. The age in which he
lived was rude and boisterous; nor did the high
cultivation of his mind entirely defend him from
the general contagion. He was subject to the
nice and irritable feelings which frequently attend exalted genius, enthusiastic in his attachment, and violent in his resentment, equally
sincere in his love and in his hatred. His friends,
among whom he numbered some of the most distinguished characters of the age, regarded him
with a warmth of affection which intellectual
eminence cannot alone secure. The general voice
had awarded him a preëminence in literature
that seemed to preclude all hopes of rivalship:
but his estimate of his own attainments was uniformly consistent with perfect modesty; and no
man could evince himself more willing to acknowledge genuine merit in other candidates for
fame. His open and generous disposition, united
to the charms of a brilliant conversation, rendered his society highly acceptable to persons of the
most opposite denominations. His countenance

was stern and austere, but his heart soft and humane. In his writings he inculcates the principles of patriotism and benevolence; and in his commerce with the world he did not forget his solitary speculations. His patriotism was of that unadulterated species which is connected with general philanthropy: his large soul embraced the common family of mankind, but his affections taught him that his first regards were due to the barren land from which he derived his birth. Though he was long habituated to an academic life, his manners betrayed none of the peculiarities of a mere pedagogue.[g] His conversation was alternately facetious and instructive. George Buchanan's wit is still proverbial among his countrymen; and a motley account of his supposed repartees and adventures is one of the most common books in the libraries of the Scotish peasantry. His humour was however of a more

[g] "Albeit, in his person, behaviour, and fashion, hee was rough-hewen, slovenly, and rude, seldome caring for a better outside than a rugge-gowne girt close about him, yet his inside and conceipt in poesie was most riche, and his sweetnesse and facilitie in a verse unimitably excellent." (Peacham's Compleat Gentleman, p. 91, edit. Lond. 1634, 4to.) "Erat austero supercilio," says David Buchanan, "et toto corporis habitu (imo moribus hic noster) subagrestis; sed stylo et sermone perurbanus, quam sæpissime, vel in seriis, multo cum sale jocaretur. Denique vir quem mirari facilius, quam digne prædicare possis." (De Scriptoribus Scotis Illustribus. MS. in Bib. Jurid.) Both these writers seem to have expressed themselves in too unqualified terms; and their observations, as must already have appeared, could hardly apply to Buchanan in his better days. In this last quotation, Love supposes the word moribus to signify morals. (Vindication of Buchanan, p. 30.) But from the rest of the sentence, as well as from the expression subagrestis, it is evident that we must understand it as signifying manners.

dignified denomination than it is there represented; nature seemed to have intended him for the ornament and reformation of a court.[h] The superiority of his talents, and the splendour of his reputation, procured him the utmost respect and deference from such of his countrymen as were not separated from him by the rancour of political zeal: and although he even assumed considerable latitude in censuring the errors of exalted station, yet the manly simplicity of his manners prevented his liberties from exciting resentment. Conscious of personal worth and of intrinsic greatness, he did not fail to assert his own dignity; nor was mere superiority of rank capable of alluring him to a servile and degrading attachment. In the course of his chequered life, he found himself not unfrequently exposed to the miseries of poverty; but in his case, prudence never subsided into a sordid love of money. Although he at length enjoyed one of the great offices of the crown, and possessed other sources of emolument, yet his liberality seems to have encreased in proportion to his opulence; he purchased no estates, and had no treasures to bequeath. Of the truth of the Christian religion, his conviction seems to have been complete and

[h] "Aiunt Buchananum," says Daniel Heinsius, "virum suo sæculo majorem ... ad reginam suam, monstrum illud fœminæ, attulisse quod mirari satis ipsa non posset. Nam cum affectaret libertatem quamdam in censura morum, diluebat specie simplicitatis omnem protinus offensam. Ut non tantum aulæ natus videretur, sed et huic emendandæ." (Burmanni *Sylloge Epistolarum*, tom. ii, p. 451.)

uniform.   Such of his contemporaries as could
best judge of his conduct and character, evidently regarded him as a man of sincere piety.   The
nature of his attachment to the reformation was
consistent with his usual wisdom: he eagerly
hailed the dawn of an æra which promised to re-
lieve the world of enormous delusion, and of enormous profligacy; but he certainly could not approve the excesses of a party which evinced sufficient inclination, as soon as it possessed sufficient
power, to tyrannize over the consciences of mankind.   The extravagances of John Knox, with
whom he appears to have been personally acquainted, and who was undoubtedly a most
powerful champion in a cause of which they
entertained the same general sentiments, have
received no splendid encomiums from the historical pen of Buchanan.   He was too enlightened
to applaud the fierce spirit of intoleration in men
who had themselves tasted the bitterness of persecution.

Nor was the genius of Buchanan less variegated
than his life.   In his numerous writings, he dis-
covers a vigorous and mature combination of talents which have seldom been found united in
equal perfection.   To an imagination excursive
and brilliant, he unites an undeviating rectitude
of judgment.   His learning was at once elegant,
various, and profound: Turnebus, who was associated with him in the same college, and whose
opinion is entitled to the greatest deference, has

characterized him as a man of consummate erudition. Most of the ancient writers had limited
their aspiring hopes to one department of literature; and even to excel in one, demands the
happy perseverence of a cultivated genius. Plato
despaired of securing a reputation by his poetry ;
the poetical attempts of Cicero, though less contemptible perhaps than they are commonly represented, would not have been sufficient to transmit an illustrious name to future ages. Buchanan has not only attained to excellence in each
species of composition, but in each species has
displayed a variety of excellence : in philosophical dialogue and historical narrative, in lyric and
didactic poetry, in elegy, epigram, and satire, he
has hardly been surpassed either in ancient or
modern times. A few Roman poets of the purest
age have excelled him in their several provinces :
but none of them has evinced the same capability
of universal attainment. Horace and Livy wrote
in the language which they had learned from
their mothers; but its very acquisition was to
Buchanan the result of much youthful labour.
Yet he writes with the purity, the elegance, and
freedom of an ancient Roman. Unfettered by
the classical restraints which shrivel the powers
of an ordinary mind, he expatiates with all the
characteristic energy of strong and original sentiment; he produces new combinations of fancy,
and invests them with language equally polished
and appropriate. His diction uniformly displays

a happy vein of elegant and masculine simplicity;
and is distinguished by that propriety and perspicuity, which can only be attained by a man perfectly master of his own ideas, and of the language in which he writes. The variety of his
poetical measures is immense, and to each species he imparts its peculiar grace and harmony.
The style of his prose exhibits correspondent
beauties; nor is it chequered by phraseologies
unsuitable in that mode of composition. His
diction, whether in prose or verse, is not a tissue
of centos; he imitates the ancients as the ancients imitated each other. No Latin poet of
modern times has united the same originality and
elegance; no historian has so completely imbibed the spirit of antiquity, without being betrayed into servile and pedantic imitation. But
his works may legitimately claim a higher order
of merit; they have added no inconsiderable in-
flux to the general stream of human knowledge.
The wit, the pungency, the vehemence, of his
ecclesiastical satires, must have tended to foment
the genial flame of reformation; and his political
speculations are evidently those of a man who
had nobly soared beyond the narrow limits of his
age.

APPENDIX.

APPENDIX.

No. I.

Georgii Buchanani Vita, ab ipso scripta biennio ante mortem.

GEORGIUS BUCHANANUS in Levinia Scotiæ provincia natus est, ad Blanum amnem, anno salutis Christianæ millesimo quingentesimo sexto, circa Kalendas Februarias, in villa rustica, familia magis vetusta quam opulenta. Patre in juventæ robore ex dolore calculi exstincto, avoque adhuc vivo decoctore, familia ante tenuis pene ad extremam inopiam est redacta. Matris tamen Agnetis Heriotæ diligentia liberi quinque mares & tres puellæ ad maturam ætatem pervenerunt. Ex iis Georgium avunculus Jacobus Heriotæ, cum in scholis patriis spem de ingenio ejus concepisset, Lutetiam amandavit. Ibi cum studiis literarum, maxime carminibus scribendis, operam dedisset, partim naturæ impulsu, partim necessitate (quod hoc unum studiorum genus adolescentiæ proponebatur) intra biennium avunculo mortuo, & ipse gravi morbo correptus, ac undique inopia circumventus, redire ad suos est coactus.

Cum in patria valetudini curandæ prope annum dedisset, cum auxiliis Gallorum, qui tum in Scotiam appulerant, studio rei militaris cognoscendæ in castra est profectus. Sed cum ea expeditione prope inutili, hieme asperrima per altissimas nives reduceretur exercitus, rursus in valetudinem ad-

X

versam incidit, quæ tota illa hieme lecto affixum tenuit.
Primo vere ad Fanum Andreæ missus est, ad Joannem
Majorem audiendum, qui tum ibi dialecticen, aut verius
sophisticen, in extrema senectute docebat.   Hunc in Galliam æstate proxima sequutus, in flammam Lutheranæ sectæ, jam late se spargentem, incidit: ac biennium fere cum
iniquitate fortunæ colluctatus, tandem in Collegium Barbaranum accitus, prope triennium classi grammaticam discentium præfuit.   Interea cum Gilbertus Cassilissæ comes,
adolescens nobilis, in ea vicinia diversaretur, atque ingenio
& consuetudine ejus oblectaretur, eum quinquennium secum
retinuit, atque in Scotiam una reduxit.

Inde cum in Galliam ad pristina studia redire cogitaret,
a rege est retentus, ac Jacobo filio notho erudiendo præpo-
situs.   Interea pervenit ad Franciscanos elegidion per otium
ab eo fusum, in quo se scribit per somnium a D. Francisco
sollicitari, ut ejus ordini se adjungat.   In eo cum unum aut
alterum verbum liberius in eos emissum esset, tulerunt id
homines mansuetudinem professi, aliquanto asperius, quam
patres, tam vulgi opinione pios, ob leviculam culpam decere
videbatur: & cum non satis justas iræ suæ immodicæ caus-
sas invenirent, ad commune religionis crimen, quod omnibus quibus male propitii erant intentabant, decurrunt: &
dum impotentiæ suæ indulgent, illum sponte sua sacerdotum
licentiæ infensum acrius incendunt, & Lutheranæ caussæ
minus iniquum reddunt.

Interea rex e Gallia cum Magdalena uxore venit, nec
sine metu sacrificulorum, qui timebant, ne puella regia, sub
amitæ reginæ Navarræ disciplina educata, nonnihil in religione mutaret.   Sed hic timor brevi secuto ejus decessu
evanuit.   Subsecutæ sunt in aula suspiciones adversus quos-
dam e nobilitate, qui contra regem conjurasse dicebantur.
In ea caussa cum regi fuisset persuasum, non satis sincere
versatos Franciscanos, rex Buchananum, forte tum in aula
agentem, ad se advocat, & ignarus offensionis, quæ ei cum

Franciscanis esset, jubet adversus eos carmen scribere. Ille
utrosque juxta metuens offendere, carmen quidem scripsit,
& breve, & quod ambiguam interpretationem susciperet.
Sed nec regi satisfecit, qui acre & aculeatum poscebat; &
illis capitale visum est, quenquam ipsos nisi honorifice au-
sum attingere.   Igitur acrius in eos jussus scribere, eam
Silvam, quæ nunc sub titulo *Franciscani* est edita, inchoa-
tam regi tradidit. At brevi post per amicos ex aula certior
factus se peti, & Cardinalem Betonium a rege pecunia vitam ejus mercari, elusis custodibus in Angliam contendit.

Sed ibi tum omnia adeo erant incerta, ut eodem die ac
eodem igne utriusque factionis homines cremarentur, Henrico VIII. jam seniore suæ magis securitati quam religionis
puritati intento.   Hæc rerum Anglicarum incertitudo, &
vetus cum Gallis consuetudo, & summa gentis humanitas,
Buchananum ad se traxerunt.   Ut Lutetiam venit, Cardinalem Betonium pessime erga se animatum ibi legatione
fungi comperit.   Itaque ejus iræ se subtraxit, Burdegalam
invitante Andrea Goveano profectus.

Ibi in scholis, quæ tum sumptu publico erigebantur, triennium docuit: quo tempore scripsit quatuor tragœdias, quæ
postea per occasiones fuerunt evulgatæ. Sed quæ prima omnium fuerat conscripta (cui nomen est Baptista) ultima fuit
edita; ac deinde Medea Euripidis.   Eas enim ut consuetu-
dini scholæ satisfaceret, quæ per annos singulos singulas
poscebat fabulas, conscripserat: ut earum actione juventutem
ab allegoriis, quibus tum Gallia vehementer se oblectabat,
ad imitationem veterum, qua posset, retraheret.   Id cum
ei prope ultra spem successisset, reliquas Jephthen & Al-
cestin paulo diligentius, tanquam lucem & hominum con-
spectum laturas, elaboravit. Sed nec id temporis omnino
ei fuit expers sollicitudinis, inter cardinalis & Franciscano-
rum minas.   Cardinalis etiam de eo comprehendendo ad
archiepiscopum Burdegalensem literas misit: sed eas forte
fortuna Buchanani amantissimis dederat. Sed hunc metum

regis Scotorum mors, & pestis per Aquitaniam sævissime
grassata sedavit.

Interea literæ a rege Lusitaniæ supervenerunt, quæ Goveanum juberent, ut homines Græcis & Latinis literis eru-
ditos secum adduceret, qui in scholis, quas ille tum magna
cura & impensis moliebatur, literas humaniores & philosophiæ Aristotelicæ rudimenta interpretarentur. Ea de re
conventus Buchananus facile est assensus. Nam cum totam
jam Europam bellis domesticis & externis, aut jam flagran-
tem, aut mox conflagraturam videret, illum unum videbat
angulum a tumultibus liberum futurum, & in eo cœtu qui
eam profectionem susceperant, non tam peregrinari, quam
inter propinquos & familiares agere existimaretur. Erant
enim plerique per multos annos summa benevolentia conjuncti, ut qui ex suis monumentis orbi claruerunt, Nicolaus
Gruchius, Gulielmus Garentæus, Jacobus Tevius, & Elias
Vinetus. Itaque non solum se comitem libenter dedit, sed
& Patricio fratri persuasit, ut se tam præclaro cœtui conjungeret. Et principio quidem res præclare successit, donec
in medio velut cursu Andreas Goveanus morte, ipsi quidem
non immatura, comitibus ejus acerba, præreptus est. Omnes
enim inimici & æmuli in eos primum ex insidiis, deinde pa-
lam animo plane gladiatorio incurrerunt : & cum per homines reis inimicissimos questionem clam exercuissent, tres
arripuerunt, quos, post longum carceris squalorem, in judicium productos, multis per eos dies conviciis exagitatos,
rursus in custodiam abdiderunt. Accusatores autem ne adhuc quidem nominarunt.

In Buchananum certe acerbissime insultabant, ut qui pe-
regrinus esset, & qui minime multos illic haberet qui inco-
lumitate gauderent, aut dolori ingemiscerent, aut injuriam
ulcisci conarentur. Objiciebatur ei carmen in Franciscanos
scriptum, quod ipse, antequam e Galliis exisset, apud Lusitaniæ regem excusandum curavit, nec accusatores quale esset sciebant ; unum enim ejus exemplum regi Scotorum,

qui scribendi auctor fuerat, erat datum. Crimini dabatur
carnium esus in Quadragesima, a qua nemo in tota Hispania est qui abstineat; dicta quædam oblique in monachos
objecta, quæ apud neminem nisi monachum criminosa videri poterant. Item gravissime acceptum, quod in quodam
sermone familiari inter aliquot adolescentes Lusitanos, cum
fuisset orta mentio de eucharistia, dixisset, sibi videri Au-
gustinum in partem ab ecclesia Romana damnatam multo
esse proniorem. Alii duo testes, Joannes Tolpinus Normannus, & Joannes Ferrerius e Subalpina Liguria, (ut post
aliquot annos comperit) pro testimonio dixerunt, se ex pluribus hominibus fide dignis audivisse, Buchananum de Romana religione perperam sentire. Ut ad rem redeam, cum
quæstores prope sesquiannum & se & illum fatigassent, tandem ne frustra hominem non ignotum vexasse crederentur,
eum in monasterium ad aliquot menses recludunt, ut exactius erudiretur a monachis, hominibus quidem alioqui nec
inhumanis, nec malis, sed omnis religionis ignaris. Hoc
maxime tempore psalmorum Davidicorum complures vario
carminum genere in numeros redegit.

Tandem libertati redditus, cum a rege commeatum re-
deundi in Gallias peteret, ab eo rogatus ut illic maneret,
pecuniola interim accepta in sumptum quotidianum, donec
de conditione aliqua honesta prospiceretur. Sed cum pro-
crastinationis, nec in certam spem, nec certum tempus, tæ-
deret, navem Cretensem in portu Olisipponensi nactus, in
ea in Angliam navigavit. Nec hic tamen substitit, quamvis honestis conditionibus invitaretur. Erant enim illic omnia adhuc turbida sub rege adolescente, proceribus discor-
dibus, & populi adhuc animis tumescentibus ab recenti motu civili. Igitur in Galliam transmisit, iisdem fere diebus,
quibus urbis Mediomatricum obsidio fuit soluta. Coactus
est ibi per amicos ea de obsidione carmen scribere, idque eo
magis invitus, quod non libenter in contentionem veniret
cum aliis plerisque necessariis, & in primis cum Mellino

Sangelasio, cujus carmen eruditum & elegans ea de re circumferebatur.

Inde evocatus in Italiam a Carolo Cossæo Brixiacensi, qui tum secunda fama res in Ligustico & Gallico circa Padum agro gerebat, nunc in Italia, nunc in Gallia, cum filio ejus Timoleonte quinquennium hæsit, usque ad annum millesimum quingentesimum sexagesimum. Quod tempus maxima ex parte dedit sacrarum literarum studio, ut de controversiis, quæ tum majorem hominum partem exercebant, exactius dijudicare posset; quæ tum domi conquiescere cœperant, Scotis a tyrannide Guisiana liberatis. Eo reversus nomen ecclesiæ Scotorum dedit. E superiorum autem temporum scriptis quædam velut e naufragio recollecta edidit. Cætera vero quæ adhuc apud amicos peregrinantur, fortunæ arbitrio committit. In præsentia septuagesimum quartum annum agens, apud Jacobum Sextum Scotorum regem, cui erudiendo erat præfectus, senectutis suæ malis fractæ portum exoptans agit.

Hæc de se Buchananus, amicorum rogatu.

Obiit Edinburgi, paulo post horam quintam matutinam, die Veneris xxviii Septembris, anno M.D.LXXXII.

ANE ADMONI:
TIOVN DIRECT TO THE
trew Lordis maintenaris of Iustice, and
obedience to the Kingis Grace.

M. G. B.

IMPRENTIT AT.
STRIVILING BE ROBERT LEKPREVIK.

ANNO. DO. M. D. LXXI.

No. II.—See p. 154.

1.—*Ane Admonitioun direct to the Trew Lordis maintenaris of Iustice, and obedience to the Kingis Grace. M. G. B.*[a]

It may seme to zour lordschippis, yat I melling with heich materis of gouernīg of cōmoun welthis, do pas myne estait, being of sa meane qualitie, & forzettis my dewtie, geuing counsal to ye wysest of yis realme. Not the les, seing the miserie sa greit appeiring, and the calamitie sa neir approching, I thocht it les fault, to incur the cryme of surmounting my priuate estait, then the blame of neglecting the publict danger. Thairfoir I chesit rather to vnderly the opinioun of presumptioun in speiking, then of tressoun in silence: and specially of sic thingis, as euin seme presently to redound to the perpetuall schame of zour lordschippis, distructioun of this royall estate, and ruyne of the haill commoun-welth of Scotland. On this consideratioun I haue takin in hand at this tyme to aduerteis zour honouris of sic thīgis as I thocht to appertene, baith to zour lordschippis in speciall, and in generall to the haill commoditie of this realme, in punitioun of tratouris, pacificatioun of troublis amangis zour selfis, and continuatioun of peice with our nichtbouris. Of the quhilk I haue takin the trauell to wryte, and do remit the iudgement to zour discretioun: hoiping at leist, that althocht my wit and foirsicht sall not

---

[a] Lekprevick, as I have already observed, published two editions of the *Admonitioun* during the same year. That which I have followed appears to have been the second; as it exhibits various corrections in the orthography and punctuation, and contains an additional paragraph, beginning, "The thrid conspiracie." Of the title of this edition, the preceding page presents a tolerably exact imitation. The *Chameleon* is here reprinted from Ruddiman's edition.

satisfie zow, zit my gude wil sall not displeis zow: of the
quhilk aduertisment ye soume is this.

¶ First, to considder how godly the actioun is quhilk ze
haue in hand: to wit, The defence of zour king, ane innocent pupill, the establisching of religioun, punitioun of
theifis and tratouris, and maintenance of peice and quyetnes
amangis zour selfis, and with forane natiounis.

¶ Item remember how ze haue vindicat this realme from
the thraldome of strangeris, out of domestik tyrannie, and
out of a publik dishonor in the sicht of all forane natiounis,
we being altogidder estemit a pepill murtherar of kingis, &
impacient of lawis and magistratis, in respect of the murther of the lait King Henry, within the wallis of the principall towne, the greitest of the nobilitie being present with
the quene for the tyme, and be zour power ane part of the
cheif tratouris tryit from amangis the trew subiectis: quhair-
by strangeris wer constranit efterwart as mekle to praise
zour iustice, as of befoir thay wrangfully condempnit zour
iniustice.

¶ Item remember how far in doing the same ze haue
oblist zour selfis befoir the haill warld, to continew in the
same vertew of iustice, and quhat blame ze sall incur, gif ze
be inconstant. For all men can beleif na vtherwyse, gif ye
tyme following be nocht conforme to the tyme past, yat
nouther honour, nor commoū-welth steirit zow vp then, bot
rather sum particular tending to zour priuate commodities.

Also remember how mony gentill and honest meanis ze
haue socht in tymes past, to caus the king be acknawledgit,
and the countrie put at rest, and how vnprofitabill hes bene
zour honestie in treitting, zour vailzeand curage in weir,
zour mercyfulnes in victorie, zour clemencie in punisching,
and facilitie in reconciliatioun.

Quhilk thingis witnessis sufficientlie, that ze estemit na
man enemie that wald leif in peice vnder the kingis authoritie: that ze wer neuer desyrous of blude, geir, nor honour

of sic as wald not, rather in making of trouhill and sedi-
tioun, declair thame selfis enemeis to God & ye kingis maiestie, nor leif in concord and amitie with thair nichtbouris
vnder the correctioun of iustice.

¶ And sen ze can nouther bow thair obstinat hicht with
pacience, nor mease thair stubburne hartis with gentilnes,
nor satisfie thair inordinat desyris vtherwyse then with the
kingis blude and souris, the distructioun of religioun, ba-
nisching of iustice, and fre permissioun of crueltie and misordour. zour wisdomes may easely considder what kynd of
medicine, is not only meit, bot alswa necessair for mending
of sic ane maladie.

¶ And to the effect that ze may the better cōsidder this
necessitie of medicine, remember quhat kynd of pepil thay
ar, that professis yame selfis in deid, and dissemblis in word
to be enemeis to God, to iustice, and to zow, becaus ze
maintene the kingis actioun,

Sum of thame ar consellaris of the king his fatheris
slauchter, sum conuoyaris of him to the schambles, that
slew his grandschir, banischit his father, and not satisfyit
to haue slane him self, murtherit the kingis regent, and now
seikis his awin blude, that thay may fulfill thair crueltie
and auarice being kingis, quhilk thay begouth to exercise
the tyme of thair gouerning.

Vtheris ar, that being alliat or neir of kyn to ye Hammiltounis, thinkis to be partioipāt of all thair prosperitie
and succes.

Vtheris being gyltie of King Henryis deith, in the first
parliamēt haldin in the kingis regne that now is, could weill
accord, that the quene sould haue bene put to deith alswa.

And seing thay could not obtene that point, the nixt
schift of thair impietie was to put doun the king, that he
sould not rest to reuenge his fatheris deith: quhilk thay
thocht could not be mair easie done, then be bringing hame
the Q. with sic a husband, yat outher for auld haitrent, or

for new couatice, wald desyre the first degre of successioun to be of his awin blude.

Sum vtheris ar praetisit in casting of courtis, & reuoluing of estatis, be raiseing of ciuile weir, and ar becum richer then euer thay hoipit. And becaus thay haue found the practise sa gude in tyme past, now thay seik all wayis to continew it, and hauing anis gustit how gude fisching it is in drumly watteris, thay can be na maner leif the craft.

Vtheris of that factioun, ar, sum papistis, sum feynit protestantis, that hes na God bot geir, & desyris agane the papistrie, not for luif thay beir to it (for thay ar scorneris of all religioun) bot hoiping to haue promotioun of idill belleis to beneficeis, and lamentis the present estait, quhair (as thay say) ministeris gettis all, and leifis na thing to gude fellowis: and to this intent thay wald set vp the quenis authoritie, say thay.

Sum thair be also yat vnder cullour of seiking the quenis authoritie, thinkis to eschaip ye punischement of auld faultis, and haue licence in tyme to cum to oppres thair nichtbouris, yat be febiller nor thay.

Now haue I to schaw zow be cōiecture, quhat frute is to be hoipit of ane assembly of sic men as for ye maist part ar of insatiabill gredynes, intollerabill arrogance, without faith in promeis, measure in couatice, pietie to the inferiour, obedience to the superiour, in peice desyrous of troubill, in weir thristie of blude, nurysseris of thift, raiseris of rebellioun, conceleris of tratouris, inuenteris of tressoū : with hand reddy to murther, mynd to dissaif, hart voyde of treuth and full of fellonie, toung trampit in dissait, and wordis tending to fals practise without veritie, be quhilk properteis, and mony vtheris thairunto ioynit, as is knawin to all men, ze that vnderstandis thair beginning, progres, and haill lyfe, may easilie remember to quhome this generall speiking appertenis in speciall : and als it is not vnknawin to sic as knawis the personis, how thay ar mellit

with godles papistis, harlot protestantis, commoun brybouris,
haly in word, hypocreitis in hart, proude contempneris or
Machisuell mockeris of all religioun and vertew, bludie
bouchouris, and oppin oppressouris, fortifiaris of theifis, and
maintsneris of tratouris.

It is alswa necessarie to zour lordschippis to vnderstand
thair pretence, that gif it be a thing quhilk may stand with
the tranquillitie of the commoun-welth, zour lordschippis
may in sũ part, rather condiscend to thair inordinate lust,
nor put the haill estait in ieopardie of battell.

First, it is not honour, riches, nor authoritie yat thay
desyre : for thay haue had, and als hes presently, and may
haue in tyme to cum sic part of all thay thingis, as a priuat
man may haue in this realme, not being chargeabill to the
countrie, or not suspectit to ane king, and vnassurit of his
awin estait.

It is not the delyuerance of the quene that thay seik (as
thair doingis contrair to thair word testifyis manifestlie) for
gif thay wald haue hir delyuerit, thay wald haue procurit
be all meanis possibill, the quene of Inglandis fauour &
support, in quhais power ye haill recouerance stuid only,
and not offendit hir sa heichlie as yai haue done, and daylie dois in participatioun of the cõspyrit tressoũ, to put hir
maiestie not only out of hir stait, bot out of this lyfe present: nor in resetting and maintening of hir rebellis contrair to promeis and solempne contract of pacificatioun betuix thir twa realmes: nouther zit haue houndit furth,
proude and vncircumspect zoung mē, to hery, burne, and
slay, & tak presoneris in hir realme, and vse all misordour
and crueltie, not onelie vsit in weir, bot detestabill to all
barbar & wyld Tartaris, in slaying of presoneris, & cõtrair
to all humanitie & iustice, keiping na promeis to miserabill
catiues resauit anis to yair mercy. And all this was done
be cõmandement of sic as sayis thay seik the quenis delyuerance, and reprochit to thame be the doaris of thay mis-

cheiffs, saying that thay enterit thame in danger, and sup-
portit thame not in mister, sa mekle as to cum to Lawder,
& luik frō thame : in quhilk deserting of yair collegis, thay
schew crueltie ioynit with falsheid, and maist heich tressoun
aganis ye quene, pretending in word hir delyuerance, and
stopping in wark hir recouerance, the quhilk (as euerie man
may cleirly se) thay socht, as he that socht his wyfe drownit
in the riuer aganis the streime.

It is not the quenis authoritie that they wald set vp in
hir absence : for gif that wer thair intētioun, quhome can
thay place in it mair freindly to hir then hir onlie sone ?
or quhat gouernour may thay put to him les suspect, nor
sic men as hes na pretens of successioun to the crowne, or
ony hoip of proffeit to cum to thame efter his deith ? or
thay that euer hes bene trew seruandis to kingis befoir him,
sould thay not be preferrit to his paternall enemeis, zea, and
slayeris of his father, and sollicitaris of strangeris to seik his
innocent blude ?

Quhat then sall we think that thir men seikis vnder pretence of the quenis authoritie, seing thay can not bring
hame the quene to set hir vp in authoritie, nor will not suffer the king lauchfully inaugurat and confirmit be decreit
of parliament, to bruik it, with sa mony of his tutouris chosin be his mother, as ar not to be suspectit to will him
harme ? I traist it is not vneasie to persaif be thair haill
progres now presently, and in tyme bypast, yat thay desyre na vther thing bot the deith of the king and quene of
Scotland, to set vp the Hammiltounis in authoritie, to the
quhilk thay haue aspyrit be craftie meanis thir fyftie zeiris
ago. And seing thair purpois succeedit not be craftie and
secreit meanis, now thay follow the same traide conioyning
to falsheid, oppin wickitnes.

¶ And that ze may se quhat meanis thay haue vsit, thir
fyftie zeiris bypast, to set vp be craft this authoritie, quhilk
now thay seik be violēce, force, and tressoun, I will call to

zour memorie sum of thair practisis; quhilk meny of zow
may remember asweill as I.

First efter the deith of King Iames the fourt, Iohne
duke of Albany chosin be the nobilitie to gouerne in the
kingis les-age, the Hammiltounis thinking that he had
bene als wickit as thay, and sould to his awin aduancement
put doun ye king, being of tender age for ye tyme, and be
the deceis of his brother left alone, and that thay wald easilie get thair hand bezond ye duke, being ane stranger and
without successioun of his body, held thame quyet for a
season, thinking that vther mēnis actioun sould be yair promotioun.   Bot seing yat ye duke, as a prince baith wyse &
vertuous, to bring him self out of sic suspitioun, put four
lordis estemit of ye maist trew and vertuous in Scotland in
that tyme, to attend on the kingis grace (to wit, the Erle
Merchell, the Lordis Erskyn, Ruthuen, & Borthick) the
Hammiltounis being out of hoip of the kingis putting doun
be the duke of Albany, and out of credeit to do him ony
harme be thame selfis, maid ane conspiracie with certane
lordis, to put the said duke out of authoritie, & tak it on
thame selfis : that all thingis put in thair power, thay
micht vse the king, and the realme at yair awin plesure.
To that effect thay tuik the castell of Glasgow, and thair
maid ane assemblie of thair factioun, the quhilk was dissol-
uit be the haistie cūming of the duke of Albany with ane
armie : for feir of the quhilk, the erle of Arrane cheif of
that cumpany, fled to his wyfis brother the Lord Hume,
being then out of court.

The secund conspiracie was efter the dukis last departing
(the foirsaidis lordis separat from attending on the king)
deuysit be Schir Iames Hammiltoun, bastard sone to the
said erle of Arrane, quha conspyrit the kingis deith, then
being in his hous in the abbay of Halyruidhous : quhilk
conspiracie efter mony zeiris reueillit, ye said Schir Iames
sufferit deith for it.

· The third conspiracie (yat come to our knawledge) was, that the kingis grace ryding oft tymes betuix Striuiling and the Downe of Menteith, to veseit ane gentill womā of his motheris, making residence in the Downe: and cōmounly accumpanyit with ane, or twa hors be nicht, the said Schir Iames proponit to certane gentil men ye slauchter of him, and assayit it not, becaus ye executaris wald tak na thing on hand without him self had bene present.

· Thir conspiracies not being exeeute, Schir Iames perseuerit in his euill intentioun, and be secreit meanis in court socht alwayis yat ye king sould not mary, that for laik of his successioun, the Hammiltounis micht cum to thair intentis. For ye king was zoung, lusty, & reddy to auenture his persoun to all hazardis, baith be sey and land, in doun-putting of theifis, and vpsetting of iustice. The Hammiltounis luikit on quhen seiknes, throw excesse of trauell, or sum vther rakles auenture sould cut him of without children: and destitute of this hoip, first he stoppit the kingis meting with his vncle ye king of Ingland, quha at that tyme hauing bot ane douchter, was willing to haue maryit hir with the king of Scotland, and maid him king of the haill ile efter him, & to haue enterit him at that present tyme in possessioun of the duchy of Zorke. Bot the said Schir Iames euer hauing eye to his awin soope, hinderit this purpois be sum of the kingis familiaris, yat he had practisit with, be giftis, and specially be the bischop of Sanctandrois Iames Betoun, vncle to the erle of Arranes mother, & greit vncle to Schir Iames wyfe, and raisit sie suspitioun betuix the twa kingis, that brocht baith the realmes in greit besynes.

This purpois, as said is, put abak, the king seing yat his ambassadouris furtherit not at his plesure, thocht meit him self in persoun to ga be sey in France: and Schir Iames Hammiltoun perseuering in his former intentioun went with him, to hinder his mariage, be al meanis yat he micht:

and to that effect, the king sleiping in the schip without
any necessitie of wynde and wedder, Schir Iames causit the
marineris to turne saill of the west coist of Ingland. bak-
wart, and land in, Galloway, quhair the king was verray
miscontent with Schir Iames, & Maister Dauid Pantar,
principall causeris of his returning, as diueris yat was in the
schip sit living câ raport. And fra yat tyme furth, the
king hauing tryit out his pretence, and persauing· his vn-
faithfull deiling euer disfauourit him, & to his greit displesure fauourit oppinlie the erle of Lennox, and his freindis
in his absence: the quhilk erle pretendit a richt & tytill to
the haill erldome of Arrane, ye present erle for that tyme
being knawin to be bastard: as also it was in mênis recent
memorie, how Schir Iames Hammiltoun had cruellie slane
ye erle of Lennox at Linlythgow, euin to the greit displesure of ye erle of Arrane, father to Schir Iames, and vncle
to the erle of Lennox, câming be the kingis commandement to Linlythgow. Sa the king, as said is, vnderstanding the priuate practick of Schir Iames, in keiping him
vnmaryit, haistit him the mair eirnestlie to mary, to the
effect, that his successioun might put the Hammiltounis
out of hoip of yair intent, and him out of danger be the
Hammiltounis. And albeit yat Schir Iames, to mak.him
self clene of that suspisioun, socht mony diuers wayis to ye
distructioû of the erle of Arrane his brother, sit he could
neuer conqueis the kingis fauour, vntill finallie he was executit for tressoun, and tuik ane miserabill end conforme to
his vngodly lyfe.

The king at last deceissit, & leuing ane douchter of sex
dayis auld, the Hammiltounis thocht all to be thairis. For
then ye erle of Arrane, ane soung man of small. wit and
greit inconstancie, was set vp be sum of the nobilitie, and
sum familiar seruandis of ye kingis laitly deceissit. for thay
thocht him mair tollerabill then the Cardinall Betoun,

quha be ane fals instrument had takin the supreme authoritie to him self.

The erle of Arrane nawit gouernour be ane priuate factioun, and fauourit be sa mony as professit the trew religioun of Christ, becaus he was beleifit then to be of the
same, howbeit he was gentill of nature, zit his freindis for
ye maist part, wer gredie baith of geir and blude, and
geuin to iniustice quhair gayne followit. Thair was in his
tyme nathing ellis, bot weir, oppressioun, and brybing of
his callit brother the bischop of Sanctandrois, sa that all
the estatis wer wery of him, and dischargit him of his office,
& chargit with it ane woman stranger.

In the beginning of his gouernment ye quene and hir
mother wer keipit be him, rather lyke presoneris nor prin-
cessis: bot sit that incommoditie was caus of preseruing of
the quenis lyfe, he beleifing to mary hir on his sone. Bot
after the erle of Lennox had delyuerit thame out of his
handis, and the nobilitie had refusit to mary hir on his
sone, howbeit he left his former freindis, & come to ye
quene, abiurit his religioun in ye gray freiris of Striuiling,
zit he could neuer cum agane to his pretendit cleaming to
ye crowne, quhilk he had lang socht, partly be fauour of
sic of the nobilitie as wer alliat with him, & partlie be
distructioun of the ancient housis that micht haue put impediment to his vnresonabill ambitioun. For hauing banischit the erle of Lennox, he thocht the erle of Angus to
be ye principal that micht resist him, & hauing enterit in
waird Schir George Dowglas, to be mair assurit he sed for
ye said erle of Angus in freindly maner, & put him in pre-
soun without any iust occasioun, and wald haue beheidit
zame baith, gif the arryuing of the Inglis armie had not
stayit his purpois: be the quhilk, and feir of the murmour
of the pepill, he was constrauit to delyuer thame. And
seing he durst not at sic a tyme put thame doun be tyrannie, he offerit thame to the sword of the enemie, to be

slane be thame. And to the effect, that thay and thair
freindis, hauing put abak ye Inglis horsmen, and ressaueing
ane vther charge; micht be the mair easilie slaine thay stā-
ding in battell & fechting for him, he in ye battell behind
fled to tyne thame: and sa thir nobill men, sa far as lay in
him, was slaine, and preseruit be the prouidence of God.

The zoung quene quhilk being in hir mothenis keiping,
he micht not put doun, nor mary at his plesure, he cōsentit
to offer hir to the stoumis of ye sey, and danger of enemeis,
and sauld hir as a slaue in Frāce, for ye duchy of Chastel-
lerault, ye quilk he bruikis in name. only, as ye crowne
of Scotland in fātasie: & ressauit sic pryce for hir as tressoun,
periurie, and the selling of fre persounis sould be recompensit
with. Bot sit ye coustice of ye crowne yat he had sauld,
ceissit not heir. for befoir hir returning hame out of Frāce,
at the troublis quhilkis began anent the repressing of the
Frenchemen, and tyrannie aganis the religioun, how many
meanis socht the Hammiltounis to haue depryuit hir of all
richt, and trāslatit the crowne to thame selfis, is knawin
baith to Scotland and Ingland.

¶Also efter the quenis arryuing in Scotland, scho seiking
a querrell aganis the said duke and sum vther lordis, under
pretence yat yai had cōspyrit against hir, for ye religiounis
caus, ye dukis freindis left him all, because that the rest of
ye lordis wald not consent to distroy the quene, or derogat
hir authoritie be ony maner of way. A lytill befoir the
quhilk tyme, the occasioun of the dukis cōspiracie with ye
Erle Bothwell, to slay ye erle of Murray in Falklād, was
na vther, bot becaus the said erle of Murray liuing, thay
could nouther do the said Q. harme in hir persoun, nor di-
minisshe hir authoritie, nor cōstrane hir to mary at thair
plesure, and to hir vtter displesure.

¶ Efter that the quene had maryit with him quhome
thay estemit thair auld enemie, & was with chylde, the
gude bischop of Sanctandrois first callit Cuninghame, estemit

Cowane, and at last awowit Hamiltoun, not only conspyrit with the Erle Bothwell, bot come with the quene to Glasgow, and connoyit the king to ye place of his murther, the bischop being ludgeit as he was saildoŭ or newer of befoir whair he micht persaif the plesure of that crueltie with all his sensis, & help ye murtheraris, gif mister had bene, & send four of his familiar servandis to the executioŭ of the murther, watching all ye nicht, and thinking lang to haue ye ioy of ye cuming of ye crowne a degre neirer to the hous of Hamiltoun. And sa greit hoip, mellit with ambitioun, inflammit his hart, for the kingis deceis, that within schort tyme he beleuit firmlie his callit brother to be king, and he (the said bischop) to be to him as curatour during the haill tyme of his nonwit: quhilk had bene a langer terme yan Witsonday or Martymes. For he thocht vn doutitly, yat the erle Bothwell sould distroy ye zoung prince, & nocht suffer him prosper to reuenge his fatheris deith, and preceid the erlis children in successioun of the crowne: and the zoung prince anis cut of, the bischop maid his rekning, yat the Q. & ye Erle Bothwell hatit alreddy for ye slauchter of the king hir husband, and mair for the innocent, wer easie to be distroyit with consent of all estatis, and the cryme easie to the bischop to be prouin, quha knew all ye secreitis of the haill disseigne. Or gif thay wald slay the Erle Bothwell, and spair the quene, thay wer in hoip sho sould mary Iohne Hamiltoun the duikis sone, quhome with merie luikis, & gentill countenāce (as scho could weill do) scho had enterit in the pastyme of the glaikis, and causit the rest of the Hammiltounis to fon for fainnes. Bot efter that ye Erle Bothwell had refusit battell at Carbarry hill, the and quene befoir the cumming of the Hammiltounis, come to the lordis, the Hammiltounis as that tyme disappointit, fosterit yair vaine hoip with a merie dreame, that the quene sould be punischit efter hir demeritis, and wer a tyme in dowbill ioy: the ane, that being red of the quene, scho sould not beir ma children to debar thame from ye crowne: and ye yther, yat thay micht haue ane easie way to calumniat the regent for distroying of the quene. Bot seing hir keipit, thay blamit oppinlie ye regent, quha keipit hir in stoir in dispyte of yame (as yai said, schawing in vnreuerend speiking quhat fauour thay bure to thair prince) to be a stude to cast ma follis, to hinder thame of the successioun of the crowne. Zit for all that, thair wald nane of thame cum to parliament to further thair desyre with ane anerlie vote, bot lay bak to keip thame selfis at libertie, to repruif all that sould be done in that conuentioun, & to sense fauour towardis the quene quhome thay haittit sa, as gif be consent of the lordis, or vtherwyse scho wer delyuerit, yai micht help hir to put doun ye lordis, yat wald not put hir doun in fauour of yame.

This thair intentioun was oppinlie schawin, quhen the quene being keipit in Lochleuin, be comandement of the haill parliament, was delyuerit be conspiracie of sum priuat men, especiallie of the Hammiltounis. For thay assemblit all yair forces to put doun the zoung king, and lordis obedient to him. Quhilk euill will thay schew towardis the lordis at the Langsyde, bringing with thame greit stoir of cordis, to murther and hang thame (gif thay had bene takin presoneris, and the victorie fallin to the Hammiltounis) and the same euill will towardis the king in keiping the watter of Forthe, that he sould not eschaip yair cruel handis, being assurit gif he come in ye quene of Inglandis power, that scho of hir accustomat clemencie and kyndnes of blude, wald not abandoun him to yair vnmercyfull crueltie experimôtit alreddy in his father. And seing yat the prouidence of God had cloisit ye dure to all yair wickednes at yat tyme, yai haue neuer ceissit since to seik enemeis to his grace in all strãge natiounis. And persauing yat thay had fair wordis of all vtheris, except of the quenis maiestie

of Ingland, quha vnderstude thair fals and tressonabill
deling, thay turnit thair haitrent aganis hir, and enterit in
conspiracie with sum tratouris of Ingland, that wer als euill
myndit towardis ye quehis maiestie yair souerane, as the
Hammiltounis wer to ye kingis hienes of Scotland. This
is nouther dremit in wardrop, nor hard throw a boir, bot a
trew narratiue, of quhilk ye memorie is ludgeit in mennis
hattis, baith Scottis and strangeris, and the veritie knawin.
be the quhilk ze may vnderstad the Hammiltounis pretence
thir fyftie zeiris and mair.

Efter sa mony wayis socht be yame to distroy the richt
successioun, & place yame in ye kingly rowme, seing all
thair practisis could not auaill, and thair forces wer not
sufficient, thay socht to augment thair factioun, adioyning
to thame all that wer participant of the kingis slauchter,
and had aspyrit to slay ye quene of Ingland. And to the
effect thay micht cū to thair wickit purpois, thay in a
maner displayit a baner, to assembill togidder all kynd
of wickit men, as papistis, renegat protestantis, theifis,
tratouris, murtheraris, & oppin oppressouris. As for yair
adherētis in Scotland I neid not to expreme thair namis,
nor the qualiteis of ye conspiratouris of Ingland, for yai
ar weill aneuch knawin to zour lordschippis. Zit ane I
can not ouerpas, being ye cheif conspiratour chosin be
thame to be king of Scotland and Ingland, I mene the
duke of Norfolk, in quhilk acte ze may se how y' thrist of
zour blude blindit thame agains thair awin vtilitie. First
yai cheisit the principall enemie of the religioun of Christ in
this ile, accumpanyit with vther fylthie idolateris, to change
the stait of the kirk in baith realmes be cutting of the twa
princes: seing that thair authoritie standing, ye conspiratouris could not cum to thair intent. Nixt thay respectit
in that proude tyrane, the vertewis that wer commoun to
him and thame, as arrogancie, crueltie, dissimulatioun and
tressoun. For euin as yai had this lang tyme in Scotland,

socht the deith of thair richteous prince: sa he in Ingland
follówing the trade of his antecessouris, diuers tymes attempting tressoun, wald haue put downe the quene of
Ingland. Heir alswa apperis the Hammiltounis crueltie
agains the nobilitie of thair awin natioun, in seiking thair
professit and perpetuall enemie of Scotland (as his badge
beiris witnes) quha sould haue spilt, the rest of the noble
blude of Scotland in peice, yat his atecessouris could not
spill in weir: be quhilk electioun, being assurit that na
Scottis hart can luif thame, sa can thay luif nane of zow,
agains quhome, yai haue vsit sa mony tressonabill actis.
" Thay do schaw alswa, how crueltie & auarice has
blyndit yame, that thay can not se, in bringing a tyrane tp
haue power ouer yame, seing yai pretending neirest chesme
to the crowne, sould be neirest the danger.
ᶫ And zit for all this could thir men be weill cōtentit, gif
be ony meanis thay could attene to thair intent, be spoyle
and rubberie, as thay did quhen as thay wer placit in supreme authoritie, or be making of zow slaues, as thay did
in selling of yair quene begin yat practise: quhairin hoy-
beit the inhumanitie was greit, zit wes it not in supreme
degre of crueltie: Bot it is na moderat, tollerabill, nor
accustomet thing that thay seik: It is ye blude first of our
innocent king, euin sic as hes bene presiquit be wyld beistis:
nixt the blude of all his trew seruandis and trew subiectis
indifferentlie. For quhat defence can be in nobilitie, or
quhat suretie agains yame yat hes murtherit ane king, &
seikis strangeris to murther ane vther king? quhome sall
thay spair for vertew and innocencie, that laithie exsortit,
and zit defendis the murther of the regent? or quha will be
ouersene for law degre, or base estait, in respect of yai yat
conductit boucheouris out of Tenidaill to slay Maister Iohne
Wod, for na vther caus, bot for being ane gude seruand to
the crowne and to the regent his maister, and had espyit
out sum of thair practisis.

Gif this thrist of blude of thay lachlechis, micht be impute to haistie hevanger, or ony suddane motioun, quhilk causis men sum tymes to forget thair dewtie, thair micht sit be sum hope yat sic a passioun ouerpast, thay wald with tyme remember thame selfis, and eftar power amend faultis past, or at leist abstene in tyme to cum. Bot thair is na sic humanitie in thair nature, nor na sie pietie in thair hartis. For not content with ane kingis blude, thay gaip for his sentis murther: not satisfyit to haue alane the regent, thay keipit ye murtherar in ye dukis hous in Arrane: maist lyke thinking as gif thay honourit not the doar, thay sould not be knawin as counsallouris of the deid, & wald tyne the gloir of that nobill act. And besydes all yis yai ar not only content to maintene Scottis tratouris, bot alswa ressaifis Inglis tratouris, and settis vp a sanctuarie of tressoun, a refuge of idolatrie, a receptacle of theifis and murtheraris.

And howbeit the bullesant blude of a king & a regēt about yair hartis, quhairof ye lust in yair appetite geuis thame lytill rest, daylie & hourlie making new prouocatioun, sit yat small space of rest, quhilk yai haue besyde ye executioū of yair crueltie, thay spend in deuysing of generall vnquyetnes throw the haill coūtrie. for not cōtent of it yat yai yame selfis may steill, brybe, & reif, thay set out ratches on euerie syde, to gnaw the pepillis banis, efter that thay haue consumit the flesche, and hountis out, ane of thame the Clangregour, ane vther ye Grantie and Clanchattan, ane vther Bakeleuch and Fairnyherst, ane vther the Iohnstounis and Armestrangis: & sic as wald be haldin the halyest amāgis yame, schew plainlie ye affectioun yai had to baneis peice and steir vp troublis, quhē thay bendit all thair fyue wittis, to stop the regent to ga first north, and syne south, to paneis thift and oppressioun: and quhē thay saw, that thair counsall wes not authorisit, in geuing impunitie to all misordour, thay spend it in putting downe of him that wald haue put all in gude ordour.

Thair is a kynd of thair theifis euin odious to mair gentill theifis, quhilk calling thame selfis greit gentilmen spoyllis trauellaris, cadgeris, and chapmen be the way, and ransounis pure men about Edinburgh for xx. schilling ye heid, quhilk vyce cā not proceid of vengeāce of enemeis, bot rather of lufe & plesure in wickidnes. This kynd of men dois not only dishonour to nobilitie in steilling, & to theifis in purspyking, bot alswa to the haill natioun of Scotland, geuing opinioun to strangeris, that sum of the Scottis be of sa law courage, that men amangis thame aspyring to ye hiest estait of a kingdome, hes crouchit thame selfis in the maist law ordour of knaifis.

¶ Now, my lordis, ze may considder, how yai that slayis, sa cruellie kingis and thair lieutennentis, will be mercyfull to zow: and quhen thay sall haue put zow doun, yat craifis reuenge of ye kingis blude, ze may vnderstand how few der craif iustice of zour slauchter. Ze may se how cruell yai will be in oppressioun of the pure, hauing cut of zow, quhilk being of maist nobill and potent housis of this realme, sufferis throw zour sleuthfulnes euerie part of this countrie, to be maid worse nor Liddisdaill, or Annanderdaill, & not only sufferis ye puspykeris of Cliddisdaill, to exercise thift and reif as a craft, bot nurysais and authorisis amangis zow, the cheif counsellaris of all misordour, as ane edder in zour bosum.

¶ Of all this ze may lay the wyte on na vther bot vpon zour selfis, that hes sufficient power to repres yair insolēcie & proudnes, hauing in zour hand the same wand that ze haue chaistisit yame with of befoir. For ze haue zour protestour the same God this zeir, yat was the zeiris bypast, vn-changeabill in his eternall counsellis, constant in promeis, potent in punisching, and liberall in rewarding: ze haif zour trew freindis yat wer with zow of befoir: ze ar delyuerit of dissimulat brether, yat had yair bodyis with zow, & yair hartis with zour enemeis: that subscryuit with zow, & tuik, remission of sour aduersaries: yat stuid with zow in battell, luiking for occasioun to betray zow, had not God bene zour protectour. Ze haif a greit nūber of new freindis alienat from yame, for thair manifest iniquitie in deid, wickidnes in worde, and treasoun in hart. Ze haue of the same enemeis that ze had then sa mony, as hes thair hartis herdinnit, & yair myndis bent agains God and lawfull magistratis. ze haue the same actioun yat ze had then, accumulat with recent murther and tresasoun, to prouoke the ire of the Eternall agains thame. How far God hes blindit thame, blind men may se, yat hauing sa etill ane actioū, & sa mony enemeis at hame, sit be hounding out of small tratouris of yair awin wickit conspiracie (men exetrabill to thair awin parentis, quhome amangis vtheris thay haue diueris tymes spoylit) be hounding out, I say, of sic persounis, to barne, murther, reif, and steill, thay prouoik the quenis maiestie of Ingland to seik vengeance of yair oppressioun agains hir realme and subiectis, quhilk vengeance iustice & honour craifis of hir sa instantlie, yat scho can not ceis bot persew thame, thair ressettaris & maintenarie, vntill sho gif sic exempill to vtheris, that althocht thay will not respect vertew, sit for feir of punitioun thay sall be content to leif in peice with nichtbouris, quhairin hir heichnes hes alreddy renewit the memorie of hir experimēnt liberalitie & tender lufe to this natioun, seiking on hir proper charges, and trauel of hir subiectis, ye punitioū of sic, as we on our charges sould haue punisit: I mene not onlie of our traitouris, bot alswa ressettaris of hir maiesties tratouria: and in doing of yis, selkis pacificatioun amangis thame thrt violatit peice with hir without prouocatioun, seuering the punischment of sic as ar gyltie in offending, frō the subiectis that hes not violatit peice. And as sho keipis peice and iustice amangis hir awin subiectis in Inglād, sa vnrequyrit sho offerit support to the same end in Scotland: and not only geuis remedie to our present calamiteis, bot cuttis the ruit of troublis to cum, & preuenis ye wickit counsall of sic, as prouoikis Inglismen, & solistis Frĕchmen to cum in this realme : to the end, that thir twa natiounis enterit in barres ye ane agains the vther, yai may saoiat thair cruell hartis of blude, yair obstinat will of vengeance, thair bothumles couatice of spoyle and thift.

Thairfoir seing God hes sa blindit zour enemies wittin, my lordis, be in gude hope that he sall alswa cast the spreit of feir and disperatioun in thair indurat hartis, & prosper zour gude actioun, to the quhilk he confortis zow with his reddie help, exhortis zow be his word, & constranis zow be the dewtie of zour estait, & necessitie of preseruing of zour lyfis and honouris. For protneis being neglectit, aith violatit, subscriptioun set at nocht, thair is na meane way left bot outher to do or suffer. And seing that baith ar miserabill amangis sic as sould be freindis, zit better it is to slay iustlie, nor to be slane wrāgfullie. For ye execu-tioun of iustice in punissing ye wickit is approuit be God and mā, & sleuthfulnes in defēce of iustice can not be ex-cusit of tressoū. And besydes that, God schewis him sa mercyfull and liberall to zow, in sending zow freindis be procuring of zour enemeis. Alswa the persounis maist re-commendit of God craifis the same : for saikles blude, op-pressioun of the pure, and of ye fatherles, cryis continually to ye heuin for a vengēce, quhilk God cōmittis to zour handis as his lieutennentis: and speciall officiaris in that part. And euin as he rewardis faith and diligence in obedi-ence of his eternall will, sa he will not neglect to punische sleuthfulnes in iust executioun of his commanditnentis.

¶ Thairfoir, my lordis, as ze wald that God sould re-mēber on zow and zour posteritie, quhē thay sall call on him in thair necessitie, remēber on zour king our souērāne, & on my lord regentis pupillis, cōmittit to zow in tutorie be the deuoir of zour office & estait anēt persounis yat ar not in age nor power to help thame selfis, and ar re-cōmēdit specially to all Christianis be God in his holy

scripture: and defend sic innocent creaturis, as may nouther
do nor speik for yame selfis, from the crueltie of vnmercyfull wolfis. Neglect not the occasioun, nor refuse not help
send to zow be God, bot recognosce thankfullie his fauour
towardis. zow, yat causis zour enemeis to procure zour help,
neglect not the offer of freindis, in caice gif ze lat slip this
occasioun, ze sal craif it in vaine in zour necessitie. Think it
na les prouidence of zour heuinlie father, than gif he had send
zow ane legioun of angellis in zour defence, and remember
that he schew him self neuer mair freindfull and succurabill
to na pepill, than he hes done to zow, and traist weill gif
ze will perseueir in obedience and recog-
noscence of his grace, he will multiplie
his benefitis to zow and zour posteritie, and sall neuer leif
zow, vntill ze forzet
him first.

F I N I S.

2.—Chamæleon, written by Mr George Buchanan
against the Laird of Lidingtone.

THAIR is a certane kynd of beist callit Chamæleon, engenderit in sic countreis as the sone hes mair strenth in than
in this yle of Brettane, the quhilk, albeit it be small of cor-
porance, noghttheless it is of ane strange nature, the quhilk
makis it to be na less celebrat and spoken of than sum
beastis of greittar quantitie. The proprieties is marvalous,
for quhat thing evir it be applicat to, it semis to be of the
samyn cullour, and imitatis all hewis, excepte onelie the

quhyte and reid; and for this caus ancient writtaris commonlie comparis it to ane flatterare, quhilk imitatis all the haill materis of quhome he fenzeis him self to be freind to, except quhyte, quhilk is taken to be the symboll and tokin gevin commonlie in devise of colouris to signifie semplines and loyaltie, and reid signifying manliness and heroicall courage. This applicatioun being so usit, zit peradventure mony that hes nowther sene the said beist, nor na perfyte portraict of it, wald beleif sick thing not to be trew. I will thairfore set furth schortlie the descriptioun of sick an monsture not lang ago engendrit in Scotland, in the cuntre of Lowthiane, not far frome Hadingtoun, to that effect that the forme knawin, the moist pestiferus nature of the said monsture may be moir easelie evitit : for this monsture being under coverture of a manis figure, may easeliar endommage and wers be eschapit than gif it wer moir deforme and strange of face, behaviour, schap, and membris. Praying the reidar to spardoun the febilnes of my waike spreit and engyne, gif it can not expreme perfytelie ane strange creature, maid by nature, other willing to schaw hir greit strenth, or be sum accident turnit be force frome the common trade and course. This monstre being engenderit under the figure of a man chyld, first had ane proprietie of nature, flattering all manis ee and sensis that beheld it, so that the common peiple wes in gude hoip of greit vertues to prosper with the time in it; other ferdar seing of greit harmes and dampnage to cum to all that sould be familiarlie aequentit with it. This monsture promovit to sie maturitie of aige, as it could easelie flatter and imitat every manis countenance, speche, and fashions, and subtill to draw out the secreittis of every manis mynd, and depravat the counsellis to his awin proper gayne, enterit in the court of Scotland the   , and having espyit out not onelie factiouns bot singular personis, addressit the self in the begyning to Iames efter erll of Murray, and Gilbert than ach of Camillis, men excellent in the tyme, in all vertuus perteining to ane nobill man, and speciall in lufe of the common welth of thair cuntre : and seing that his nature could not bow to imitat in veritie, but onely to contrafat fenzeithe the gudnes of thir two personis, nor zit change thame to his nature, thocht expedient to leane to thame for a tyme, and clym up be thair branches to hiear degre, as the wod bind clymeth on the oik, and syne with tyme distroyis the tre that it wes supported be. So he having cum to sum estimatioun throw hanting of thir nobill lordis (quha wer than estemit of every man as thair vertuus meritis) wes sone he gud report of thame, and ane fenzeit gudnes in him self, put in credeit with the quene regent, verelie an nobill lady and of greit prudence, bot zit could not espy the gilt vyces under cullour of vertew hid in the said monster, speciallie being clockit be favour of the two forsaid lordis, in quhais company hir grace wald nevir have belevit that sic ane pestilent verm could have bene hyd. The first experience the said quene had of him wes in sending him to France for cartane bissines occurrent for the tyme, quhair he did his commissioun sa weill to his awin intention, and sa far from the quenis mynd, that he dissavit the cardinall of Lorayne ; quha, untill that day, thocht him self not only auld practicien, bot als maister, zea doctour *subtilis*, in sic matters of negociatioun. His fals dealing being sone persavit, and he greitlie hatit, zit sche being ane lady of greit prudence, could not defend hir self frome subtilkie, bot within schort tyme, be meanis of sic as belevit him to be thair freind, he crap in credence agane be ane other dur, and under ane other cullour : bot zit could not sa weill as he wald, invent new falshead, becaus of the auld suspitioun, and being of auld suspectit, sone persavit, and in dangerie to be taken reid hand and puneist efter his meritis, he fled out of Leyth, and coverit himself with the cloik of religioun sa lang as it could serve, bot nevir sa closse bot he keepit ane refuge to

sum sanctuarie of the Papistis, gif the court had changeit;
as to the bischoppis of Santandrois and Glasgow, and
utheris diverse, quhais causis wer in his protectioun: and
thairfore the haly Doctour Cranstoun deptit to him largelie
of the speyle of Sanct Salvatoris College, and wes mantenit
be Chamæleon aganis all law and ressoum; beside that he
wes ane man contaminat in all kynd of vyceis. How far
afoir the cumming hame of the quene the kingis moder, he
wes contrary to all hir actiouns, and favourabill to hir adversaries, and inclynit to hir deprivatioun, it is notourlie
knawin bayth in Ingland and Scotland, be sic as mellit
than with the affairis of the estait in bayth the realms.
Efter the quenis cumming hame he enterit schortlie be
changeing of cullouris, and turning out the other syde of his
cloik, and halding him be the branches of the erll of Murray, and for ane tyme applying him to the quenis G. heir,
that he allone wes hard in all secreit matteris, casting of
lytill and lytill the erll of Murray, and thinking that he
wes strang aneweh to stand by himself, on leaning to the
erll of Murray. And becaus the erll of Murray pleasit
not mony interprysis of marriage than attemptit, as with
the princes of Spayne, with the duke of Anjou, with the
empriaris brother, the said Chamæleon applyit himself to'
all thir partilis, and changeing hew as the quene sweyit the
ballance of hir mynd, and followit the appetyte of hir lust.
And at lang the quene, be avyis of hir oncles, devysit to
destroy the erll of Murray, thinking him to be ane greit
brydill to refrane hir appetitis, and impediment to leif at
libertie of hir plessoure; not that evir he usit ony violence
amentis hir, bot that his honestie wes sa greit that sche wes
eschamit to attempt ony thing indecent in his presence.
Sche than being deliberat to distroy him be the erll of
Huntlie, went to the north, and he in hir company; and
howbeit the tressoun wes oppynnit planelie, and Johnne
Gordoun lying not far of the town [Aberdeen] with an

greit powar, and the erll of Murray expresslie ludgeit in
an hous separate frae all uther habitatioun, and his deid
be diverse wayis socht; this Chamæleon, quhether of sempilnes, or for layk of foirsicht, or for bauldness of courage, I
refer to every manis conscience that doith knaw him, he
alone could se no tressoun, could feare no dangear, and wald
nevir beleif that the erll of Huntlie wald take on hand sie
ane interpryis; howbeit thair wes gevin advertisement of it
out of Ingland and France, letteres taken declarand it, and
the mater manifest, before all menis ene.   It wer to lang to
reherse, and not verie necessar for the present, it being
knawin to sa mony, quhat diverse purposis wer tane,
quhat dangearis eschapit all the tyme of that voyage,
untill the quene come to Abirdene again, and how miracu-
lous wes the victorie : bot ane thing is not to be pretermit-
tit, that the said Chamæleon wes ane of the reddiest to gnaw
the bainis of the deid, to spoyle the qwyck, and mak his
proffeit at that marcat.   Efter this the oursey traffeque of
mariage growing cald, the said Chamæleon going in Ingland, delt sa betuix the Protestantis and Papistes, that he
changeit dalie colouris, sumtyme flattering the ane, sumtyme the other, and making every ane of thame beleif that
he labourit onelie for thame; and amangis other thingis, be
ane prevy intelligence with the quene, and verie few of the
nobilitie, practizit the marriage of the quene and Henry
Lord Dernlie, of the quhilk he mad nevir the erll of Murray prevy, untill all wes endit.   Howbeit the erll of Murray did nevir thinge, nor tuke nevir propose without his advise and counsale. Heir the mater quhilk he had rasshelie
brocht on, wes neir the point. Seing that the quene of
Ingland dissagreit with it for certane respectis, and the lordis
of Scotland for the cause of the religioun, to the mantein-
ance of the quhilk thay dessyrit an premeis of the quene
and the said Lord Dernlie, the Chamæleon in secreit flatterit the quene, and openlie tuke the colour of religioun :

and at the lang (seing my lord of Murray, for being precise and plane in all doingis, cast out of court) cled himself onelie in the quenis colouris, untill that David prevalit agains him, and had in a manner the haill credeit of all wechtie materis. At this poynt thinking himself in werse caise than he beleivit, socht to make an other change of court, and set up new play again, awaytit on the court sumpart disgracit, louking for sum new cullour to apply himself to. In this mene tyme the quene seking to move sum thing in the religioun, made ane querrell agains certane lordis of the principallis of Scotland, the quhilkis, albeit that ane ressonabill power faillit thame not, and that the favouir of the cuntre wes for thame, xit to schaw thair innocency, quhen thai could not breke the quenis obstinat mynd of thair destractioun be prayer and sollicitacioun of freindis, thay left the cuntre and went in Ingland, zit Chameleon held the small grip that he had in court, secunding to David. In this mene tyme the parliament set to forfalt sick leudis as had fled in Ingland, except the duke, quha did be intercessioun of silver by his remissioun fra David. The rest of the lordis quhilk were of wisdome or estimatioun, partlie requirit be the king, quha wes in na credit in respect of David, partlie for thair awin libertie, conspyrit the deid of the said David, and executit the same. Chameleon, cheifest enemy to David, eftir the kingis grace, xit not being advertisit be the lordis of thair enterprise, and suspectit of the quene, knawing his dowbilness, quhyther for verie feare, or preparing ane entre to the quenis favour, fled as uthers did; and eftir lang fetchis brocht agane to the court, kest clene frae him all colouris of the kingis, and cled him agane in the quenis colouris, and wes ane of the principal instrumentis that incressit dissensioun betwix hir and the king: the quhilk practise, howbeit he wald have dissimulatit, sum tyme brake out with him; as to ane nobill woman praying *God to gif the king and the quene grace to agrie*, he answerit, *God let thame nevir agre:* for thay leving in dissensioun, he thocht that his dowbilnes could not be espyit out. And than seing the Erll Bothuile cum in credeit, he flatterit him; and evin as thay agreit in all pointis to put down the king, seing that he prospering thay could have na lyff, sa eftir the king deid, the Erll Boithuile, having in that practize knawin his falset, and fearing his inconstancy, and desyring to be deliverit of sio an witnes, socht his deid: and he having na refuge to the quene for the samyn cause, tuke for a tyme the erll of Mortonis collouris, and being borne furth be him agains the erll of Boithuiles power and hatrent, sa lang as he wes in feare lurkit under the erll of Mortonis wingis, and the feir past schew himself the said earls enemie: and having no sufficient cause, nor appearand indice of separatioun of company and kyndnes, he fenzeit that the said erll of Mortun had conspyrit his deid, to be execute by some of the erllis friendis; and to prove the said conspiracy, alledgit an famous witnes (*majorem omni exceptione*) the nobill and virtuus Lady Gyltoun. Now to returne agane to our propose, eftir the deid of the king devysit be him, executit be the Erll Bothuile, for feir of the said erll he lurkit a quhile out of court, untill the tyme the quene at Carberrie-Hill come to the lordis, and the Erll Boithuile fled to Dunbar. Than he come to parliament, and with sume otheris participant of the kingis slaughter, wald have had the quene slane be act of parliament; and not finding mony consenting thairto, and speciallie the erll of Murray, than chosen regent, being in the contrair, he sollicitat some previe men to gar hang hir on hir bed with hir awin belt, that be that way he and his partinaris in the kingis murthoure mycht be deliverit of an witnesse; knawing weill the quenis nature, that quhen she wes miscontent of ony man, sche wald tell all sic secreittis as sche did knaw of him. This propose not proceeding as he desyrit, he turnit him first in flattering with the quene, and send to hir, being in Lochlevin, ane picture of the deliverance of the lyoun by the mouse; and nist turnit his haill wit to the distruction of the erll of Murray, thinking that the wickit could not proffeit greitly, so just a man having the supreme power; and als seing that the quenis craftiness wes abill at the lang to overthraw the erll of Murrays sempilnes. So he bendit all his wittis to the said erllis eversioun, and the quenis restitution, and procedit in this cause, partlie be making an factioun of the counsalleris, and partakeris of the kingis murthoure, of men lycht of fantasie and covatous of geir; partlie be correpting of my lord of Murrayis freindis and servandis, and travellit principallie with the laird of Grange, thinking that it sould be an greit strenth to the factioun, to have the castell of Edinburgh at thair command. The regent being divers tymes advertiset of thir practizis, wes of so upright nature, that he wald beleif na thing of ony that he had takin in freindschip, quhilk he wald not have done himself; and als mony of the factioun in the begyning thocht it had bene bot ane ligue defensive againis the power of the great, that is accustimat to overthraw the small in tyme of troubill.

In this mene tyme come the deliverance of the quene out of Lochlevin, the quhilk he wes not ignorant of, and specially be the meanis of his cousing Johne Hamiltoun of the Cochnoch [al. Coheugh]: zit he tareit with the regent to keip ane cullour of honestie, and that with the quenis consent, quha had given him, and divers otheris that were in my lord of Murrayis company, fre remissioun for all by past.

Bot the battel chansing utherwaies than he desyrit and belevit, zit he persistit in his propose to destroy the regent, not opinlie, bot be secreit meanis: as being sent divers tymes to commune with the Lord Flemyng, evir did the contrair of the propose that he wes send for, and evir tendit to hald the cuntre in unquietnes; and in all assembleis for appointment, tendit to have all by past remittit, to keip ay thevis and revaris in courage, and to abase the hartis of

trew subjectis, that sould haif na hoip of redresse of wrangis
done to thame be the kingis rebellis. Efter that, be the
dilligence and wisdome of the regent, the cuntre wes brocht
to sum stay, and justice lyke to haif the over hand, the
kingis rebellis purchassit at the quene of Inglandis handis,
that sche sould consider the greit wrangis (as thai said)
done to hir nixt nychtbour, and being nixt of blude to hir,
and other be hir requeist or puissance caus hir be restorit
agane to her formar authoritie. The quenis majestie of
Ingland having zit no less regaird to justice nor to consan-
guinitie, desyrit some of the principallis of the nobilitie to
repair to hir or hir deputties for thir requeistis and com-
playntis, and my lord deliberat to go in persoun wes in
doubt, having ellis enterit in sum suspicionis of this Chamæleon, quhethir he sould tak him with him self, or leif
him beheind: for taking him he doubtit not bot he wald
hinder the actioun in all manner possibill, and leaving him
behind, that following his natural complexioun he wald
trubill the cuntre, in sick maner that it sould not be easelie
in lang tyme brocht to rest agane. At lang having deliberat
to take him with him, and perswadit him bayth be giftis
of landis and money, he fand to be trew in deid all that he
suspectit afore ; for everie nycht in a manner he commu-
nicat all that wes amangis us with sum of our adversaris,
and armit thame sa far as he could agains the said regent.
Bot the force of the ressonis, and cleirnes of the haill de-
ductioun of the caus that my lord regent usit, wes sa per-
swasive to the auditouris, that be Chamæleons advertisement, the kingis mother disschargeit hir commissiouners to
proceed forther, and differrit to ane mair commodious tyme
for hir: for it wes weill knawin to hir that the quenis majestie of Ingland and hir counsall had allowit the said regentis procedingis ; and the ambassadour of Spayne seing
the horribill cryme sa abhominabill to all honest men, refused to speik ane word in the-mater, and the Frensche am-

bassadour excusit himself that he spake be command of [his] maister.

· In this mene tyme the said Chamæleonis secreit practize with the duke of Norffolk, suspectit afore, begouth to brek out be sum letters of Maister Johne Lesskis callit bischope of Ross, and als be the duke himself, put in hoip of mariage of the Scottis quene be thame, the quhilk practize wes handillit: sumpart putting feir to the regent, that he could not returne in Scotland with his lyff without the dukis favour, be reassoun of greit preparationis that wes maid aganis the regent on bayth the bordoris of Scotland and Ingland: partlie be tempting of the said regentis mynd, quha answerit to the duke of Norffolk, *That he wald be glad that the quene recognoscing hir falt, and repenting, sould marry ony gude Christian man of nobill house.* The rumour of this dealing wes sa openelie spoken in the court of England, that the quenis majestie wes constraynit to wryte to hir lieutenentis to mak the regent be put sauf in Scotland; and so he wes without any recounter, bot of the erll of Westmureland not far frome Durame, quho seing the regentis company, and ryding throw thame, thocht not best to matche with thame. The next assemble wes at Glasgow, quhair the Hamiltonis bragging, bot could not be party, be meanis of him and otheris thair favoureris with the regent, wer ressavit to sic an appointment as wes greitlie to thair advantage, and the said regentis dissadvantage. And quhen thai sould haif gevin pledgis to performe the said appointment, as wes compromittit, thay did bot seke delay; and so the principallis of thame [wer] committit to ward in the castell of Edinburgh. The haill mater wes secreitlie handillit be the Chamæleon. The quhilk handilling apperit more planelie at an conventioun at Sanctandrois; quhair thair wes twa headis principallie disputit: first, *Gif the erll of Huntlie sould haif general remissioun for all reif and oppressioun done be him and his friendis in all tymes bypast;*

er, gif the kingis actioun pardonit, prevat men sould have
actioun to crave thair awin geir: nixt, *Gif the erll of*
Huntleis haill assiestaris sould be comprehendit in ane remis-
sioun with him. The quhilk twa headis the Chamæleon
and his complices preassit ernistly be all meanis to be ressavit, as said is, and that not without boisting of Franche
men and Spanzaris, and mony uther inconvenientis; and
all this done to disscourage the kingis trew liegis, and lycht-
ning the hartis of rebellis in hoip of impunitie of all wrongis
that thai sould do in tyme to cume, and to hald the haill
cuntre in rebellioun and inquietnes, to consume at the lang
the regent, quhilk thai knew to be puir of substance and liberall of courage. And zit wer not thir thingis mair sub-
tilly devysed, nor thai wer constantlie resistit be the regent
and his trew counsall. And seing that thai could not come
to thair propose this way, thay causit new articles to be de-
visit in Ingland, towching the quenis cuming hame: to
the quhilk albeit thair wes sufficient answer mad in London, zit for the samyne caus wes devysit ane assemble of
lordis in Sanct Johnestoun, with ane additioun of ane commissioun of divorcement of the Erll Boithuile and the quene,
and to the effect of the haill, mony writingis [wer] purchassit of boith wise men and greit men of Ingland, schawing planelie that it wes ane foly to Scotland to presse to resist the marriage betwix the quene and duke of Norffolk;
for it wes devysit be sic wisdom, and to be executit with sic
force, as Scotland wes not abill to resist; and not without
consent of the quenis majestie of Ingland. Heir, albeit
Chamæleon and all his quhelpis ragit nevir sa fast, the contrair wes concludit, and schawen to the quenis grace of Ingland be Alexander Hume, gentleman of my lord regentis
hous. And becaus the quenis majestie wes not fully satis-
feit at that tyme, ane uther convocatioun wes hald at Stirling,
to the quhilk the Chamæleon, assurit of my lord regentis
clemencie, and proude in his awin consait, bot feiring for

his demeritis, efter sum dubitatioun come to Stirling; and
wes in doubt not without caus. For about this tyme, my
lord regent, advertisit that the Hamiltonis had decreitit to
murthoure him, he schew bayth the taill and the authour
to the Chamæleon, of the quhilk the Chamæleon reprovit
vehemently the Hamiltonis that could not keip thair coun-
'sall mair secreit; and this advertising being schawin be
sum of the Hamiltonis to my lord regent, zit he sufferit
pacientlie. At Stirling the articles being declarit at greiter
length, the Chamæleon wes attecheit be justice, and chargit
of the kingis murthoure, the quhilk greivit him havelie,
and pressit at my lord regentis hand the cryme to be changeit, and he to be accusit of the troubles lyke to ryis in Ingland and Scotland throuch the forspoken mariage; for he
thocht that mater to be consavit and devysit sa substantial-
lie, that nouther force nor wit could maik impediment to
the performance of it, and belevit suirlie that sic ane cryme
sould redound to his greit prayse and opinioun of wisdome.
This not obteinit, he obteinit aganis all the said regentis
friendis will, to be send to ward in the castell of Edinburghe;
quahir he wrocht againis the nature of the Chamæleon, for
he changeit the greitar part of thame of the castell to his
collour sa weill, that the conspiracy of the regentis deid,
lang afoir consavit, wes than brocht to effect. Eftir the
quhilk he wrocht be sic meanis, that he perswadit the haill
lordis than present in Edinburgh to be enlargit of his ward,
under promeis to compeir and answer to the cryme of the
kingis murthoure layd to his charge, at sic day as he sould
be callit, and under hoip to be an gude instrument of concord amangis the lordis; and ane day prolongit to sick of the
Hamiltonis as wald purge thame sellfis of the murthoure of
the regent unto the first day of Maii: bot sone being ad-
joinit with utheris of his factioun, he changeit that collour,
and perswadit utheris complices of the murthoure for feir,
and sum sempill persones be ane fals collour of proffeit, to

convene to an schorter day, viz. the tent day of Apryle, assuring thame that the castell (as it wes) being thairs, and the town als, (for the capitane of the castell wes proveist) that this rumour sould caus mony to convéne to thame, and thair adversaris disagracit sould haif na place to convene togidder; and that the quene of Ingland, troublit alreddy with civile warre at hame, mycht the mair eselie condiscend to that syde, wrait to hir letteres partlie flattering, partlie threatning; and to schaw hir thair greit power, send ane roll of the lordis of thair syde, quhairin wes comprehendit sum lordis neutrallis, and mony of the adversaries, beleving that leyis maid in Scotland could not be tryit in Londoun. And seing that the town of Edinburgh could not be perswadit to rebell with thame, and that the cuntre convenit not as thai hoipit, and the breking of the bordouris succedit not to thair proffeit, the most part flittit camp, and went to Lynlythquow, and thair set furth thair proclamatioun dytit be Chamæleon (as wes afore the erll of Westmuirlandis second proclamatioun) and thairby set up the quenis authoritie, quhairof he (tarreing in the castell of Edinburgh) kepit himself clene, as Pilat wesching his handis of the deid of Chryst. And sens that tyme, as afore, this gud subjecte and servand to the kingis grace confortit with counsale, and conveyit out of the cuntre the rebellis of Ingland, the samyne being enemies to the king of Scotland; and prattit proudlie, vanting that his pen sould be worth ten thousand men; and threitnit schamefullie (gif he had reservit any schame) the quenis majestie of Ingland with wordis of quhilk the memory sould be rather abolishit be punitioun of him, than rehersit for thair impudencie; and feirit not to maik sa opin a leye to nobillmen of Ingland, as that the kingis trew subjectis acknawledging his authoritie wer not able to assembill togidder fyve hundred horse, quhair thai saw, within few days, moir than fyve thousand assemblit out of ane cornar of Scotland. And ay sensyne he hes bene at all convocatiouns of the kingis professit enemies in Scotland, in Dunkeld, in Athol, in Strabogie, in Braidalbine, and ellis quhair, and kepis contrebank to Mr Johne Leslie of Kingusce, in all directionis to put the king out of his estait, his realme, and at lenth out of this erdlie lyffe.

Now, I pray you, espy out quhat proffeit the quene, our kingis modder, sall gadder of him that hes bene (as sche knawis) sa oftentyme traitour to hir modder, to hir selfe, to hir sone, to hir brother, and to hir cuntre. Sche will be exemplis considder, that how mony collouris that evir this Chamaleon change, that it can nevir, aguinis the nature of it, turne perfytelie quhyte.

Respice finem,
1570.   *Respice finem.*

No. III.—See p. 178.

Buchanan's Opinion anent the Reformation of the Universitie of St Androis.

(From a MS. in the Advocates' Library.)

The ordinar Expenses of the Colledge of Humanitie.
Persons.
The Principall.
Ane Lector publick.
Sex Regents.
Servants.
The Principall, 2 servants.
The Lector publick, j servant.
The Cook.

The Porter.

The Steuart.

The Pantriman.

For the principall and tuo servants, tuo quarts of ale, tuo bread of 16 unce the bread, ane quarter of mutton, or equivalent in silver on the fish day, tuo shilling.

Summa.

Of malt fiftein bolls and ane half, at tuelve gallons the boll.

It. in bread of uheat sex bolls.

For kitchin meatt threttie sex punds.

For the publick lector a quart of ale, ane bread and ane halfe. It. half ane quarter of mutton at the principalls table. If he be maried, or had house out of the college, that it shall befall to him to have ane boarder in the colledge at the principalls table in his place, or els the price of the boarding above uritten.

Summa.

Of mault, seven bolls and three furlitts.

In bread, four bolls and tuo furlitts.

In silver, eightein punds.

The sex regents, every man three chopins of ale, and tuentie unce of bread daylie; and amongst them ane quarter of mutton and ane halfe, or equivalent; that is, for fish or flesh on the day, five shilling; viz. on the fish day, tuo courss of fish, and every man ane egg at the melteth, aftir the   and opportunitie.

Summa.

Of malt, threttie five bolls.

Of wheat, tuentie tuo bolls, and ane furlitt.

Of silver, nintie one pund, seven shilling.

The cook, steuart, porter, and pantriman, ilke ane of them ane bread, ane pint of ale, in the day, and halfe ane quarter of mutton, or equivalent among them, ane courss of fish att melteth; sextein pennies the day.

Summa.

Of malt, eleven bolls, tuo furlitts, tuo pecks.

Of oatmeall, fiftein bolls.

Of silver, tuentie four punds, sex shilling, eight pennies.

Wadges of the persons.

The principall, ane hundreth punds.

The publick lector, ane hundreth merks.

The sex regents, sex score of punds to be divydit at the principalls discretion, and paction made uith them.

The cook and porter, tuelve merks.

The steuart to be payed be the principall off the professor of the portionists.

For coalls, naperie, and vessells, and other extraordinars, and concerning the hall and kitchin, fourtie punds yeirly.

For reparation of the place, fourtie pundes yeirly. Of the whilk reparations the principall shall give compt yeirly to the censors and rector for the tyme.

The haill soume.

In drink of malt, sextie nine bolls, four furlitts, tuo pecks.

In wheatt, threttie one bolls.

In silver, five hundreth fourtie seven pund, ten shilling, ten pennies.

It. for ilk bussar, so many as shall be thought necessary to be in the College of Humanitie, one bread and ane pint of ale in the day, the sexth part of ane quarter of mutton, or the value therof.

The Order of the Colledge of Humanitie.

The scholars that comes of neu shall adress him to the principall, who shall cause them to compeir, and examin them, and, eftir ther capacitie, send them to ane regent with his signet: and the regent shall writt them in his roll, aud assigne them place in his class, divydit in decurys.

The bairns of this colledge shall hear no other lessens

but ther regents; and the leetor publict in humanitie, so many as shall be found able by the principall: and that which is read in the college shall not be read in others.

The bairnes of this college shall not goe furth by them selvs, nor yet uith ane regent without the principalls leave.

All other things pertaineing to discipline scholestick, to be done as comoditie and time occurrs.

The number of the classes at the least sex.

The louest class is for those that should declin ther nouns, and the verbs, actives, passives and anomales, and aftir that learn Terence and the rudiments of grammer, as followes. They shall bring to ther class peaper and ink; and ther regent shall cause them to writt tuo or three lines of Terence, telling not only to them the letters and the word, but also the accent, in such leasure that the bairnes may easilie writt aftir his pronunciation. And aftir that, he shall give the interpretation in Scotts correspondant to the Latine, garring them all writt: syne he shall decline every word, and cause them to writt severally all the nouns and the verbs that be in ther lesson, give comand to learn them against the next lessone, and also bring that lesson whilk was made in the class, without any fault written. The nomeclators to have charge to gather the lessons written, every one in his oune decurie, and bring them to the regent, and schou him who hes faults. And if the regent find fault wherof the nomeclator hes not advertised him, then he shall punish both the writter and the nomeclator to make them more dilligent in tyme to come; and no man shall mend others faults whill they come to the regent. In this class they shall be constrained to speak Latine, and daylie to compon some small thing eftir ther capacitie.

The fifth Class.

This class shall read Terence and some of the most

facil epistles of Cicero alternarim [alternatim], and also
the rules of grammar assigned to them, without commen-
tair bot only the express words and sentence of the rule:
and they shall writt both Terence and Cicero, every man
with his oune hand.

The fourth Class.

This class shall read of Terence and Cicero some thing
maire then the classes under them; and also *de construc-
tione octo partium*, and the latter half of the year shall read
some epistles of Ovid or other of his elegies; and also writt
all ther lessons except the grammar, and compone larger
thames than the other classes. And all ther classis shall be
visit every quarter of a year, and promovit them aftir ther
merits.

The thrid Class.

This class shall read the grammar in Greek, the epistles
of Cicero, and some of the most facil orations, with some
bookes of Ovid, and the qualities [quantities] of syllabs,
and some introduction of rhetorick, and some of the books
of Lineesters [Linacre's] grammar, and shall be maire
exercised in composition then the others louer.

The second and first Class.

Ther classis shall read the rhetorick of Cicero and his
orations, and for part Virgill, Horace, Ovid, and some of
Homer or   . The auditors shall be dilligently
exercised in verss, and oration, and declamation, every month,
ilk ane ther cours about. Item, general disputasiones to be
had every Saturnday frae on aftirnoon to four houres, ane
class against another, fixing thames alternatim; and syne
componeing, or thames dited by regents of other classis, or
other maisters.

At the end of the year in the month of August or therby,
all the haill classis shall propon thames openlie, and affix
them upon the college walls, or in the great schooll, or
halls. The principall shall chuse ane certane of the best

of the first classe and second, and send thames to some of the honest men of other colleges, or some other learned man being present for the tyme, and desyre that he propon them ane thame in prose and ane other in verse. Ther shall be tuo bonnetts proponed to be given solemnly to the tuo that makes best composition, with honorable word to encourage others in tyme to come to emulation; and that the honest and principall persons in the universitie assistand, and exhorting the students to be dilligent, and raise ther courage.

Hereftir, because the maist part of the countrey will be glad to see ther bairns, and make them cloathes, and provide to ther necessities the rest of the year, ther may be given some vaccans unto the first day of October; on the whilk day, all lessons begins again in all colleges. At the whilk day, nane shall be promovit to no class without he be examined by the principall and regents comittit thereto.

The principall shall be dilligent that every regent doe his dutie, and that the bairnes be obedient; and to that effect make some particular rules, sick as shall be found gud be the rector and the censors for peaceable governing of the college; and at the begining of October the principall shall present before them the said report. And gief any inlak be sickness or other necessitie, he shall present ane qualified person to them: and geif the principall inlake, the universitie and conservator or his deput shall convein, and chuse of the haill universitie foar of the best qualified persons to that office, and writt ther names; and eftir prayer made that God of his gudness would send the tort upon some that were ablest to exerce that estat to his glory and comon weill, ane barn shall drau of the foare one, the whilk shall be principall; and this to putt auay all deception and ambition.

The principall shall support the defects of absence of the public reader, and repeat. And sicklyke, in the prin-

cipalls absence, every man in his order shall have his jurisdictione and correction of the students.

The porter shall abide continually at the zeatt and receave the principalls signet of them that desires to pass
furth. Item, in Summer he shall ring daylie at five houres
to the riseing; at sex to the lesson public; befor eight
tuice to the ordinar lection; at ten he shall knell ane halfe
houre; to eleven knell; at eleven ring to the dinner; at
grace knell; to repetition aftir grace ring; or three houres
ring tuice; at halfe houre to five knell; at five ring.

All the students remaineing in the colledge shall be dis-
tribut be chalmers, and under care of the principall or some
regent or padagoge, learned and of judgement, who shall
have care of ther studie and dilligence; but not to read any
parlant lection to them, but to cause them to give count of
it that they read in the classe: nor yet shall it be laufull
to the said pedagoge to ding ther disciples, but only to declair the fault te the principall or to ther regent, and refer
the punishment to them.

In this college nane shall persever regents in humanitie
above the space of seven or eight years.

The three lou classis shall not be subject to come to
preachings or exercise publict except on the Sonday. The
other preaching and exercise dayes, ane regent shall be
comissionat to see that they be deullie exercised, and specially in learning to writt.

The College of Philosophie.

Persons.

Ane Principall.
Ane   in Medicine.
And Regents four.

Servants.

The Principall, tuo servants.
The Medicine, one servant.
The Cook.

The Portar.

The Steuart.

The Pantriman.

The principalls portion and sallarie as in the College of Humanitie.

The medicins as in the lector public of humanitie.

The rest ut supra proportionally.

Summa.

In bread

In drink

In silver

The bursars tuelve ut supra; each one sextin pund the year, or ut supra.

For coalls, candle, naperie, and vessells, fourty punds yeirly.

For reparation of the place, fourty pund yeirly.

The haill subject to compt ut supra.

The principall to be ane man of honour, and sufficient doctrin to supplie the regents absence in reding in ther sickness or laufull bussines. Item, to have all sick autoritie over regents, and students, and servants, in the college, and to give compt to the rector and censors, as foirsaid is in the College of Humanitie, at every visitation.

The first regent read the dialect, analiter [analytics], and moralis, in the first year and halfe; and the other year and halfe, the naturall philosophie, metaphisick, and principis of mathematick. Sua in the year ther regents shall pass by degrees the haill cours of dialect, logick, phisick, and metaphisick : the rest of the tyme to repeat, and pass ther acts. They shall read such books of Aristotle or other philosophers as the principall shall prescribe to them.

No man shall be admitted at the begining of the year to the philosophie, that hes not past by the first or second class of humanitie ; or, geif he be ane stranger, be inputt worthie of the first and second class, be triall of composition in versse and prose.

The Order of Reading.

All the regents shall begin, both Summer and Winter, at sex hours in the morneing to ther ordinar lessons; and at the begining, shall make ane short prayer for promotion of learning and the estate of the comon well. They shall read unto eight hours; and uhilk being strokin, the bell shall ring to the medicinis lesson; quha shall read on to nine hours: and frae nine to ten shall be intermission. In the rest of the hours they shall be exercised in disputeing and reading, as the College of Humanitie; and the regents in every class shall cause the one part to disput against the other. On Saturnday, every class shall propon certan propositiones, whilk afoir noon shall be examinat and disput again by the regents betuixt eight and eleven houres; and aftir noon the disciples of the superior class shall disput against the inferior betuixt ane and three hours.

The Promotion of ther Degrees.

At the end of the first two years, they shall be made batchelors, wher not only they shall declare publicly what they have profited by ther industrie and labours, but alsua they shall ansuer privatly to four examinators deputt by the universitie, of the dialect, logic, and moralis: and uha beis not found able, shall he deposed to ane louer class. And so sicklyk, at the end of the year and halfe follouing, to be examinat of the naturall philosophie, metaphysicks, and mathematicks. The examinators shall be graduat, and [ane] in theologie, ane that hes read in philosophie, ane of profession of medicine passed master, and ane regent in humanitie: quha on ther conscience shall declare to the rector and censors quha are worthie of promotion or not. Eftir the whilk declaration, the rector shall decern the unworthie to be deposit for time convenient to ane inferior class: sua that na man be admitted to receave degree except that he have promovit in letters.

To the banquet of acts of bachelar, and liseuce, the rich shall not pay above fourtie shilling, the puir ten shilling, to augment the comon portion of the college; sua that the convention of honest men of the universitie be with modestie and temperance. Item, so many of the asisstands to this act as be graduat in divinity, laus, or medicine, or presently regents in philosophie or humanitie, shall have for ther presence and decreeing of the act, ane pair of gloves. And the principall of the said colledge shall take hoad [heid] that thir things be performed as he will ansuer to the judgement of the rector and censors.

The number of bursars sustained, tuentie four, as is prescrivit in the College of Humanitie.

Naine shall persever regent in this colledge longer then the space of tuo courasses.

The medicin shall read four dayes in the week, ane houre every day, in medicine: and if he inlake, the principall shall deduce so meikle of his wage, to be used to the comon profit of the college.

The College of Divinitie.

Personis.

Ane Principall, to be Reader in Hebreu.

Ane Lauer.

Servants.

The Principall, tuo servants.

The Lauer, one servant.

Cook.

Pantriman.

Steuart.

Porter.

Ther expensis ut supra: viz. the principall as other prinpalls. The lauer fourty punds. The cook, porter, steuart, and pantriman, ut supra. Bursars, eightein of them; sex in lau, and tuelve in theologie: ther expensis ut supra.

In this college, becaus that the students are in number feuer, and of greater age then in the others, the principall and lector in Hebrew may be ane person. The uhilk shall read four dayes every week.

The Thursday, ane student in divinitie shall expone ane peice of the scripture the space of ane hour; and this being done, shall answer to the objections of every man that pleases to disput against him, the space of ane hour and ane halfe. The principall shall see that good order be keepit in disputing, without superfluitie of words, nothing pertaineing to the purpose, without dinrie or pertinacitie in contention; and that every auditor in divinitie answer his courss about, as shall be ordained by the principall. To speak in the public exercise and expone the scriptur, shall entice not only the auditors of divinitie, sick as shall be thought expedient, but also the regents in other faculties.

The lauer shall read daylie ane hour in lau, except on the Thursday.

Ther shall be eightein bursars in this college: viz. sex in lau, and tuelve auditers in divinitie.

The Comon Magistrats and Officiars of the Universitie.

Ane Rector.

The rector most be ane discreit and grave person, doctor or bachelar in the higher faculties, principall of ane college or presently regent in divinitie, lau, or medicine, of age above threttie years; and shall be chosen by the haill graduats of the universitie, within ane of the three colleges, the conservator or his deputt being present: quha shall require the convention in ther conscience, that out of every college ther be ane chosen, quha shall declair the votes of the college faithfullie gathered; and declare him rector who hes maniest votes, sua that he have not been rector within tuo yeares befor.

The rectors office is principally in keeping of the disciplin scholastick; as in visitation of the colleges twice or thrice in the year, so that the order be keepit in teaching; in uisitations of classis; in disputationes als uell privat as publick: item, that no idle man be holden on the wage or expensis of the universitie, nor unworthie promovit to degree. The rectors time to be ane year, without continuation: and if by ambition or otherwayes, the most part of the votes continou him, all ther votes that tends to continuation, to be null. And make ane register of all that entars in the number of the universitie, and shall enjoy the previledges therof.

Conservator.

The conservator of priviledge most have autoritie to call befor him all actiones or questiones moved by them of the universitie against any persons in maitters tuitching students as being students: and his decreit shall have ready execution, notuithstanding any appellations, without delay or appellation out of the universitie. His wage to be payed to him, or his deputt, of the archdeanrie; becaus in tymes bypast the archdean or bishop uas conservators, or some deputt for them; and nou is reasonable that they sustain the samen charge.

The thesaurer shall be chosen once in the year, the samen day that the censor beis chosen; and shall give compt at the yeares end to the censors, the day aftir the choiseing of the neu censor.

The sellary of the rector, thesaurer, and censor, to be payed off the casualities of the universitie, as it that comes of the entries of the students in the rectors book, and of the degrees. Also the beddell to be payed of the samen. The wages of the rector, censor, thesaurer, and beddell, and als all ther casualities, to be so moderat that they be not excessive in no qualitie.

Item, that the Queens Grace and Lords of the Parlia-

.ment be required to pass ane act, that three years aftir the performing of this reformation, na man be provydit to sustaine office of preacher or lector in the kirke, except they have been deullie graduat in the schoolls.

The Rentall of St Leonards College.

In silver	- -	132 lib. 2 sh. 4 d.
In wheat	- -	2 chal. 12 bolls.
In bear	- -	13 chal. 11 bolls, 2 fur. 2 pecks.
In meall	- -	8 chal. 8 bolls.

Sanct Salvators, all being free.

In silver	- - - - -	642 lib. 00 00
Wheatt	- - - - -	3 chal. 13 bolls.
Bear	- - - - -	8 chal. 2 bolls.
Aits	- - - - -	19 chal. 3 bolls.

The Neu College, all being free.

In silver, besides	when it shall vaick,	110 lib.
Wheatt	- - - - -	3 chal. 8 bolls.
Bear	- - - - -	6 chal.
Aits	- - - - -	5 chal.

The haill Soumes.

In silver	-	1284 [884] lib. 2 sh. 4
Wheatt	- -	10 chal. 1 boll.
Bear	- -	27 chal. 13 bolls, 2 furl. 2 pecks.
Aite meall	-	8 chal.
Aits		24 chal. 3 bolls.

No. IV.

Notices of George Buchanan; communicated by the Rev. John Lee, M.D. Professor of Ecclesiastical History in New College, and Rector of the University of St Andrews.

GEORGE BUCHANAN was not, as is commonly imagined, a student in St Salvator's College. In the year 1525, the names Patricius Balquhannan and Georgius Balquhannan both stand in the list *Incorporatorum in Pædagogio*, that is, of those who were matriculated in the seminary afterwards distinguished by the name of St Mary's, or New College; which seems to have been for the first time designed *New* in 1538, when its foundation was new-modelled by Archbishop James Beaton, its greatest benefactor. John Mair was one of the masters in the Pedagogy when Buchanan entered this college. Mair had become a member of the university only a year or two before, as appears from the following entry in one of the records of the university: " Die nono mensis Junii anno Dni Im. V^c. XXIII. incorporatus erat venerabilis vir Mg^r nr. Mg^r Johannes Major, Doctor Theologus Parisiensis, et Thesaur^{ius} Capellæ Regiæ. Eodem die incorporati sunt Mg^r Patricius Hamilton et Mg^r Ro^{tus} Lauder in ara. universitate." [This Patricius Hamilton was the abbot of Fearn, who was burnt as a heretic four years afterwards.] That Mair was not at this time a member of St Salvator's College (as has been generally believed) is evident from his appointment in 1523 and 1524 as one of the deputies who assisted the rector in the annual visitation of that college. The following minute mentions his nomination in 1523. " Congregatióne Univ^{tis} Sancti Andr. in ecol^{ia} S^{ti} Johannis Evang^tes Pædagogii intra civitatem Sancti Andr. die XVII. Mensis Ja^m anno dni Im. V^c. XXIII. in qua congrega. pro electione deputatorum ad visitandum Collegium S^ti Salvatoris, de mandato egregii viri Mg^d Georgii Lockhart, Rectoris dicti Univ^tis electi fuerunt per Univer^tem congregatam venerabiles et egregii viri Mg^ri Mg^r Johannes Mayr, Thesaur^ius Capellae Regiae Strevilens. venerabilis vir Mg^r Georgius Fern, Præcentor Brosbinens. Mg^r Johannes Lockhart, Rector de Innerkeithe, una cum D^no Rectore Universitatis, pro visitatione antedicta, per nationes Laudoniae, Albaniae, Anguaiae et Britanniae, ad visitand. praefatum collegium hoc anno instante vigesimo tertio, ut moris est."—The name of John Mair disappears from the registers of the university in 1525, and does not occur again till the year 1533, when he is mentioned as one of the rector's assessors, without any other official designation. An instrument of seisin still extant of the date 21 Jan. 1532, styles him "Vicarius de Dunloppie Glasg. diocæs." In 1533 he became provost of St Salvator's (Ecclesiae Collegiatae Divi Salvatoris praepositus), having succeeded Hugh Spens, who had possessed that dignity nearly thirty years. Mair continued to hold his office till 1549, about which time he was succeeded by Martin Balfour.

While Mair was provost of St Salvator's, the college of St Mary had for its principals Robert Bannerman, Archibald Hay, and John Douglas, all secular priests; and St Leonard's College was under the superintendance of a succession of learned men, all of them regular clergy; namely, Thomas Cunningham, Alexander Young, John Annan, and John Law. This last was succeeded by John Duncanson, one of the brethren of the Augustinian priory, who became principal of St Leonard's College in 1556, and who having been converted to the reformed religion, retained his office in the college as well as his share of the rents of the convent. Whether he acted as minister of St Leo-

nard's church is not certain; but as he was in orders, and
as St Leonard's was a parish long before the reformation,
it might be presumed that he did, if it did not appear from
the minutes of the kirk session of St Andrews, that immediately after the reformation the inhabitants of St Leonard's
were in the habit of attending the Trinity Church of St
Andrews. When Duncanson retired from the principality
in 1566, he gave to the college a great cup or mainer,
double gilt, and other articles to the value of 80 pounds;
also 20 pounds to purchase coals, and 100 pounds to the new
work of the college, with 50 pounds of his yearly pension
from the abbey of St. Andrews. In addition to these dona-
tions, amounting to 200 pounds, he gave two tin flagons for
the use of the college, and (what appears to have been
much more valuable) all his books, both great and small.

The office of principal of St. Leonard's College is thus
described in the original statutes enacted by the prior John
Hepburn, and confirmed in the year 1544 by James commendator of the priory, and Alexander (Myln) abbot of
Cambuskenneth, administrator, with the approbation and
consent of John Winram, subprior, John Annand, principal, Thomas Fyff, sacrist, Jo. Lamont, provisor, and Jas.
Wylkie, David Guild, John Scheill, and David Gardyn,
regents. " Volumus ex fratrum nostrorum Collegio, viz. ex
Capitulo Sancti Andreæ per priorem ejusdem, perpetuis fu-
turis temporibus, unum aliquem canonicum, virum gravem,
prudentem et doctum, in sacris literis doctorem, licentiatum
aut bachalarium, seu alium quemvis eruditum ex Capitulo
Sancti Andreæ canonicum, eligi et nominari, ac dicto nostro
pauperam Collegio præfici, locique magistrum principalem
nuncupari, cui omnes alii presbyteri, regentes et discipuli
humiliter obediant, ad ejus monita et directiones diligenter
auscultent, correctiones pro delictis ab ipso benigne susci-
piant, eumque in ea quæ decet reverentia semper et ubique
tueantur et habeant. Singuli etiam loci officiarii sibi que-

tiescunque voluerit de bonis collegii rationem reddant. Ipse
vero semel in anno domino priori computum de rebus ipsis
exhibere teneatur. Et in festis majoribus vesperas cum
missa, et collectas post salve cantabit, omnibusque feriis
quartis et sextis presbyteris, regentibus, et aliis quibuscunque
interesse volentibus, lectionem in sacris literis aut in specu-
lativa theologia scite et mature docebit. .... Ipse etiam
principalis, presbyteri et regentes pro. suis laboribus habe-
bunt intra locum cameras et victum quotidianum honeste
ut decet. .... Et praeter victum ac ea quae ei debentur ex
monasterio, principalis habebit pro stipendio annuo decem li-
bras, una cum juvene servitore qui acyphario in magna mensa
adjumento sit," &c.

The original statutes continued in force after the reform-
mation (till the year 1579) in so far as they were consistent
with the purity of religion.

George Buchanan succeeded John Duncanson as principal of St Leonard's in the year 1566. The following is
the earliest notice of him which occurs in the rector's books.

" Septimus decimus Rectoratus Magistri Johannis Dou-
glasii, praepositi Novi Collegii Mariani, 1566.

" Electores hoc anno fuerunt viri praeclari, ex Laudonia
Magister. Jacobus Vilkie, Regens Collegii. Leonardini, ex
Albania Magister Johannes Lamond, ejusdem Collegii
Provisor, ex Angusia Magister Guilielmus Skein, juris li-
centiatus, ex Britannia Magister Georgius Buchananus,
Collegii Leonardini Gymnasiarcha, hujus seculi Poetarum
facile princeps, Assessores ex Laudonia Magister Johannes
Vinram, superintendens Fyffiae, Magister Jacobus Vilkie,
et Magister Alexander Hammyltoun, junior, Regentes, ex
Albania Magister Gulielmus Ramsay,* secundus princi-

---

* John Rutherford and William Ramsay, both of whom are named in
the first edition of the Memoirs of Buchanan, p. 81. are frequently mentioned in the university books. The one was minister of Cults, as well as
provost of St Salvator's College, and the other was minister of Kemback.

palis magister Collegii Salvatoriani, et Magister Joannes
Brown, Causarum procurator, ex Angusia Mg* Gulielmus
Skein, juris licentiatus, Magister David Guild, tertius ma-
gister principalis Collegii Salvatoriani, et Magister Johannes
Carnegie, Novi Collegii regens, ex Britannia Magister
Georgius Buchananus, Magister Johannes Rutherford,
Collegii Salvatoriani praepositus, et Magister Robertus
Hammyltoun, minister verbi Dei, &c.

" Deputati per Universitatem designati, qui vicem Rectoris absentis gerant hoc anno, fuerunt viri praestantissimi
Magister Johannes Vinram, superintendens, &c. Mg* Georgius Buchananus, gymnasiarcha, &c. Magister Joannes Re-
thurfurd, praepositus, &c. et Magister Robertus Hammyltoun, minister," &c.

The minute on occasion of the next election of the
rector in 1567 is exactly the same as in 1566. It is remarkable that no students are enrolled as belonging to St
Leonard's College either of those years, though the numbers both in St Mary's and St Salvator's are considerable.
In 1568 more students entered St Leonard's than even St
Mary's, which had generally been the most numerously attended of all the colleges; and in 1569, the numbers enrolled for the first time in St Leonard's were 24, while those
entering at St Mary's were only 11, and those at St Salvator's only 8. Buchanan's name appears in this book
for the last time in 1568. His name is mentioned, as before, among the electors, the assessors, and the deputies
of the rector; and each of these three times he is called
" Poetarum nostrae memoriae facile princeps." Buchanan's
colleagues in St Leonard's College were James Wilkie,
eldest regent, and vicar of Eglisgreg, Nicol Dalgliesh, Robert Wilkie, and William Collace.

The masters in St Mary's College in 1569 were Jo.
Douglas, principal, Robert Hamilton, licentiate in divinity,
second master, Archibald Hamilton, bachelor in divinity,

third master, William Skene, professor of law, and commissary of St Andrews, (brother of Sir John Skene, the lawyer, who had himself been a regent in 1564 and 5,) Alexander Hamilton, John Hamilton, James Hamilton, George Gillespie, and John Carnegie.

The principal, professors, and regents of St Salvator's were John Rutherford, William Ramsay, David Guild, James Martyn, John Ker, Thomas Brown, and John Arthur.

In the dean of faculty's register, the name Magister Georgius Buchananus occurs three times, viz. 2d Nov. 1567, 3d Nov. 1568, and 2d Nov. 1569, always as one of the dean's assessors. He was never either rector, or dean of the faculty of arts.

In the register of the faculty quaestor's accounts from Nov. 1566 to Nov. 1567, he signs the discharge as one of the auditors. Thomas Buchanan,[b] one of the regents of St Salvator's College, had been elected quaestor for that year: but as he left the college in the course of the year, James Martyn, another regent, and afterwards provost of the same college, was appointed to act for him. The other auditors of accounts, besides Buchanan, are John Douglas, rector, (afterwards archbishop of St Andrews,) John Rutherford,

---

[b] Two persons of this name were enrolled in St Mary's College in 1556, Thomas Buchanan senior, and Thomas Buchanan junior. The one, who was George Buchanan's relation, was afterwards a distinguished minister and professor. Was the other Buchanan of Ibbert, keeper of the privy seal? [The former is thus mentioned by J. Melvin: " Mr Tho. Buchanan, first schoolmaster in Stirling, and syne provost of Kirk-heugh in St Andrews, and minister of Syres, a man of notable gifts and learning, natural witt, and uprightness in the cause of the kirk against the bishops, but had his own imperfections, namely of extreme partiality in the cause of his friends and dependars." (MS. Life of James Melvin, p. 110.) This writer describes him as the cousin of G. Buchanan. D. I.] Rollock, in the dedication of his commentary on the epistles to the Thessalonians " Thomæ Buchanano, fliresenais ecclesiæ pastori," says, " cum in schola tua educarer, quam tum Steelini magno republicæ nostræ bono spernisti, non sine auspiciis Georgii Buchanani patrui tui, viri omnium quos tulit hæc natio literatissimi."

dean of faculty, provost of St Salvator's College, James
Wilkie, Buchanan's successor as principal of St Leonard's,
Robert Hamilton, minister of St Andrews, and a professor
of divinity, afterwards principal of St Mary's College. The
signature of George Buchanan is remarkably neat (more so
than in the report of the commissioners of visitation); and
he does not prefix Mr to his name, as was the general practice at that period. There are more deviations from this
mode of subscription before than after Buchanan's time.
In 1558 the accounts are signed by Jo. Douglas, Jo. Rutherford, James Wilkie, Alexander Arbuthnot, and Thomas
Smeton, all afterwards principals of colleges; and the only
one who writes Magister before his name is Wilkie, the
least considerable person of the whole number. From the
year 1566 to 1617, when doctors of divinity were again introduced into Scotland by James VI. I have not observed one
instance in which any subscriber of the quaestor's accounts
omits the Mr before his name, except that of Andrew Melvin, principal of St Mary's College in 1581. I find him
however conforming to the usual mode in 1588. But his
signature wherever else I have seen it, forms an exception
from the rule to which masters of arts in this country generally adhered.

I have not been able to discover the name of George Buchanan in any of the other records of this city. The books
of the kirk session contain the names of most of the professors and other persons of education, who were generally,
elected elders every year, at least from October 1560 to
October 1597. All the men of learning were required by
the first book of discipline to attend the weekly exercise of
expounding the scriptures, in which all ministers and ex-
pectants within six Scotish miles of every principal town were
obliged to take their turn, on pain of subjecting themselves
to discipline in case of refusal. At this exercise all masters and students in the three colleges of St Andrews were

required to be present, by a statute of the university dated 7th January 1561.

George Buchanan's predecessor as principal was a minister, as was also his immediate successor James Wilkie; and indeed all his successors have been ministers. It may be presumed, therefore, that Buchanan was as much in orders as any of the other ministers admitted into the Scotish church, about the time of the reformation, none of whom was set apart by the imposition of hands. On account of the omission of this ceremony, Archbishop Adamson chose to say in 1586, that Robert Wilkie, moderator of the synod of Fife, was a layman: but the synod said that he had been upon the exercise for sixteen years before, and been ordained by the presbytery of St Andrews at its first erection in 1581; and besides they declared that it was heresy to maintain that the office of *doctor* is no ordinary ecclesiastical function. When Maxwell, bishop of Ross, in the year 1646 asserted that laymen had sometimes presided in presbyteries and general assemblies, he did not repeat this instance; probably because Wilkie had afterwards submitted to episcopacy, without however being reordained: but he referred to the cases of Robert Yule, Andrew Melvin, and George Buchanan. Principal Baillie, in his *Historical Vindication*, p. 21, after animadverting on the two first assertions, adds, " George Buchanan had sometimes, as I have heard, been a preacher in St Andrews : the eminency of this person was so great that no society of men need be ashamed to have been moderated by his wisdom." Baillie having been born in 1599, only 17 years after Buchanan's death, might have enjoyed many opportunities of ascertaining the fact from some of his contemporaries ; but his information concerning this and several other topics introduced in that tract is less satisfactory than might have been expected. Whether George Buchanan was a parochial minister or not, it is certain that he was at least a *doctor* or professor of divinity, and in this capacity was entitled to a seat in all church courts, as a teaching elder or presbyter.[c]

The chamber which George Buchanan is said to have occupied, as principal of St Leonard's College, is now part of a private dwelling-house, and is supposed to have undergone scarcely any transformation. It is about 18 feet long by 16 in breadth, having a window to the south and another to the east, which last commands a view of the bay of St Andrews and the rocks of Kinkell. It is on the second floor of the building, and was formerly entered by an outer stair, having no communication with any other apartment. All the rooms, I believe, were constructed on a similar principle, being separated from one another by thick stone walls, and each having a door to the front; but there were no stairs or passages within the walls.

As a specimen of the comfort of living in colleges about this period, I shall insert the inventory of the most splendidly furnished chamber in St Leonard's College in the year 1544, the very chamber I believe which was allotted to the principal.

" In camera quae est prima versus orientem proximior templi in parte australi, fuerunt hæc bona communia pertinentia ad locum collegii. In the first, twa standard beds; the foreside of aik, and the northside and the fuits of fir. Item, ane feather bed, and ane white plaid of four ells, and ane covering woven o'er with images. It. another auld bed of harden, filled with straw, with an covering of green. It.

[c] If Buchanan had ever performed the ordinary functions of a clergyman, it may, I think, be presumed that such a fact would not have been left doubtful by the ecclesiastical writers of his own age.—It appears from the accurate researches of Dr Lee, that he was not appointed principal of St Leonard's College till 1566; but he is known to have been a member of the general assembly in each of the three preceding years. When I formerly described him as a *lay* elder, I ought to have added that the term was not recognized in that age. D. I.

ane cod. Item, an inrower of buckram of five buds, part
green, part red to zaillow. Item, ane Flanders counter of
the middling kind. It. ane little buird for the studie. It.
ane furm of fir, and ane little letterin of silk on the side of
the bed, with an image of St Jerome. It. an stool of elm,
with an other chair of little price. It. an chimney weighing   . Item an chandler weighing   .

In the year 1599, the furniture of the college is as fol-
lows.

Impr. In the hall four fixed boards. The hale beds
almaist fixt. In every chamber ane board and ane furme
pertainand thereto, w! glassen windows, and the maist part
of all the chambers cieflered abone, and the floars beneath
laid with buirdis.

Compt of Vessels.

2 Silver pieces, ane maizer w! common cups and stoups.

3 Doz. silver spoons, ane silver saltfat, a water basin, ane
iron chimney fixed in the hall.

In the kitchen, an iron chimney, w! sic vessels as is necessar therein, with fixed boards and almeries.

With respect to the books which Buchanan is said to
have presented to the library of St Leonard's College, [d] I
have been able to lay my hands only upon nine.

1. Hieronymi Osorii de Gloria libri V. Conimbr. a
Francisco Correa, A. D. MDXLIX. This volume has this
inscription at the bottom of the title: " Ex libris commu-
nis bibliothecæ Collegii Leonardini, ex dono doctissimi
Magistri Georgii Buchanani, principalis ejusdem." The
inscription is repeated at the end of the volume in the same
handwriting, not Buchanan's own, it is almost unnecessary
to add.

---

[d] " Est etiam in eo collegio librorum, eidem a Buchanano donatorum, ca-
talogus : qui omnes adhuc in bibliotheca extant." (Sibbaldi *Comment. in
Vitam Buchanani*, p. 66. Edinb. 1702, 8vo.)

2. Ησιοδου Ἀσκραιου Ἰατρου ἀριστου βιβλια ἐστιν. Venetiis, in ædibus Aldi et Andreæ Asulani soceri, M.D.XXVIII. fol. This is a very beautiful copy of the *editio princeps*.

3. Homeri Poetarum Supremi Ilias per Laurentium Vallensem in Latinum Sermonem traducta: accuratissimo ac solerti cura impressum ac emendatum hoc opus per venerabilem d. presbyt. Baptistam Farfengum, impensa vero d. Francisci Laurini civis Brixiani, MCCCCLXXXXVII. With regard to the accuracy of the impression, the following specimens taken from fol. 1. may suffice. Agros for Argos, gratia for grata, fasta for festa, argis for rogis, innuet for juvet. These errors are corrected on the margin, in Buchanan's handwriting I think. I see many others corrected in the handwriting of Professor Francis Pringle.

4. Marci Antonii Sabellici Annotationes veteres et recentes, ex Plinio, Livio, et pluribus Authoribus. Philippi Beroaldi Annotationes centum. Angeli Politiani Miscellaneorum centuria, &c. (8 other tracts). Impressit volumen hoc Jacobus Pentius de Leuco, Impressorum omnium accuratissimus M.D.II.—Many marginal notes in this volume seem to be in our poet's handwriting.

5. Augustini Steuchi Eugubini Bibliothecarii contra Laurentium Vallam de falsa Donatione Constantini libri duo. Ejusdem de Restituenda Navigatione Tiberis. Ejusdem de Aqua Virgine in Urbem Revocanda. Lugd. ap. Seb. Gryphium, M.D.XLVII. These three last are in folio.

6. Arithmetica Integra, authore Michaele Stifelio, cum præfatione Philippi Melanchthonis. Norimbergæ, ap. Johan. Petreium, anno Christi M.D.XLIII. A quarto of 640 pages.

7. Terentiani Mauri venustissimus de Literis, Syllabis, et Metris Horatii Liber. (Johan. Petit.) Venundantur Parisiis in vico Divi Jacobi sub leone argenteo, apud Joannem Parvum. Bound up with this is Probi Grammatici Instituta Artium. Parisiis, 1.5.1.0.

8. Ephemerides Nicolai Simi, Mathematici Bononiensis, ad annos xv. incipientes ab anno Christi MD. LIIII. usque ad annum MDLXVIII. cum meridiano inclytæ civitatis Bononiæ diligentissime collatæ, &c. Venetiis, ex officina Erasmiana Vincentii Valgrisii, MDLIIII.

9. Le Epistole Famigliari di Cicerone, tradotte secondo i veri sensi dell' autore, et con figure proprie, della lingua volgáre. Con privilegio del sommo Pontifice et della illustrissima signoria di Venezia. M.D.LII. (8vo.)—All these books are marked in the same manner as No. 1, both on the first and the last page.

There is also a copy of Buchanan's translation of Linacre's rudiments, printed at Paris in 1540, with a great number of interlineations and marginal notes, written in a very small hand, whether Buchanan's or not, I am not able to ascertain.

I cannot take upon me to say that the above are all the books presented by Buchanan; but I have reason to believe that not many more are now in the university library. There is still preserved in some of our registers a catalogue of books, subscribed by Robert Wilkie, principal, and laid before a commission of visitation in the year 1599. The number of titles is not quite 300; but Wilkie says that there was not time to take a complete list. I have looked carefully at all of them, which can now be found, and I perceive that a considerable number had belonged to the Augustinian convent; many of them had been given by the regent Murray, when commendator of that priory; some of the oldest were a legacy from John Hepburn, prior of the convent, and founder of the college; some had once been the property of William Shivez, archbishop of St Andrews; many had been given by Thomas Cunningham, principal of the college about the year 1537; and several more by John Duncanson, who was principal from 1556 to 1566. Some of the books are classics, and not

a few relate to the school divinity. The name of *Joannes
Major* occurs very often in the list, but most of the copies of his works have been lost. The only Scotish authors
whose names I have noticed are, Hector Boyce, Alexander
Aless, John Hamilton, archbishop of St Andrews, Archibald Hamilton, John Mair, and John Winram. The
work of this last author, entitled *Catechismus D. Joannis
Winram supprioris*, is not known to exist. It is possible
that all the copies may have been studiously destroyed after the reformation. Some of the finest copies of the classics in the library of St Leonard's College were the gift of
Robert Wilkie, by whom the catalogue is subscribed. He
was principal from 1589 to 1611.

No. V.

1.—*Writ of Privy Seal for Buchanan's Pension.*
See p. 123.

(From Ruddiman's Animadversions, p. 96.)

AWE Lettre maid to Maister George Buchquhannane,
for all the dayis of his liffe, of the gift of an seirlie pen-
sioune of the sowme of five hundred pundis usuale money
of this realme, to be seirlie uptakin be him, his factoris
and servitouris in his name, at twa termes in the seir,
Whitsounday, and Martimes in winter, be equale portionis,
of the reddiest fruittis and emolimentis of the abbay of
Corsragwell, now vacand and being in hir Majestie's handis
throw the deceis of umquhile Master Quintene Kennedie,

2 B

last abbot thairof. ' 'And, for payment of the said zeirlie pensioun, assignis to him the haill temporalitie of the said abbay, with the place, manes, orchardis, mains, woodis, coilheuchis, and pertinentis quhatsumevir pertaining thairto : with power to him to set and rais the said temporalitie, outputt and imputt the tennentis thairof, and utherwise to use the samyn als frelie in all sortis as the said umquhile abbote mycht have in his liftyme. And gife the samyn sall not be fundin sufficient and aneuch for zeirlie payment of the said soume of five hundredth poundis, in that case her Majestie assignis to him sa mekle as he sall inlaik of the said temporalitie, of the reddiest teyndis and fruitis of the spiritualitie of the said abbaye, viz. of the kirkis of Girvane and Kirk-Oswald belangand thairto. And that the said Lettre, &c.

At Halirudhous the nynt daye of October, the zeir of God. M. V^c. LXIV. zeiris.

2.—Act of Privy Council relating to Buchanan.— See p. 156.

(From Ruddiman's edition of Buchanan's Life, p. 9.)

The Lords of Secret Council and others of the Nobility and Estates, being conveened for taking order in the affairs of this common-wealth, among other matters being carefull of the King's Majestie's preservation and good education, and considering how necessary the attendance of Mr George Buchanan, Master of St Leonard's Colledge within the University of St Andrews, upon his Highness shall be, and that it behoves the said Mr George to withdraw himself from his charge of the said colledge, if he makes continual residence with his Majesty, no ways willing that the said colledge, and youth being therein, shall be destitute

1

of regiment and good instruction, through the said Mr
George's absence : he therefore compearing personally in presence of the said Lords of the Council, Nobility, and others
of the Estates above-written, at their desire, and of his own
free will and proper motive, dimitted and gave over his
charge and place of master of the said colledge in the favours of his well beloved Master Patrick Adamson, and no
otherwise : of whose honesty, qualification, literature, and
sufficiency to administrate the said charge and place, not
only the said Mr George, but the said Lords, Nobility,
and Estates, have good opinion and certain experience.
And albeit the presentation, nomination, and admission of
the master of the said colledge pertained of old to the prior
of St Andrews, yet the same right and patronage presently
appertains to our sovereign lord, as well by reason of the
laws of the realm, as because the priory of St Andrews presently vaiks destitute of a prior or commendatar : and seing it tends to God's glory, and the advancement of the
common-wealth, that good letters flourish and increase, and
that delay in not placing or admitting of a qualified and
sufficient master to the said colledge may greatly prejudge
and hinder the same, and if [gif] the students occasion to
skail and separate themselves ; the said Lords, Nobility,
and Estates, therefore, in respect of the present necessity,
in our sovereign lord's name received the said Mr George's
dimission, and thereupon received and admitted the said
Mr Patrick to the said charge and regiment of the said
colledge of St Andrews, as principal master thereof, with
all immunities, priviledges, commodities, and duties belonging to the same, sicklike as the said Mr George, or
any other masters of the said colledge, used and brooked
the same of before ; and ordain him to be answered and
obeyed therein in time coming, and none other, &c.

3.—A Circular Letter.

(From Wodrow's MS. Life of Buchanan.)

Trustie Freind, we greet you well. We have, upon knouledge had by us of the conveening of some of our nobility and others in armes, appearendly to trouble the present estate, taken occasion to write to you and others our trustie subjects, desiring you effectuously, that you fail not wt your freinds, houshold servants, and dependants, well boden in feir of warr, to be at us with all possible diligence, provided to remain and serve us, as ye shall be comanded; for 15 dayes, as ye will declare your good affection to our service, and do us pleasure. Thus we committ you to God: From our castle of Stirling, July 29, 1578.

JAMES REX.

GEORGE BUCHANAN.

No. VI.—See p. 70.

Candido Lectori Joannes Retorfortis S. P. D.

(Preface to the second edition of Rutherford *De Arte Disserendi*. Edinb. 1577, 4to.)

SÆPE amici et familiares qui mecum in Galliis et alibi philosophati sunt, a me contenderunt, ut aliquando me,

commentariosque de arte disserendi a me conscriptos, ab
injuria typographi qui me inscio et inconsulto eos innumeris erratis fœdissime conspurcatos, et turpissime depravatos
typis excussit, liberarem.   Sed quoniam id perquam labo-
riosum videbam, et alia graviora urgentioraque negotia me
totum occupabant, amicorum postulationi parere antehac
nec licuit nec placuit.   Verum cum hisce diebus superiori-
bus me mea quædam negotia Edinburgum pertraxissent,
vir integerrimus, jurisque consultissimus, et bonarum omnium artium et literarum genere ornatissimus, *Eduardus
Henrisonus*, mecum graviter expostulando (pro suo erga
nos amore, et studiorum conjunctione) eandem causam
egit : hortatusque est, ut et mei nominis, et studiosorum
commodi rationem ut decet haberem, ipsosque commentarios diligenter repurgarem et restituerem.   Ego vero, cum
eruditissimi viri et nostri studiosissimi opinionem a sententia et judicio amicorum non dissentire animadverterem, de-
crevi pro viribus utrisque satisfacere.   Itaque (candide lector) multo limatiores, et majori diligentia et perspicuitate
illustratos accipies.   Et si quid fructus ad te posterosve
ex illis pervenerit, id omne bonarum literarum literato-
rumque hominum studiosissimo *Eduardo Henriseno* acceptum feres.   Nam illius solius suasu et consilio calamum
ad eos perpurgandos converti : quos si censero a doctis ap-
probari, alios ad Aristotelem de rebus physicis intelligen-
dum, non minus utiles et accommodatos (Deo favente)
mox parabo.   Vale, ex Servatoriano nostro gymnasio 5 Kalendas Maias.   1576.

No. VII.—See p. 102.

Henricus Stephanus Georgio Buchanano S. D.

(Dedication of *Davidis Psalmi aliquot.* Ex officina H. Stephani, 1556, 4to.)

Nimium diu latuisti, mi Buchanane : jam tibi, ut vides, in publicum prodeundum est : ego te, velis nolis, ex istis educam latebris. Tun' mihi succenses hoc nomine ? atqui, aut ego fallor, aut mea efficietur opera ut posthac Georgius Buchananus, vir Scotus, supra Gallos omnes atque Italos nostri seculi poetas *Laudetur, vigeat, placeat, relegatur, ametur.* Utor enim libenter Augusti versu in tam augusto poeta celebrando : ac nisi vererer laudare te in os, quiddam etiam non paulo augustius proferrem. Quanquam quid meo tibi opus est praeconio, qui quot scripsisti versus, tot fere habeas summi ingenii tui praecones ? Hoc igitur unum his dicam : quum nihil praeclarius, nihil splendidius sit, quam, aliis omnibus superatis, seipsum tandem superare : te in exprimendis his psalmis hunc laudis gradum foelicissime, meo quidem judicio, assequutum esse. In transferendis enim reliquis hujus sacrosancti poetae odis, Buchananus fuisti, id est, inter reliquos omnes interpretes tantum quantum luna inter minora sidera, enituisti : at postquam ad psalmum CIII ventum est, quem tu ita inchoas, *Te Deus alme omnem rerum dominumque patremque,* Buchananum vicisti : ut non jam inter caeteros interpretes, tanquam luna inter minora sidera, fulgere : sed tanquam sol, coruscis radiis stellas omnes obscurare videaris. Quod si dicebat poeta profanus in opere profano, *Est Deus in nobis, agitante calescimus illo :* & Callimachus hymno decoraturus Apollinem, ita praefatur, Οἷον ὁ τῶ πόλλωνος ἐσίσατο δάφνινος ὄρπηξ, Οἷα δ᾽ ὅλον τὸ μέλαθρον (ἱκὰς ἱκὰς ὅστις ἀλιτρὸς) Καὶ δήπου τὰ θύρετρα καλῷ ποδὶ Φοῖβος ἀράσσει. si inquam illi talia jactare audebant, quis Buchanani poetae Christiani pectus in opere sacro non existimet Dei Optimi

Maximi motu & agitatione vero incaluisse? Euge ergo euge,
huic tam insigni operi, in cujus primordiis tantam Dei fa-
vorem expertus es, extremam manum tandem impone. Jure
enim scilicet Christianorum nomen sibi vendicant poetæ
illi, quibus magis arridet in carmine Deus ales, aut volu-
cris, aut penniger, quam Deus exercituum. Equidem non
possum continere me quin exclamem, *Illi sub terris fiant
mala multa poetæ*, qui primus (de Christianis loquor) ejus
nomen a suo versu arcere ausus est, cujus beneficio et mentem ad cogitandum, et manum ad ea quæ cogitaverat, scribenda, accepisset. Itane vero? Nonnus poeta non ignobi-
lis quum antea Dionysiaca, materiam idololatriæ suæ con-
venientem, delegisset, simulatque abjecto idolorum cultu,
Evangelio nomen dedit, nulli alii quam vero Deo cui
servire cœpesat, venam etiam suam servire voluit: nos,
qui Christiani ex Christianis nascimur, iis ipsis idolis,
quibus jam inde a matris alvo renuntiavimus, poesim
nostram dicabimus? Quod siquis objiciat, literas sacras
ejusmodi esse quæ ornatum non admittant: idem ego
quod abhinc quadriennium Romæ homini Italo respondi,
nunc quæque respondebo. Quum enim orto de Flaminii
versibus sermone, ejus ego laborem atque operam quam in
transferendis psalmis posuisset, laudarem: Imo, inquit ille
(verbis quidem Italicis, sed in hunc sensum) ô factum male: ex quo enim istis sacris se addixit, multum illius car-
mini de solita elegantia et lepore decessit. nam quum omne μυσθίκον respuant illa, nescio quomodo ita descivit ab
illis quibus antea uti solebat ornamentis, ut quum, sacris
omissis, profana repetere vellet, in Flaminio Flaminius non
agnosceretur, utpote qui a seipso prorsus degenerasset. Tunc
ego, Si, inquam, in transferendis sacris, muliebri cuidam
vel potius meretricio ornatui locum esse negas: tibi assen-
tior: (nihil enim magis ab illis alienum) sin virilem quen-
dam ornatum et majestatis plenum mihi narras, toto te,
quod aiunt, cœlo errare existimo: hunc enim illa ornatum

postulant. ideoque ego contra, male factum dico quod Flaminius, antequam ad psalmorum interpretationem venisset, jam illis amatoriæ poeseos lenociniis nimium effœminatis Musam suam ita fregisset & enervasset: ut quum altius attolere se deberet, videlicet in gravi argumento, ad sublime carminis genus aditus ei non pateret. Hæc ego tum de Flaminio, mi Buchanane: quibus hæc addo in præsentia: si ille se antea in componendis aut vertendis de Græco tragœdiis (quo ex labore magnum tibi jampridem nomen quæsitum est) multum diuque exercuisset: non idem tibi fortasse quod nunc, contingeret, ut tu victoriam adeo facile & propemodum sine pulvere reportares. Sed qualis qualis est Flaminius, hoc ego ingenue fateor, quum a Buchanano discessi, me, quem illi comparem, non reperire. Nam Salmonius noster (amica enim patria, sed amica magis veritas) Flaminio non solum sermonis puritate longe est inferior, sed versus etiam elegantia ei cedit: & ut minus cultus, quam ille, versum facit, ita multo magis humi serpit. Nec vero hæc eo dicuntur a me, ut animum lectoris (siquis teretes afferens aures, & acri ingenio, acriori etiam judicio fretus, judex esse volet) quodam veluti præjudicio occupem: sed quoniam stultus tuæ poeseos prædicator & admirator haberi possim, nisi quid potissimum admiratione dignum in ea mihi videatur, ex aliorum comparatione ostendam. Verum dixerit aliquis fortasse, Quæ tu in Buchanano admiraris, in Italo autem Flaminio & Salmonio Gallo desideras, ea in Eobano Germano, aut in Rapicio, Italo & ipso, reperiri poterunt. πολλῶ γε καὶ διϊ. nam (ut de Eobano taceam, cujus versuum bona pars, siquis metrum detrahere velit, nihil commune cum poesi habere comperietur) Rapicius certe dicenda tacenda loquitur. fere enim unicuique non omnino malo versui pessimum subjungit, dum copiam ostentat: & verba quidem affert multa, sed in quibus nihil præter verba multa invenias. Ejus tamen lyricos versus tuis, (quum nec Flaminii nec Salmonii ullos habebam) opposui:

nec enim te in arenam sine adversario producere volebam.
Quem vero alium tibi dare potuissem? an eum qui ex theo-
logo factus typographus, ex typographo poeta: malus theologus, peior typographus, pessimus poeta : in extremo illo suæ
ἐγκυκλομωρίας vel potius ἐγκυκλομανίας curriculo, sacrum poetam
pessime profanavit? dum invita Minerva, iratis Musis,
adverso Apolline carmina, non sublimia illa quidem, qualia
narrat Flaccus, sed puerilia & quidvis potius quam Davidem
exprimentia, ructatur? Ructatur autem dico, quia—nunquam nisi potus ad illa Prosiluit scribenda. Sed de his
hactenus. *Nanque animus meminisse horret.* Audies præ-
terea hic (& hoc velut corollarium accipies) Henricum tuum
Davidis aliquot hymnos Græca lingua modulantem: siqua
tamen modulatio in tam inconditis versibus inveniri potest.
Nam quanvis illos ad regulam poeseos quam potui maxime
severam exegerim, & in ea multorum satisfecerim non rusticis
auribus: ipse tamen meis, ut ingenue fatear, non satisfacio.
quare de illis tuum quoque expectabo judicium: quod si cum
reliquis consentire intellexero, fortasse experiar an aliquid
ætas attulerit: & utrum paulo meliora iis quæ dedi adhuc
pene puer, nunc, pene vir factus, dare Græcæ Musæ stu-
diosis possim. Vale. Ex Musurgeo nostro.

No. VIII.—See p. 181.

*A List of Books which Buchanan presented to the
University of Glasgow.*[b]

(From the Annales Collegii Glasguensis, tom. i, f. 166-7.)

Eustathii Commentarii in Homerum, quatuor voluminibus, Græce, in folio, Romæ, 1549.

[b] This list was transcribed from the records of the university by John
Riddell, Esq. by whom it was politely communicated through Sir William

Plutarchi Opera,[c] Græce, duobus voluminibus, fol. Basil. *Frobenius*, 1542.

Platonis Opera, Græce, fol. Basil. 1534, *Valderus*.

Procli in Platonis Tym. [Timæum] Commentarii, Græce, fol. Basil.

Demosthenis Opera, cum Conamentariis Ulpiani, Græce, fol. Basil. 1532, *Hervagius*.

Lycophronis Cassandra, Græce, cum Commentariis Tzetzæ, fol. Basil. 1546, *Oporinus*.

Commentarii Græci in Aristotelis Rhetoricam anonymi, fol. Parisiis, *Neobar.* 1539.

Apollonii Argonautica, Græce, in quarto, Florentiæ, 1496.

Aristophanes cum Commentariis, Græce.

Basilii Opera, Græce, fol. Basil. 1532, *Froben.*

Euclides cum Commentariis, Græce.

Stephanus Byzantinus de Urbibus, Græce.

Omnes ex dono viri optimi et doctissimi Georgii Buchanani, regii magistri.

Strabo, Græce, fol.

Athenæus, Græce, fol. Basil. 1535.

Suidas, Græce, fol. Venetiis, *Aldus*, 1514.

Manuelis Moschopuli de Ratione Examinandæ Orationis Libellus, Græce.

Ex dono pariter Georgii Buchanani, regii magistri.

Hamilton. For some additional information I am indebted to my learned friend Lockhart Muirhead, A. M. professor of natural history, and librarian to the university of Glasgow. " Thus, I have no doubt that every book which that eminent poet and historian gave to our library, is still preserved. In none of them can I discover the donor's name in his own handwriting; but on the title-page of Strabo, *Patricius Buchanan* appears in very legible characters. In a few instances, short manuscript running titles or various readings occur on the margin; but whether from the pen of Buchanan, I have no means of ascertaining."

* This book, says Mr Muirhead, ought to have been entitled *Moralia Opuscula.*

No. IX.—See p. 309.

Buchanan's Testament Dative.

(From the Records of the Commissary Court.)

Maister
George Buchannane
Vigesimo Febr[ii]
1582.

The Testament Datiue, & Inuentar of ye gudis, geir, soumes of money, & dettis, pertening to vmquhile ane rycht venerabill man, Maister George Buchannane, preceptour to ye kingis majestie the tyme of his deceis, quha deceist vpoun ye xxix day of September,[c] the zeir of God j[m] v[c] lxxxii zeris, faithfullie maid & gevin vp be Jenet Buchannane, relict of vmquhile Mr Thomas Buchannane of Ibert, his bruyer sone, executrix datiue, decernit to him be decreit of ye commissaris of Ed[r] as ye same decreit of ye dait ye xix day of December, the zeir of God foirsaid, at lenth proportis.

In the first, ye said vmquhile Maister George Buchannane, preceptour to ye kingis majestie, had na uyer gudis nor geir (except ye dett vndirwrittin) perteining to him as his awin proper dett ye tyme of his deceis foirsaid : viz. Item, yair wes awand to ye said vmquhile Mr George be Robert

---

[c] The notice subjoined to Buchanan's sketch of his own life, refers his death to the 29th of September; and some of the early editions mention not only the day of the month, but also the day of the week, and even the very hour of the day. I have thought it more safe to follow this account; especially as the old register of testaments not unfrequently exhibits erroneous dates. In this very document we find another error; namely, *gratus* instead of *gratis*. It is also to be considered that in a record of this nature, it is of no importance to ascertain the particular day of the person's death.

Gourlaw, custumar burges of Ed[r] for ye defunctis pensioun
of Corsraguell, restand of ye Witsonday terme in anno
j[m] v[c] lxxxii zeris, the soume of ane hundreth pundis.

  Summa of ye inuentar . . . . j[c] l.
  No diuisioun.
  Quhairof ye quot is gevin gratis.

 . We, Maisteris Eduard Henrysoun, Alex[r] Sym, & Johne
Prestoun, commissaris of Ed[r] specialie constitut for con-
firmatioun of testamentis, &c. vnderstanding yat efter dew
summonding & lauchfull warning maid be forme of editt
oppenlie, as efferis, of ye executouris intromettouris with ye
gudis & geir of vmquhile Mr George Buchannane, & of
uyeris hafand entreis, to compeir judicialie befoir us at ane
certane day bypast, to heir & sie executouris datiuis decernit to be gevin, admittit, & confermit be us in & to ye
gudis & geir quhilk justlie pertenit to him ye tyme of his
deceis, or ellis to schaw ane caus quhy, &c. we decernit
yairintill as our decreit gevin yairupoun beris; conforme
to ye quhilk we in our soverane lordis name & autoritie
makis, constitutis, ordanis, & confermes ye said Jonet Buchannane in executorie datiue to ye said Mr George, with
power to hir to intromet, vptak, follow & persew, as law
will, ye dett & soume of money abone specifeit, & yair-
with outred dettis to creditouris, and generalie all & sindrie
vyer thingis to do, exerce, & vse yat to ye office of executorie datiue is knawin to pertene; prouiding yat ye said
Jonet, executrix foirsaid, sall ansuer & render compt vpoun
hir intromissioun quhan and quhair ye samin salbe requirit
of hir, & yat ye said dett & soume salbe be furthcumand to
all parteis haifand entres, as law will; quhairvpoun scho hes
fundin cautioun, as ane act maid yairvpoun beris.

No. X.—See p. 240.

Notices of James Crichton.

. Crichton appears to have been born in 1560, and he was killed at Mantua in 1582.[h] The unrivalled fame of this young scholar is certainly allied to romance: but, on the other hand, it is very difficult to imagine that it was not originally founded on some qualities, which eminently distinguished him from other forward and aspiring youths, who at that period were extremely numerous in the more learned countries of Europe. A reputation so splendid, and so uniformly maintained, cannot reasonably be ascribed to a mere concurrence of accidental circumstances. The specimens of his Latin poetry which have been preserved, do not indeed contain any thing remarkable: but these are very inadequate specimens; nor does his reputation depend on one species of excellence.[i] He is celebrated for the wonderful facility with which he composed verses; for his knowledge of ten or twelve different languages; for his acquaintance with the writings of the fathers; for his uncommon powers of memory; for his promptitude and acuteness in public disputation; and for his superior proficiency in every manly exercise suitable to his rank. We

---

[h] The will of Robert Crichton of Eliok, king's advocate, which is dated at Edinburgh on the 18th of June 1582, mentions that his son James was then in Italy. This will was not confirmed till the 24th of January 1586-7. (*Register of Testaments*, vol. xvii.)

[i] Nec placet ante annos vates puer: omnia justo
Tempore proveniant: ah! ne mihi olentia poma
Mitescant prius, autumnus bicoloribus uvis
Quam redeat, spumetque cadis vindemia plenis.
Ante diem nam lapsa cadent, ramosque relinquent
Maternos, calcabit humi projecta viator.

               VIDÆ Poeticorum lib. i, v. 334.

must not therefore hastily conclude that he " was in Italy
considered as one of those literary mountebanks who were
numerous in that age;" or that his reputation chiefly de-
pends on the romantic flights of Sir Thomas Urquhart,
who wrote about seventy years after his death. Joseph
Scaliger, who flourished at the same period with himself,
who professes to have obtained his information in Italy, and
who besides was not too prone to admiration, mentions
Crichton as a prodigious genius, and indeed enumerates all
the most essential qualifications that are commonly ascribed to
him.[k] This testimony, which is entirely overlooked by the
ingenious biographer of Tasso,[l] is certainly of considerable
weight and importance. Crichton is likewise extolled in
terms of the highest admiration, in a work published so
early as the year 1609 by Dr Adam Abernethy, a native
of Edinburgh, and a member of the university of Mont-
pellier.[m] The subsequent verses, though not conspicuous

[k] " J'ay oüy parler d'un Critton Escossois en Italie, qui n' avoit que
21 ans, quand il a esté tué *par le commandement du duc de Montoué;* et qui
sçavoit 12 langues, avoit leu les peres, poëtes, disputoit de omni scibili, et
respondoit en vers. C'estoit ingenium prodigiosum, admiratione magis
quam amore dignum. Il estoit un peu fat. Ei judicium non tantum ad-
fuit. Principes solent illa ingenia amare, non vero bene doctos. Manutius
præfatione ad Paradoxa, quam dicat Crittonio, meminit illius ingenii."
(*Scaligerana,* p. 58.) Gabriel Naudé speaks of Crichton's orations being
printed ; but he probably confounded him with George Crichton, who published various orations in a detached form. " Tel negligera, par exemple,
les Oraisons de Jacques Criton, parce qu' elles ne se trouvent qu' imprimées
separément, qui aura dans sa bibliotheque celles de Raymond, Gallutius, Ni-
gronius, Bencius, Perpinian, et de beaucoup d'autres autheurs, non pas qu'
elles soient meilleures ou plus disertes et eloquentes que celles de ce docte
Escossois, mais parce qu' elles se trouvent reserrées et contenuës dans de cer-
tains volumes." (*Advis pour dresser une Bibliotheque,* p. 76, edit. Paris,
1644, 8vo.) His *Appuleus* appears to have been printed in 4to in the year
1580. (Renouard, *Annales de l'Imprimerie des Aldes,* supp. p. 39.)

[l] See Dr Black's Life of Tasso, vol. ii, p. 413. Edinb. 1810, 2 vols. 4to.

[m] Adam Abernethy took the degree of A. M. at Edinburgh on the 7th
of August 1594. He afterwards took that of M. D. probably in some foreign university, He is described as " Monspeliensis academiæ moderator."

for their original merit, possess some value as an historical document. They are introduced by this inscription.
" D. M. popularis sui Jacobi Chrichtoni a Cluny, juvenis
incomparabilis, tam acumine, judicio, memoriaque omnium
literarum oblivisci nescia, quam equestri, gladiatoria, omni-
umque armorum exercitatione, quo ad majorem stuporem
totius Italiæ, ita et ejusdem mœrorem, indigne trucidati.
A G. G. D. M. D. S."

O felix animi juvenis Chrichtone vigore
Ingenii volitante supra, qui vectus in astra
Humanam sortem, et mortalis culmen honoris!
Seu placuit Musas colere, aut glomeramine campum
Tundere cornipedis, pictisve ardescere in armis. [a]
Grandia sublimis nuper miracula mentis
Monstrasti attonito, et rapuisti protinus orbi.
Tuque licet princeps, peperit quem Mantua clara,
Gonsaga infelix, tua quem temeraria dextra!
Heu decus Aonidum fixisti vulnere fudo,
Doctoremque tuæ, formatoremque juventæ, [o]
Quo nimium, nimium infœlix Chrichtonus obivit,
Ætheris invisas auras, lucemque relinquens! [p]
Nunc facinus pueri deplora ætate senili.
Illum Antenoridæ flerunt, Phaetontias unda
Deflevit miserum, flevit Venetusque senatus,
Matronæ Adriacæ, simul Italidesque puellæ.
Flevit olorifero peramœnus Mincius amne.
Illum omnes Athesisque deæ, et Benacides omnes

[a] Cui studia aut pernicis equi compescere cursum,
 Aut galeam induere, et pictis splendescere in armis.
  FRACASTORII Syphilis, lib. i, v. 388.
[o] Doctoresque rudis formatoresque juventæ.
  BUCHANANI Silva iv, v. 207.
[p] Quo tandem infelix fato, post tempore parvo
 Ætheris invisas auras, lucemque reliquit.
  FRACASTORII Syphilis, lib. i, v. 407.
 These two verses I quote from the third edition of Fracastorii Opera Om-
nia. Venet. 1584, 4to. They do not occur in Peters's elegant edition of
the Syphilis. Lond. 1720, 4to.

Flevere[q] At doctæ ante alias flevere sorores.
Quin popularis adhuc gemitum Fortha abdit in alveo,
Fortha Caledoniis fœcundans arva colonis.
Ergo flos juvenum, Scotiæ spes, Palladis ingens,
Ereptumque decus Musarum e dulcibus ulnis;[r]
Te quamvis sileant alii Chrichtone poëtæ,
Teque tuamque necem nunquam mea Musa silebit.
Flebilibusque modis semper tua fata queretur,
Sæpe iterans luctus, et singultantia verba.[s]

These verses serve to establish the disputed fact, that Crichton was killed by his own pupil, a prince of the house of Mantua. Manutius had only ventured to hint that he died a violent death. Abernethy has added an epigram in the same strain of commendation.

Si videas, quæ mira, diu, mirabere non plus;
 Sin semel, in totos mira loquere dies.
Chrichtonum hinc superi voluere ostendere mundo
 Tantum, non mundo hunc hi voluere dare.

Borrichius mentions the hexameters of Crichton with some degree of approbation. "Jacobo Crittonio Scoto non ignotum fuisse Pegaseium melos docent heroica, quibus suum in urbem Venetam appulsum designat. Plus tamen vividi caloris cultusque in epicis Georgii Crittonii."[t]—George Crichton, doctor of the canon law, was a professor in the

[q] Illum Alpes vicinæ, illum vaga flumina flerunt;
Illum omnes Ollique deæ, Eridanique puellæ
Fleverunt, nemorumque deæ, rurisque puellæ;
Sebinusque alto gemitum lacus edidit amne.
FRACASTORIUS, lib. i, v. 409.

[r] Spes Latii, spes et studiorum, et Palladis illa
Occidit; ereptum Musarum e dulcibus ulnis, &c.
FRACASTORIUS, lib. i, v. 456.

[s] Musa Campestris, &c. authore Adamo Abrenetheo ex Scoto-Britannia, Edinburgeno. Monspelii, 1609, 8vo.—This rare volume was pointed out to me by Sir William Hamilton; to whose extensive learning and obliging disposition I have frequently been indebted.

[t] Borrichii Dissertationes Academicæ de Poetis, p. 151. Francof. 1683, 4to.

.university of Paris, and the author of various works. [u] It may not be improper to add that there was another scholar of this surname; Robert Creyghton, D. D. professor of Greek in the university of Cambridge, and afterwards bishop of Bath and Wells.. He was a native of Dunkeld. [x]

—————

No. XI.—See p. 205.

Notices of Alexander Cunningham.

THIS distinguished scholar was the son of the Rev. John Cunningham, minister of Cumnock in Ayrshire. In the same county his father possessed the small estate of Block. It appears from the public records that he was served heir to his father in the year 1677.[y] With respect to the time of his birth, and the place of his education, I have not hitherto been able to obtain any authentic information. It however seems probable that he studied in the university of Edinburgh. We afterwards find him employed as tutor to Lord George Douglas, a younger son of the first duke of Queensberry. In the university library there is a rare book containing the subsequent notice : " This volume presented to the library be Mr Alex[r] Cuninghame of Block, preceptor to the Lord George Douglass." Above this no-

[u] Niceron, Memoires des Hommes Illustres, tom. xxxvii, p. 346.

[x] Wood's Fasti Oxonienses, vol. i, col. 243, edit. 1721. Godwin de Præsulibus Angliæ, a Richardson, p. 392. Cantab. 1743, fol.—See likewise Dr Zouch's notes to Walton's Lives, p. 311, 2d edit. York, 1807, 8vo. Creyghton's edition of Syropulus is mentioned by Gibbon, vol. xii, p. 99. He is celebrated by N. Heinsius, Poemata, p. 202, and by Duport, Musæ Subsecivæ, p. 340.

[y] Inquisitionum Abbreviatio, vol. i, Ayr, 612.

tice, but in a different hand, the following inscription occurs: "Serveti Opera, [z] donata Bibliothecæ Edinburgenæ a Domino D. Georgio Douglassio, filio Illustriss. Ducis de Queensberrie, A. D. 1695." This young nobleman died in the year 1693. [a] It appears from Henderson's catalogue that the book was presented by Cunningham, " to preserve the memory of his dear pupil."

It was probably through the influence of this noble family that he was appointed professor of the civil law in the university of Edinburgh. By an act of the Scotish parliament, 1 Sept. 1698, the revenue arising from a tonnage to be levied on certain ships is burdened with a salary to Cunningham: " and further, with the burden of one hundred and fifty pounds sterl. yearly, as the yearly fee and sallary granted to Mr Alexander Cunninghame as Professor of the Civil Law, nominat and designed to that profession." This act was to continue in force for the space of five years; and the same provision is renewed in another act, 26 Aug. 1704: " and the superplus (if any be) to the payment of one thousand eight hundred pounds yearly to Mr Alexander Cunninghame, Professor of the Civil Law." [b] In the latter act, the sum is specified in Scotish currency. If we estimate the value of money at that period, a salary of one hundred and fifty pounds will appear very ample.

These acts of parliament do not mark his connection with any university: but according to the notions of that age, a professor must be connected with some university or college; for the public was yet unacquainted with such literary

---

[z] Christianismi Restitutio, &c. 1553, 8vo.

[a] Douglas's Peerage of Scotland, by Wood, vol. ii, p. 380.

[b] The professor of the civil law has been erroneously described as an advocate. In the records of the faculty for that period, I find no advocate of the same name. The act of the dean and faculty for the augmentation of Ruddiman's salary as librarian, is subscribed, not by Al. but by Ad. Cuningham.

4

denominations as " professor of the piano forte," and " professor in animal medicine." As no university is specified,
it is natural to infer that which belonged to the seat of the
legislature. The university records are so extremely mea-
gre that they reflect no light on the subject; but we are
again relieved by an occasional notice in a book belonging
to the library : ᶜ " Returned for that which was lost by Mr
Alexʳ. Cuninghame of Block, Profess. of Law." This notice seems to afford sufficient evidence of his having been a
professor in the university of Edinburgh. But in the records of the town council I find an entry, on the 18th of
October 1710, which may perhaps be supposed to render
the fact more than doubtful.

" The Councill, with the Extraordinar Deacons, taking to
their consideration that the colledge of this citie, from the origi-
nall and foundation thereof by King James the Sixth of ever-
blessed memory, being erected into ane universitie, of which
they as patrons were endued with the priviledge of erecting
professors of all the liberall arts and sciences ; and particularly considering that throw yᵉ want of professors of the civil
law in this kingdom, the youth who have applied themselves
to that studie, have been necessitate to travell and remain
abroad a considerable time for their education, to the prejudice of the nation by the necessarie charges occasioned
thereby, untill of late some gentlemen having undertaken
that profession altho' only in a private capacity, have given
convincing proofs how advantageously that study might be
prosecute at home, if countenanced and encouraged by publick authority; and understanding the ability and good
qualifications of Mr James Craig, Advocate, doe therefore
elect, nominate, and choice the said Mr James Craig to be
Professor of the Civill Law in the said university." ᵈ

ᶜ Pauli Voet Jurisprudentia Sacra. Amst. 1662, 12mo.
ᵈ Register of the Town Council, vol. xxxix, p. 948.

These contradictory accounts may however be reconciled without much difficulty. The magistrates of Edinburgh, regarding themselves as the proper patrons of the university, have always entertained the greatest jealousy of any interference on the part of the crown; and as Cunningham must have held a regius professorship, they would studiously decline to recognize his appointment. His salary would cease to be paid at the expiration of the second term of five years, that is, in 1709; and it was in the course of the ensuing year that the magistrates established another chair. It may also be proper to observe that this new foundation took place after the death of the second duke of Queensberry, who had acted as her majesty's commissioner at the important crisis of the union.

So early as the year 1590, the lords of session, the town council, and the advocates and clerks to the signet, had raised a fund of L.3000 for the endowment of a professorship of the laws; each of these three parties contributing an equal portion. Adam Newton, an advocate, was first appointed to the office; but having neglected to obtain the approbation of the magistrates, he was dismissed in the year 1594. * He was succeeded by Sir Hadrian Damman of Bistervelt, who was born in the Danish dominions, but was then the Dutch resident at the court of Scotland. Both these professors taught humanity, without reading any public lectures on law. Damman having resigned his chair, the interest of one third of the sum formerly contributed was in 1597 allotted for a professor of humanity, and the

---

* Adam Newton, the son of a baker in Edinburgh, was successively tutor and secretary to Prince Henry. Though a layman, he held the deanry of Durham from 1606 to 1620, when he resigned it. During the latter year he was created a baronet. He translated into Latin King James's book against Vorstius, and the first six books of Father Paul's history of the council of Trent. The two last were translated by Dr Bedell. (Birch's *Life of Prince Henry*, p. 14, 218. Lond. 1760, 8vo.)

interest of the remainder for the maintenance of six bursars or exhibitioners. The first professor of humanity was John Ray, A. M. who superintended the edition of Buchanan's poems published in 1615.[f]

Cunningham had equally devoted his attention to the study of philology and the civil law, which at that period were very little cultivated in his native country. Most of the Scotish advocates continued till a later period to be educated at Leyden and Utrecht; and it is highly probable that he had likewise completed his studies in one of those universities. He at length fixed his residence in Holland, where his favourite studies were prosecuted with uncommon ardour and success. The following quotation from a work published in 1707, renders it probable that he was then residing in that country. "Sed et insuper," says Best, "nc quid dubites, idem mihi adseveravit vir doctissimus Cunninghamius, natione Scotus, qui præclara ingenii monumenta, quibus jurisprudentiam arctissime sibi devinxit, non diutius, ut speramus, erudito orbi invidebit, quum id ipsum sæpius percontatus didicisset ab accuratissimo Jacobo Gronovio."[g] Best apparently alludes to an edition of the Pandects, which Cunningham long meditated, and for which he made great preparations. From a letter of Cuper, dated on the twelfth of November 1709, it appears that this project had then excited high expectations. He quotes the subsequent passage from a letter which he had lately received from Leibnitz. "Tibi rem (ut opinor) non ingratam nuntio, ut aliquam vicem reddam pro lætis literariæ rei novis, quæ significasti. Nempe cuique auctoris libro sua reddita sunt verba in Pandectas Justiniani relata. Tantum jam reliquum est, ut edantur hæc Redigesta, sed sine aliquo

---

[f] Crawford's Hist. of the University of Edinburgh, p. 34, 40. Edinb. 1808, 8vo.

[g] G. Best Ratio Emendandi Leges, p. 17. Ultraj. 1707, 8vo.

cultu, itaque optandum foret emendationes ex Pandectis
Florentinis accedere; et cum intellexerim Cunninghamum
Scotum doctrina et ingenio valentem multum in constituendo
textu laborasse, non video ubi melius emendationes vel col-
lationes suas collocare posset." Cuper subjoins, " Ce q'il
dit de Mr Cunningham est vray: je le connois, et j'espere
de pouvoir luy parler bientôt, s' il est encore à la Haye, ou
je dois aller."[h] Cunningham appears to have resided at the
Hague during the remainder of his life; but I find no
evidence of his having there taught " both the civil and
canon laws." He apparently lived in Holland as a private
gentleman, supported by the rent of his estate, and probably by an annuity from the noble family with which he
had been connected. Long before he published his edition
of Horace, he enjoyed a very high reputation as a classical
scholar. That edition appeared in 1721. His notes are
brief, and relate to the various readings; but he announced
his intention of preparing another edition, illustrated with
more copious annotations. At the same time he published
a separate volume, consisting of animadversions on the notes
and emendations of Bentley, whose edition of Horace had
been printed ten years before. This volume displays much
learning and sagacity, and evinces the author to have studied
the art of criticism with uncommon assiduity and success.
He has prefixed an address to Dr Bentley, whom he every
where treats with much freedom and even severity. Bentley
was a man of great vigour of intellect, and of erudition not
less accurate than extensive. Of the Greek language he
possessed a masterly knowledge; and he had studied the
ancient metres with a degree of nicety unknown to former
critics. His principal defect seems to have been a want of
taste; for when he quits the mechanical part of language,
and the mere structure of verse, he cannot be regarded as a

---

[h] Lettres de Gisbert Cuper, p. 233. Amst. 1742, 4to.

safe guide in subjects of polite literature. His conjectural emendations often display singular felicity; but at other times they are chiefly remarkable for their audacity. Many of his rash conjectures on Horace are very successfully exposed by Cunningham. One of the emendations on which he seems to congratulate himself with most complacency, is the substitution of *ter natos* in the subsequent verse of the art of poetry.

> Et male *tornatos* incudi reddere versus.

A reading more repugnant to every principle of taste could not easily have been devised; and yet his learned correspondent Grævius speaks of it in the following terms: " Eam qui videt et non probat, is in his litteris cæcior est quavis talpa. Quid enim tórno cum incude ?"[1] Bentley professes to be offended at the incongruity of Horace's metaphor, and asks the same question with Grævius. But he perceives no incongruity in an animal being produced at three births, and being moreover hammered upon an anvil. Cunningham, who was fully aware of this absurdity, has unnecessarily adopted the reading *formatos*, which appears somewhat flat. There is in truth no occasion for any change. When an artist has turned a piece of iron, without being able to give it the shape or polish which he intended, he very naturally brings it back to the anvil, and a second time prepares it for the lathe. The metaphor therefore which occurs in this passage, is at once consistent and expressive.

The vanity and arrogance with which Dr Bentley exercised his critical functions, are likewise exposed by this formidable antagonist. Cunningham appears to have been the friend of Le Clerc,[k] and on that account he may have point-

---

[1] Bentleii Epistolæ, p. 137. Lond. 1807, 4to.
[k] Bentleii Epistolæ, p. 202.

ed his animadversions with more keenness. The English
critic had attacked Le Clerc's edition of the reliques of
Menander and Philemon, and had exulted over him with
all the insolence of critical superiority.[1] Of this very respectable character it has lately become fashionable to speak
in terms of disparagement. It must indeed be admitted
that Le Clerc was indifferently qualified for publishing an
edition of a Greek poet; but he possessed a very considerable share of ingenuity, and was distinguished by a liberal
and speculative turn of mind. To these qualifications he
added much learning, more valuable in itself than the knowledge of Greek metres; and his writings, which were very
numerous, had no inconsiderable influence on the age in
which he lived.

Jani, a recent editor of the odes of Horace, has formed
so just an estimate of the critical merits of Bentley and Cunningham, that I shall transcribe his account of their respective editions.

" Sed clarissimam hujus sæculi haud dubie editionem
dedit *R. Bentleius*, maximum profecto ingenium criticum,
quod umquam vixit. Is Horatium tam ex codd. MSS.
quos plurimos habuit, quam ex suspicione, amplius DCCC
locis emendavit. Sed tanta est ejus in hoc conatu audacia,
ut, si qua illi semel placuerit lectio, omnes libros asperne-
tur, argutiisque sæpe tanto viro indignis vulgatam lectionem sine ulla necessitate exagitet. Interea plurimum sane
Horatius debet tanto critico, estque hic, etiam ubi errat, ab
ingenii doctrinæque magnitudine semper admirabilis ac
venerandus. Prodiit prima ejus editio a. 1711. notis ad
calcem libri subjectis : emendatior, et cuivis paginæ substra-

---

[1] " Quod enim," says Dawes, " in me præstandum recipio, centum ut
minimum Clerici errores intactos præteriit, centum insuper ipse erravit.
Sed neque erga Clericum viri ingenui officio functus videtur." (*Miscellanea
Critica*, p. 215. Cantab. 1745, 8vo.)

tis notis, repetita Amstel. a. 1713. et 1728. item Lipsiæ
1764. Londini 1765. Recusa etiam est, sed notis in compendium missis, Cantabr. 1713. cura Th. Bentleii.[m] Nactus est Bentl. (quod ipsum magnæ utilitati fuit Horatio)
adversarios plurimos. Fuit eorum primus anonymus, cujus extat *Aristarchus ampullans in curis Horatianis, auctore
Philargyrio Cantabr.* Londin. 1712. 8. Secutus est *Richardi Johnsoni* (ludi magistri Nottinghamiensis) *Aristarchus
Antibentleianus,* Nottingham. 1717. 8. Fuit in hoc viro
major adversus Bentleium acerbitas, quam doctrina.

" Omnium doctissime in hoc castigando versatus est.
Alexander Cuningamius, vir summus et doctissimus, unus
omnium, qui in Horatium scripserunt, criticorum princeps, ipsique Bentleio, si quid intelligo, anteferendus. Is
a. 1721 (Hagæ Com.) non solum edidit *Horatium, ex antiquis Codd. et certis observationibus* (quas inprimis ex codice
Blandinio antiquissimo Cruquii et Pierio Valeriano sibi in-
formasset) *emendatum,* cum variis lectt. sed subjecit etiam
huic editioni *Animadversiones in Bentleii notas et observationes,* doctissimas illas, et unde eximios fructus capere
possit critices studiosus. In Londinensi ejusdem anni edit.
accedunt *observationes criticæ* textui subjectæ. Amplius
CCCC locis emendatiorem esse suam recensionem Bent-
leiana affirmat Cuningamius, superbior justo, si verum
dicendum, et in Bentleium acerbior. Tantum est illius
adversus hunc odium, ut, si lectionem Bentleianam amplec-
tatur, eam numquam Bentleio debere videri velit, sed semper studiose alios quosvis fontes indaget. Quos ubi non

---

[m] Thomas Bentley, LL. D. senior fellow of Trinity College, Cambridge,
and rector of Nailston in Leicestershire, died on the fourth of March 1786,
at the age of eighty-two. Among other works, he published an edition of
Callimachus (Lond. 1741, 8vo.) which has lately been ascribed to his uncle.
Not to mention the internal evidence, it was soon after its appearance advertised with the editor's name, in a list of publications subjoined to Dr Tun-
stall's *Epistola ad Conyers Middleton.* Cantab. 1741, 8vo.

reperit, quamvis ei placere appareat Bentleianam, aliam adoptare mavult; ita non potest invidiam vincere. Emendationes autem ejus fatendum est omnium doctissimas esse ac ingeniosissimas, sæpe, si ad leges artis criticæ excutiantur, pro unice veris lectionibus habendas. Sæpius tamen non minor in iis, quam in Bentleianis, audacia est, sed illa melior profecto aliorum indocta modestia."[n]

Klotzius remarks that Sanadon has pilfered much from both Bentley and Cunningham.[o] Jani's estimate of the latter differs very widely from that of Wakefield; who styles him " ille criticus illaudabilis,"[p] and repeatedly honours him with some of the peculiar graces of his elocution. Of his own character as a critic, I shall here produce the opinion of Herman : " In quo viro quum quantum ingenii, tantum effrenatæ temeritatis, Græcæ autem linguæ haud accuratior, quam Latinæ, cognitio sit, debet ille aliquam sane, sed non eam auctoritatem habere, quam apud nostrates, nimis æquos exterorum judices, consequutus est."[q]

The reputation of Cunningham was now completely established ; and he seems to have been intimately connected with most of the eminent scholars and civilians who then flourished in Holland. In France he had several learned correspondents ; and from the following passage of his animadversions, it may be inferred that he was acquainted with Addison : " Cum autem hoc argumentum, quod tuam emendationem penitus evertit, cum Josepho Addison excellentissimi ingenii viro communicarem, ei quoque idem in mentem venisse animadverti : neque sua laude fraudandus

---

[n] Jani de Horatii Editionibus, p. xxxviii.—See likewise his preface to the second volume. Gebaver has remarked of Cunningham, " sobriæ criticæ fuisse studiosissimum." (Narratio de Henrico Brenkmanno, p. 10. Gottingæ, 1764, 4to.)

[o] Klotzii Vindiciæ Q. Horatii Flacci, p. 206. Bremæ, 1764, 8vo.

[p] Wakefield ad Lucretium, lib. v, v. 205.

[q] Hermanni præf. in Euripidis Hecubam, p. iv. Lipsiæ, 1800, 8vo.

est vir egregius Carolus Stanhope, is enim *versus male ter natos incudi reddere* eadem ratione adductus ferri non posse observaverat."[r] Dukerus and various other critics mention him in friendly, terms.[s] When Otto published his great collection of tracts on the civil law, he professed to have been chiefly indebted to Bynkershoek, Cunningham, and Brenkman, for their advice and assistance. " Post virum illum primarium, alios quoque recolere juvat, qui re et judicio suo hoc opus instruxerunt. Hos inter haud postremum locum obtinent Alexander Cuninghamus, et Henricus Brenkmannus, viri clarissimi, et optima fide de republica literaria pariter ac jurisprudentia merentes, qui repetitis deliberationibus ad dilectum librorum institutis, adfuerunt, dignoscere cauti quid solidum crepet."[t]

Cunningham appears to have died in the year 1730. The auction of his library commenced on the twentieth of November, and he may be supposed to have died some months before.[u] His collection of books was very curious and valuable, particularly in the departments of philology and jurisprudence. The catalogue describes it as a most

---

[r] Cuningamii Animadversiones, p. 214.

[s] Dukeri præf. in Florum. Lugd. Bat. 1722, 8vo.

[t] Thesaurus Juris Romani, præf. Lugd. Bat. 1725, seq. 5 tom. fol.—Cunningham is said to have assisted in revising a French translation (Haye, 1725, 2 tom. 4to.) of the first volume of Bishop Burnet's *History of his own Time.* " Nous avons appris que M. Cunningham, connu par son edition d'Horace en Hollande, et M. Johnson, seigneur Ecossois, ont revû cet ouvrage posthume de M. Burnet, et en ont retranché un grand nombre d'endroits injurieux à des personnes respectables. Ce qu' ils ont laissé fait assez voir l'indulgence de ces reviseurs." (*Journal des Sçavans, pour l'année 1726,* p. 669.)

[u] Bibliotheca Cuningamia, continens Selectissimos, Rarissimosque omni in Lingua Libros. Hos omnes multo judicio, vigilantia ac labore collegit Celeberrimus ac Eruditissimus Vir D. Alexander Cuningamius, Jurisconsultus et Polyhistor eximius. Lugd. Bat. 1730, 8vo. Pp. 130.—The notice on the back of the title-page contains a curious prohibition : " verum ne quis palliatus aut toga Japonica indutus accedat, rogamus."

splendid library, and mentions that the greater part of the books were in gilt vellum or calf.

Alexander Cunningham, the author of the *History of Great Britain*, who has often been identified with this learned critic and civilian, died in London on the fifteenth of May 1737. His will is registered at Doctors Commons. It is certainly a curious circumstance, that at so barren a period of its literary annals, Scotland should have produced two learned writers of the same name. From the subsequent notice it may be inferred that the historian had likewise cultivated the study of criticism. " I had a visit," says Dr Lister, " from Mr Cunningham, tutor to my Lord Lorne, a very learned and curious man in books. I askt him (knowing him to have been lately at Rome) very particularly about the papers of Monsieur d'Azout. He told me, that he saw him not above half a year before he died, and was very intimately acquainted with him, and saw him for a twelvemonth very often. That he told him, that he had about 80 difficult passages in Vitruvius, which he had commented and explained; and the correction of a great number of *errata* in the text. Also that upon Julius Frontinus (though that was a much less book) he had much more to say, than he had upon Vitruvius."[x] About the same period there was a third scholar of the name of Alexander Cunningham, professor of humanity in the university of Edinburgh. His testament was confirmed by the commissary court on the 26th of March 1697.[y]

The real and personal estate of the critic and civilian ap-

[x] Lister's Journey to Paris in the year 1698, p. 99, 2d edit. Lond. 1699, 8vo.—One of the Cunninghams is mentioned in a letter from Colonel Codrington to Dr Charlett, written in June 1702. (*Letters written by Eminent Persons*, vol. i, p. 133. Lond. 1813, 3 vols 8vo.)

[y] There is a Latin poem by the professor of humanity, subjoined to a work entitled *Grammatica Latina. Authore Patricio Dykes, Perthensi.* Edinb. 1679, 8vo.

pears to have descended to his nephew the Rev. George
Logan, A. M. afterwards one of the ministers of Edinburgh;
A letter from Sir John Pringle to Forbes of Culloden,
contains some information relative to his papers.

" I wrott to Mr Logan of Dunbar, as I told you I would
do, both in your name and mine, about his uncle Mr Cunningham's papers; and I have since had an evening's conversation with him; the sum of which was, that his uncle has
not left one single scrape of any thing ready for the press, or
even in any tolerable order. His notes on Horace are written on the margin of six volumes; whereof three are the
text of Horace, as he published it; and the other three are
his animadversions on Bentley. The use of all these, I
am promised again next week: the Lord have mercy on
the patients till I have done with them! His notes on
Phædrus are likewise only on the margins of two editions
of Phædrus; but he thinks them fuller than the others,
and is talking of giving them to Mr Ruddiman, if he will
be at pains to putt them in order and publish them. He
has marginal notes upon several other authors; as Virgil,
Statius, Quintillian, Cicero; any of which he offers to send
me after I have done with Horace. His notes on the Corpus are larger than any of the rest, and not writt on the
margin, as the rest. His copy of the Corpus is interleaved
with clean paper; so that there is a leaf of written notes,
for every printed leaf. He told me, the Advocat's Library
has applyed to him to have it; but he has given the cura-
tors no answer as yet, nor did he seem determined when he
spoke to me.

" What will surprise you most is, that he has left nothing of his scheme of the Christian religion. Mr Logan
told me, he had inquired at him about it when he was in
his perfect senses; but that he declared to him that he had
never putt it in writing, and that he would dictate it to
him any day, for he had it all in his head, and that it

could be contain'd in four or five sheets of paper; however, every day that Logan pressed him to do it, he found always some reason for shifting it, till he was incapable of doing any thing." This letter is dated at Edinburgh on the thirtieth of January 1731; and on the second of February, he writes thus: " I have gott two volumes of Horace, with Cunningham's marginal notes; but the hand is so bad, and the lines so close on one another, that I have difficulty to make sense of them, tho' I perceive no *siglæ*, or secret marks, among them. However, I design to give true pains, and you will see probably the fruit of my labours when you return." [z]

Cunningham's edition of Virgil was printed at Edinburgh in 1743 in small octavo. The preface was written by John Clerk, M.D. [a] An edition of Phædrus, with the text as revised by Cunningham, was published by Dr Clerk [b] in 1757. It contains a preface by the editor, but no annotations. It is thus described by Schwabe, a late editor of Phædrus: " Splendida et characterum nitore commendanda editio! Variæ lectiones et conjecturæ Cuninghami, antea in Germania minus notæ, a me insertæ sunt parti iii. Phædri, p. 134. sqq. (Hal. 1779–1781.) ubi vide. Sunt tamen non paucæ, quæ displicere possint, vel justo audaciores, vel non necessariæ." [c]

In the Advocates' Library are copies of Vinnius's first edition of the Institutes, [d] and Best's *Ratio Emendandi Leges*, with manuscript notes ascribed to Cunningham. These books appear to have been presented in 1763 by David

[z] Culloden Papers, p. 120–1. Lond. 1815, 4to.

[a] Ruddimanni Bibliotheca Romana, p. 10. Edinb. 1757, 8vo.

[b] Catalogue of the Library of the learned Dr John Clerk, Physician in Edinburgh, and of Dr David Clerk, his son, p. 72. Edinb. 1768, 8vo.

[c] Notitia Litteraria de Phædro, p. 104, prefixed to Schwabe's second edition. Brunsvigæ, 1806, 2 tom. 8vo.

[d] Lugd. Bat. 1646, 12mo.

Clerk, M.D. the son of the learned physician lately mentioned. The greater part of the notes were apparently written by some other person. One of these books enclosed a Latin poem, in the hand-writing of Cunningham, and exhibiting such erasements and corrections as an author may be supposed to make in his own composition. This poem I shall insert, together with the various readings.

Dum propriis urbem Neptunus ponere in undis
    Ardet, aquas Venetis jussit abire locis.
Æternas Batavus dum condere cogitat urbes,
    Neptunum propriis cogit abire locis.
Dedecus hoc patiar? non, non, deus inquit, et urbes
    Structoresque imo contumulabo solo.
Jamque parat bellum instructus magno agmine aquarum,
    Ingentesque* animos Æolus adflat aquis.
Belga gigantæo nova mœnia construit ausu,
    Debellatque deos ætheris atque maris.
Tum pacem deus ipse orat, juratque futuras
    Felices Batavis per sua regna vias.
Per montes ducti duros, per mœnia fontes
    In domibus certant currere, Roma, tuis:
Damnoso hos ductus redimi reficique labore,
    Fluminis ut tibi sit copia, forte doles.
Hæc urbes Batavæ molimina cara recusant,
    Quas gratis almæ copia nutrit aquæ.
Blande emendicans populi suffragia magnis
    Romanus ludis, nobilis exit inops.
At Batavus frugi virtutibus ambit honores,
    Nec domina accisis imminet hasta bonis.
Quin hyeme est illis per flumina, per mare docto
    Ære pedem armatis carpere ludus iter:
Hunc pueri atque senes, hunc exercentque puellæ,
    Ocius et tua quam, f Parthe, sagitta, volant.
Acrior at juvenis rapit æquora, continuo stat,
    Refrenans, agitans brachia, crura, latus.
Hic labor actori jucundum atque utile præstat:
    Spectantem casus spesque metusque tenet.

* Immanesque.
f His tua nec citius.—This reading requires the further change of *volat.*

Vidisses, Roma, hæc spectacula, forte putasses
'Non hæc magnificis cedere parva tuis.
Latas, Roma, vias tibi muniit undique saxum :
Quid, saxum ? hic omnes sternit et unda vias :
Alta hic se mirans secat agros puppis et urbes,
Ac stupet ad nitidas anchora jacta domos.
Arbore velifera ratis hic amat ire sub ipsis
Pontibus, immensus quos numerare labor.
Hic quoque celsæ ædes pelago fundantur in imo,
Nec domus in mediis ulla vacillat aquis.
Atque modis flagrant [g] miris commercia, credas
Hic nasci quicquid mundus [h] uterque parit.
Te, pax, Belga colit : sed, Gallo bella minante,
Militibus terras, classibus implet aquas.
Dum fingis classes [i] ex bellis bella serendis,
Innocuas gentes, martia Roma, domas,
Imperiumque tuum non ullo fine coerces :
Artior est Latio terra Batava solo.
Rex maris ecce stupet, rate quod se crebrius urguet
Amstelis urbs quam orbis, Roma superba, tuus.
Hanc deus aspectans propius, sic triste [k] profatur :
Sedibus est Venetis cultior illa meis :
Artsæque, ait, Batavi quæ talem ponere ssistis,
Qualem cœlicolæ non posuere dei.

These verses in celebration of the Dutch bear an allusion
to the famous epigram of Sannazarius, for which he received
so large a sum from the republic of Venice.

Viderat Hadriacis Venetam Neptunus in undis
Stare urbem, et toto ponere jura mari :
Nunc mihi Tarpeias, quantumvis, Juppiter, arces
Objice, et illa tui mœnia Martis, ait.
Si pelago Tibrim præfers, urbem adspice utramque :
Illam homines dices, hanc posuisse deos. [l]

Dr Pitcairne has written an epigram on the Dutch,

---

[g] Fervent.
[h] Quævis orbis.
[i] So this word is spelt in the MS. See Dausquii *Orthographia Latini
Sermonis*, vol. ii, p. 78.
[k] The adverb *triste*, though it may be found in dictionaries, seems to be
of very doubtful authority.
[l] Sannazarii Epigrammata, lib. i, 35.

which it may be curious to compare with both these poems. " Sannazarii in urbem Venetam hexastieho," says Toland, " inventionis tahtum gloria cedere videtur hocce Pitcarnii carmen; cæteroquin excellentius, ut mea fert sententia, et multo excelsius." [m]

> Tellurem fecere dii, sua littora Belgæ;
> Immensæque fuit molis uterque labos.
> Di vacuo sparsas glomerarunt æthere terras,
> Nil ubi quod cœptis possit obesse fuit.
> Ast Belgis maria, et cœli, naturaque rerum
> Obstitit: obstantes hi domuere deos. [n]

I am indebted to the politeness of Sir William Hamilton for a transcript of fourteen letters from Cunningham to J. P. d'Orville, and of several others connected with his history.[o] The originals are preserved in the Bodleian Library at Oxford. In this collection are several letters addressed to D'Orville by John Cunningham, who was a friend, and probably a relation of the critic. A. Cunningham's letters are partly written in English, partly in French. I shall subjoin a few as a specimen.

Sir,   *Hague, December 15, 1724.*
    My good friend Dr Mitchell is well versed in the

---

[m] Tollandi Gállus Aretalogus, p. 107.
[n] Pitcarnii Selecta Poemata, p. 3. Edinb. 1727, 12mo.
[o] George Waddel, one of Cunningham's learned friends, is likewise mentioned in D'Orville's papers. The following is an extract of a letter from Oudin, dated at Dijon on the 30th of July 1726: " Le correspondent de Mr Waddell m'a ecrit de Bezançon: il ne scait on est à present Mr Waddell; qui a eu le deplaisir de voir mourir Mr Racoff, seigneur qu'il conduisoit à Rome." He is the author of a little volume entitled " Georgii Waddeli Animadversiones Criticæ in Loca quædam Virgilii, Horatii, Ovidii, et Lucani; super illis Emendandis Conjecturæ." Edinburgi, 1734, 8vo. Pp. 159. There is likewise an anonymous tract ascribed to Waddel: " Remarks on Mr Innes's Critical Essay on the Ancient Inhabitants of the Northern Parts of Britain, or Scotland." Edinburgh, 1733, 4to. Pp. 32.

belles lettres, and well known to Prof. Burman. He will
do you all the services he possibly can : and my cousin Mr
Cuningham, who has a plantation in St Christophers in
the West Indies, will procure you the acquaintance of Bri-
gadier Hunter, one of my truest friends. You will profit
much in his conversation ; for he is a good *literator*, and a
very good poet both in Latin and in English ; and I kno
he will be ready to doe you all sort of good offices.   Now I
am extremely sorry to hear of the bad estate of your health:
and, with my affectionate humble service to your fellow
traveller, I am, with much passion and esteem,
>   Sir,
>> your most humble
>> and most obedient servant.
>>> ALEX. CUNINGHAM.P

SIR,   *Hague, June 7, 1726.*
   The very day you parted for Paris, I finally resolved
to publish my conjectures and corrections in Phædri Fabb.
and therefore the same day, which was a Saturday, and the
following Monday, Tuesday, and Wednesday, were only
employed in considering all the places which seemed to me to
be vitious, and in distinguishing the incurable ones from the
curable.   On the Thursday I went to Leyden ; and on the
Fryday I shewed my conjectures and corrections, fairly
written, to Mr Gronovius; and afterwards being with Prof.
Burmannus, I was upon the point of shewing them to him,
when his surgeon came to dress his legg, and so I took
leave of the prof. not having then the opportunity of com-
municating them to him.   The Saturday I returned to the
Hague, and the Monday following I had resolved to send
the conjectures to my printer.   But Mr Gosse having sent

P This letter is followed by a postscript of nearly the same length, respecting D'Orville's French servant.

me a copy of the *Epistola Critica*,[q] which he received a week sooner than it was expected, I altered my mind, since I could not pretend that my conjectures were printed before I had seen the *Epistola Critica*. The author of it quotes me, pag. 37: " ob hæc pluribus eum castigavit acutissimus et infinitæ diligentiæ vir, Alex. Cuninghamnius, in doctissimis Animadversionibus, quas dedit ad Bentleium,"[r] etc. and immediately followeth his correction of the 317 v, of Hor. Serm. lib. ii, 3,[s] which is,

Quantane? num tantum, sufflans se, magna *fuit?* tum
Major dimidio.

His reason is, that " *num fuisset* dici nequit, sed *num fuit;*"

[q] Written by Dr Hare, afterwards bishop of Chichester. This epistle relates to Bentley's notes and emendations on Phædrus. Of this great critic he had formerly expressed the highest admiration, and had even commended him with enthusiasm in an anonymous tract, entitled " The Clergyman's Thanks to Phileleutherus, for his Remarks on the late Discourse of Free-Thinking. In a Letter to Dr Bentley." Lond. 1713, 8vo. Pp. 48. He published his edition of Terence in 1724; and when Bentley's followed in 1726, the editor never mentioned the name of his former friend, but frequently took occasion to expose his errors. Hare endeavoured to avenge himself by the publication of his *Epistola Critica;* which it is amusing enough to compare with his former letter of thanks.

[r] Hare's Works, vol. ii, p. 328.

[s] This disputed passage is very successfully illustrated by Waddel; who shews that there is no occasion for any change in the text. He retains *fuisset,* and, with Dr Hare, is of opinion that *major dimidio* is a part of the narrative : " cum mater se eo usque inflasset, ut jam dimidio major esset, quam quum se primo inflare cœpisset." He mentions his having communicated this explanation to Dr Snape, and to the masters of Eton school, four years before the publication of the critical epistle. (*Animadversiones Criticæ,* p. 66,) Any sober explanation seems preferable to the bold conjectures of Bentley and Cunningham.

I avail myself of this opportunity of defending a reading, which the learned Dr Hunter seems very judiciously to have admitted into his late edition of Horace, printed at Cupar in 1813, 2 vols 8vo.

Indeque decerptam fronti præponere olivam.

                                                      Lib. i, od. vii, v. 7.

which reason I have confuted, and at the same time I
shewed that *num fuit* after *rogare*, *sc. cœpit*, in *præt. per-*
fecto indicativi modi, is not Latin, but *num esset*, as Phædrus expresses it, or *num fuisset*, as Horatius does. Then
he says, " cum ex pulli silentio mentem ejus satis intelli-
geret, se iterum sufflans, et jam *major dimidio facta iterum*
interrogat *num tantum?*" which explanation contains two
great mistakes, as I shall shew in my observations on
Phædr. I shall only at present take notice of the auth.
of the Epist. his saying in one place of his Epist. " tanta
est affinitas temporum imperfecti et plusquamperfecti sub-
junctivi modi, ut alterum pro altero poni soleat." I did
not doubt, as you can remember, but that the author of the
Epist. had found some of my corrections, and especially
such as the rule of the construction suggests. I shall only
add at present the last 4 lines of the Epist. Crit. " Prelo
parantur Animadversiones in Terentium Bentleianum, quibus præstantissimi scriptoris textus repurgatur ab innumeris
corruptelis, quibus viri doctissimi critica temeritas eum com-
maculavit."

Pray, Sir, let me kno if you have seen the Epist. Crit.
for if it is not to be had in Paris, I shall write out some pas-

---

It has, as I understand from a mutual friend, been objected by the respectable head of a public school in England, that the adverb *inde*, with the en-
clitic *que*, " is not to be found in the whole compass of the Latin classics."
This objection seems to have been somewhat hastily advanced ; for *indeque*
occurs twice in a single act of the *Aulularia* of Plautus.

Indeque observabo, aurum ubi abstrudat senex.
Act. iv, sc. vi, v. 13.
Indeque aspectabam ubi aurum abstrudebat senex.
Act. iv, sc. viii, v. 7.
The same phrase is likewise to be found in prose writers. " Flamen Dialis
fictus, quod filo assidue veletur. *indeque* appellatur flamen, quasi filamen."
(Pompeius Festus *De Verborum Significatione*, p. lxii, edit. Scaligeri.)—It
may be proper to add, that before the publication of Jones's edition, and long
before that of Schrader's *Emendationes*, the reading *indeque* had been ad-
opted by Dr Wade in his edition of the odes of Horace. Lond. 1731, 4to.

sages, which it's likely you would be glad to be apprysed of. Now I beg your pardon for not sending you the note of the Italian books. It shall be delivered to your father some time next week, who will take care to direct it so that it may come to your hands. I need not put you in mind of what I mentioned to you respecting P. Sanadon; and pray present my most humble respects to the very worthy and very learned president Bohier. So wishing you a very hap＋ py voyage, I remain, with a very great affection and esteem, Sir,

> your most oblidged
> and most obedient servant.
> > ALEX. CUNINGHAM.

SIR,   *Hague, July 17, 1726.*

I need not advise you to buy all the classicks, and good modern Lat. and Ital. poets, and histories Lat. Ital. as likewise all the editions of the classicks of the Alduses, if cheap and fair, but especially Horat. Virgil, and some other poets printed by old Aldus; all the old editions of classicks before the 1480, if cheap; for you kno, I suppose, that the prices of the old edd. and of all the Alduses, Juntas, Torrentinos, are much lower than they were 3 years ago. I cannot at present send you so full a *notitia* of curious books best to be had in Italy, for I find that I have left in London, with other papers and books, the catalogue I had made of them : so at present I have set down such as my weak memory has retained, and such as I found in a paper I have here. I shall add no more, but my most earnest wishes that you may continue in perfect health, and all your good designs be attended with success : and I am, with very much affection and esteem, Sir, yours entirely.

> > A. C.

* This letter is not printed entire.

Sir, I had almost forgotten to tell you that the British envoy is or will be with the king of Sardinia, where his Majestie drinks the waters; and therefore I have not desired the envoy here to give me a letter of recommendation in your favour to the British envoy at that court. I long to hear from you what the learned president has communicated to you upon Horace; and I desire [you], if you have any time, to look into 2 or 3 MSS. of Horace, which are said to be very ancient, in the king of Sard. his library, and to take cheifly notice of the order of the words in the Sermones, Epist. and A. Poet. You will do well to buy a copy of the *Pandectæ Florent.* if you can have them for 4 Rom. crowns.

Sir, such as I have marked with a cross, you can safely exceed the prices marked. I desire that you would be so kind as to see if in the Ambrosian Library, or any other library in Milan, there is a manuscript without Accursius's glosses in 2 voll. fol. The 2d vol. begins with the 1st tit. of the 36 book, *Ad senatusconsultum Trebellianum;* and if you find it, I earnestly entreat you would see if in the 37 book, the title 9th *De ventre in possessionem mittendo,* is postponed to the title *De conjungendis cum emancipato liberis ejus.* The books I have sent this note of are saleable books, and such if you have a mind to retain a copy for your own use, you will do well to buy more than one copy of them. Those that you purchase at Genua, Turin, Milan, it is best to send from Genua; and those that you purchase iu Piacensa, Parma, Modena, Bologna, Lucca, Piza, Ligorno, Fiorenze, to send them to [from] Ligorno. Nor do you forget to find out the shops of old books in every town you pass thro, and to find one of the booksellers who uses to get books out of private libraries, and out of the libraries of the cloysters. I have writ this in great haste, nevertheless I hope you shall find it legible: and I am again and again, Sir, yours entirely.

ALEX. CUNINGHAME.

I shall close this article with a list of Cuningham's publications.

1. Alexandri Cuningamii Animadversiones in Richardi Bentleii Notas et Emendationes ad Q. Horatium Flaccum.

Laudis amore tumes, sunt certa piacula, quæ te
Ter pure lecto poterunt recreare libello.

Horat. Epist.

Hagæ Comitum, apud Thomam Jonsonium, 1721, 8vo.

2. Q. Horatii Flacci Poemata. Ex antiquis Codd. & certis Observationibus emendavit, variasque Scriptorum & Impressorum lectiones adjecit Alexander Cuningamius. Hagæ Comitum, apud Thomam Jonsonium, 1721, 8vo.

3. P. Virgilii Maronis Bucolica, Georgica, et Æneis. Ex recensione Alexandri Cuningamii Scoti, cujus emendationes subjiciuntur. Edinburgi, apud G. Hamilton & J. Balfour, 1743, 8vo.

4. Phædri Augusti Liberti Fabularum Æsopiarum libri quinque. Ex recensione Alexandri Cuningamii, Scoti. Accedunt Publii Syri, et Aliorum Veterum Sententiæ. Edinburgi, apud G. Hamilton & J. Balfour, Academiæ Typographos, 1757, 8vo.

No. XII.—See p. 113.

An Explanation of some Passages in the Latin Poems of Dr Pitcairne.

(From a MS. in my possession.)

P. 8.—Ad Robertum Lindesium.

Robert Lindsay, grand-child, or great-grand-child, to Sir David Lindsay of the Mount, Lyon King at Arms, &c.

being an intimate condisciple with Arch^d Pitcairne, they bargained, anno 1671, that whoever died first, should give account of his condition if possible. It happened that Lindsay died about the end of 1675, when Arch^d Pitcairne was at Paris; and the very night of his death, A. P. dreamed that he was at Edinburgh, when Lindsay attacked him thus. Archie, said he, perhaps ye heard I'm dead? No, Robin. Ay, but they bury my body in the Grey Friers. I'm alive tho' in a place whereof the pleasures cannot be exprest in Scotch, Greek, or Latin. I have come with a well-sailing small ship to carry you thither. Robin, I'll go with you: but wait till I go to Fife and East Lothian, and take leave of my parents. Archie, I have but the allowance of one tide. Farewell: I'll come for you at another time. Since which time, A. Pitcairne never slept a night without dreaming that Lindsay told him he was alive. And having a dangerous sickness anno 1694, he was told by Robin that he was yet delayed for a time; and that it was properly his task to carry him off, but he was discharged to tell him when.

P. 15.—Ad Marcum Lermontium.

Mark Lermont, Advocate, supped with me on a 29th May, when our forces could not go to the fields, when Charleroy was taken, &c. and the secret peace was made. You know that the French king's device was a sun.

P. 16.—Ad Greppam.

Mrs Henderson, by a nickname called Greppa, kept the best wine in town. When our wine was at 32 pence the Scots pint, she suddenly sold hers at 20 pence. This was obliging; but she knew that new French wine would be suddenly home, which the other vintners knew not, but kept up their price. We did ourselves the pleasure to drink in

Greppa's ill wine in the end of the year at the old Scots price, whereby she sold all her wine; whereas the other vintners were forced to give theirs by hogsheads, at 20 shillings a piece, to be turned to aquavitæ. A little time thereafter Greppa died, was put in St Giles', our high church, and so is supposed to be married to St Ægidius; which is an honour next to her who is married to the chief of such sort of saints.

P. 17.—Ad Gualterum Danistonum.

Explained by what is said in the former. For Watty Danistone died a few days before Greppa, and so could not be at her marriage with Ægidius. *Nota*, That Ægidius's wooden statue was, in a procession by the rabble, drowned in the Nore Loch, with a stone about his neck. This is " Limosoque iterum," &c.

P. 18.—" Annam dum sitiens vocaret Hugo."

Hugh Cunninghame, a profest, and a true Presbyterian, but who eternally intruded himself into honest men's company : and in faith I could not be free of him, for he spoke as we did. This Hugh drank always in Greppa's, and ruined Mark Lermont, my easy friend. Our present Greppa is Ann Stanfield, a worthy woman, and whose wine ye drank lately, then servant to old Greppa. Hugh always called for her.

The above explications appear to have been communicated by Dr Pitcairne to some friend. They were copied from a manuscript of Dr Andrew St Clair's.

No. XIII.—See p. 312.

Davidis Doig, LL. D. ad Georgium Buchananum,
ob Columnam ipsi mox erigendam, Apostrophe.[a]

Ex Buchanane! pii, longo post tempore, cives
Ingenio statuunt hæc monumenta tuo,
Scotia te natum, te Gallia jactat alumnum ;
Te canit Europe, qua plaga cumque patet.
Nil opus est saxo, nil indice : læta sonabunt
Carmine Levinium sæcula cuncta decus.
Seu decoras Latio divina poemata cultu,
Seu recinis nugas, ludicra, festa, sales ;
Grandia seu tragico devolvis verba cothurno,
Seu reseras varii claustra viasque poli ;
Æmula seu captas Patavi præconia linguæ,
Fœdera dum patriæ, bella virosque refers ;
Eloquio, gravitate, sono, vi, lumine, verbis
Æquiparas veteres, exsuperasque novos.
Quod Graii potuere simul, quod Romula virtus,
Tu solus numeris, arte, lepore potes.
Sin aliqua titubas patriæ labefactus amore,
Aut nimium vera pro pietate pius,
Ipsa notam lecti Libertas plorat alumni ;
Ipsa tegit lauri Calliopea comis.
Sæpe nitor veri spissis latet obrutus umbris,
Nec semper Lynceus cuncta videnda videt.

[a] These verses were politely communicated by the Right Rev. Bishop
Gleig, through my learned friend Dr Barclay.

No. XIV.

A List of Publications relating to Buchanan.

ADAM BLACKWOOD. Adversus Georgii Buchanani Dialogum, de Jure Regni apud Scotos, pro Regibus Apologia. Pictavis, 1581, 4to. Pp. 341.

NINIAN WINZET, D.D. Velitatio in Georgium Buchananum circa Dialogum quem scripsit de Jure Regni apud Scotos. Printed with Winzet's *Flagellum Sectariorum.* Ingolstad. 1582, 4to.

WILLIAM BARCLAY, LL.D. De Regno et Regali Potestate adversus Buchananum, Brutum, Boucherium, et reliquos Monarchomachos, libri sex. Paris. 1600, 4to. Pp. 549.

GEORGE EGLISHAM, M.D. Duellum Poeticum, contendentibus Georgio Eglisemmio, medico regio, et Georgio Buchanano, regio præceptore, pro Dignitate Paraphraseos Psalmi centesimi quarti. Adjectis Prophylacticis adversus Andreæ Melvini Cavillum in Aram Regiam, aliisque Epigrammatis. Lond. 1618, 4to.

ARTHUR JOHNSTON, M.D. Consilium Collegii Medici Parisiensis de Mania G. Eglishemii. Paris. 1619, 8vo. Onopordus Furens. Paris. 1620, 8vo.

WILLIAM BARCLAY, M.D. Judicium de Certamine G. Eglisemmii cum G. Buchanano. Lond. 1620, 8vo. Pp. 54.

SIR GEORGE MACKENZIE. Jus Regium: or, the Just and Solid Foundations of Monarchy in general, and more especially of the Monarchy of Scotland; maintain'd against Buchanan, Naphthali, Dolman, Milton, &c. Edinb. 1684, 8vo. Pp. 200.

SIR ROBERT SIBBALD, M.D. Commentarius in Vitam

Georgii Buchanani, ab Ipsomet scriptam. Edinb. 1702,
8vo. Pp. 84.

THOMAS CRAWFORD, A. M. Notes and Observations on
Mr George Buchanan's History of Scotland. Edinb.
1708, 8vo. Pp. 187.

JOHN LOVE. Buchanan's and Johnston's Paraphrase of
the Psalms compared. Edinb. 1740, 8vo. See above,
p. 115.

A Vindication of Mr George Buchanan. Edinb.
1749, 8vo. Pp. 93.

WILLIAM LAUDER, A. M. Calumny Display'd: or,
Pseudo-Philo-Buchananus couch'd of a Cataract. Edinb.
1740, 4to. Pp. 36. See above, p. 115.

WILLIAM BENSON, Esq. A Prefatory Discourse to a
New Edition of the Psalms of David, translated into
Latin verse by Dr Arthur Johnston: to which is added a
Supplement, containing a Comparison betwixt Johnston
and Buchanan. Lond. 1741, 8vo. Pp. 119.

JAMES MAN, A. M. A Censure and Examination of Mr
Thomas Ruddiman's Philological Notes on the Works
of the great Buchanan. Aberdeen, 1753, 12mo. Pp.
574.

THOMAS RUDDIMAN, A.M. A Vindication of Mr George
Buchanan's Paraphrase of the book of Psalms, from the
Objections rais'd against it by William Benson, Esq.
Auditor in Exchequer. Edinb. 1745, 8vo. Pp. 390.

Animadversions on a late Pamphlet, intituled, A
Vindication of Mr George Buchanan. Edinb. 1749,
8vo. Pp. 110.

Anticrisis: or, a Discussion of a scurrilous and mali-
cious Libel, published by one Mr James Man of Aberdeen. Edinb. 1754, 8vo. Pp. 226.

Audi alteram partem: or, a Further Vindication of
Mr Tho. Ruddiman's Edition of the great Buchanan's
Works. Edinb. 1756, 8vo. Pp. 62.

GEORGE CHALMERS, Esq.   The Life of Thomas Ruddiman, A. M. to which are subjoined New Anecdotes of
Buchanan.   Lond. 1794, 8vo.   Pp. 467.

ROBERT MACFARLAN, A. M.   George Buchanan's Dialogue concerning the Rights of the Crown of Scotland
translated into English : with two Dissertations prefixed; one Archeological inquiring into the pretended iden-
tity of the Getes and Scythians, of the Getes and Goths,
and of the Goths and Scots ; and the other Historical
vindicating the character of Buchanan as an historian,
and containing some specimens of his poetry in English
verse.   Lond. 1799, 8vo.   Pp. 205.

ADDITIONS.

GESNER relates the following anecdote of Buchanan, without mentioning from what source he derived it. "Quum illi aliquando alterutra, nescio utrum sua regina, an Elisabetha, objecisset ejus paupertatem, ' Buchanane,' dicens, ' Pauper ubique jacet:' ille non cunctatus illico explevit versiculum ita: ' Si pauper ubique jaceret, In thalamis hac nocte tuis regina jacerem." (*Primæ Lineæ Isagoges in Eruditionem Universalem*, tom. ii, p. 181.) In the same page, this learned writer imputes to Buchanan what belongs to Sir James Melvil, and to Milton what belongs to Waller.

Brucker informs us that Buchanan's dialogue *De Jure Regni* was translated into Dutch: " mox Anglico quoque sermone, et tum Belgico comparuit." (*Historia Critica Philosophiæ*, tom. iv, par. ii, p. 796.)

The subsequent notice I found written on the cover of a book, in a hand which appears to have been formed in the earlier part of last century. " Scheriffhall near Dalkeith, said to be the place of Buchanan's residence, where he wrote his history : this room is pointed out to the visitors of the place."

INDEX.

2 E

FINIS.

Edinburgh:
Printed by A. BALFOUR.

DIRECTIONS FOR PLACING THE PLATES.

The portrait of Buchanan to front the title-page.
The facsimiles to front p. 1.
Buchanan's skull to front p. 310.

THE BORROWER WILL B
AN OVERDUE FEE IF THIS B
RETURNED TO THE LIBR/
BEFORE THE LAST DAT
BELOW. NON-RECEIPT O
NOTICES DOES NOT EX
BORROWER FROM OVERD

Montclore   128

Sambucus   217
(that letter)